Twentieth-Century
Europe

Twentieth-Century
Europe

Unity and Division

P.M.H. BELL

First published in Great Britain in 2006 by
Hodder Education, part of Hachette UK,
338 Euston Road, London NW1 3BH

www.hoddereducation.com

The advice and information in this book are believed to be true and
accurate at the date of going to press, but neither the author[s] nor the publisher
can accept any legal responsibility or liability for any errors or omissions.

British Library Cataloguing in Publication Data
A catalogue record for this book is available from the British Library

Library of Congress Cataloging-in-Publication Data
A catalog record for this book is available from the Library of Congress

ISBN: 978 0 340 74055 2

Typeset in 10.5/12.5pt Apollo by Phoenix Photosetting, Chatham, Kent

What do you think about this book? Or any other Hodder Education
title? Please send your comments to educationenquiries@hodder.co.uk

CONTENTS

LIST OF ILLUSTRATIONS

MAPS

PREFACE

'European unity. We hear the cry on all sides.' So wrote a great Dutch historian in 1959.[1] Nearly 50 years on, little has changed. In Britain, the questions of whether the country should ratify the treaty establishing a constitution for Europe, or adopt the euro as our currency in place of sterling, have provoked debate and disagreement. A whole new vocabulary has grown up around the prefix 'Euro' – Eurobabble and Eurospeak, Eurocrat and Eurocracy, Eurofanatic and Eurosceptic.[2] The word 'Europe' itself is used in different senses: to denote the geographical continent and to describe the organizations that have been called successively the European Economic Community (EEC), the European Community (EC) and the European Union (EU). A veritable academic industry has developed to describe, analyse and theorize about these organizations. We hear on all sides not so much a cry as a cacophony.

This book is an attempt to stand aside from the cacophony and the Eurobabble, and consider our debates and our present discontents in the perspective of a century of European history. It is often said that the idea of European unity makes most sense when there is more that unites the continent than divides it, and we must ask when that has been true during the hundred years or so since about 1900. Moreover, the unity of Europe can only be understood in the context of the separate nations that make up the continent, whose histories shape their current attitudes. The book is therefore a history of Europe in the twentieth century, written from a particular perspective. It starts before 1914, because in many respects Europe was more cohesive at that time than at any stage up to the present, and it comes as close as possible to the present day, ending in 2004.

In brief, the book argues that in the few years before 1914 there was a form of European unity that was largely taken for granted and reinforced by a general feeling of superiority to other continents and peoples. This sense of identity had no need of precise definition or of expression in institutions, except for limited and practical purposes, such as ensuring that trains could cross the continent on time or shipping could pass along the Danube without hindrance. There followed a period between 1914 and 1945 in which two great wars and intense ideological struggles tore the continent apart; and yet these years also witnessed attempts to restore the unity of Europe, in some cases by visionary schemes, in others by the use of force. After the Second World War the continent was divided between east and west, along lines which seemed so definite and rigid as to be final, if not fatal. Yet this was not so, and since about 1990 a new form of unity has been taking institutional form over a large part of the continent, west and east, in the shape of the European Union. One of the pressing questions of our own day is how this form of European unity will develop, and how its elaborate structures will accommodate the divisions and diversities which have marked European history in the past century. The book sets out to put flesh on these bare bones, and to examine some of the complexities of an absorbing and momentous theme.

This book is written for the informed and interested general reader as well as for students of history. I have therefore passed lightly over some vigorous academic debates. For example, I am aware of recent controversy about the exact status of the Schlieffen Plan, but accept the influence of the Plan, in a modified form, in 1914; and I have chosen one of the many definitions of totalitarianism which have preoccupied political theorists. I hope that the book will be read both as a contribution to history and as a vital background to our current debates, in the belief that the past and the present can illuminate each other.

P.M.H.B.
Kew, April 2005

ACKNOWLEDGEMENTS

I am deeply grateful to all those who have helped in the writing of this book, and am delighted to take this opportunity to say thank you to them. Christopher Wheeler kindly suggested that I embark on the enterprise in the first place, and oversaw its early stages. My forbearing, not to say long-suffering, friends, David Dutton, Mark Gilbert, John Lukacs and Ralph White, read all or large parts of a draft version, suggesting far-reaching improvements and saving me from many errors (the conclusion, in particular, owes much to Ralph's perceptive comments). None of these readers, of course, bears any responsibility for the imperfections that remain. David Annett has repeatedly helped me through computer problems which threatened to bring the project to a halt. The London Library is a wonderful place to work, with a remarkably helpful and erudite staff, and opportunities for serendipity among its vast holdings of books on open shelves.

As ever, my greatest debt is to my wife, who has lived with this book for a long time, read drafts at their messiest stage and helped tirelessly with all kinds of difficulties. It may be a cliché to say that the book would not have been written without her, but it is true all the same.

P.M.H.B.
Kew, April 2005

Introduction

WHAT IS EUROPE?
A HISTORICAL PERSPECTIVE

THE IDEA OF EUROPE

What is Europe? Most people in Britain would probably reply 'The European Union', or perhaps 'Brussels' for short. This is the Europe of common parlance and political controversy, and its most obvious embodiment is the euro, the single currency adopted at the beginning of 2002 by 12 of the 15 states of the European Union. By long custom, banknotes and coins display symbols of the state which issues them. The European Union is not yet a state, though it may eventually become one. Meanwhile, its currency displays an idea of Europe in visible form. The banknotes depict Europe as a geographical land mass, including western Russia and most of Turkey, and without frontiers. They show no national emblems, but evoke European history and civilization by displaying windows, gateways and bridges in different styles of architecture. The coins depict national emblems on one side. On the other side, three coins pick out Europe on a world map; another three outline the countries of the European Union; and two others show Europe as a land mass in the same way as the banknotes. The new currency thus highlights certain aspects of European identity: geography and a historic civilization. The coins also display what the banknotes seek to transcend: the diversity of national histories and identities.

The designers of the euro have tried to wrestle with the age-old problem of the identity of Europe. Others have blazed a trail before them. Fifty years before the advent of the euro Oscar Halecki, a Polish historian writing in exile in the USA, defined European history as: 'The history of all European nations considered as a whole, *as a community clearly distinct from any other*'.[1] In the 1990s Norman Davies found the subject matter of European history in '*the shared experiences* which are to be found in each of the great epochs of Europe's past.'[2] Luigi Barzini, an Italian journalist trying to explain Europe to

Americans, wrote that 'in spite of the infinite diversities…we [Europeans] are all *basically the same kind of people*, comfortable in each other's countries and in each other's homes'.[3] These writers get further than the currency designers, and provide three keys to European identity: a community distinct from any other, shared experiences and the same kind of people. These keys open new questions. Where is that distinct community to be found? What are the experiences shared by its peoples? How can we describe Europeans as the same kind of people when they differ so widely from one another?

Where is Europe? It is almost a commonplace to describe Europe as a peninsula of the great land mass of Eurasia. A peninsula must start somewhere, and a widely accepted baseline is that of the Ural Mountains. 'From the Atlantic to the Urals' has a resounding ring to it, especially with the authority of General de Gaulle behind it. 'Yes, it is Europe, from the Atlantic to the Urals, it is the whole of Europe, that will decide the fate of the world', proclaimed the General in 1959.[4] It is not wholly convincing as a geographical thesis. The Urals rise to no great height and display no continuous crest, and their acceptance as the natural eastern frontier of Europe dates only from the early eighteenth century. But generations of rail travellers have seen the evocative border sign pointing to Europe in one direction and Asia in the other, and many more have seen it depicted on photographs. The Urals may not be very high, but they have left their mark in the maps of the mind. To the south, the Mediterranean Sea, from the Straits of Gibraltar to the Bosphorus, has long marked the boundary of Europe. To the west, the Atlantic is unchallenged as a marker, though Iceland forms a far-flung outpost.

Geography offers a reasonably confident answer to the question 'Where is Europe?', but then history sows doubts. For much of its history, Europe has not coincided with the geographical area between the Atlantic and the Urals, or indeed with any fixed area at all. Its boundaries have moved to and fro, with little regard for mountain ranges or even the sea. From the ninth to the fifteenth centuries the Iberian peninsula was wholly or partially held by the Arabs. The Ottoman Empire controlled the Balkans for some 500 years. Both areas were thus excluded from European civilization, which was long identified with Christendom. On the other hand, Europeans spread beyond the geographical confines of their continent. The Greeks were long established on the coasts of Anatolia. The French settled in Algeria, and Algiers became a French city in many respects. The Mediterranean was a highway rather than a barrier, and the historical frontiers of Europe were fluid, not fixed.

It was in the Mediterranean that European civilization began, in the threefold shape of ancient Greece, classical Rome and Christianity. In this trinity, Christianity assumed a particular importance. As recently as 1935, H.A.L. Fisher wrote in his immensely influential *History of Europe* that religion was the key test of European identity. 'To be a Christian was to be admitted…into the fellowship of the European nations. To be a non-Christian was to be an outcast and enemy.'[5] The very existence of Europe was saved in battle when Charles Martel defeated the Saracens at Poitiers in 732. Over 800 years later, in 1565, the Turks attacked Malta; and as late as 1683 they besieged Vienna. The historical character of Europe was thus forged and maintained in repeated struggles against Islam. At a deeper level, the combined influences of Greece, Rome and Christianity produced cultural, intellectual and moral effects which shaped European civilization for centuries and created the idea of a European identity, which was long bound up with the concept of Christendom. In our own day this identity between Europe and Christianity has diminished markedly. Many Europeans (especially in the West) have become secularized, post-Christian or simply non-Christian. Other religions have become implanted within Europe, with Islam particularly prominent in France and Britain. The predominant current of west European opinion, expressed by governments, elites and the mass media alike, asserts the virtues of multiculturalism and a multi-faith society, and rejects any exclusive affiliation with Christianity. The constitution of the European Union signed in Rome in November 2004 omitted any reference to the Christian roots of European civilization, despite the efforts of some member governments and the Vatican to insert one.

The twentieth century, indeed, brought a new approach to the idea of Europe. Intellectuals and politicians came to think of Europe, not as something which has grown, as Christendom did, but as something to be built. The leaders of the Second Socialist International before 1914 dreamed of creating a benevolent socialist Europe, where war would be impossible. After the disasters of the Great War, a new generation of European thinkers produced schemes for European unity, of which the best known were Coudenhove-Kalergi's idea of 'Pan-Europe' and Aristide Briand's plan for a European federation in 1929–30. During the Second World War the German victories in 1940–41 presented Hitler with an opportunity to build a Nazi Europe, which he might well have seized if he had had enough time. After 1945 Stalin actually established a communist Europe over the eastern part of the continent. In the 1950s the practical prophets of European unity, Monnet, Schuman, Adenauer and De Gasperi, devised schemes which produced a series of European Communities and eventually the European Union, a steadily growing building in which a succession of elaborate treaties are piling up. European unity, which was once a vision akin to Utopia, has been taken up and transformed by politicians and administrators. 'Building Europe' has become largely an economic proposition, and the concept of Europe has assumed legal and bureaucratic forms.

Geography offers us a Europe from the Atlantic to the Urals. History tells us that Europe has not always corresponded to that geographical area. Ideas of the identity of Europe have assumed different forms. The question 'What is Europe?' arises very sharply in relation to certain countries and regions. Two such cases are Russia and Britain. Seen from other continents, both are undoubtedly European. When the Japanese proclaimed 'Asia for the Asians' in 1941, they did not include the Russians; and when the Afro-Asian movement took shape at the Bandung Conference in 1955, the Soviet Union was not invited. Seen from America, Britain is obviously in Europe, 'over there', beyond the Atlantic. But viewed from within the two countries themselves, the situation looks very different.

RUSSIA

The Russians themselves have long been divided over whether their country is part of Europe or not. Peter the Great tried to settle the issue by building his new capital, St Petersburg, on the Baltic Sea, facing westward and in a European architectural style. By the nineteenth century the Russian aristocracy was largely European in outlook and habits. They spoke French and often spent the winter in the south of France. (There was a special train from St Petersburg to the Riviera, called *Le train des ducs*.) Later, Russians in exile after the Bolshevik Revolution took comfort in their European identity, and sought to 'mitigate their painful awareness of being exiles by the sense of belonging culturally to Europe'.[6] But against these 'Westernizers', the Slavophiles have maintained that Russia is or should be separate from Europe, cultivating its own civilization, which is implicitly and often explicitly deemed superior to that of Europe. In the nineteenth century Dostoevsky, and in the late twentieth century Solzhenitsyn, championed the Slavophile cause with all the weight of their prestige as writers and prophets.

In practice, and rather prosaically, Russia has been both in and out of Europe. No one can discuss European literature or music in the nineteenth century without including the great Russian writers and composers, who form a significant part of European culture. Yet at the same time, in political terms, tsarist Russia, with its absolutist tradition, was alien to the parliamentary institutions and limited monarchies of most of Europe. Under Communism, when Stalin ruled as a Red Tsar, more absolute and arbitrary than any of the Romanovs, Russia was in many ways completely cut off from the rest of Europe, and yet it also had close links with the European communist parties, which regarded the Soviet Union as the workers' fatherland. Russia was sometimes in Europe, sometimes out of it, and sometimes both at once – an uncertainty which has not been resolved since the fall of communism in 1991. Broadly speaking, there has been a part of Russia which has been geographically, culturally and sometimes politically part of Europe, and a Russian empire (whether tsarist, Communist or post-Communist) which is largely Asiatic, or perhaps Eurasian.

BRITAIN

Britain too is semi-detached in its relations with Europe. Geographically Britain belongs to Europe, lying merely a few miles offshore. Britain has been part of European civilization from the time of the Roman Empire. In literature, music, art and architecture British culture is part of the European mainstream. In politics Britain took its own path towards constitutional monarchy and parliamentary government, while remaining part of European political society, and often serving as a model for European liberals. Yet in important respects the British saw themselves as separate from the continent. An influential school of historical writing emphasized this individuality, sometimes in almost mystical terms. G.M. Trevelyan, for long the doyen of English historians, wrote of England in the early sixteenth century, on the eve of Atlantic voyages and settlements: 'She has long been half European; she shall now become oceanic – and American as well, and yet remain English all the while.'[7] Successive British statesmen, from Canning to Churchill, saw their country as standing outside Europe, intervening in its affairs to redress the balance of power or to save the continent from tyranny in various forms, from Napoleon to Hitler.

In 1940 Britain stood alone against the might of Nazi Germany. It was, in Churchill's words, 'their finest hour', which stamped its memory on a generation and more of the British people. It was a long time before any British government would contemplate joining any sort of united Europe. Even when governments changed their policy and eventually joined the EEC in 1973, this had only a limited effect on British feelings. A series of public opinion polls between 1974 and 1986 showed positive British approval of membership of the EEC never rising above the high 30s in percentage terms, while disapproval hovered around 30 per cent. In 1992 a poll showed that only 25 per cent would regret the possible demise of the European Union; 28 per cent would be relieved at its disappearance; while the rest would greet the news with indifference or had no opinion at all.[8] In 1983 Luigi Barzini made the point impressionistically, writing that 'If one asked a Briton "Are you European?" the answer was always "European? Did you say European? Er, er" – a long thoughtful pause in which all other continents are mentally evoked and regretfully discarded – "Yes, of course I'm European". This admission is pronounced without pride and with resignation.'[9] Geographically and culturally Britain is part of Europe. Politically the country has often stood aside from the continent, and is still not fully committed to the idea of European integration. This situation may change with the generations, but still prevails substantially in the early twenty-first century.

TURKEY

Another doubtful case, presenting crucial questions about the identity of Europe, is that of Turkey. For centuries there was no doubt about the matter in European minds. The Ottoman Empire had been the enemy of Europe, and the Turks were not Europeans. During the nineteenth century the peoples of the Balkan peninsula broke free from Turkish rule and rejoined Europe. The long Greek war of independence fired the imagination of many Europeans, attracting the support of Byron and other philhellenes, at a time when most educated men were raised on the literature and history of ancient Greece. Other countries, though outside this classical tradition, still had their champions. Gladstone took up the cause of the Bulgarians in 1878, denouncing the Turks for the Bulgarian massacres and demanding that they should be driven 'bag and baggage' out of Europe. The Russians felt a particular kinship with the Serbs, who were Orthodox in religion and Slavonic in race. The elites in the new Balkan states found their inspiration in European-style nationalism and adopted European institutions as signs of modernity.

In international affairs the situation was different, in that Turkey was regarded as 'the Sick Man of Europe' (not Asia), and the Ottoman Empire formed part of the European balance of power. In 1914 Turkey took the German side in the First World War, acting as both a European and an Asian power. After the war, Mustafa Kemal created a new secular Turkish Republic, and moved the capital to Ankara in the Anatolian highlands. This left Turkey largely, though not completely, outside Europe, with a very small portion of its territory in Europe, but the bulk, including the new capital, in Asia.

After 1945, with the onset of the cold war, the situation changed again. For the USA, and to a lesser degree for west European countries, Turkey became a valuable ally against the Soviet Union, with a vital strategic position at the Straits. In 1952 Turkey joined the North Atlantic alliance, and for a time Turkey was the only state contiguous to Greece which was not under communist rule. Turkey could also claim better democratic credentials than a number of west European countries, when Spain and Portugal were dictatorships and Greece was controlled by a military regime.

At the same time, west European states accepted Turkey into parts of their movement towards unity. As early as 1949 Turkey was invited to become a member of the Council of Europe, whose avowed purpose was 'to bring European states into closer association', and whose members declared their 'devotion to the spiritual and moral values which are the common heritage of their peoples'.[10] In principle, this meant that European countries accepted Turkey as one of their own, and Turkey for its part assented to European values. This was a remarkable development, which attracted curiously little attention, perhaps because the Council of Europe was a purely consultative body (or, less politely, a talking shop), so that few practical consequences were expected. After the EEC was founded in 1957, Turkey became an associate member in 1964, under an agreement which envisaged a long transition before the country could apply for full membership. There followed a prolonged period of uncertainty, during which Turkey repeatedly pressed to open negotiations for entry, and the member states of what was successively the EEC, the EC and the European Union hesitated to agree. Only at the end of 2004 did the members of the European Union finally agree to open negotiations for Turkish entry, still amid widespread misgivings and doubts.

The position of Turkey presents a crucial test for the identity of Europe. Geographically, a small part of the country is on the European side of the Bosphorus, but to include the whole country in Europe would mean pushing the frontiers of the continent to the headwaters of the Tigris and Euphrates and to the borders of Syria, Iraq and Iran, something never previously contemplated. Historically Europe has had to be defended against Ottoman invasions, and the Balkan states were formed by breaking free from Turkish rule. The Turkish state is secular, but the population is overwhelmingly Muslim, which raises problems at a time of tension between militant Islam and the West. As a practical matter, European governments and their peoples are reluctant to admit some 70 million Turks to the freedom of movement which is extended to all members of the European Union. Yet despite all these difficulties the question of Turkish membership of the European Union remains open. Some politicians (notably Giscard d'Estaing, a former president of France) oppose Turkish membership on the fundamental grounds that Turkey is not European and its entry would call into question the whole idea of Europe. The arguments in favour of Turkish entry rest mainly on the balance of political and strategic advantage, and on the dangers of alienating Turkey from the European Union, and regard questions of history, geography and European identity as secondary. Yet at some point these issues of principle will have to be faced. If Turkey joins the European Union during the next ten years or so, the question 'What is Europe?' will be given a new answer, ignoring geography and history, and appealing to different criteria.[11]

DIVISION AND UNITY

The political geography of Europe is thus uncertain, with important countries remaining on the margins, within Europe in some respects, but outside in others. The continent is also divided within itself. The most persistent division has been between east and west, though the actual line of demarcation has shifted over time. The frontier of the Roman Empire along the Rhine and Danube left a lasting distinction between the lands which were Romanized and those which were not. The later division between Catholic and Orthodox Europe followed a different line, most obviously between Catholic Poland and Orthodox Russia. At the time of the Reformation and Counter-Reformation, a new line was drawn between the Protestant north and Catholic south. In the nineteenth century there were marked differences between an industrialized Europe in the west and an agrarian Europe in the east. In the twentieth century the two great wars of 1914–18 and 1939–45 were fought very differently in western and eastern Europe, and produced widely divergent results. The imposition of Soviet domination in eastern Europe after the Second World War severed east from west with a harsh brutality, and the Iron Curtain marked a physical, political and psychological barrier between the two, which for a long time seemed destined to be permanent. Even after that barrier disappeared in 1989 the re-creation of a single European society has been a painful and uncertain venture.

East–west divisions split Europe into two parts. The force of nationalism has split it into fragments. The principle of nationality threatens constant division, because there are no precise criteria by which we can define a nation. Language, race, territory, religion, a common history can all be advanced as the basis of nationality, but all break down or admit of exceptions in one case or another. Nationalists themselves cling to whatever symbol they feel is most important, and people can claim to form a nation when enough of them believe that they do. They can then press their claim upon others when even a few are prepared to kill and to die for their cause.

In practice, nationalism has operated in Europe in two main directions: the demand for the *union* of peoples of the same nationality in a single state (for example, the unification of Italy and Germany in the nineteenth century); and the demand for *separation* by national groups living within an existing state (for example, the nations which once formed part of the Habsburg Empire, the Irish seeking independence from Britain, or the Basques from Spain and France). The unifying effects were largely accomplished by the end of the nineteenth century. During the twentieth century, the divisive effects reached remarkable proportions. In 1914 Europe was made up of 22 separate states. In 1995 there were 39, or 40 if Serbia and Montenegro were counted separately rather than remaining part of the Yugoslav federation. (These figures do not include the tiny states which contribute to Europe's infinite variety – Andorra, Liechtenstein, Monaco, San Marino and the Vatican – which mostly represent the persistence of tradition rather than the triumph of nationalism.)

In the first part of the twentieth century, the divisive force of nationalism proved stronger than the cohesive sense of European unity. The peace settlement of 1919–20, heavily influenced by the idea of national self-determination, produced a Europe that was more divided than before the Great War. In the 1920s and 1930s fascism and Nazism introduced a new brand of nationalism – intense, vocal and highly visible – which for a time tore the continent apart. After the convulsion of the Second World War it seemed for some time that the force of nationalism was spent. In western Europe there was a strong sense that the nation state had failed, and governments and peoples were willing to embark on a new search for European unity. In eastern Europe the predominance of the Soviet Union and communist ideology appeared to iron out many of the differences between separate countries.

In the 1990s the movement towards unity continued in the West, with the nation state yielding ground to the European Union, which took the remarkable leap (at once symbolic and practical) of adopting a single currency for 12 of its 15 member states. In the East, on the contrary, the collapse of the Soviet empire revealed the survival and even the intensification of national feeling. The Baltic states of Estonia, Latvia and Lithuania recovered the independence they had lost in 1940. Ukraine, Belarus and Moldova emerged as nation states – though Ukraine itself shows dangerous fault lines between east and west. Czechoslovakia separated peacefully into the Czech Republic and Slovakia in 1993. Yugoslavia split into six countries, amid fierce fighting, massacres and expulsions – euphemistically called 'ethnic cleansing'. The chaos and barbarism of these conflicts were so far removed from the intricate politics and bureaucracy of the European Union that it was sometimes hard to believe that they coexisted on the same continent. The contrast stands as stark testimony to the continuing division of Europe.

In the past hundred years Europe has gone through an identity crisis in its relations with other continents and peoples. Before 1914 Europeans were conscious of their superiority to the rest of the world, which was itself a part of their identity. European powers controlled almost the whole of Africa and most of Asia. For most of the nineteenth century their armies had been capable of defeating almost any African or Asian opponents, with the occasional exceptions only tending to prove the rule. European companies and banks controlled the world economy. European migrants settled over great tracts of the globe, especially in America and Australasia, where offshoots of European society were transplanted with remarkable success. European ideas, science and technology prevailed throughout the world. Europeans largely took their superiority for granted, but when they thought about it they were proud of it. Empire and imperialism were words of praise, and European self-confidence was immense.

By the end of the twentieth century all this had changed. The predominance of Europe and the self-confidence that went with it had vanished. The European empires had dissolved. Even the Soviet empire, which lasted longest, collapsed in 1991. In warfare the tables were turned with a vengeance and (with rare exceptions) it seemed virtually impossible for a European army to defeat Asian or African opponents. The French lost long wars in Indochina and Algeria. Even the Soviets, with powerful forces and few inhibitions, could not win a war in Afghanistan in the 1980s. Economic power moved away from Europe, so that a decision made by a Japanese car firm or the collapse of a North American company could settle the fate of European workers and investors. The tide of migration turned. Immigrants from Asia, Africa and the Caribbean came to Europe in large numbers, changing the character of the population in certain areas, notably in Britain, France and the Netherlands. At the same time Europe's demographic position in relation to the rest of the world was transformed. In 1900 the population of Europe made up about 28 per cent of the total world population. By 1995 that had fallen to about 12 per cent. Moreover, the European population was ageing and failing to reproduce itself.[12] These changes were accompanied by a profound loss of self-confidence. Europeans became ashamed of their former empires and no longer claimed any superiority for their civilization. Christians often became hesitant and uncertain in their beliefs and claims. Even the movement towards

European unity, which was in part a sign of vigour and innovation, could also be seen as a huddling together against the rest of the world.

Among all these changes, how far has European identity itself survived? Do the concepts of forming a distinct community, sharing common experiences and being basically the same kind of people still hold good? It remains true that Europeans are conscious of what they are *not*. They are not Asians or Africans. They are distinct from Americans, even though most Americans are the descendants of Europeans. But negatives do not suffice to make up an identity. Who *are* the Europeans? Many of them belong to the European Union, but that organization does not cover the whole of geographical Europe, and so far has been a construct of governments rather than an organic growth. Politicians and administrators have 'built Europe', but they have not yet made many Europeans. What *is* Europe? The old foundations of European civilization in ancient Greece, classical Rome and Christianity have been largely eroded, and it is not clear what, if anything, has replaced them.

How do we answer these questions, and how do we approach the issue of the unity and division of Europe, which now figures so prominently in political debate? It has been said that the unity of Europe depends on there being more that unites the continent than divides it. When has that been true, and what characteristics do we regard as elements of unity? There are different Europes – geographical, historical and political. During the past century there have been several different concepts of Europe: one before 1914, when European identity was largely taken for granted; another during the First World War, when Germany threatened to impose its own order on the continent; another between the world wars, when idealists tried to find a formula for voluntary unity; then Hitler's Europe and Stalin's Europe; and more recently the Europe of the EEC and the European Union. Methods of building Europe have included brute force, appeals to reason and idealism, economic cooperation and bureaucratic organization. Motives have swung between an optimistic faith in the shared characteristics of the European peoples on the one hand, and on the other a fear that Europe can only be saved from self-destruction by devising some form of institutional unity. Let us look at the different visions of Europe in the past hundred years, and at the opposing forces pressing towards unity or division.

PART ONE

EUROPE BEFORE 1914

1 Europe in 1914

1

THE LAND OF LOST CONTENT

That is the land of lost content,
I see it shining plain,
The happy highways where I went
And cannot come again.

A.E. Housman

THE GOLDEN AGE?

The Great War of 1914–18 marked a profound and terrible rupture in European history, opening a period of turmoil that shaped the world in which we now live. When it was over, many men looked back to the years before the war with longing and regret, as to a golden age. In large part this was an illusion. The years before 1914 were not much of a golden age, except for a privileged few, and they gleamed more brightly in memory than they had at the time. But in a sense that scarcely mattered. Europe before 1914 *came to seem* a land of lost content. Many people wanted to go back to it and for a long time refused to believe that they could not do so. This feeling became a part of European consciousness, and in some ways we are trying even now to return to the sunlit plateau which still lies, unattainable, beyond the fatal cleft of the Great War. The first Europe we must examine is Europe before 1914, when the continent enjoyed, if not a golden age, at any rate a period of remarkable cohesion in economics, politics, international affairs and relations with the rest of the world. It was a time when there was no doubt as to the reality of European identity and coherence.

This cohesion and identity was manifested in a number of features which crossed state boundaries and were shared across much of the continent. It was demonstrated in the conduct of international relations, and in the development of practical organizations which managed certain aspects of European life. But above all it was largely taken for granted by Europeans who

1 A golden age for a privileged few: at the races, Budapest, 1902 © Ullstein-Imagno

sensed the identity of their own continent without needing to define it or set up institutions to formalize it. After two great wars (which were in part European civil wars) this situation changed. The cohesion of Europe had been shown to be too fragile to be taken for granted, and a quest for European institutions began – at first hesitantly, in the 1920s, and then with greater intensity and success from the 1950s onwards.

Before 1914 the population of Europe was showing a marked increase, as it had done throughout the nineteenth century. In 1881 the total population stood at about 344 million, and by 1911 it was about 464 million (these figures include the Asian as well as the European provinces of Russia, so that the actual European total was rather lower). This trend affected the whole continent, with only two exceptions: France, where the growth rate was tiny, and Ireland, where the population was actually falling. Demographic trends were not uniform across the continent, but showed marked differences between the northern and western areas and the south and east. Average life expectancy in western and northern Europe was about 50 years, and in the east and south no more than 30–40 years – low by present-day standards, but still showing that people were living longer than before. Birth rates were high in eastern and southern Europe. The Russian birth rate was the highest in Europe, at 45.8 per 1000 in the period 1906–10. In the west and north, birth rates were falling, and in France the birth rate was only 19.9 per 1000 in the same period. This French experience proved to be the precursor of a demographic transition which was to affect almost the whole continent. As the twentieth century progressed, birth rates declined while expectation of life increased, producing an ageing population.[1]

It was a striking fact that the population of Europe was increasing *despite* large-scale emigration to other continents. Between 1870 and 1914, 35–40 million people left Europe for overseas destinations, mainly the USA, Canada, Australia, New Zealand, South Africa, Latin America and North Africa. In the early years of the twentieth century, the main sources of this vast exodus were Russia, the Scandinavian countries, Ireland, Greece, Italy, Spain, Portugal and Austria-Hungary. There were fewer emigrants from Britain and Germany, and from France very few indeed.[2]

Some of these migrants were escaping political or religious persecution, but the overwhelming motive for emigration was economic. It was noticeable that emigration decreased as economic conditions improved, as they did in Scandinavia (slowly) and in Germany (rapidly) about the turn of the century. For any emigrant, the wrench of uprooting from one's home, the costs and miseries of an ocean crossing, and the hardships of settling in a new country presented enormous obstacles. Only very harsh conditions, a fixed determination to escape and a powerful hope for a new life could bring people to overcome such difficulties. The emigration figures show beyond doubt that for many Europeans the period before 1914 was by no means a golden age.

Migration was largely one-way. Some emigrants returned home, and there was some migration into Europe from other continents. There were some Chinese, mainly in the ports; and migrants from European colonies (for example, Indochinese and Algerians in France, and West Indians and Indians in Britain). But their numbers were small. Even in France after the upheaval of the Great War, the census of 1921 showed only 36,300 North Africans living in the country.[3] Europe before 1914 was an exporter, not an importer, of people.

Important consequences followed from this one-way movement of population. Emigration acted as a political safety valve, draining away some of the discontented. Economically it had the negative effect of removing many of the most vigorous and enterprising among the population; though successful migrants often sent back money to their families 'at home', giving a useful boost to many a household economy. Emigration with little immigration meant that the remaining populations in European countries tended to be stable and homogeneous. In previous centuries, Europe had absorbed successive waves of immigration, and been something of a melting pot, but at the beginning of the twentieth century the population had reached a state of equilibrium.

THE ECONOMY

Emigration was to a large degree an index of poverty. Yet in the period before 1914 the European economy was expanding rapidly. About 1895–96, after some 20 years of economic difficulties, a new surge of growth began. New industries (chemicals, motor vehicles, electricity) developed at such a rate as to amount to a new industrial revolution. International trade flourished, encouraged by the free movement of capital and stable exchange rates based on the gold standard. Between 1900 and 1913 the external trade of almost every European country increased in value considerably.[4] Banks and insurance companies provided a web of services across the continent. Railways moved goods quickly and efficiently. Department stores and chain stores marked the growth of a new consumer society, reflecting the rising prosperity of the bourgeoisie in the big cities of Europe.

The main powerhouse of this economic growth lay in western Europe, in Britain, Germany, France, Belgium and northern Italy. In 1913 Britain, Germany and France provided about 70 per cent of total European manufacturing capacity, producing 93 per cent of Europe's coal and 78 per cent of its steel.[5] Of these three countries, Germany was the young giant, with a rapidly rising population (45 million in 1881 and nearly 65 million in 1911) and a booming economy (steel production rose from 2.3 million tons in 1890 to 13.8 million tons in 1910 – a six-fold increase in a mere 20 years).[6] Led by these three big industrial countries, Europe was at the centre of the world economy. Other continents provided raw materials for European industries and food for its peoples, and most of the world's business was run from Europe. This division of functions was taken for granted in Europe, and went largely unchallenged outside. Even the USA – which was already an economic great power, with steel production well over double that of Germany in 1913 – played only a modest part in world trade and remained a field for inward rather than outward investment.

Looking back after the Great War of 1914–18, the young John Maynard Keynes depicted the workings of the pre-war economy in almost lyrical terms. 'The inhabitant of London could order by telephone, sipping his morning tea in bed, the various products of the whole earth, in such quantity as he might see fit, and reasonably expect their early delivery upon his doorstep...' Within Europe, he went on, 'The interference of frontiers and of tariffs was reduced to a minimum, and not far short of three hundred millions of people lived within the three Empires of Russia, Germany and Austria-Hungary. The various currencies, which were all maintained on a stable basis in relation to gold and to one another, facilitated the easy flow of capital and of trade... Over this great area there was an almost absolute security of property and of person.'[7]

There was a marked difference between the industrialized areas of Europe (mostly in the north and west) and the mainly agricultural countries in the south and east. Broadly speaking, southern and eastern Europe were poorer than the north and west, with lower incomes per head. Even so, the general progress of the European economy affected the whole continent. Western Europe invested in the developing countries – German firms supported new

chemical industries in Russia, the British invested in Caucasian oil, and French investment helped to finance the Trans-Siberian railway. In the other direction, grain from Ukraine was exported to feed the urban populations of western Europe. The countries of advanced, industrial Europe and those of developing, agricultural Europe worked in symbiosis.

Industry and agriculture also overlapped a good deal in individual countries. Even in Germany, the growing industrial giant, agriculture occupied about 40 per cent of the active population and provided 20 per cent of the national income in 1914. In France, the equivalent figures were even higher, with 40–45 per cent of the active population engaged in agriculture, providing 30–35 per cent of the national income. Only in Britain had the balance swung decisively towards industry, with agriculture occupying only 12 per cent of the active population and producing only 9 per cent of the national income.[8] In all three countries the political and social influence of landowners and the countryside remained considerable. In Germany the Junker landowners of Prussia held a predominant place at the imperial court and in the army. In France it was virtually impossible for any government to go against the interests, or even wishes, of the countryside and small towns, whose representatives controlled parliament. In Britain the possession of great estates conferred great prestige, and the landed aristocracy took a prominent role in political life.

Large-scale emigration showed that large numbers of Europeans were voting with their steamship tickets to leave their own countries in search of a better life, often at the cost of immense hardship. A mass of individual decisions thus revealed a determination to escape from poverty in Europe. Yet at the same time other indicators told a different story, of a rising population (in spite of emigration), growing industrial production, flourishing foreign trade and in much of northern and western Europe an improving standard of living and longer expectation of life. This formed the background to the cohesion which the continent displayed in several other respects.

THE POLITICAL LANDSCAPE

Politically, almost every country in Europe was a monarchy, which was still the most widely practised form of government and the accepted basis for a state's legitimacy. When Balkan countries gained their independence from the Ottoman Empire during the nineteenth century, they set out to find kings, usually from among the established royal families of Europe. (The one exception, Greece's attempt at a republic, was short-lived.) In Scandinavia, when Norway separated from Sweden in 1905, it was taken for granted that a monarchy was essential for the respectability of the new state, and King Haakon filled the role to perfection from 1905 to 1957. Only the Swiss, with their long-established republican tradition, France under the Third Republic and Portugal after the deposition of the king in 1910 stood outside this monarchical monopoly.

2   Monarchs and relatives: King George V and Tsar Nicholas II © Hulton Archive/Getty Images

The role of the monarchs was in part decorative and symbolic, setting the tone for the upper echelons of society and providing a focus for the rituals of state. They also exercised practical power and influence in varying degrees, ranging from the autocracy of the Russian tsars, which was scarcely diminished by the introduction of a Duma after 1905, to the limited role of constitutional monarchies in Britain and the Scandinavian countries. In Austria-Hungary the Emperor Franz Joseph played a vital part in holding his diverse empire together by his sheer longevity (he reigned from 1848 to 1916) and his diligent application to his duties. In Germany the kaiser held a key position, as the head of the armed forces, with the title of Supreme War Lord; in addition, the chancellor was responsible to the kaiser, not to the Reichstag. Wilhelm II played his role to the full. He has been well described as an actor who overplayed his part and sometimes wrote his own lines. It was the kaiser himself, addressing German troops departing for China in 1900, who urged them to follow the terrifying example of the Huns under Attila, thus leaving the Germans with the nickname of 'Hun' for many years to come.[9]

At the same time almost every European country accepted the principle of representative democracy, though its application varied widely. Parliamentary

government was well established in Britain, France, the Low Countries and the Scandinavian states, though in different forms. France practised manhood suffrage, while Britain operated a restricted franchise based on property. In Germany the Reichstag was elected by manhood suffrage, but exercised more limited powers than the British and French parliaments. Russia remained an autocracy for most practical purposes, but the revolution of 1905 compelled even the tsar to accept a form of parliament.

A historian writing in 1910 could confidently claim that 'the steady advance of democracy' had been the most remarkable feature of the last 40 years of European history. Moreover, it appeared to be a characteristically European form of government: 'a European invention, and perhaps only suited to the European race and European culture'.[10] This growth of democracy and parliamentary institutions seemed at the time an inevitable part of the progress which had characterized Europe in the nineteenth century. Outside Russia, a reversion to autocracy seemed unthinkable. No one would have imagined that by the late 1930s most European countries would be ruled by dictatorships of one sort or another, and parliamentary democracies would have become an endangered species. In this respect, at any rate, it is not surprising that the period before 1914 took on the aura of a golden age.

THE CLASS SYSTEM

Alongside this mixture of monarchy and representative institutions which gave Europe its political cohesion there stood a class system shared in essentials by the whole continent. Class might be defined legally (for example, by the possession of a patent of nobility), by occupation (the professions were bourgeois, manual labourers were working class) or, more subtly, by modes of speech (Eliza Doolittle could pass as a lady by changing her accent and idiom), but in any case it was all-pervasive.

The aristocracy, meaning 'a hereditary, legally privileged, socially dominant ruling class', retained an important place in most countries.[11] In British politics the long-lived influence of the aristocracy seems surprising in retrospect, but at the time was largely taken for granted. Lord Salisbury's last Cabinet, formed in 1895, was headed by a marquess and included seven other noblemen and two baronets; out of its sixteen members only six were commoners – and one of those, Arthur Balfour, was Salisbury's nephew. The House of Lords, mainly made up of hereditary peers, retained its unrestricted powers over legislation (except in financial matters) until the Parliament Act of 1911. In Germany the Junkers exerted immense influence through the officer corps, the administration and the imperial court. The aristocracy held powerful positions in the Austro-Hungarian and Russian Empires. The great exception was France, where the aristocracy had little political influence in the Third Republic, though retaining some standing in the army and the diplomatic corps.

Aristocratic society worked in similar ways over most of Europe, and especially in the great capital cities. A British nobleman was entirely at home in Paris, and reasonably so in St Petersburg – though he would have found the rules for the leaving of visiting cards stricter in St Petersburg than in London. Russian aristocratic families often spoke French at home and employed British or Swiss nannies and governesses to raise their children. Across the continent, great landowners followed similar ways of life and pursued the same sports and recreations. Their most natural profession was the army, particularly in the guards and cavalry regiments.

The bourgeoisie was more amorphous, displaying an immense variety, from great bankers to small shopkeepers, and yet it had common characteristics over most of Europe. In contrast to the aristocracy, bourgeois families preferred saving and investment to ostentatious expense, seeking to pass on the family fortune undiminished, and if possible increased, to the next generation – a task which was made easier in an age of stable prices and sound money. Families insisted on a good education for their sons, and sometimes for their daughters too. Perhaps above all, the bourgeoisie had attained respectability, and intended to retain it – not an unworthy aim, though one despised by some artists and intellectuals, who delighted in shocking the bourgeoisie. Members of the European bourgeoisie were easily recognizable across Europe, though they travelled less freely and transplanted less easily than aristocrats.

Europe also included a large and mostly urban working class, engaged in industry, mining, building and transport. There were wide differences between skilled and unskilled workers, the migrant builders of the construction industry and the settled communities of mining villages. Skilled workers formed a sort of aristocracy, protecting their privileges as zealously as did the landed aristocracy, and often with equal success. In western Europe industrial workers were increasingly organized in trade unions: in 1911, German trade unions numbered 3,061,000 members, British 3,010,000 and French 1,029,000. Industrial workers were also organized in socialist parties, strongest in Germany but influential in many countries; the Second Socialist International, founded in 1889, brought together socialists across the continent (see below, pp. 23–4).

Across most of Europe, agriculture remained a vital (and sometimes the predominant) sector in the economy. In 1914, it was estimated that two-thirds of the active population was engaged in agriculture; in France, the figure was between 40 and 45 per cent. Agriculture itself was changing in character in much the same way, though at different speeds. New crops were being introduced; farm implements were being improved (for example, with the introduction of the iron plough, or something so simple as the replacement of the scythe by the sickle); breeds of livestock were being improved. The development of railways in the second half of the nineteenth century allowed bulky, and sometimes perishable, agricultural produce to be transported quickly, and also brought farmers in different countries into direct competition with each other, and above all with the farmers of the American Middle West, whose crops were now transported by railway and steamship. This was followed by a demand for protective tariffs, which were introduced in nearly every country (with Britain as the only important exception). There were differences in these developments, both across the continent and within countries – in Italy, agricultural practices and conditions in the Po valley in the north and Calabria in the south were very different – but in general the same changes were taking place in the practices of agriculture.[12]

THE ROLE OF THE STATE

Before 1914 all European states carried out much the same functions – modest in comparison to the all-embracing state of our own day, but still significant. The basic tasks of the state were to maintain order, administer law and conduct foreign policy; and in addition governments assumed three further roles: the maintenance of armed forces, the education of children and the provision of social legislation.

Of these functions, the most prominent and most expensive was the military role. In the period before 1914 every major state in Europe except Britain, and most of the minor ones as well, imposed some form of compulsory military service, for periods of between two and four years. These conscript armies were regarded as military necessities, but they also served social and political purposes, notably in France and Italy, where conscription helped to consolidate the nation state. The cost was enormous, not simply because of the sheer numbers of men called up, but also because equipment, especially artillery, was constantly improving. Navies were also extremely expensive, as warships became larger, more heavily armed and more complicated in their machinery. The armed forces absorbed a high proportion of government expenditure; for example, in 1904 France spent 36 per cent of its budget on the army, and Germany 20 per cent.[13]

In later years it came to be taken for granted that these massive armaments were one of the main causes of war in 1914, but at the time it was generally believed that they had a stabilizing effect. The presence of large armed forces had accompanied 40 years of peace in Europe, from 1871 onwards, and had perhaps even contributed to that peace. In 1910 a British historian argued that 'On the whole, the existence of this tremendous military equipment makes for peace', because governments and peoples shrank from the prospect of war between such vast forces.[14] Up to a point that proved to be the case, but after that point had been passed and war had begun, the immense effort put into armaments and the involvement of so large a part of the population meant that it was very difficult to bring a conflict to an end. In earlier times, a monarch could accept defeat or stalemate and negotiate terms, in a way that whole peoples could not. Winston Churchill prophesied in 1901 that the wars of peoples would be more terrible than the wars of kings, and events were to prove him right. But meanwhile the maintenance of great armed forces was a common feature of European life, and appeared to contribute to the stability of states and the cohesion of the continent.

States mobilized their citizens. They also educated them and made some provision for their health and welfare. By 1900 primary education, concentrating on reading, writing and arithmetic, was compulsory and free in the countries of northern and western Europe. Governments used education for their own purposes, to inculcate patriotism and reinforce social cohesion; for example, in France by insisting on the French language in schools instead of Breton or Provençal. But individuals also gained enormously. For industrial workers education offered access to skilled jobs. Farming families moving into the market economy were glad to have children who could read and do accounts. A new mass readership for newspapers, magazines and books developed – in Britain the *Daily Mail* was launched in 1896 and the *Daily Express* in 1900. The situation was different in southern and eastern Europe. In Italy in 1901 about half the adult population could neither read nor write, and the illiteracy rate in parts of the south was as high as 70 per cent.[15] Much of the Russian population remained illiterate, though primary schools were increasing in number.

Over most of Europe governments were also embarking on a new role as providers of social insurance and welfare legislation. In Germany, as early as the 1880s, Bismarck introduced compulsory state insurance against sickness, industrial injury, disability and old age (though the old-age pension only came into effect at the age of 70, which was too late for most people). The Scandinavian states, though at that time far from wealthy, became models for social legislation. Denmark introduced old-age pensions, based on need, in 1891; Sweden initiated compensation for industrial accidents in 1901 and universal old-age pensions in 1913. In Britain the Liberal governments of 1905–14 were keenly interested in the German system, which was used as the basis for legislation on old-age pensions and insurance against illness and unemployment. France introduced compensation for industrial accidents between 1898 and 1902, and old-age pensions in 1910. The outlines of what was to be the characteristically European phenomenon of the welfare state were already visible in large parts of the continent, though not yet in Russia or the Balkan countries.

POLITICAL MOVEMENTS AND IDEAS

The cohesion of Europe was also marked by the presence of various political movements and ideas which were common to the continent as a whole. For most of the nineteenth century the main progressive force in European politics was liberalism, characterized by an emphasis on individual freedom, the rights of man, parliamentary institutions and the rule of law. Liberalism transcended class differences, so that many industrial workers supported liberal parties; the bourgeoisie was often liberal in politics though socially conservative; and many aristocrats were devoted to liberal ideas, especially in

Britain, where Whig nobles formed an important element of the Liberal Party up to the 1880s. It was also largely taken for granted that liberalism went hand in hand with nationalism, and that there was no fundamental conflict between the two.

At the end of the nineteenth and in the early twentieth centuries liberalism was under challenge on the left by socialism. Socialist parties were thriving across much of Europe, united by Marxism as a political doctrine and linked by the Second Socialist International, with its permanent bureau in Brussels – already a significant international centre.

Among the European socialist parties, the German Social Democratic Party (the SPD – *Sozialdemokratische Partei Deutschlands*) was by far the strongest, with 1.7 million members in 1913, a strong administration, its own newspapers and a web of social activities. The party's vote in parliamentary elections showed a remarkable upward trend: 1.4 million votes and 35 seats in 1890, 3 million votes and 81 seats in 1903 and 4.25 million votes and 110 seats in 1912, when the SPD became the largest single party in the Reichstag. It was true that the party was rent by theoretical disputes between orthodox Marxists, proclaiming the class struggle and advocating revolution, and revisionists, who preferred evolution to revolution; but in practice the German socialists were able to unite in securing material advantages for the working class, in which they achieved much success. In France, a number of socialist groups came together in 1905 to form the *Section Française de l'Internationale Ouvrière* (SFIO), which won 1.3 million votes and 101 seats in the legislative elections of April–May 1914. The Austrian socialist party secured just over a million votes and 51 seats in the Vienna parliament in 1907. In Italy the socialists won 900,000 votes and 51 seats in 1913, in the first Italian elections held under manhood suffrage. The advance of socialism seemed inexorable.[16]

Every three years the Socialist International held great congresses, with lively social programmes as well as ardent political debates. These congresses were much concerned with the danger of European war and the best means of preventing it. The Stuttgart Congress of 1907 passed unanimously a long resolution declaring that the working classes had the duty to prevent the outbreak of war 'by whatever means seem to them most effective...'[17] These means were left undefined; a proposal to prevent war by calling a general strike was put forward in 1910, but deferred until the next Congress, fixed for 1913. That Congress was itself postponed until 1914, when it was overtaken by the outbreak of war. The debates on war revealed a deep-seated problem within the socialist movement. Many socialists were conscious that, whatever Marx had said about the worker having no fatherland, this was frequently untrue. German socialists instinctively supported their own country against Russia – a hereditary enemy which was also an enemy of socialism. French socialists were loyal to France – as Jean Jaurès (the most inspiring figure in the whole socialist movement) declared in 1910: 'Those Frenchmen, if there are any left, who say that it is all the same to them whether they live under the German troopers or the French troopers...commit a sophism which by its very absurdity makes refutation difficult.'[18] The unpalatable truth was that, despite its name, the Socialist International was riven by nationalism. The International itself was organized in sections by countries, which made much practical sense but raised problems about nations which did not yet have a country. Polish members within the German socialist party demanded, and eventually achieved, a separate section. A Czech socialist party was established by breaking away from the Austrian party. The debates on war in the Socialist International were at once passionate and hollow, because at bottom, with very few exceptions, socialists were more loyal to their own country than to socialism – or at any rate believed that the two loyalties were compatible. The outbreak of war in 1914 was to see the collapse of the Socialist International.

We should not allow this final failure in a great crisis to obscure the significance of the Socialist International, which was for a quarter of a century a powerful expression of European, as well as socialist, solidarity. Moreover, socialism itself survived the disaster of 1914, and in different forms has remained a vital and distinctive element in European politics.

On the right wing of European politics, conservatives shared no all-embracing political doctrine comparable to Marxism on the left. Instead, they assumed certain truths to be self-evident. They preferred continuity to change, and evolution to revolution. They supported religion and legitimate authority – 'Church and King' or 'King and country' were still resonant watchwords. They respected hierarchy, as against equality. In such ways conservatism existed in all countries, though in diverse forms and under different names. Indeed, it is a curious fact that conservative parties rarely called themselves such – the British Conservative Party was an exception. Across the Channel France was in many ways a profoundly conservative country, but right-wing parties felt bound to call themselves Republican or Popular, or even Radical.

In the late nineteenth century it seemed possible that political Catholicism might provide a basis of unity for a large section of European conservatism. From 1870 onwards the papacy offered strong social and political leadership, based negatively on opposition to socialism and liberalism, and positively on the idea of a Catholic social order that would transcend the materialist values of capitalist society. But politically active Catholics were themselves divided between conservatives, prepared to follow Pope Pius IX in rejecting all compromise with the modern world, and liberals, anxious to come to terms with democracy and even with socialism. In these circumstances the safest course was often to stand aside from politics in general, intervening only in defence of specific Catholic interests (for example, church schools or the appointment of bishops). The Catholic Centre Party in Germany, which took a full part in the activities of the Reichstag, was an exception in this respect;

and in general political Catholicism remained a latent, rather than an active conservative force.

Towards the end of the nineteenth century a new force emerged on the right wing of European politics, in the shape of radical nationalism. This new nationalism broke away from the long-standing alliance between nationalism and liberalism, because its adherents rejected the tolerance and regard for individual freedom that were characteristic of liberalism. It was also, almost by definition, opposed to socialism, which was *international* in its nature, asserting the primacy of class over nationality. Later, in the twentieth century, a new amalgam was to be formed: national socialism (in Germany, Nazism for short), which brought the two ideas together in an explosive mixture; but that is another story. The adherents of the new nationalism were mainly found among the young, who were not conservative but radical or even revolutionary, and were often fiercely xenophobic, identifying nation with race.

This new nationalism was often linked to a revival of anti-Semitism, an ancient and deep-rooted sentiment (often amounting to a mania) which sprang into renewed life towards the end of the nineteenth century. Pogroms in Russia in the 1880s drove Jews out of Russia, often to settle in Warsaw, Vienna and other cities in eastern or central Europe, where they attracted much hostility as a result of their distinctive dress and way of life. Anti-Semitism was far from being confined to such cases, but was directed even against Jews who had long been assimilated into the societies where they lived. The old hatred of the Jew as usurer was transformed by anti-capitalist sentiment into hostility to the Jew as sophisticated banker or speculator. Anti-Semitism was reinforced and given pseudo-scientific support by racial theories expounded by Gobineau and Houston Stewart Chamberlain. An offshoot of these views appeared in Edouard Drumont's *La France juive*, published in 1886 and reprinted 200 times by 1914. Anti-Semitism, long endemic in France, burst into public view in the Dreyfus affair. In 1894 Captain Dreyfus, an assimilated Jew serving in the French Army, was wrongly accused of passing secret information to the Germans. He was found guilty, at least partly because he was Jewish, and sentenced to imprisonment on Devil's Island. Many Frenchmen (mostly not Jewish) rallied to his defence, and his case became the centre of a legal, political and moral storm which attracted attention and aroused emotions throughout France and Europe. Ultimately Dreyfus was pardoned by the president of the Republic, returned to the army and served in the Great War. In retrospect it seems astonishing that such widespread and intense feeling could be aroused by an unjust verdict in a case brought against a single man; but so it was. The Dreyfus case was both a sign of the strength of anti-Semitism and a testimony to the quality of French political life. The Third Republic was in many ways corrupt and time-serving, but many of its politicians and writers were capable of great courage and persistence. Europe too showed the virtues of its liberal tradition in the widespread concern for the fate of Captain Dreyfus.

When Dreyfus was stripped of his rank on the barrack square, the event was witnessed by a Jewish journalist, Theodore Herzl, representing the *Neue Freie Presse* of Vienna. Herzl heard the crowd in the street shouting 'Death to the Jews', and rapidly concluded that the only long-term security for his people lay in the establishment of a Jewish state. He became the founder and moving spirit of Zionism; wrote a book, *Der Judenstaat*, to expound his ideas; and organized the first Zionist Congress in 1897. This set in train a movement which eventually culminated in the establishment in 1948 of the state of Israel, which has in turn become the focus of fierce conflict and renewed anti-Semitism. In the intervening years, European anti-Semitism reached an unheard-of intensity and violence in Nazi Germany. The Dreyfus affair called out some of the best qualities in European politics; and later the anti-Semitism of Nazi Germany called into question the whole nature of European civilization.

Another 'ism' was also active in Europe: feminism, in the sense of 'the doctrine of equal rights for women, based on the theory of the equality of the sexes'.[19] This movement was largely middle class in its make-up, and was led by a small number of educated and articulate women, with the time, energy and social standing to make themselves felt. Their aims were in the first place economic: access to education, and by that means entry into the professions; and the right for married women to control property and money. They were also moral: the pursuit of equal standards for women and men in sexual morality; the regulation or abolition of prostitution; and support for temperance movements and the control of alcohol. The securing of the franchise (votes for women) was both a practical means of achieving these aims and a symbol of the feminist cause.

The nature of feminism, and the degree of its success, varied widely. There was a marked difference between Protestant Europe, where the movement flourished, and Catholic Europe, where it was slow to start and gained little support; and also between countries dominated by the Napoleonic Code of 1804, which allotted rights to fathers of families, and the countries of northern Europe which followed a common-law or Nordic tradition. Among individual countries, Britain had the largest and most active feminist movement, and produced its most distinguished theorist in John Stuart Mill. The Scandinavian movements achieved the greatest successes, with women gaining the vote in Finland in 1906, and Norway by stages in 1907 and 1913; Denmark followed in 1915. In France, a number of feminist movements developed, notably the National Council of French Women (which claimed 100,000 members in 1914) and the French Union for Women's Suffrage (with 12,000 members). But these movements worked under a double disadvantage in the firm establishment of the Napoleonic Code and the opposition of the Catholic Church; and they attracted little support from republicans and anticlericals, who were afraid that the influence of women voters would strengthen the right wing – and who were against change anyway. Secondary education for girls made rapid progress, but with little follow-up in entry to higher education and the professions – only 3 per cent of French doctors were women in 1910.[20] In most of Germany, women were prevented by law from forming political associations (the German Union for Women's Suffrage was founded in Hamburg, where this legal ban did not operate). Women secured entry to universities between 1902 and 1908, but married women still had no control over property. In Austria-Hungary there were feminist groups in the big cities (Vienna, Budapest and Prague), but these made little headway against the prevailing climate of opinion. In Italy there was only a weak feminist movement, and an even weaker demand for the vote. Feminism was thus unevenly represented across Europe, and was far from being solely European, flourishing strongly in the USA. In Australia and New Zealand women gained the vote well before 1914, but even changes far from Europe had their effects on the 'old continent'.

Behind the activities of the feminist vanguard and its specific demands there lay changes in the position of women in much of Europe. In northern and western Europe women were having fewer children, and were free from some of the burdens of constant pregnancy and childbirth. This did not 'release' them to work, as is sometimes said, because most women had *always* worked – on farms, in factories, in shops or in domestic service. But it did open the way in the future for girls who had achieved a secondary education to have a better chance of going to university and pursuing a career.

THE INTERNATIONAL STAGE

In the years before 1914 Europe was in many ways a coherent whole, with similar political institutions, social classes and political movements spanning the continent. This common European identity was also apparent in the conduct of international relations.

In part this was a response to practical problems and requirements. A Telegraphic Union was set up in 1865 by representatives of 20 states, and comprised a total of 48 states or colonies by 1911. (This was primarily a European body, of which the USA was not a member.) An International Railway Convention to ensure the smooth working of rail transport was formed by the governments of Austria-Hungary, Belgium, France, Germany, Italy, Luxembourg, the Netherlands, Russia and Switzerland. Conventions governing navigation on the Rhine and Danube were concluded by the various riparian states in 1868 and 1878 respectively. There was a sign of a new era in the signature of a convention on road vehicles in 1910. The interests of private enterprise were advanced by the founding of an International Chamber of Commerce in 1905, with the purpose of bringing about a unification of national laws on matters affecting international trade. By 1914 this body had established a permanent executive committee and bureau, with their headquarters in Brussels – a presage of things to come. The protection of workers' rights also became an international matter, and by 1914

22 European states belonged to the International Association for the Protection of Labour.[21]

These different bodies (and this list is by no means complete) demonstrated the need for a large measure of European administration to meet the continent's requirements in communication, transport, commerce and industry, which all had to operate across state boundaries. For example, a train would leave Paris every night in the near certainty of arriving in Constantinople at its scheduled time after passing a number of frontiers during its journey. Before 1914, this degree of European administration was successfully achieved by international agreements and cooperation between governments, and was part of that cohesion which Europeans largely took for granted.

Where high politics and foreign policy were concerned, European governments also achieved at least some degree of cooperation. Statesmen liked to refer to 'the Concert of Europe', an attractive idea implying that their countries shared certain interests, and invoking comparison with an orchestra, in which different instruments played their parts in a harmonious whole. In practice, the Concert of Europe worked only occasionally, notably in dealing with the problems of the Ottoman Empire, which was an outsider, and the Balkan states, which were weak enough to be coerced. In 1878 the great powers met at the Congress of Berlin, under Bismarck's chairmanship, and settled a long and difficult Balkan crisis. In 1897 the powers intervened in a war between Greece and Turkey over Crete, imposing a settlement under which that island was garrisoned for a time by forces from the great European states – an unusual and largely forgotten example of European cooperation. In 1913 a Conference of Ambassadors of the great powers, meeting in London under the chairmanship of Sir Edward Grey, did much to resolve the problems left over by the Balkan Wars of 1912–13. This was the last success for the old Concert of Europe. When Grey tried to call a similar conference in the crisis of 1914, he failed – the members of the orchestra no longer responded to the conductor. The Concert had never lived up to the aspirations of its admirers, but it had provided a useful means of European cooperation.

Europe also enjoyed the benefits of a well-organized system of diplomacy, which had evolved over some four centuries. The diplomats who represented their respective countries in foreign capitals were often aristocrats, with the same polished manners as well as professional customs. They conducted their negotiations in secret, usually with patience, and in careful and precise language. After the Great War this 'old diplomacy' was widely attacked for its secrecy and its immunity from popular control, and critics demanded its replacement by a new, democratic and open diplomacy. Yet in fact the old diplomacy possessed great virtues and provided a stable framework for the conduct of foreign policy throughout Europe. Its successors, whether in the form of the 'open diplomacy' advocated by President Wilson, or the ideological diplomacy of Communist Russia or Nazi Germany, had little to commend them, and divided Europe when the old diplomacy had brought it together.

Under the guidance of these accepted diplomatic methods, Europe developed a system of alliances and alignments. Germany and Austria-Hungary were linked from 1879 in a Dual Alliance, joined by Italy in 1882 to form a Triple Alliance. France and Russia concluded an alliance against Germany in 1894. In 1904 Britain and France signed an entente, settling various disputes and providing for diplomatic cooperation in the future; and in 1907 Britain and Russia also reached an entente, registering agreement on problems between the two countries in parts of Asia. Europe thus became divided into two blocs. Germany and Austria-Hungary (the Central Powers) faced France and Russia, with Italy loosely connected to one side and Britain to the other. Like the old diplomacy, this alliance system came to be seen as one of the causes of the Great War, but for many years the division did not seem unduly dangerous. The old antagonism between France and Germany, recently sharpened by the Franco-Prussian War in 1870–71, appeared to be diminishing. In France, the call for revenge against Germany lost some of its appeal, and it seemed that the people of Alsace-Lorraine were becoming accustomed to their place in Germany. The endemic rivalry between Russia and Austria-Hungary in the Balkans had also abated. The two great power blocs balanced one another, offering a sort of stability to Europe as a whole.

Hopes ranged beyond mere stability to the prospect of a lasting peace. The Nobel Peace Prize was first awarded in 1901, and was shared by Henri Dunant, the founder of the Red Cross and a principal architect of the Geneva Convention of 1864, and Frédéric Passy, a French economist and ardent pacifist. Just two years earlier, in 1899, Tsar Nicholas II had invited all countries with diplomatic representatives at his capital to hold a conference on the limitation of armaments. His ministers were largely influenced by practical issues, notably the heavy expense of introducing a new type of quick-firing field gun to match Austrian artillery of the same kind; but the tsar himself was young, idealistic and eager to promote the cause of peace. Other governments were sceptical, but none cared to decline. From 18 May to 29 July delegates from 26 countries met at The Hague and agreed on three conventions, dealing with arbitration, the laws and customs of war, and regulations for the use of various weapons, including poison gas. These agreements were often disregarded in later conflicts, but the basic attempt to establish laws and customs of war was never abandoned. Once started along this road, governments felt bound to go on. A second Hague Conference met in 1907, attended by 44 countries and lasting four months. There probably would have been a third conference, but the Great War intervened, bringing a sad and ironic end to this search for peace.

We know the tragic end of the story, but in pre-1914 Europe hopes for peace were strong and apparently well founded. Since 1815 Europe had enjoyed a long period of comparative peace – not free from conflict (as the Crimean War, the Franco-Prussian War and other hostilities remind us), but without war on a continental scale. In 1910 Norman Angell's book, *The Great Illusion*, demonstrated (with apparently unanswerable logic) that economic self-interest would prevent the powers from going to war. In the eleventh edition of the *Encyclopaedia Britannica*, published in 1911, the article on 'Peace', by Sir Thomas Barclay, declared that 'war is coming, among progressive peoples, to be regarded merely as an accidental disturbance of that harmony and concord among mankind which nations require for the fostering of their domestic welfare.'[22] It was true that different sentiments could be heard, for example in Berlin, and that some Europeans felt a sense of impending doom and heard 'voices prophesying war'.[23] But rational men, of whom there were many, could discern a sure progress towards peace, order and prosperity. Since then we have supped so deep on horrors that it is almost impossible to recapture, or even comprehend, that mood, which was in itself a striking sign of the stability and coherence of Europe.

This same Europe exerted an almost unquestioned superiority in the world. In 1910 a Cambridge historian wrote that 'in the world-wide struggle for life, wealth and power the Europeans have for the moment proved their indisputable predominance.'[24] European states controlled almost the whole of Africa and most of Asia. Even countries which remained nominally independent, like China, were compelled to accept European intervention and influence. In the American hemisphere the independent states which had replaced former European colonies remained partly European in character. Australia and New Zealand were essentially European states at a vast distance from the mother continent. The full geographical extent of this predominance was strikingly recent, testifying to the rapid growth of European influence in the nineteenth century. In 1800 about 35 per cent of the earth's land surface was under European control, whether as actual or former colonies; in 1878, 67 per cent; and in 1914, a remarkable 84 per cent.[25] Most European countries had colonial possessions of one sort or another, from the great powers (Britain, France, Germany, Italy and Russia) to the medium-sized (Spain) and the small (Belgium, the Netherlands, Portugal). Even Denmark held three islands in the Caribbean. Only Norway, Sweden, Switzerland, Austria-Hungary and the newly emerged Balkan states took no part in imperial expansion. Most empires were seaborne, but Russia expanded overland, conquering Central Asia and pushing the frontier of settlement across Siberia to the Pacific. This had the curious result that Russia was often not regarded as an imperial power at all. The Russians conquered Uzbeks and the British conquered Zulus; Russian migrants settled in Bokhara and French in Algeria. There was very little difference, especially from the losers' point of view, and yet it is the British and French rather than the Russians who have usually been described as imperialists.

Territorial control was accompanied by an immense self-confidence and sense of cultural superiority. A British historian wrote in 1910 of his country's 'consistent and sustained attempt to ameliorate the condition of the Indian peoples, to confer upon them the benefits of Western knowledge and Western ideals of government...'[26] The French similarly had no doubt of their civilizing mission. Only the Dutch, it seems, cared little for spreading civilization or religion, and simply got on with trading. All European countries were confident of their right and ability to impose their will by force. In the space of a few years the British sent an expedition to Lhasa (1904); the Germans crushed rebellions in East and South-West Africa (1905–7); and the Dutch completed the occupation of Sumatra (1908). These events were regarded as the small change of imperialism and passed with little notice in London, Berlin and The Hague.[27]

All in all Europeans saw the world as their oyster, and opened it more or less at will. Migrants went in large numbers to North America, Australasia, Latin America, Algeria, South Africa, Central Asia and even Siberia. Investments went mainly to the USA, and to the colonies of white settlement (plus India), which offered high and usually safe returns, rather than to the new colonies in Africa, which were risky ventures. Trade and raw materials were sought where they could be found. The Christian churches, faced by increasing secularization at home in Europe, threw themselves with enthusiasm into missionary activities in Africa and Asia. Plant hunters penetrated the fastnesses of China and Sikkim to send specimens to botanical gardens in Kew or Paris. European mountaineers explored the peaks, passes and glaciers of the Himalayas, while sturdy women travellers such as Isabella Bird and Marianne North journeyed to remote parts of the earth, often with sketchpads and easels.

As the nineteenth became the twentieth century there were signs that the tide of imperialism was beginning to turn. In 1900 the partition of China seemed almost certain to follow that of Africa. The ancient empire was in decay and the European powers, plus Japan, were staking their claims. In 1900 the Boxer Rising in China led to the siege of the foreign legations in Peking, and an international relief force (Austrian, British, French, German, Italian and Russian, along with Japanese and American contingents) marched from Tientsin to relieve the siege and occupy the Chinese capital. This was Europe in action, with the Americans and Japanese being treated as honorary Europeans for the purposes of the expedition. The final dissolution of China seemed imminent. Yet it did not occur. Russia, which might have taken the lead in partitioning China, instead went to war with Japan and was defeated in the war of 1904–5. The other powers were content with commercial advantages and hesitated to take on new territories. The wave, apparently about to break, instead receded.

At much the same time, the world's greatest imperial power, Britain, was suffering a bloody nose and a severe jolt to its self-confidence at the hands of the Boers. In the Boer War of 1899–1902 the British had to deploy 400,000 men to defeat the Republics of the Transvaal and the Orange Free State. After winning the war in the field they had to win the guerrilla war by criss-crossing the veldt with fences of barbed wire and gathering Boer families into what the British themselves called concentration camps – an ill-omened name, though as yet without the terrible connotations it later acquired. The British won the Boer War, but it was a Pyrrhic victory. 'The imperial idea had...suffered a contraction, a loss of moral content, from which it never completely recovered.'[28]

There were other signs of European decline. In 1898 the USA went to war with Spain and won, 'liberating' Cuba and annexing the Philippines, putting an end to the Spanish Empire in the Caribbean and the South Pacific. In 1904–5 Russia went to war with Japan and lost. A Russian fleet was annihilated at the battle of Tsushima, and the army lost a long campaign in Manchuria. These two wars were won respectively by a country of European origin (the USA) and a country which had modernized on European lines (Japan). It is true that Spain was one of the weaker European powers and Russia was fighting far from its main centres, but even so, these wars were portents. The tide of European dominance in the world had reached high-water mark and was beginning to turn.

2

THE DIVERSITY OF EUROPE: CONTRASTS AND DIVISIONS

Europe before 1914 displayed a cohesion probably greater than at any previous time in its history. Yet alongside that cohesion there existed contrasts and divisions which marked the diversity of the continent. Europe was the smallest of the continents but also the most varied in its make-up. Liberalism and autocracy, dynamism and inertia, orderly progress and violent upheaval all coexisted with one another. It is time to look at what divided the continent.

FRANCE

Liberal Europe was represented above all by France and Britain. France enjoyed the prestige of being the home of the Enlightenment, the revolutionary tradition and the Rights of Man, representing an immense attraction for progressive and liberal political thinkers everywhere. Paris was also the cultural capital of Europe, a magnet for writers and artists. Stravinsky, though born in Russia, flourished in France and became a naturalized Frenchman; his ballet *The Rite of Spring* had its premiere in Paris in 1913, and it is hard to see where else it could have been performed. In 1900 some 50 million people visited the Paris International Exhibition, a showcase for French culture and commerce. It was true that French political life was tainted by corruption, as in the affair of the Panama Canal shares, and by anti-Semitism, displayed in the Dreyfus affair; and that the Third Republic suffered from chronic ministerial instability, with governments lasting on average no more than a year. But the Dreyfus case brought out the best as well as the worst in French politics, and much of the political instability was superficial. As one French politician remarked at the end of the 1890s, 'We present the spectacle of a tranquil people with agitated legislators.'[1] Even the legislators were only superficially agitated, because they were usually long-serving representatives of their home areas, and firmly grounded in local politics and interests. France, with its advanced democratic constitution, based on manhood suffrage and with an elaborate system of checks and balances to control the power of the state, was a leader of European liberalism as well as civilization.

BRITAIN

While France was the home of the revolutionary tradition, Britain prided itself on having avoided revolution since the seventeenth century. Tennyson's lines in praise of 'A land of settled government / …Where Freedom slowly broadens down / From precedent to precedent' still commanded general consent. At the end of the nineteenth century the unwritten British constitution combined monarchy, aristocracy and democracy in what the British believed to be the most mature and stable form of government in Europe – a view with which many Europeans agreed. It was true that early in the twentieth century the British had their difficulties, with widespread strikes, a suffragette movement which the government did not know how to deal with, and a crisis over Home Rule in Ireland which threatened the country with civil war – a famous book about this period was entitled *The Strange Death of Liberal England*[2] – but liberal (with a small 'l') England did not die, and Britain was to prove a sturdier bastion of parliamentary democracy than some feared in 1912–14. During the Great War both Britain and France were to show that their forms of government had deep reserves of resilience and adaptability.

RUSSIA

Geographically at the opposite side of Europe from France and Britain, and at the far end of the political spectrum from their liberal regimes, lay Russia, as usual partly in and partly out of the European mainstream. In some ways, Russia was becoming a modern European state. Economically the country was growing at extraordinary speed – more rapidly in percentage terms than any other European country, though starting from a very low base. Oil production (soon to become a great asset in a modern economy) was the highest among European states, at 10.28 million tons in 1913. There was a large-scale movement of population from the country to the towns, with the urban population reaching about 27 million by 1914, about double the figure for 1910.[3] Stolypin, one of the tsar's most energetic ministers, embarked in 1906 on a programme of agrarian reform which he called 'the wager on the strong', designed to consolidate peasant landholdings and create a new class of prosperous and efficient landowning farmers. This enterprise achieved considerable success, improving Russian agriculture and providing a stabilizing force in the countryside.

Yet in other respects Russia was neither modern nor European. Against the trend in the continent as a whole, Russian politics moved back towards unrelieved autocracy. In 1905, in the face of revolution at home and defeat by

Japan abroad, the tsar had set up an elected Duma, or parliament, with legislative powers. But in 1906 the tsar promulgated new Fundamental Laws which reclaimed wide powers for the monarch, and in 1907 used these powers to change the methods of election to the advantage of the gentry and to the detriment of the peasants and industrial workers. Russia thus veered back towards autocracy only two years after its move towards constitutional government. Moreover, Tsar Nicholas II was that most dangerous of rulers, a weak autocrat. He was much influenced by his wilful and unstable wife, Alexandra, who was herself rendered desperate by the illness of their only son, a haemophiliac. In her desperation, Alexandra fell under the spell of Rasputin, a fantastic and sinister figure, at once monk, healer, voluptuary and charlatan. Only in Russia, among all the European countries of that time, could such an extraordinary creature have attained so influential a position at court. It was a sign that Russia was neither a fully modern nor a fully European state.

In September 1911 there was another sign. Stolypin, the driving force of agrarian reform, was assassinated in extraordinary circumstances, being shot by a police secret agent who was associated with the revolutionaries on whom he was supposed to be spying. As Barbara Tuchman commented, 'The half-lunatic world of the Romanov twilight had so darkened that it was never clear whether the assassins were genuine revolutionaries or *agents provocateurs* of the police.'[4] G.K. Chesterton's *The Man Who Was Thursday*, in which the leading anarchist turns out to be also the chief policeman, published in 1908, had been translated into real life.

Russia was in limbo. Constitutional government might conceivably have worked, if it had been tried seriously. Autocracy could have worked, if applied with enough ruthlessness and efficiency, as Stalin was to show some years later. But Russia before 1914 achieved neither constitutional government nor efficient autocracy. The country stood in stark contrast to almost anywhere else in Europe. Neither the life of Rasputin nor the death of Stolypin was conceivable in any other country in the continent.

GERMANY

There was no doubt of the European character of Germany and Austria-Hungary, neighbours, allies and in many ways the heirs of a common history and culture. Yet in other ways these two countries displayed the remarkable diversity of Europe in the contrast between German dynamism and Austro-Hungarian inertia.

The dynamism of the newly created German Empire was astonishing. The population was increasing rapidly (41 million in 1871, 65 million in 1913). All the economic indices showed remarkable growth. Germany had the strongest army in Europe, and from about 1900 set out to build a great navy as well. German universities and schools were admired and emulated throughout Europe. German philosophers and biblical scholars were the leaders in their fields. German social legislation set standards for others to follow. Yet this dynamism was in some ways febrile, and the country was uncertain of itself. Even the greatest German successes seemed precarious. The booming German industries had to find ever increasing markets for their products, and there was a constant fear that these markets might at any time be closed by protectionist tariffs. After all, the Americans already had the McKinley tariff, and even Britain, that home of free trade, was debating tariff reform. Germany was the strongest military power in Europe, and yet the Germans felt constantly insecure, fearing encirclement by their French and Russian enemies, or alarmed at the prospect of a pre-emptive British strike against their growing navy. Germany was politically divided, including four kingdoms, six grand duchies, five duchies and three free cities, the remnants of a diverse history which still had practical effects. The Prussian aristocracy, which dominated the imperial court and the officer corps, was in many respects opposed to the industrialists of the Ruhr, who dominated the economy. Both were deeply disturbed by the growth of socialism among the working class. The German mind seemed possessed by a strange combination of nagging fears and a self-confidence which often spilled over into arrogance, and Germany's neighbours observed her with a mixture of admiration and anxiety.

AUSTRIA-HUNGARY

Germany was dynamic, occasionally to the point of appearing febrile. Austria-Hungary, by contrast, was passive. Its very existence required a balancing act which discouraged change or movement. The *Ausgleich* (compromise) of 1867 provided that the Empire of Austria and the Kingdom of Hungary should be autonomous and equal. They were ruled by the same monarch, so that the Emperor of Austria was also the King of Hungary, and they acted as one unit in foreign policy and defence, with a single diplomatic service and regular army. At the reviews of the *Ausgleich*, which took place every ten years, the Hungarians sought to edge nearer to full independence; for example, in 1907 they sought to set up a regular Hungarian Army, using Magyar as the language of command. The balance between the two halves was thus precarious, but it was maintained, not least by the presence of the aged Emperor Franz Joseph, who had come to the throne almost unimaginably long ago, in December 1848, and held his diverse realms together by respect and force of habit.

The Austro-Hungarian Empire included a diverse array of nationalities. In the Austrian half there were German-speaking Austrians, Czechs, Poles, Ruthenians, Slovenes, Croats and Italians; the Austrians, though a minority, exercised political control. In the Hungarian half there were Hungarians, Germans, Slovaks, Romanians, Serbs and Croats; the Hungarians, who made up about half the population in 1900, controlled the country through a limited franchise and the use of Magyar as the language of education and the courts. As yet, few among the diverse nationalities actually wanted to break free from the empire and establish their own states. Some Italians wanted to join a united Italy; some Serbs and Croats sought union with Serbia or a potential South Slav state; but elsewhere even ardent Czech militants were mainly looking for improved status within the empire, while the Poles knew that they were better off in Austria-Hungary than their fellows in Russia or Germany. Some nationalists condemned the empire as the 'prison of nations', an accusation which later came to appear an absurd exaggeration in an age when nations really *were* imprisoned. In fact, the Austro-Hungarian Empire before 1914 was a remnant of a very old form of state, going back to the sixteenth century and beyond, whose principle of unity was allegiance to the Habsburg dynasty. In an age of growing nationalism the empire was under constant tension and strain, and the safest course seemed to lie in immobility.

After 1918–19, when the empire finally broke up after defeat in the Great War, there were those who regretted its passing. The Austro-Hungarian customs union, which had given some economic cohesion to the Danube basin, contrasted favourably with the destructive economic rivalries between the successor states, and there was some talk of creating a Danubian confederacy to replace the old empire. Before 1914, however, it was Germany which seemed to represent the new Europe, while Austria-Hungary was almost a fossil of the old. They presented a striking contrast in the centre of the continent.

SCANDINAVIA

There was an even starker contrast between Scandinavia and the Balkans, which differed so widely from one another that they hardly seemed to belong to the same continent, except in the simple geographical sense. It was certainly difficult to envisage them as part of the same civilization.

We have already seen that the Scandinavian countries (Sweden, Norway and Denmark) were stable constitutional monarchies, with parliaments elected on manhood suffrage. Norway was a pioneer in the extension of the franchise to women, and all were to the fore in the introduction of old-age pensions and other forms of social insurance – the start of what eventually became the most elaborate social security systems in Europe. Danish farmers were innovators in setting up cooperatives in agriculture – their first cooperative slaughterhouses for pigs were established as early as 1887, and set a pattern for other ventures and other countries.

To these admirable activities was added in 1905 an object lesson in the peaceful settlement of an international dispute. In 1814, as part of the continental settlement at the end of the Napoleonic wars, Norway had been incorporated in a union with Sweden, though retaining its own parliament and judiciary, and exercising a large degree of autonomy in domestic affairs. The union was never an entirely happy one, and by about 1900 the Norwegians were pressing strongly for independence. A plebiscite in Norway

(13 August 1905) showed virtually unanimous support for separation. Negotiations with the Swedish government were difficult and sometimes on the point of breaking down; but in the event the union was dissolved by agreement under the Karlstad Convention of September 1905. The long dispute left some bitterness. It is likely that the lingering shadow of being incorporated in an unpopular union with Sweden played some part in the Norwegian people's refusal, by a referendum in 1972, to join the European Economic Community. But in 1905, at a time when nationalism was becoming more virulent in some parts of Europe, the peaceful separation of Norway from Sweden stood out as a beacon of forbearance and good sense.

THE BALKANS

In striking contrast to this Scandinavian story of orderly politics, social progress and avoidance of war stood the states of the Balkan peninsula, five in number in 1900 (Serbia, Montenegro, Romania, Bulgaria and Greece), plus the European territories of the Ottoman Empire, which at the turn of the century still stretched across what is now northern Greece and Albania to the Adriatic Sea. The Balkan states were all struggling to achieve order and stability at home after winning their independence from the Turks. Montenegro, a wild mountain country which had never been entirely conquered by the Turks, was ruled by the long-lived King Nicholas, who introduced a constitution in 1905 but still governed essentially in his own individual and sometimes despotic manner. Serbia was torn by factions, and in 1903 the ruling Obrenovic dynasty was overthrown by a violent coup, in the course of which the king, the queen and her two brothers, the prime minister and a number of generals were brutally murdered by a group of army officers who restored the rival Karageorgevic dynasty to the throne. This dreadful event shocked civilized Europe, and the British government withdrew its minister from Belgrade. King Edward VII tried to insist that diplomatic representation should not be resumed until the regicides were dismissed from the Serbian Army, but this proved easier said than done. In fact, the conspirators maintained their association as the nucleus of a secret society, called The Black Hand, whose plots eventually culminated in the assassination of the Archduke Franz Ferdinand at Sarajevo in 1914.

The Balkan states all had territorial claims against one another or against the Ottoman Empire, which could not be settled by any known principle, and certainly not by the principle of nationality. In Macedonia, for example, there were a number of different nationalities all mixed up with each other – Albanians, Bulgarians, Greeks, Macedonians, Serbs and Turks; and two principal religions, Greek Orthodox and Muslim, which in many ways counted for more than nationality. The territory of Macedonia, still part of the Ottoman Empire up to 1912, was claimed by three neighbouring states – Bulgaria, Serbia and Greece; and the Bulgarians reinforced their claim by asserting that the Macedonians were themselves Bulgarian, whether they knew it or not.

In 1912–13 several of the Balkan territorial claims were settled by the only means available – war. In the first Balkan War, the Balkan League (bringing together Serbia, Montenegro, Greece and Bulgaria) attacked the Turks and almost drove them out of Europe altogether – the advancing Bulgarian Army was checked only a few miles from Constantinople. But then the victors quarrelled over the spoils, and in a second Balkan War the Bulgarians rashly attacked Serbia and Greece, only to be themselves assailed and defeated by all their neighbours, including Romania and Turkey. At the end of this second war, Macedonia and Thrace were divided between Serbia and Greece, which emerged as the major victors. Serbia in particular gained much in territory, and even more in self-confidence and ambition, which were later turned against Austria-Hungary.

The story of international affairs in the Balkans was one of almost anarchic violence. The European powers sometimes tried to control events. Russian diplomacy played a key part in the creation of the Balkan League, only to find, like the sorcerer's apprentice, that they could not control the force they had conjured up. In 1913 a Conference of Ambassadors representing the six great powers, under the chairmanship of Sir Edward Grey, tried to negotiate settlements in the two Balkan Wars, with only limited success. At other times the European states were tempted to regard the Balkans as a sort of barbaric quarter, which should be isolated or put in quarantine so as not to harm the rest of the continent. But this was impossible. Russia and Austria-Hungary both had interests in the Balkans. All the European powers were concerned in the fate of the Ottoman Empire, and interested in the control of the Straits between the Mediterranean and the Black Sea. In 1914 there began a conflict which might have been only a third Balkan War, between Austria-Hungary and Serbia, but which in fact became the Great War. Balkan politics might be dominated by conspiracies and violence which seemed un-European, and were certainly a far cry from the moderation and good sense of the Scandinavian countries, but it was impossible to prevent them from affecting the whole continent – a lesson which had to be relearned in the crises following the dissolution of Yugoslavia in the 1990s.

TURKEY

The Balkan states, however disorderly and rough-hewn, were part of Europe. Turkey, it was generally assumed, was not. H.A.L. Fisher, a historian of impeccable liberal and internationalist credentials, had no hesitation in describing the Turks at the start of the twentieth century as 'that barbarous Asiatic people'.[5] And yet the position was already growing less clear-cut. In the latter part of the nineteenth century the Ottoman Empire had been trying to modernize itself by introducing a European-style officer corps and administration. In 1908 the Young Turks, a group of middle-ranking army officers, seized power in a *coup d'état* with the aim of modernizing Turkey on European lines. This eventually proved to be the start of a transformation of

Turkish life, but at the time was ambivalent in its significance. The Young Turks wanted to borrow from Europe certain elements that suited them, but with the ultimate object of *diminishing* European influence in Turkey, not of drawing their country into Europe.

Cultivated Europeans regarded Turkey as part of Asia, or even part of barbarism; modernizing Turks wanted to copy Europe in order to remain separate from it. It was the start of an ambiguity which was to persist throughout the twentieth century and into the twenty-first.

SPAIN, PORTUGAL AND ITALY

There were other territories which, though undoubtedly European by both geography and history, were separated from the bulk of the continent by their poverty, economic backwardness and isolation. Spain was a country of uneven economic growth at best; a distinguished historian has written that 'the Spaniard ate more frugally than anyone else in Europe outside the Balkans and southern Italy'. Politically, conservatives tried to maintain traditional values in separation, while progressives looked towards the rest of Europe as an inspiration for change. Negrin, who was later to be prime minister under the Republic, joined the Socialist Party because he believed it was 'European'.[6] Portugal was even more isolated, its only neighbours being Spain and the Atlantic. Italy presented the spectacle of a country which had proclaimed its unification in 1860, but still had not achieved it, so that many Italians (perhaps most) felt more attachment to their own city or province than to Italy itself. Economically, northern Italy moved towards an advanced industrialization, with firms such as Pirelli and Fiat; while the south and the islands of Sicily and Sardinia remained agrarian and backward, with no capital even to improve their agriculture. It was almost true to say that half of Italy was in the early twentieth century, and the other half in the early nineteenth.

In these various ways, Europe was a continent of contrasts and divisions as well as of cohesion. Yet if a rough indicator of the state of European unity is to be found by comparing what draws Europeans (whether states or people) together with what divides them, then Europe before 1914 showed a substantial balance on the side of unity. It was a state of affairs which would not be repeated for a long time to come. As events turned out, this cohesive and in many ways unified Europe was about to plunge into a terrible and destructive war, which almost destroyed the old Europe and brought into being a new one which was weakened by the conflict and riven by ideological divisions. We must look next at the act of near-suicide which contemporaries called Great War, and which we know as the First World War.

PART TWO

THE FIRST WORLD WAR AND THE DESTRUCTION OF EUROPE, 1914–1918

3

THE TRAGIC MYSTERY OF 1914

Europe before 1914 was not perhaps the golden age, but it was full of promise compared with what was to follow. The disasters and fatal divisions of Europe started with the Great War. We still live in its shadow. Its dead are remembered each year with solemnity and awe. The war gave birth to fascism, Nazism and communism, which between them tore the continent apart for decades. It wrecked the European economy. It weakened European predominance in the world, and heralded the end of European imperialism, with effects which persist to this day.

Thus many of the bases of Europe's cohesion before 1914 were undermined, some of them for ever. After the war, this provoked the emergence of a more explicit and self-conscious attempt to assert a European identity. Pre-war self-confidence, when European cohesion was taken for granted, gave way to a growing conviction that, as a result of the war, Europe faced problems so serious that they crossed national boundaries and demanded European solutions of one sort or another. In our own time, the modern movement towards European union has been a deliberate attempt to prevent another suicidal European war, to guard against totalitarian ideologies and to strengthen the continent in face of the rest of the world. The fate of Europe in 1914–18 is not simply a matter of history. It still affects us.

Moreover, it still baffles us. How could it happen? How did the wealthiest and most civilized continent in the world, with a mature and elaborate system of diplomacy, come to embark on *and persist in* such a dreadful and destructive conflict? This remains one of the strangest and most tragic mysteries of modern history. Why did the war start? Why did it assume its particular character? Why did it go on so long?

THE BACKGROUND TO THE GREAT WAR

There has been no shortage of answers to the question of how the war came about. Almost from the start, a number of profound causes were advanced.

One favourite, especially on the political left, was imperialism, which was itself regarded as the product of capitalism. Competition for the markets, resources and territories of the rest of the world brought the European states into conflict with one another, especially when the other continents had been so completely divided up that there was no more room for manoeuvre. Another explanation was found in the arms races which marked the period before 1914. 'Great armaments lead inevitably to war', wrote Sir Edward Grey in his memoirs, finding ample support in the Anglo-German naval rivalry and the competition in land armaments between Germany, France and Russia.[1] Other causes were found in the pre-war alliance system and secret diplomacy. The alliance system had created a chain reaction which caused an apparently minor dispute in the Balkans to escalate into a European war, while the aristocrats who conducted high-level diplomacy were accused of being out of touch with the peace-loving sentiments of the people. And yet, by contrast, another explanation traced the origin of the war to the people themselves, or at any rate some people, on the grounds that the war arose from a conflict between Serbian nationalism and the Habsburg Empire.

Each of these alleged causes of the war suggested a solution, like the antidote to a poison, which could prevent the outbreak of war in the future. The imperial rivalries produced by capitalism could be removed by embracing socialism, which would eliminate capitalism and thus do away with war. Arms races could be prevented by disarmament. Alliances and secret diplomacy could be replaced by creating a new international organization and introducing democratic diplomacy, so that relations between states would be conducted openly and under the control of public opinion. The tensions created by frustrated nationalism could be relieved by accepting national self-determination as a guiding principle of European politics.

All these remedies for the presumed causes of the Great War achieved wide acceptance and long life, and some continue to flourish into our own day. Much of the appeal of socialism and communism arose from the belief that they held the key to peace. Disarmament has been pursued by many conferences and through elaborate negotiations, as well as by organized movements appealing to public opinion. New international organizations have been established, first in the League of Nations and later in the United Nations. The self-determination of peoples has become the aspiration of the whole world, though it is not always (and perhaps can never be) fully put into practice. All these remedies for the assumed causes of the Great War pointed the way – or sometimes different ways – to a new Europe when the war was over.

At the time of the war itself, and for many years to come, these explanations seemed to make much sense. Before 1914, underlying forces (imperialism, arms races, alliances and nationalism) brought about a series of crises, in Morocco in 1905 and 1911, in Bosnia in 1908–9 and in the Balkan Wars of 1912–13. For a time, European diplomacy did its work and found ways to resolve these crises. In 1914 it did not. There seemed no way out. The assassination of the Austrian Archduke Franz Ferdinand presented the Habsburg Empire with a challenge from Serbian nationalism which could not be ignored or tolerated. Russia supported the Serbs, and Germany supported Austria in the belief that if European war was to come, it would be better then than later, when Russia would be catching up in the arms race. France had to support Russia, through the workings of the alliance system.

In these ways historians reached a sort of explanation for the outbreak of the Great War, and up to a point it seems convincing. Yet it is hard to avoid the impression that the sums do not quite add up, and that the explanations do not match the war that followed. After all, the underlying forces were not overwhelmingly strong. Imperial disputes between the great powers had mostly been settled by agreement before 1914, when hardly any colonial questions remained open. The naval race between Britain and Germany was slackening, as the Germans diminished their battleship programme. Alliances were open to interpretation: Italy was allied to Austria and Germany, but remained neutral in 1914 and was to join the war on the opposite side in 1915. Nationalism had flourished, not least in the Balkans, for most of the nineteenth century, without producing a European war.

If these conventional explanations for the outbreak of the Great War seem inadequate, it is natural to ask whether something more was at work. If wars come to an end because people grow war-weary, do they break out because men are weary of peace? In 1914 Europe had not experienced a general war since 1815, though there had been several limited conflicts. At least some of the articulate and literary members of 'the generation of 1914' felt obscurely that war would open up new horizons and act as a kind of release. Rupert Brooke famously wrote: 'Now God be thanked Who has matched us with His hour / And caught our youth, and wakened us from sleeping'. Psichari and Péguy in France, and d'Annunzio and the Futurists in Italy gave voice to a similar mood.[2] Moreover, if the arts somehow convey in advance a crack in civilization, there were ample signs before 1914: in painting, Picasso and the Cubists; in music Schoenberg and atonal scores; in ballet the shock of *The Rite of Spring* by Nijinsky and Stravinsky. The idea of a widespread restlessness culminating in war, presented in Eksteins's book *Rites of Spring*, is striking.[3] But is it true? Do governments go to war because poets are discontented or artists change their styles, or as a result of 'mysterious forces swirling in the air'? It seems highly unlikely.[4]

Yet that only brings us back to those same reasons which seem inadequate to explain the catastrophe which wrecked Europe between 1914 and 1918. There is too great a gap between the explanations of the origins of the war and the appalling events that followed. But the mystery is not so great, and the answer may be found in the mentality and circumstances of 1914.

ATTITUDES TO WAR

At that time, war was not a calamity but simply part of life, as it had always been. For governments it was, as Clausewitz had explained, the continuation of policy by other means, and a measure used when necessary or advantageous. During the half-century before 1914 all the European great powers had engaged in warfare: Prussia against the Habsburg Empire in 1866 and against France in 1870–71; Russia against Turkey in 1877–78 and against Japan in 1904–5; Britain against the Boer Republics in 1899–1902; Italy against Turkey in 1911–12; not to mention many small colonial wars. There was little in the experience of these conflicts to indicate that war was about to become a massive human disaster, for which someone must be held responsible – or guilty. In the Europe of 1914 the concept of 'war guilt' meant nothing. What could states be guilty of, when all held the same view of war as something which was necessary, and indeed normal, in certain circumstances? For people too war was part of life. Most of the men who answered their mobilization orders in 1914 had been raised as patriots and trained as soldiers under systems of military service which were generally accepted. Moreover, their normal civilian lives were often harsh and uncomfortable, so that they were not unduly perturbed by military life. There were indeed peace movements in several countries, and many socialists were genuinely opposed to war; but, as we shall see, their repugnance was quickly overcome. It is now almost impossible for us to recapture the state of mind of the men of 1914, yet our understanding of events depends on our making the attempt.

Throughout Europe governments and peoples believed that when they embarked on war they were not plunging into catastrophe but undertaking something comparatively ordinary. This belief was all the stronger because almost everyone was sure that the war would be short. Geoffrey Blainey hits the nail on the head. In 1914 governments were not facing the war of 1914–18, but only 'the beginning of what they hopefully believed would be the war of 1914 or, if the worst happened, the war of 1914–15'.[5] Moreover, everyone believed they were going to win. The Germans aimed to surround Paris within six weeks. The French intended to cross the Rhine and advance into Germany. The Austrians were sure that Belgrade was within their grasp. The Russians advanced into East Prussia. Obviously not all these hopes could be fulfilled; but meanwhile everyone expected that the war would be short.

In the light of these assumptions, the conventional explanations of the war of 1914 no longer seem out of proportion, but perfectly adequate for the war which everyone expected – not the Great War of 1914–18, but only the War of 1914. The key question for the future of Europe therefore becomes: why did the war of 1914 become the war of 1914–18? It was the length and ferocity of the war, and the implacable determination with which it was waged, that brought Europe to ruin.

The popular image of the outbreak of war in 1914 is one of cheering crowds in great cities, bands playing and flags waving. In France the moment is caught by photographs of soldiers with flowers in their rifles at Paris railway stations. There is another famous photograph of a packed square in Munich, with Adolf Hitler as a face in the crowd caught up in the fervour of the moment. These pictures do not lie, but they tell only part of the story, and not the most important part. Enthusiasm is a bubble that can soon burst, and if the cheering crowds had told the whole story the war might well have been very different, and might indeed have been the war of 1914–15. But there lay behind the crowds and the flowers something very different: *a determined acceptance of war* which was to decide the character of the conflict.

BELGIUM

It helps to look first at Belgium. In 1831, when the European great powers recognized the independence of Belgium, they imposed on the new state a condition of permanent neutrality, to be observed towards all other countries. This governed all Belgian foreign and military policy. With regard to any external threat, the official interpretation of neutrality was that Belgium was ready and determined to resist attack from any quarter – Germany, France or Britain. In 1914 the reality was very different. Belgium was by no means ready to resist attack, because its army was ill-equipped and its only strategic plan (drawn up in 1905) was to make no attempt to defend the whole country, but to protect only a national redoubt round Antwerp, in the north of the country. (If this plan had been followed in 1914, it would have given the Germans free passage for their invasion of France through Belgium.) Indeed, there seemed no necessity to be determined to resist attack, because the country had implicit faith in its neutral status, which had protected the Belgians from war for over 80 years, even during the Franco-Prussian War.

The European war crisis in July 1914 took Belgium completely by surprise. On 15 July the 1913 class of conscripts, comprising nearly half the army, was actually sent home on a month's leave, which was not cancelled until 27 July. As the crisis deepened, the government was determined to observe not merely neutrality but impartiality, seizing all copies of the French-language newspaper *Le Petit Bleu* when it appeared on 2 August with the banner headline *HONTE A LA BARBARIE! VIVE LA FRANCE!* ('Shame on barbarism! Long live France!'). The Belgian government thus tried to avoid offending the Germans, but it was wasting its time. The German military plans for war against France depended on passing through Belgium to avoid the French fortifications. At 7 p.m. on 2 August (the same day that *Le Petit Bleu* was seized) the German minister in Brussels presented an ultimatum, prepared well in advance, demanding that the Belgians accept the passage of German troops. If they did so, Germany would guarantee Belgian independence and territorial integrity, and would evacuate Belgian territory when peace was made. If not, Germany would regard Belgium as an enemy and undertake no obligations towards it. Belgium was given 12 hours to reply.[6]

This formidable document confronted the Belgian government with an appalling choice. To accept would open the path for a German attack on France and incur the immediate hostility of the French, and probably the British too. To refuse would result in an instant attack by Germany, for which Belgium was completely unprepared. What was to be done? The underlying currents of elite opinion and strategic assumptions tended towards acceptance, in that the diplomatic service was largely pro-German in sympathy and the army had no plans to defend the frontiers against invasion. Calculations of Belgian interests were finely balanced and depended heavily on guesswork – in the long run, would it be more dangerous to be invaded by the Germans or protected by the French?

King Albert summoned a Crown Council which discussed the German ultimatum from 9 p.m. on 2 August to the early hours of the next day, and after agonized debate agreed unanimously to reject it. Belgium would defend its territory at all points (thus scrapping the only plan the army had), and appeal for French and British assistance while retaining political and military independence. In the long midnight discussions, pragmatic arguments which might have led to acceptance were overborne by a sense of duty as a neutral state and an acute resentment against German bullying. As the king said the next morning, speaking of Kaiser Wilhelm: 'What does he take me for?'[7]

The decision to reject the German ultimatum was supported unanimously by parliament and welcomed with enthusiasm in the country. Later, when the Germans had occupied all but a small corner of the country, the Belgians maintained a widespread passive resistance against the occupying power. The Germans appealed with some success to Flemish separatist sentiment, but on the whole the unity achieved in 1914 remained remarkably solid. In the words of a Dutch historian, 'The mass of the population was inspired by an unsophisticated form of patriotism...strong, straightforward and widespread...'[8] The Belgian government and people alike reacted to the German ultimatum and invasion with an instinctive patriotism and a deep anger in which there was a strong moral element.

FRANCE

The situation in Belgium was revealing, but it was not going to decide the fate of Europe. France was another matter, and it so happens that we know more about how the French people entered the war than we do about any other country.[9] The war came as a surprise to everyone – politicians and civil servants, businessmen and bankers, trade unionists and intellectuals. This meant that there was very little calculation in French actions. For a few crucial days in July, the president of the Republic, Poincaré, and the premier, Viviani, were at sea, returning from a visit to St Petersburg, and out of contact with their own country. In their absence French policy was largely passive, and after their return it remained cautious. On 31 July the government ordered the army to withdraw 10 kilometres from the German frontier, to ensure, in the event of fighting, that there was no doubt that the Germans were the aggressors. Germany declared war on France on 3 August, on the transparently false pretext that French aircraft had bombed Nuremberg. France then fought because the country was attacked.

The French people accepted war with calm determination. Even at protest meetings held by socialists and trade unionists before war began, speakers concentrated their oratory on general denunciations of war and on urging the French government to maintain its peaceful stance. Here lay a crucial point. Even left-wing leaders were convinced that France wanted peace and was not responsible for the crisis. Throughout the country people suddenly discovered a remarkable unity, soon called the *union sacrée*. The government played its part by making gestures of goodwill towards both left and right. Towards the left, it made no arrests among the socialists and trade unionists who were suspected of planning to oppose war and obstruct mobilization; towards the right, attacks on the religious orders were suspended. But the same spirit welled up throughout the country, where old opponents were suddenly reconciled with one another. Parish priests and atheist schoolteachers, who had long headed rival factions in small towns, shook hands. An ageing aristocrat stood up for the *Marseillaise* for the first time in

3   French mobilisation, 1914: women saying goodbye to soldiers © THE BRIDGEMAN ART LIBRARY

his life. Old quarrels were suspended in the shadow of a greater conflict. The National Assembly reflected this unity. War credits were voted without opposition, even from the socialist deputies who in the past had been vocal opponents of war and militarism. At the end of August the premier, Viviani, reconstructed his government to bring in two socialist ministers, Sembat and Guesde.

The acid test was mobilization – the call-up of nearly 3 million reservists, starting on 1 August and lasting 15 days. Some trade unionists, notably in the postal services and on the railways, had planned to obstruct mobilization, and the General Staff had feared that significant numbers of reservists might refuse to answer their mobilization orders. In the event the whole process went through in an atmosphere of calm and good order, and reports from all over the country spoke of a widespread conviction that France had been attacked without provocation – even the most determined pacifists had never imagined such an event. The vast majority of Frenchmen had no doubt that their country had been attacked, and had no hesitation in defending it. The calm resolution evident throughout the country was more impressive than the occasional displays of enthusiasm, and much more likely to endure.

BRITAIN

In Britain the situation was different, in that no one attacked the country, but the final outcome was very similar. The war crisis developed almost unobserved, while attention was concentrated on the Home Rule crisis in Ireland. Only on 29 July did the Cabinet take serious note that war was impending on the continent, and begin to discuss whether Britain should intervene or stand aside. There was a strong case that Britain should support France in order to prevent German domination of Europe, but such an argument based on the balance of power was by no means universally acceptable. The Liberal government of the day and its supporters in Parliament were divided. The Labour Party was instinctively opposed to war and distrustful of power politics. The Irish Nationalists (with 84 MPs) were not certain to support a British war. The Conservatives advocated intervention on the side of France, for reasons of national security, but they were in opposition and their influence was limited. The Liberal press opposed intervention in a continental war, and on 1 August the leading article in *The Economist* made the remarkable claim that a war between France and Germany need concern Britain no more than one between Argentina and Brazil. In these circumstances, the furthest the Cabinet would go was to decide on 2 August that the fleet would defend the French Channel coast against attack by German warships; and four ministers offered their resignations rather than accept even so limited a commitment.

If this hesitation had persisted, Britain might (and probably would) eventually have gone to war rather than see France defeated and Germany dominate Europe, but only half-heartedly and with a divided parliament and public opinion. But the situation was transformed by the German ultimatum to Belgium. King Albert appealed for British help and the Cabinet made up its mind at once. Unless Germany retracted its demands on Belgium and withdrew its invading forces, Britain would go to war. War was actually declared at the fatal hour of 11 p.m. on 4 August (midnight in Berlin). Two Cabinet ministers (Burns and Morley) resigned, but they were lone voices. The Irish Nationalists, led by John Redmond, supported war. The Labour leader, Ramsay MacDonald, had some reservations, but war credits were voted without a division. Calculations of British interests and the balance of power probably required British intervention, but they could never have taken the country into war united, with a firm will and a clear conscience. Only the German attack on Belgium achieved that remarkable result. Britain had not been attacked, but the British knew that they were right to go to war.

Lloyd George, a radical Liberal and formerly an opponent of the Boer War, made a public speech on 19 September, declaring that the British people stood on 'an elevation where we can see the great everlasting things that matter to a nation – the great peaks we had forgotten, of Honour, Duty, Patriotism, and, clad in glittering white, the great pinnacle of Sacrifice pointing like a rugged finger to Heaven.'[10] The sacrifice was to be greater than anyone expected, and Lloyd George himself was to be appalled by it. But at the time he did not mistake the mood of the country. One sign of this was the number of men who volunteered for the army: 298,923 in August, and an astonishing 462,901 in September.[11] These men doubtless had many different motives for enlisting, but by sheer weight of numbers they showed the strength of support for the war. Another indication may be seen in an extraordinary gathering which took place on 2 September at the office of C.F.G. Masterman, the head of the government's Propaganda Board. No fewer than 25 of the country's most distinguished writers attended, including J.M. Barrie, Arnold Bennett, Robert Bridges, G.K. Chesterton, Conan Doyle, John Galsworthy, Thomas Hardy, Anthony Hope, John Masefield, Gilbert Murray, Henry Newbolt, G.M. Trevelyan and H.G. Wells. Rudyard Kipling and Arthur Quiller-Couch were unable to be present but sent letters of support. These men were widely different in political persuasion, temperament and beliefs, but all were agreed in their desire to serve their country by their literary talents. This meeting represented the mobilization of some of the best minds in the land, and is as impressive in its way as the hosts of volunteers for the army.[12]

From events in these three countries (Belgium, France and Britain) a crucial pattern emerges. When countries go to war for pragmatic reasons, based on calculation, it is possible for them to make peace on the same grounds. But in these countries this was only very partially the case. For Belgium, a cold assessment of national interest would have been finely balanced, but the sense of outrage at the German ultimatum outweighed all such considerations. In France, the government would certainly have gone to war for reasons of national security in the event of a German attack on Russia, but in the event the need for such a decision never arose. Germany attacked France, and the French fought in self-defence. In Britain, there was a strong balance-of-power reason for fighting in support of France, but what actually united government, parliament and people was the German attack on Belgium. All three countries were convinced that they were fighting for *right* in a just war. Later, compromise might well have been possible on questions of material interest, especially when the costs of the war increased to such an extent as to make any material gain seem dubious. But it was very difficult to compromise in the cause of right, especially when people had entered the war with such unity and determination. The exceptional character of the war thus took shape in these three countries from the very start.

GERMANY

Seen from the outside, the position of Germany seemed very different. In the past the posturing of the kaiser had created an impression of arrogance and belligerence. In 1914 the sheer crassness of the German invasion of Belgium and the unprovoked assault on France demonstrated that Germany was the aggressor. But within the country this picture was completely reversed. Gordon Craig has summed up the situation: 'Most Germans believed as fervently as most Englishmen and most Frenchmen that their country was the victim of a brutal assault; "We did not ask for it, but now we must defend the homeland" was the common response, and it led to an impressive closing of the ranks'. One crucial element lay in a deep-seated hostility to Russia, arising in part from fear. Russia was the ancient Slav enemy, the barbarian who might yet overthrow German civilization, and also the tsarist tyranny which would destroy German socialism. When Russia mobilized its army, the first among the great powers to do so, it was a threat that struck home to all Germans. The Social Democrats in the Reichstag voted for the war credits. The kaiser declared on 4 August: 'I no longer recognise parties; I recognise only Germans.'[13] The Germans too were fighting for right.

THE SIGNIFICANCE OF SOCIALISM

In both France and Germany the reactions of the socialist parties to the outbreak of war were of crucial importance, and it is worth pausing to consider the conduct of the socialists in 1914. For many years, as we have seen, the Socialist International and its constituent parties had proclaimed their opposition to war and debated the question of how to prevent it. As the crisis developed in July 1914 the signs were that the French and German socialists would indeed throw their weight against war. On 25 July the German Social Democratic Party issued a declaration in favour of peace, and organized meetings and demonstrations, which in turn were prominently and sympathetically reported in *L'Humanité*, the principal French socialist newspaper. On 27 July the French syndicalists held a big demonstration against war in Paris. Strikingly, the German and French governments, which had prepared plans to arrest socialists and syndicalists in the event of war, both moved to head off opposition to war by means of conciliation. The German chancellor, Bethmann-Hollweg, got in touch with socialist leaders and assured them that there would be no government repression as long as the socialists did not obstruct mobilization. In France the government succeeded in persuading Jaurès, the socialist leader, that France was working for peace.

The socialist leaders themselves continued to advocate a common policy against war, and called a special meeting of the Bureau of the Socialist International, held in Brussels on 29–30 July. This meeting decided to bring forward the next full Congress of the International, due in September 1914, to 9 August, and to change the venue from Vienna to Paris. In retrospect this came to seem a wholly inadequate response to the crisis, but at the time it was a bold move, designed to bring hundreds of socialists (including many Germans) to the most famous city in Europe to exert a peaceable influence on governments. In making these plans the socialist leaders assumed, not unreasonably, that the crisis of 1914 would resemble earlier ones over Morocco or the Balkans, which had all rumbled on for six months or a year. On these precedents, there was time in hand. But there was not. Instead of rumbling along, events moved like an express train. Before the Socialist Congress could meet in Paris, Europe was at war.

In this desperate crunch, the French and German socialists accepted war with almost no dissent, and often with wholehearted assent. In France, it seemed briefly that the assassination of Jaurès, the charismatic socialist leader, on 31 July might swing left-wing opinion against war, but it did not. Jouhaux, a syndicalist leader who had often differed from Jaurès while he was alive, made an impassioned and patriotic speech at his funeral, and the socialist deputies went straight from the graveside to the Chamber, where they voted for the war credits. The German socialist deputies, after painful discussions among themselves, took the same line and voted for the war credits in the Reichstag, unanimously except for one member who left before the vote. All the passions and oratory of the Socialist International, perfectly sincere in their time, vanished in the crisis of 1914. This was due partly to the sheer speed of events, which overtook the slow movements of the International, and partly to the tactics of the French and German governments, which succeeded in persuading their respective socialist parties that they were working for peace. But above all it was due to a surge of patriotism which proved stronger than all the claims of class solidarity, however sincerely meant. Looking back in September 1919, the French syndicalist leader, Alphonse Merrheim, declared that 'At that moment [in 1914], the working class, moved by an immense wave of nationalism, would not have left it to the government to shoot us; they would have shot us themselves'; on which a left-wing historian commented 'This has never been contested.'[14] The worker *did* have a country. French and German socialists alike believed that the war was necessary and right. It was to take two or three years for that conviction to be shaken, and even then only among a minority of socialists. The majority, in both countries, supported the war to the end.

In these ways, in western Europe, the war assumed from the start the character of a moral struggle as well as a conflict waged for reasons of state. In retrospect, this came to be denounced as a grave mistake. Put crudely, 'If you are quarrelling about Alsace, you had better say that you are quarrelling about Alsace, and not that you are fighting for righteousness.'[15] As the war went on, it would have been easier to compromise about territorial questions than about moral issues. But at the time there was no mistake. Governments and peoples alike (though doubtless peoples more than governments) believed that they were indeed fighting for righteousness, or at any rate in self-defence, which for most people came to the same thing.

EASTERN EUROPE

In eastern Europe the situation was rather different. In Austria-Hungary the government and a substantial part of public opinion accepted the necessity for war to preserve the existence and the status of the empire, to eliminate the threat from Serbia, and to stand up to Russia. There was a rallying of opinion – the Hungarian political parties came together in a sort of 'sacred union'. But there was no sense of total unity like that which prevailed in the countries of western Europe. Austria and Hungary had two separate governments, which did not see eye to eye about the conduct of the war. Indeed, Austria-Hungary was fighting two different wars, which were hard to coordinate: one against Serbia and one against Russia. The various nationalities had diverse interests and feelings, though for some time they held together reasonably well. In the army, soldiers proved willing to fight against their fellow-nationals – for example, some of the divisions which took part in the invasion of Serbia were 20–25 per cent Serb in their personnel.[16] But the Habsburg Empire never achieved the solid unity which prevailed in France, Britain and Germany.

Russia too had strong motives for going to war, according to the reasoning prevalent in 1914. The government could not abandon the Serbs, nor give way in face of Austria-Hungary and Germany; and they dared not allow the French to think that Russia was an unreliable ally. The articulate sections of public opinion rallied behind the entry into war with patriotism and even enthusiasm. The Duma met for a single day to vote for the war credits. The Labour Group (with 10 deputies) and the Social Democrats (with 14) abstained on the issue of war credits, and the Social Democrats actually put forward a resolution condemning the war. Otherwise, opinion in the Duma was solid, and there was evidence that factory workers supported the war. But in the long run the sprawling empire had none of the coherence of west European nations, and the government proved too inefficient to wage war successfully. The situation was to be different during the Second World War, when Russian patriotism was reinforced by the iron hand of Stalin's dictatorship, which was far more severe and effective than the tsarist autocracy.

The contrast between western and eastern Europe came to a head in 1917, the year of trial for all the belligerents in the Great War. Under the strain of war, Austria-Hungary and Russia began to disintegrate. Austria-Hungary had to be sustained by German assistance, which came to approach domination; Russia collapsed in revolution. Austria tried to make peace by secret negotiations, and Russia (under a new regime) actually concluded an armistice at the end of 1917 and a peace treaty in March 1918. It was in western Europe, between the countries which had shown such remarkable unity and determination in 1914, that the war was fought to a finish. So it was that the political conditions for a long and pitiless war, which ultimately destroyed the old Europe, were established at the very start of the conflict. The military conditions which completed the deadlock were soon to follow.

The war of 1914 eventually became the 'First World War', which is in many ways a misnomer. The war was European in its origins. As it developed, it spread to other continents, and non-European powers (notably the USA) became involved, but it remained essentially a European war − which, because of the cohesion of the continent before 1914, was a *European civil war* − in which like-minded states and peoples tore themselves apart. Yet with time the war itself became a shared experience and a common tragedy, which eventually led to the emergence of new forms of European identity from the wreckage of the old.

4

THE GREAT WAR AND THE END OF THE OLD EUROPE

The outbreak of war in 1914 meant that for the first time since 1815 the fate of Europe was to be settled by force. The continent, or at any rate most of it, was going to war, and devoted its energies to self-destruction. Armies were mobilized; warfare assumed new forms; resources had to be organized; governments took new powers; the war spread and drew in new belligerents. Efforts at a compromise peace failed. Slowly and relentlessly the old Europe was consumed in the fires of war. How did this come about?

MANPOWER

In the first place, the armies of the belligerent powers were to decide the course of the war, and with it the future of the continent. In some apparently dry facts and figures lay the shape of things to come.

Germany possessed a standing army of about 800,000 men, plus another 4 million well-trained reserves to be called up on mobilization. The Germans were able to achieve these large numbers while calling up only about half of each 'class', or yearly age group, and they therefore had access to a further reservoir of men who had not yet been recruited for the army. The French mustered a standing army of 813,000, with nearly 2,900,000 trained reserves; but with a smaller population than Germany they could only attain these figures by calling up 86 per cent of each age group. French manpower was therefore almost at full stretch when war began, and came under intense strain as casualties mounted up. Among the other continental powers, Austria-Hungary had 480,000 men in the standing army, with two different reserve armies in the Austrian and Hungarian parts of the country. Russia maintained a large standing army of 1.4 million men, with vast numbers of reserves who had passed through the conscription system. The soldiers were mostly peasants, immensely hardy and stoical, but ill-educated for the needs of modern warfare, especially in comparison with the German army, which drew on a well-educated population.[1]

Britain was in a different position to the continental powers. The country did not practise conscription. The regular army was made up of just under 250,000 men, of whom nearly half were stationed in the overseas empire. There were 210,000 reserves (mostly ex-regulars), and a Territorial Army 269,000 strong, intended only for service at home. When war began, volunteers poured in, and over a million men enlisted by the end of 1914; but they then had to be armed, trained and organized for war, a prodigious task which was far from complete when the New Army went into battle on the Somme in 1916.[2]

Germany and Britain thus had resources of manpower to draw on over the long term. France was already at full stretch in 1914. Neither Austria-Hungary nor Russia had armies capable of meeting the demands which were about to be imposed on them. The military situation closely paralleled political circumstances, where neither the Habsburg Empire nor Russia was solid or efficient enough to wage a long war. In the long run, therefore, the make-up of the various armies did much to decide the course of events. But first it had to be decided whether there was to be a long run, or whether the war would be over in a few months, as most people expected.

PLANS AND STRATEGIES

In the west, the war opened with two great offensives, by the Germans and French respectively. The Germans broadly followed the Schlieffen Plan, devised by a former chief of staff, under which the bulk of their forces advanced through Belgium into northern France, and then towards Paris. The objective of the Schlieffen Plan was to knock France out of the war in six weeks, and at first all went well. For five weeks the German armies pressed on almost unchecked, with the French forces and the small British Expeditionary Force retreating before them. The Germans came within a few miles of Paris, and the French government withdrew to Bordeaux. A French defeat like that of 1870 seemed imminent, but it did not come. By early September the German troops were weary after their long march, and their commanders were in some confusion. The German offensive lost its impetus. On the other side, the French commander-in-chief, Joffre, was able to regroup his forces and organize a counter-offensive. At the Battle of the Marne (5–11 September 1914) the tide turned. On 11 September the German chief of the general staff, Moltke, ordered his armies to retreat to the River Aisne, and issued the fateful instruction that 'The lines so reached will be fortified and defended.'[3] The 'lightning war' against France had failed. The war of fortifications was about to begin.

While the Germans were advancing towards Paris, the French launched their own offensive in Alsace-Lorraine, to recover the lost provinces. In fact they suffered a crushing defeat, and lost some 300,000 dead and wounded in the Battle of the Frontiers. So in the first few weeks of the war neither side achieved the decisive victory for which it had planned. For some time the opposing armies continued to manoeuvre, seeking a gap between their enemy's flank and the Channel coast. They failed, and by the end of November a continuous front stretched from the English Channel near Nieuport (in Belgium) to the Swiss frontier near Belfort.

The war in the west then assumed the form it was to take for the next four years. The opposing armies dug themselves in, establishing systems of trenches and barbed wire along the whole front, but in different ways and for contrasting purposes. The Germans settled down to hold what they had won: a large part of north-eastern France and nearly the whole of Belgium. They constructed permanent, well-engineered defences, sometimes using concrete and even installing electric light. The French, conversely, had to recover the territory they had lost. They could not settle down, and their trench lines were not intended to be permanent, but merely starting points for attack. The British, who took over more of the line as their forces increased, conformed to the French strategy.

Here lay the key to what followed on the western front. The Allied offensives in France and Flanders are often described as 'senseless', and indeed they often cost appalling casualties for little gain. But there was sense behind their purpose, if not their methods. The French, and the British with them, had to drive the Germans from the territories conquered in 1914. Otherwise, the Germans would have won the war and would eventually impose their terms. The Germans, on the other hand, were usually content to stand on the defensive, and chose to attack only twice, at Verdun in 1916 and in the spring of 1918, for reasons which will be examined later. This was of crucial importance, because the combination of fortifications and firepower along the trench lines gave the defence an immense superiority over the attack. The armies repeatedly sought to break this deadlock, without success. Massed artillery produced immense destruction but only limited advances; poison gas could achieve dramatic but temporary effects; tanks, when they were first used in 1916, were too few and too unreliable. It seemed that neither generalship nor technology could find a way out of the impasse created by the power of the defence.

These conditions created the appalling character of the war on the western front, which left a lasting mark on all the combatants and on Europe as a whole. Two of the greatest battles may stand as archetypes: Verdun and the Somme.

VERDUN AND THE SOMME

The Battle of Verdun lasted from February to December 1916 – a length which was in itself unprecedented in the history of war. It was a rare case of the Germans taking the offensive, with the intention of drawing the French into a fatal struggle on unequal terms and bleeding their armies to death. The

4 'He who has not seen Verdun has not seen the war.' Destruction on the Verdun battlefield, 1916
© akg-images

Germans began their assault with a superiority of two to one in men and three
to one in guns, and their commander (Falkenhayn) reckoned on inflicting
casualties at a rate of three to one in the German favour. Falkenhayn chose
Verdun for its symbolic and psychological, rather than strictly strategic
importance, and he was proved right, in that the French command decided
that the city must be held at any cost. Retreat was not an option. In the
ensuing 10-month struggle the casualties were enormous, but much more
equal than the Germans had anticipated: some 377,000 on the French side and
337,000 on the German, including in both cases a high proportion of men
killed.[4] The battle assumed an overwhelming importance. 'He who has not
seen Verdun has not seen the war', wrote a French infantryman; and indeed
most of the French Army *did* see Verdun. Both sides suffered grievously in
mind as well as body. A German soldier wrote to his mother: '...we must give
up all hope of taking Verdun. The war will continue for an indefinite period,
and in the end there will be neither victors nor vanquished.' A French
lieutenant wrote in his diary: 'You wonder with anguish when and how this
unprecedented struggle will end. There is no solution in sight. I wonder if it
will end simply for lack of fighting men... Yes, humanity has gone mad. We
must be mad to do what we are doing.'[5]

The British Army endured its own martyrdom on the Somme, where the
British, along with the French, opened a great offensive on 1 July 1916. The

first day on the Somme has achieved a grim distinction in military history, with British casualties totalling over 59,000, including 19,000 killed. The attacks continued until November, with the British gaining a few square miles marked by names which still haunt the memory – Beaumont Hamel, Delville Wood, Thiepval. British losses (killed, wounded and missing) were estimated at about 400,000; French at 200,000; German at 500,000 to 600,000 – in all, some 1,200,000. 'Decades later, the sum of anguish which these figures represent horrifies us', wrote a professional soldier turned historian.[6] No one is likely to say otherwise.

Verdun and the Somme were to affect the French and British peoples and their governments for many years to come. For the British, the Somme came to symbolize the dreadful futility of the Great War, and perhaps of war itself. For the French, Verdun was a calamity, but it also exemplified the heroic tenacity of the French soldier defending his country. From this arose the immense reputation of General Pétain, the French commander at Verdun for a short but crucial part of the battle, later a marshal of France and the head of the Vichy Government during the Second World War. Because Verdun embodied French patriotism, it could also become a focus for Franco-German reconciliation at a later time. In 1984 President Mitterrand and Chancellor Kohl met at Verdun in a joint act of remembrance, at which they were photographed holding hands in an awkward yet moving gesture. A wooden cross was placed at Le Mort-Homme, one of the central points of the battle, inscribed: '1916–1984. Pardessus les tombes, l'amitié franco–allemande' ('Above the tombs, Franco–German friendship').[7] Verdun thus made its contribution to another, very different phase of European history.

THE EASTERN FRONT

The vast distances and open country of eastern Europe meant that the war there was very different to that in the west. Troops dug in, but did not establish continuous and virtually impregnable trench lines. A war of movement developed, in which offensives captured vast areas rather than a few devastated square miles.

In August 1914 the Russians invaded East Prussia, to the alarm of the German high command, but were later defeated and thrown back at the battles of Tannenberg and the Masurian Lakes. In the south, the Austrians invaded Russian territory in Galicia, only to be defeated so severely that they had to call on German reinforcements. In the Balkans, where the war had started, the Austrians launched an attack on Serbia on 12 August 1914, but were driven back with heavy losses; at the end of the year, Belgrade, though only just across the border, remained firmly in Serbian hands. Austria was thus held back by the Serbs and had to be saved from the Russians by German help. It was a bad start.

In 1915 the Germans turned their main efforts to the east. In the five months from May to September they advanced up to 100 miles, occupying most of

Russian Poland and Lithuania. The Russians lost about 2 million men, nearly half of them taken prisoner – a sign of disintegration in their armies.[8] Against the Austrians, however, the Russians continued to gain successes, winning a great battle in Galicia (June–August 1916), inflicting some 370,000 casualties and taking 380,000 prisoners. Encouraged by these Russian successes, Romania – thus far neutral – chose to enter the war on the Allied side in August 1916, only to be crushed by the Germans in November and December.[9]

In sharp contrast to the stalemate in the west, the eastern front thus produced sweeping movements and decisive results. By the end of 1916 Germany was already the victor, making large territorial gains, which brought with them new resources – not least the oil wells of Romania. Austria-Hungary was holding on only with German support. The Russians had won victories against the Austrians, but had been repeatedly defeated by the Germans, suffering casualties which included most of the pre-war officers and NCOs, who had formed the backbone of the army. The Russian army was losing its cohesion, with potentially fatal consequences.

The war on the eastern front decided the fate of Russia and the Habsburg Empire. In 1917 Russia collapsed in revolution – in fact, two revolutions: the fall of the tsar in February, and the Bolshevik seizure of power in October. By the end of 1918 the Habsburg Empire, worn out by defeat, broke up into fragments.[10] These events in their turn decided the fate of Europe for many years ahead.

The war also spread into new areas. In October 1914 the Ottoman Empire entered the war on the side of the Central Powers, extending the conflict to the Middle East, as far as Mesopotamia (Iraq) and the border of Egypt. In the Dardanelles campaign of 1915–16 the British tried to knock Turkey out of the war by an attack on the Straits between the Mediterranean and the Black Sea. The attempt failed, and Allied and ANZAC troops endured appalling hardships to no ultimate purpose. In retrospect, the Dardanelles campaign has assumed the status of one of the great 'might-have-beens' of the war. A victory, with the capture of Constantinople and the opening of the Straits to pass supplies through to Russia, might have had far-reaching effects. It might have bypassed the deadlock on the western front, and so saved innumerable lives. It might have strengthened Russia and so prevented the Bolshevik Revolution – at which point the 'might-have-beens' become dizzying. In practice, it is more likely that such far-ranging consequences would have been ruled out by the dreary facts of production and shipping. At the time, the British and French did not have enough shells for their own operations, without sending munitions to Russia; and it was in any case doubtful whether there were enough ships available to carry the supplies. So we must come back to earth. What actually happened was that the Allies transferred their attentions to Salonika, in northern Greece, where a French and British force remained until 1918, when it made a sudden and valuable contribution to final victory. As another consequence of the Dardanelles campaign, one of the Turkish generals, Mustafa Kemal, made his reputation as 'the saviour of Gallipoli', which eventually helped him to emerge after the war as the maker of modern Turkey.

OTHER FRONTS

Another front opened in 1915, in Italy. At the outbreak of war Italy had remained neutral, and the belligerent powers then tried to enlist Italian support in a sort of clandestine auction. Eventually the Allies made the best offer of territories to be gained by Italy after victory (in the Treaty of London, 26 April 1915), and Italy entered the war on 24 May. The Italian Army attacked the Austrians in the only area open to them, on the River Isonzo, in north-east Italy, in difficult terrain and an often harsh climate. Between 1915 and 1917 they fought in all 12 battles of the Isonzo, showing great courage and suffering heavy losses for little result. They eventually became exhausted, and were heavily defeated at the Battle of Caporetto in October 1917. Despite these failures, the Italian front placed a heavy burden on Austria-Hungary, which in 1916 had to deploy over half its forces against the Italians, and once again had to call on support from the Germans in 1917. So the Italian intervention played a significant part in the war. It also had long-term, and quite unexpected, political consequences. Italy expected much from the war, in terms of both territory and prestige. At the peace settlement many of these hopes were disappointed, as we shall see later; and the consequent disillusionment was one of the factors that led to the rise of Mussolini and the Italian Fascist Party, with far-reaching effects for Italy and Europe.

The war was also fought at sea, in largely unexpected ways. At the start, all eyes were on the two great battle fleets, British and German, which confronted one another across the North Sea. In the event, the only large-scale encounter between them, at the Battle of Jutland (31 May 1916), resulted in a draw. The British Grand Fleet suffered the heavier losses, in ships and men, but the German High Seas Fleet never took to the high seas again, thus effectively conceding defeat. The British continued to exercise command of the surface of the sea, as they had done since the start of the war. Troops and supplies crossed the Channel without interruption, while imports flowed into Britain and France from all parts of the world. The Allied navies blockaded the Central Powers, cutting off most of their supplies from overseas, with increasingly severe effects, especially on food supplies.

But there was now a new weapon in the war at sea: the submarine. In February 1915 Germany declared the imposition of a 'war zone' surrounding the British Isles, in which all vessels (belligerent or neutral) were liable to be sunk without warning by German submarines. The attempt was premature. During the whole of 1915 the Germans had no more than 45 U-boats available at any one time, and of these only one-third were actually on station, with the other two-thirds either in transit or refitting. Even so, U-boats sank about 750,000 tons of shipping in 1915, including the British liner *Lusitania*, with a large number of Americans on board. Eventually, for fear of offending the Americans too far, the German government relaxed the blockade by ending the policy of sinking without warning. The first attempt at a submarine blockade thus proved no more than a limited success. There was to be a different story later, when the venture was resumed in 1917.

RESOURCES

Blockades were a part of the war of resources which lay behind all the military campaigns. When the war began, all the belligerents expected it to be short, and relied on getting through on their existing stocks of arms and ammunition. The call-up of vast armies resulted in a fall in production of all kinds, industrial and agricultural. In France the fall was particularly steep, because the Germans occupied the north-east of the country, with its coal mines, heavy industry and arable land. French coal production fell from 40.8 million tons in 1913 to 19.5 million in 1915, and steel production from 4.7 million tons to 1.1 million in the same years.[11] The situation was less drastic, but still serious, in other countries. By the autumn of 1914 governments began to realize that the war was not going to be short, and production must be revived. A war of resources and organization began.

In resources, the Allies were superior to the Central Powers. A calculation of world manufacturing production in 1913 showed Germany and Austria-Hungary together as providing 19.2 per cent of world production, while Britain, France and Russia totalled 27.9 per cent.[12] On the Allied side, resources were distributed in a way which proved highly significant for the future of Europe. French manpower had been almost at full stretch before the war began. By the end of 1915, after heavy casualties, reserves were almost exhausted, and France became largely dependent on British military support. By contrast, the British role in the conflict increased enormously. In August 1914 the original British Expeditionary Force (BEF) comprised only seven divisions. By spring 1916 there were no fewer than 70 British and imperial divisions on the western front. In 1914 the British armaments industry produced only 91 guns, 300 machine guns and 200 aeroplanes. In 1916 it produced 4314 guns, 33,500 machine guns and 6100 aeroplanes – a prodigious increase.[13] Yet at the same time both Britain and France were becoming dependent on the USA, partly for munitions and even more for food, raw materials and machine tools. The value of sterling and the French franc fell against the dollar, and from August 1915 onwards Britain and France had to raise loans in the USA to pay for their imports. The war of resources thus produced a new structure of power in western Europe and the North Atlantic, with France relying increasingly on Britain and both countries on the USA, with consequences that persisted long after the war was over.

The efficient use of resources demanded organization, and above all decisions on priorities. Was manpower best used in the armed forces, industry or agriculture? For example, was one man more useful as a shepherd, or another as a coal miner, than either would be as a soldier? Were supplies of nitrates better used to manufacture explosives or as fertilizers in agriculture? Who was to resolve such problems, which occurred at every turn? The answer was that the state must decide, and the war therefore saw a rapid extension of government control in all aspects of life.

The results were far-reaching and often unexpected. For example, at the outbreak of war the French government at once fixed the price of bread, as a vital element in national life and the morale of the people. As the war went on, this apparently simple act involved an increasingly complicated attempt to control the whole chain of production and pricing, which ran from the baker to the miller, and then to the farmer and to his suppliers, so that the reach of price controls had to be extended constantly. Moreover, when the price of wheat was fixed farmers had an awkward tendency to change to barley, or some other crop whose price was not controlled, so that government regulation had to be expanded further still.

Britain entered the war under a Liberal government, opposed by tradition and instinct to state control over the economy. But the slogan of 'business as usual' quickly proved impossible to sustain. In the first month of war a Royal Sugar Commission was set up to control the purchase of sugar, a vital element in the nation's diet. The BEF in France needed unforeseen quantities of shells, and a Ministry of Munitions was set up, under Lloyd George, in May 1915. The use of shipping for the country's needs demanded increasing government intervention: a scheme for state requisition of shipping was introduced in November 1915, and a Shipping Control Committee was set up in January 1916. Most serious of all from a political and psychological point of view, conscription for the armed forces was introduced, first for unmarried men in January 1916, and then for all men between the ages of 18 and 41 in May of the same year. This was a drastic departure from British tradition, and was at first hotly contested, but eventually conscription came to be accepted as both fairer and more efficient than voluntary recruitment.[14] These changes were made piecemeal, to meet the demands of war as they occurred; but when Lloyd George became prime minister in December 1916 he introduced new methods of running the war as a whole. He set up a small War Cabinet, with a secretariat to ensure that its business was done efficiently, and transformed the system of Cabinet committees. Among the new committees were two whose titles summed up the demands of war: the Tonnage Priorities Committee and the War Priorities Committee. To set priorities was the problem, and the committee system provided the answers.

To wage war by committee was something that came naturally to the British, but not to the Germans. Germany was accustomed to an authoritarian form of government, with the kaiser as an active head of state. As the war went on, the kaiser was relegated to the sidelines, and by the end of 1916 Germany was in practice a military dictatorship dominated by two generals, Hindenburg and Ludendorff. In August 1916 the Hindenburg Programme for 'total war' set immense targets for industrial production, which meant that large numbers of men had to be released from the army to work in the factories. Agriculture, on the other hand, was given a low priority in the allocation of resources, resulting in a severe fall in agricultural production.[15] This drop in production, together with the Allied blockade, resulted in serious food shortages. Bread was rationed as early as January 1915, and in 1916 rationing was extended to potatoes, meat, sugar, butter and milk. The rationing system itself was ill-managed, with too many food authorities, and responsibilities being divided between the central government and the separate states of the German federation. There was a dismaying contrast between low civilian rations and large supplies for the army, which received (and often wasted) vast quantities of food. The civilian population did not starve, but there was much hardship, resulting in occasional food riots.

The enormous German war effort was largely financed by borrowing, with only 6 per cent of the cost being raised by taxation, as against 20 per cent in Britain. The federal system of government caused difficulties because direct taxation was controlled by the separate states, and the central government could only raise indirect taxes. On the whole, the German government, despite its military traditions and authoritarian nature, proved less efficient at organizing the country for war than the British. Jay Winter, after careful examination, concluded that the German war economy was 'one of the...least successful examples of a "military-industrial complex" in action.'[16]

The other two European empires could scarcely produce a military-industrial complex at all. Austria-Hungary failed to meet the demands of total war. The separate governments of Austria and Hungary failed to agree on raising taxes, and the war was mainly financed by borrowing and printing money, with consequent high inflation. In 1915 Hungary actually reduced its normal pre-war grain supplies to the Austrian part of the empire. Food distribution was mismanaged, and there were shortages of food in Vienna as early as October 1914. Russia, on the other hand, managed to achieve substantial increases in the production of arms and ammunition during the war, but failed (through faulty administration and a poor transport system) to make sure that the material reached the armies. The Russian management of war finance proved disastrously inflationary: the retail price index rose from 100 in June 1914 to 700 in June 1917.[17]

In sum, the campaigns of 1914–16 brought stalemate in western Europe, but sweeping German victories in the east. In the west, Britain, France and Germany organized themselves for total war, and were prepared to pay the costs, human and material. In the east, Austria-Hungary and Russia were incapable of such a tremendous effort. Their armies were on the verge of breakdown, and Russia was about to collapse in revolution.

BREAKING POINT?

The third full year of the war, 1917, was a time of crisis for all the major belligerents. On the Allied side, France came near to breaking point. The French Army had suffered terribly between 1914 and 1916, and was reaching the end of its endurance. In the spring of 1917 a new commander-in-chief, General Nivelle, claimed to have the secret of a successful offensive; and he also undertook that if he did not achieve a breakthrough he would at once call off the attack. Perhaps in desperation, he was widely believed, by soldiers and politicians alike. Nivelle began his attack on 16 April 1917, at the Chemin des Dames. By the standards of the western front in previous years, the offensive did not go too badly – the French gained some ground, and casualties on the two sides were not drastically uneven. But compared to the expectations built up by Nivelle it was a disaster. There was no breakthrough, and yet Nivelle did not call off the attack for over a month, thus breaking both his promises. Overwhelmed by a cruel disillusionment, parts of the French Army broke down. Beginning in mid-April 1917, reaching a peak in May–June, and continuing sporadically until January 1918, acts of mutiny broke out in much of the army. In all, 49 divisions out of 110 on the western front were affected at one time or another.[18] At the front, troops in the line were prepared to defend their trenches, but refused to attack. In the rear, there was widespread ill-discipline and drunkenness, with some demonstrations in favour of peace. The crisis was severe, but the army survived. Nivelle was dismissed and replaced by Pétain, the hero of Verdun, who had a high reputation for being sparing with the lives of his men, and who showed a remarkable touch in his dealings with the ordinary soldier. Pétain gradually restored order by a combination of improved conditions (regular leave, more rest periods and smaller rations of wine) and carefully judged repression. Above all, he gave up the idea of great offensives. He undertook a few limited attacks, thoroughly prepared and successfully executed, with a minimum of casualties, to restore morale. But essentially he decided to wait, as he put it, for the tanks and the Americans. French tank production was increasing in 1917, and the USA entered the war in April of that year, though it was to be a long time before American troops reached France in large numbers. This strategy proved a success, and the French Army recovered its fighting power to a degree which has not always been appreciated.

The French civilian population was also feeling the strain of war. With no end in sight, a pall fell over the land, and prefects' reports on morale grew gloomy. In politics, the 'sacred union' of 1914 broke down in 1917, and the socialists left the government. A movement for a compromise peace, led by Joseph Caillaux, grew in strength in the autumn of 1917. As events turned out, this actually stiffened the French determination to continue the war. When the choice became clear between attempting a compromise peace, which would almost certainly prove to be on German terms, and continuing the war, there was little hesitation. The president of the Republic, Poincaré, overcame his personal dislike of Clemenceau, and asked the aged but still formidable Tiger to form a government. Clemenceau's programme was simple: 'I wage war'. His ministry was narrowly based compared with those of the sacred union, but it proved solid, and endured until the war was won. France survived the troubled year of 1917.

The British crisis in 1917 came from an unexpected direction. In home politics, Lloyd George had become prime minister in December 1916 in order to prosecute the war more vigorously, and his coalition government held an overwhelming majority in Parliament. At the front in Flanders, the BEF fought the terrible Third Battle of Ypres, which has entered the language under the name of Passchendaele. The army suffered grievously, losing about 245,000 casualties to gain at most five miles of ground, but did not break. The actual crisis came at sea, where Britain was thought to be strongest. In February 1917 Germany renewed its submarine blockade, reverting to the practice of sinking without warning, and this time could deploy some 120 ocean-going U-boats. The results were impressive. In April 1917, the most successful month for the submarines, the total shipping sunk was 881,017 tons, of which 545,282 tons were British. That month, about one-quarter of all the vessels leaving British ports did not return. Only two U-boats were sunk. Between April and June, total shipping losses were about 3,300,000 tons.[19] At one point there was only about six weeks' supply of grain left in the country; at another there was only four *days'* supply of sugar. Eventually the answer was found in the convoy system, which reduced losses of merchant ships and increased sinkings of U-boats. In September a statistical turning point was reached when more U-boats were sunk than were launched. The Battle of the Atlantic, 1917, was a close-run thing, but Britain survived.

Russia did not survive. At the beginning of 1917 the army at the front was near breaking point, and at home was neither willing nor able to maintain order in the cities. In the capital, Petrograd, there were plenty of troops, many of them in the supposedly elite Guards regiments; but they were mostly raw recruits and inexperienced officers. The use of force to disperse rioters proved impracticable and the tsarist regime collapsed. The tsar abdicated, on behalf of himself and his son, in favour of his brother, the Grand Duke Michael, who refused to serve. The Duma appointed a provisional government, headed by Prince Lvov; but at the same time the Petrograd Soviet of Workers and Soldiers (at that stage dominated by the Mensheviks, or moderate socialists) emerged as a rival body to the Duma, and issued on its own initiative 'Order No. 1' to the army, declaring that all military units should be controlled by elected committees, with officers issuing orders only during actual operations – which effectively completed the dissolution of discipline which was already well under way. Despite this, the provisional government sought to continue the war, and attempted one last offensive in Galicia in July 1917. It failed and Russia ceased to be an active belligerent. In November Lenin and the

Bolsheviks seized power in Petrograd with the slogan of 'Peace, Bread and Land', of which peace was the easiest to deliver. On 15 December 1917 (a date rarely remembered in western Europe) the Bolsheviks made an armistice on the eastern front. Russia left the war, and indeed for some time Russia almost ceased to exist as an organized state, breaking up into fragments and civil strife.

The Central Powers also faced difficulties in 1917. The German Army had endured much, and suffered heavy casualties (not least at Verdun and the Somme, which are often seen as disasters only for the Allied side). In July 1917 General Ludendorff became afraid that morale was failing, and ordered a campaign of 'patriotic instruction' to be undertaken throughout the army. At home, the optimism of the early years of the war had given way to a mood of stoical endurance. There were shortages of food, clothing and coal, causing much hardship and some vocal discontent. The Socialist Party had split, with a minority opposing the war. The Reichstag actually passed a vaguely worded 'peace resolution' in July 1917. There was no crisis to compare with that in France, and still less Russia, but there was a growing uneasiness about the war.

THWARTED PEACE EFFORTS

In Austria-Hungary the aged Emperor Franz Joseph died on 21 November 1916, after a reign of 68 years. His death removed an intangible yet vital bond of unity in the divided empire. His successor, the new Emperor Karl, believed that the only way for Austria-Hungary to survive was to escape from the German domination which had steadily increased as the war went on, and to make peace; which he attempted to do in 1917.

1917 was indeed a year of many peace moves. In January President Wilson of the USA called, in ringing tones though obscure language, for 'peace without victory'. Between March and May Emperor Karl of Austria-Hungary made secret approaches to the Allies for a compromise peace, on terms which would have included acceptance of 'the just claims' of France in Alsace-Lorraine. This came to nothing, partly because the Allies insisted on Austrian concessions of territory to Italy; but in any case there was no chance of Germany giving up Alsace-Lorraine without being beaten first. But it was remarkable that the venture was even tried.

In April 1917 the Socialist International stirred into life with a suggestion by the Secretary of the Bureau (which had moved to the Netherlands when the Germans invaded Belgium) that socialists from neutral and belligerent countries should hold a conference in Stockholm to discuss a compromise peace. In May the Petrograd Soviet supported this appeal, and for a time the proposed conference became the centre of much activity. The French Socialist Party and the British Labour Party agreed to send delegates, though in the event their respective governments refused permission to travel. The conference never actually convened, but the proposal revived the idea of peace among European socialists. In Germany, the Socialists combined with the Catholic Centre Party to propose a 'peace resolution' in the Reichstag, calling for a peace of understanding, without forced territorial acquisitions, which was passed by 212 votes to 126 (July 1917). The wording was ambiguous, and was later stretched to allow approval of the Treaty of Brest-Litovsk, which brought Germany immense advantages without formal territorial gains; but even so a vote of this kind would previously have been inconceivable.

There followed a number of appeals for peace from widely disparate sources. In August 1917 Pope Benedict XV called for peace based on a return to the territorial status quo of 1914 and a renunciation of all financial demands or reparations. In November Lenin, the leader of the new Bolshevik government in Russia, appealed to the peoples of Europe for a peace without annexations or indemnities, which amounted to much the same thing. On 29 November the London *Daily Telegraph* published a letter from Lord Lansdowne, calling for a compromise peace before it was too late: 'What will be the value of the blessings of peace to nations so exhausted that they can scarcely stretch out a hand with which to grasp them?'[20] Lansdowne was a Conservative, a former viceroy of India and Foreign Secretary, and a great Anglo-Irish landowner – just about as far removed from Lenin as it was possible to be, and none too close to the Pope.

When the Pope, Lenin and Lord Lansdowne spoke in much the same vein within three months of one another, it was surely time for others to listen. Above all Lansdowne was plainly right to assert that the war was costing more in lives, economic exhaustion and social dislocation than could ever be regained, even by victory. Yet none of these peace moves came to anything. The war went on, and Europe continued to destroy itself. Why?

Part of the answer lay in the war aims which the principal belligerents had formulated, and which they were reluctant to give up. As early as September 1914 the German chancellor, Bethmann-Hollweg, had drawn up a far-reaching programme. In the west, Germany was to control Belgium and annex some territory from France; in the east, Russia must hand over territory in the Baltic provinces and Poland, which would become dependent on Germany. Economically, most of Europe (including Scandinavia) was to form a customs union under German control. *Mitteleuropa* was to be firmly under German predominance. (*Mittelafrika* was to follow, though that was less important.) The main body of these aims became firmly established, and German governments were to stick to them as long as was conceivably possible; in the east they were actually implemented in the Treaty of Brest-Litovsk in March 1918.

On the other side, the Allied powers also developed far-reaching aims. France was determined to recover Alsace and Lorraine. Russia aimed at territory in East Prussia, Posen and Galicia. The British intended to take over the German colonies. But Britain and France went further than territorial aims. As early as 9 November 1914, Asquith, the British Liberal prime minister, declared that Britain would not make peace until Belgium was restored, France was made secure from aggression, and *'the military domination of Prussia is wholly and finally destroyed.'*[21] On 22 December 1914 the French premier, Viviani, proclaimed as a French war aim (along with Alsace-Lorraine and the restoration of Belgium) *the crushing of Prussian militarism* – almost a repetition of Asquith's phrase. It was an extraordinary objective, because to 'crush Prussian militarism' meant breaking the traditions, customs and social organization which were ingrained in the Prussian state, and by extension in Germany. The French and British also set out, at an Allied Economic Conference in Paris in June 1916, economic war aims, designed to protect them against German economic domination.

It is striking that Asquith and Viviani, and the liberal parliamentary democracies which they represented, produced demands which were as drastic in their own way as those devised by the German chancellor and endorsed later by Hindenburg and Ludendorff as military dictators. If these aims were taken seriously – and they were – there was little room for compromise. The war was fought, not for limited aims, but for total victory. Moreover, the issues at stake involved much more than territory. The Germans sought security through the control of Europe. The British and French intended to change the very nature of German society. These were deep issues.

The entry of Italy into the war confirmed the point. At one level, Italy fought almost blatantly for territorial gains. The Treaty of London set out what Italy was to receive: the Trentino, the South Tyrol, Trieste and most of the Dalmatian coast, part of Albania, the Turkish province of Adalia and unspecified colonies in Africa. These terms represented the hardest sort of political bargaining. Yet there was more to Italian intervention than that. Italian nationalists, notably the future standard-bearers of Fascism, Benito Mussolini (formerly a socialist opponent of war), Gabriele D'Annunzio and Tomaso Marinetti (Futurist poets), helped to propel Italy into war by their propaganda and demonstrations, believing with an almost desperate urgency that they had to force a reluctant and stagnant country into war in order to 'save its soul'. Such an aim could scarcely have been further removed from the detailed and sometimes cynical negotiations of the Italian politicians. This contrast of motives was probably clearer in Italy than in other countries, but it was present everywhere. The war was about *both* territory (and other material matters) and ideas – even ideals. This meant that the war was particularly difficult to get out of, even in 1917, when its costs had become painfully clear and its length was still unpredictable.

The war aims on all sides made a compromise peace very difficult to achieve. Only victory would do, and only victory could justify the sacrifices made in the war. And, crucially, *victory was still possible for both sides*, as a result of two great events in that same year of 1917: the collapse of Russia and the entry of the USA into the war.

THE LONG ROAD TO ARMISTICE

Russia ceased to be an effective combatant in 1917 and concluded an armistice in December that year. Germany won the war in the east and was able to move men, guns and munitions to France for a last great effort to win in the west as well. Even though the Germans and Austrians left about a million men in the east as occupying forces, that did not prevent Germany from transferring 53 divisions from east to west between November 1917 and May 1918.[22] There was therefore little incentive for Germany to seek a compromise peace when victory had been won on one front and seemed within reach on the other.

But as Russia dropped out of the war the USA came in, declaring war on Germany on 6 April 1917 – a crucial date in European as well as North American history. The exact reasons for American intervention remain unclear, even at this distance in time. President Woodrow Wilson had long been ardently neutral – 'impartial in thought as well as in action', he had declared in 1914. American public opinion had been divided or indifferent, and American interests largely unaffected. Early in 1917 the second German submarine campaign changed the situation. American trade suffered badly; American pride was hurt and lives lost. The USA faced the possibility of an Allied defeat, the loss of their war loans to the Allied powers, and the potential consequences of a German-dominated Europe. Wilson himself, who had previously hoped to bring about a righteous peace by remaining neutral, now adopted the equally attractive idea of imposing righteousness through victory.

Whatever the American motives for intervention, the consequences were immense. Wise heads among the Europeans had long known how important the Americans might be. In 1915 Grey declared that 'the blockade of Germany was essential to the victory of the Allies, but the ill will of the United States meant their certain defeat.' In Germany, Falkenhayn warned the advocates of U-boat warfare that 'we could not withstand a war with America on the side of our enemies.'[23] Falkenhayn was proved right. Slowly at first, but later at a remarkable rate, the American Expeditionary Force crossed the Atlantic. In October 1917 there were three American divisions in France, and in March 1918 still only five. By July 1918 there were 25; in October 32; and in November 42.[24] By that time in the war, an American division was double the strength of a British or French division; and though the Americans were inexperienced, they were fit, fresh and confident. The outcome of this military arithmetic was certain. If the Western Allies could hold on long enough for the Americans to arrive, they would win the war. Why then should they settle for a compromise peace?

If 1917 presented the last chance to save something from the wreck by bringing the conflict to a negotiated end, it was lost. The Great War ground on, to the final destruction of most of the old Europe. What the year had brought, in the shape of the American entry into the war and the Bolshevik Revolution, were two events which were to shape a new Europe.

The German government had high hopes that 1918 would be the year of victory, but it was to prove an extraordinary roller coaster of a year. They began by imposing a drastic peace settlement on Russia. At the peace conference, at Brest-Litovsk, the Russian delegation was headed by Trotsky, and included a worker, a peasant, a soldier and a sailor, to show that a new revolutionary era had begun. Trotsky hoped for much from revolutionary diplomacy. The Bolsheviks handed out subversive leaflets to German soldiers at the Brest-Litovsk railway station. At one point Trotsky tried a new trick in the annals of diplomacy, declaring that the war was over even though no peace had been concluded – 'no war, no peace', he proclaimed, and left the conference. The Germans were not impressed, and simply resumed their advance into Russian territory. Revolutionary diplomacy proved no match for old-fashioned force. To save the revolution, and his own authority, Lenin sent Trotsky back to the conference to accept the German terms, which had grown harsher in the meantime. By the Treaty of Brest-Litovsk, signed on 3 March 1918, Russia was reduced roughly to its territories before the reign of Catherine the Great. Finland and Ukraine became independent states. Poland and the Baltic provinces were left for Germany to organize at leisure. Territory in the southern Caucasus passed to Turkey. It was a treaty of extraordinary severity and showed the Western Allies the consequences to be expected from a German victory.

Despite these gains, Germany was on the verge of exhaustion. The reserves of manpower that had been so deep in 1914 had been used up, and the next class of conscripts (that of 1900) would not be available until autumn 1918. Astonishingly, the Germans had done almost nothing to supplement men with machines – at the beginning of 1918 they had only 20 tanks in service, mostly captured from the British and French.[25] The civilian population was hard-pressed, and in January and February 1918 there were strikes in several cities, including Berlin, demanding more food and an end to the war. If Germany was to complete its victory by winning the war in the west as well as the east, it would have to be done quickly.

The Germans began their effort on 21 March 1918, with a great offensive against the British in Flanders. They made spectacular gains, advancing 40 miles and threatening to drive a wedge between the British and French armies. Other attacks followed. At the end of May the Germans attacked the French, advanced 30 miles in three days and came within 40 miles of Paris. (Trains out of the city were suddenly packed.) Yet the Germans never achieved the complete breakthrough they sought. The Allies appointed for the first time a single supreme commander, General Foch, to coordinate their operations, and they eventually checked the German advance. By the end of July the Germans had suffered heavy losses, which they could not replace, and even their successes in capturing territory left them with the disadvantage of a longer line to hold than when they began their offensives in March.

At the same time, the French home front suffered a sharp crisis, with big strikes in the Paris region during May and a sudden wave of antiwar feeling. The shock was sharp but short-lived. The strikers wanted peace, but were not prepared to accept defeat in order to get it. They were not ready for 'revolutionary defeatism' on the Bolshevik model. Jean-Jacques Becker concluded his analysis of these events by observing that 'the anti-war movement never managed to break down the invisible and apparently insurmountable barrier of national sentiment.'[26] The solid resolution with which the French people entered the war in 1914 survived the crisis of 1918, and reminds us again of why the war lasted so long.

The Germans had made their last throw, and failed. The Allies then struck back. On 18 July 1918 the French and Americans attacked on the Marne, using 750 tanks and 1000 aircraft in an offensive that foreshadowed a new form of warfare. On 8 August the BEF attacked in Flanders, a date which Ludendorff was to call the Black Day of the German Army. After that, successive Allied offensives drove the Germans back to the positions from which they had started in March. At the end of September the BEF breached the Hindenburg Line, which had been thought impregnable, and the French and Americans were advancing towards Sedan. The German high command recognized defeat. On 28 September Ludendorff told the chancellor that he must ask for peace while the army was still intact. On 4 October the German government sent a note to President Wilson seeking peace on the basis of the Fourteen Points which he had set out in a speech on 8 January 1918, and which the Germans hoped would provide them with lenient terms.[27]

For nearly three weeks the Germans and the USA communicated solely with each other, disregarding the French and British, who had been at war with Germany for over four years. It was an extraordinary state of affairs, and showed how the European situation had been transformed by recent events. For a time President Wilson held the vital threads of European diplomacy in his own hands. The war had been made in Europe, but it seemed that the peace was going to be made in America. Clemenceau and Lloyd George, who rightly felt that their countries had borne the heat and burden of the day, intervened by instructing General Foch, the Supreme Allied Commander, to draw up his own terms for an armistice. Foch produced a set of demands which were intended to cripple the Germans militarily and politically: the surrender of 5000 guns, 25,000 machine guns and large quantities of railway rolling stock, plus the evacuation of all occupied territory (including Alsace and Lorraine, which pre-empted a vital political issue) within a fortnight and all territory west of the Rhine in four weeks. These terms were accepted by all the Western Allies, including the Americans, and then imposed upon the Germans. They came into operation at the fateful hour of 11 a.m. on 11 November 1918.

MYTHS AND CONSEQUENCES

In subsequent years two myths grew up about these events. In Germany, many soldiers and politicians (not least the Nazi Party) were to make much of the idea of 'the stab in the back' – that defeatists and socialists at home had betrayed an unbeaten army in the field. This turned the chronology of events back to front. Ludendorff knew that his army was beaten at the end of September, and the government asked for peace on 4 October. Revolution *followed* these events. Mutiny broke out in the High Seas Fleet at Kiel on 1 November; a left-wing coup seized power in Munich on 7 November; the kaiser abdicated on 9 November; and on the same day the chancellor, Prince Max of Baden, handed over his office to the socialist Friedrich Ebert – a poisoned chalice if ever there was one. The story of a stab in the back was a falsehood, but it was to have great influence in Germany and to assist the rise of the Nazis.

Another influential belief grew up among the victors. Many years later, when Germany had launched another European war, it was widely asserted that the Allies had made a mistake in concluding an armistice in November 1918. Instead, they should have continued the war, invaded German territory and driven home the lessons of defeat, so deterring the Germans from trying again. There were advocates of such a course at the time, including President Poincaré of France and General Pershing, the American commander, whose troops had only recently entered the fray and had not yet suffered heavy casualties. But the tough old Clemenceau, who could not be accused of weakness, would not hear of it. If the Germans were ready to admit defeat, he would have no more Frenchmen killed merely to carry the war onto German soil. Moreover, the longer the war went on, the greater would be the role of the Americans and the weaker the position of the European Allies. The British leaders, civilian and military, agreed. The arguments were surely unanswerable. What would have been the popular verdict on politicians and generals who prolonged the war and sent soldiers to their death merely for the satisfaction of invading German territory? Only during the Second World War did the armistice seem mistaken, and the Allies adopted instead the policy of 'unconditional surrender', which was in its turn denounced on the basis that it prolonged the war unnecessarily. The verdict of history, so often appealed to, can produce some contradictory results.

So much for the myths and the might-have-beens. At the time, the facts were eloquent enough. The year 1918 produced an extraordinary combination of events. Germany defeated Russia, which for a time vanished from the scene as a great power, and became instead the home of Bolshevism and the 'workers' fatherland'. Then Germany itself was defeated by the Western powers. The armistice of 11 November 1918 annulled the Treaty of Brest-Litovsk and required German troops to withdraw from the occupied territories.[28] At the end of 1918 the Austro-Hungarian Empire broke into fragments. On 28 October Czechoslovakia declared independence, and Thomas Masaryk moved into the palace in Prague where his father had been an imperial coachman. A newly established Hungarian National Council declared the separation of Hungary from Austria. On 11 November Polish independence was declared. On 4 December the newly proclaimed Kingdom of the Serbs, Croats and Slovenes took over parts of the former Habsburg Empire. The Emperor Karl remained like a wraith in the palace of Schönbrunn.

These three great powers – Russia, Germany and Austria-Hungary – had long controlled eastern Europe. Their collapse left a vacuum, which a number of new states emerged to fill. But these circumstances were fleeting. The Habsburg Empire had indeed vanished for ever, but the fall of Germany and Russia proved short-lived. When they recovered their strength, it became apparent that the new states of eastern Europe had been founded on a sandbank, at the mercy of the rising tides of German and Soviet power. By 1940 most of them had been submerged again, or were struggling for survival.

The slaughter and destruction wrought by the Great War demolished the old Europe that existed before 1914, and it was a new and strange continent that emerged from the wreckage. Moreover, the damage wrought by the war was moral and psychological as much as material. Europe had lost its pre-war self-confidence and faith in progress. Yet partly because of this loss of confidence, new concepts of European identity, rooted in tragedy and division, were to emerge as one legacy of the war.

PART THREE

THE ILLUSION OF PEACE AND THE EUROPE OF THE -ISMS, 1919–1939

2   Europe in the 1920s

5

EUROPE SURVIVES, 1919–1929

PEACE AND REVOLUTION

When the Paris Peace Conference opened on 18 January 1919, the delegates looked out on the wreckage of the Europe of 1914. The empires of the Hohenzollerns in Germany, the Habsburgs in Austria-Hungary and the Romanovs in Russia had all disappeared, and various successors were struggling to replace them. In some areas there was no effective government at all. Revolution was in the air. The Bolsheviks had seized power in Russia and were appealing to the proletarians of all countries to overthrow their rulers. There was a revolution in Berlin in November 1918. A Soviet Republic was declared in Bavaria in March 1919. Bela Kun's communist regime held power in Hungary from March to the end of July 1919. Workers occupied factories in northern Italy. It seemed that the flames of revolution might spread further still.

Another revolutionary principle was at work: the self-determination of peoples. During the war, both the Allies and the Germans had tried to use self-determination to undermine their enemies. When the war was over, the victors could not simply turn the idea off like a tap, even if they had wished to do so. President Wilson, indeed, sought to make self-determination one of the guiding principles of the peace settlement, though he had little idea where it would lead. In a rare moment of self-doubt, he admitted to the United States Senate that 'When I gave utterance to those words [that all nations had a right to self-determination], I said them without the knowledge that nationalities existed, which are coming to us day after day…'[1] The American Secretary of State, Lansing, prophesied gloomily: 'It [self-determination] will raise hopes which can never be realised. It will, I fear, cost thousands of lives.'[2] He suffered the fate of Cassandra, in that his prophesy was true but in vain. Self-determination raised more hopes than could be satisfied. In eastern Europe almost any frontier, no matter how carefully or sensitively drawn, was certain to leave national minorities under foreign rule.

The Peace Conference which met to re-order the continent was a large and unwieldy body, representing 32 states. The list included some surprising names. It was strange – and before 1914 it would have been inconceivable – to see Guatemala, Liberia and Siam taking even nominal responsibility for the settlement of Europe. The conference met in plenary session only eight times, and the main work was done by the Council of Four, made up of the prime ministers of Britain, France and Italy and the president of the USA, whose influence was far-reaching. The presence of Guatemala was merely an oddity; but the power of the USA was an ominous sign that Europeans were losing control of their own continent.

A NEW EUROPE?

Where was Europe to go in this new situation, and could any form of European cohesion be restored? At first, the answer seemed to be a resounding 'no'. In western Europe the map at least remained recognizably similar to that before 1914, though with some transfers of territory. By the Treaty of Versailles of 1918, Germany lost Alsace and Lorraine to France, Eupen and Malmédy to Belgium, and part of Schleswig to Denmark. Germany was also separated from the victorious powers by a series of conditions very different from anything known in Europe before 1914. The country was disarmed, with an army restricted to 100,000 men, the navy limited in tonnage and no air force at all. Moreover, the German General Staff, formerly a powerful element in the government of the country, was to be dissolved. These were extraordinary interventions in the affairs of a sovereign state. Germany was to pay reparations, set by the Reparations Commission in 1921 at the enormous figure of 132 million gold marks; though the Commission also declared that the payment of 80 million gold marks would be indefinitely postponed. At the head of the reparations section of the Treaty of Versailles stood an article (number 231) laying down that Germany accepted responsibility for the loss and damage suffered by the Allies 'as a consequence of the war imposed on them by Germany and her allies.' The Germans soon denounced this as 'the war guilt clause', though the word 'guilt' was not used. In practice this scarcely mattered. The idea of 'responsibility' for starting the war was quite enough in itself, and the shift to the simpler word 'guilt' was an easy one. Moreover, another section of the treaty demanded the trial of the former Kaiser Wilhelm II for 'a supreme offence against international morality and the sanctity of treaties', and of other unnamed persons for violations of the laws and customs of war.[3] Little immediate or practical result followed from this. The kaiser had taken refuge in the Netherlands, and the Dutch refused to give him up. Only a few alleged offenders against the laws of war were brought to trial in Germany. But the concept of war crimes, and that going to war might in itself be a crime, had been propagated, and Germany had been accused on both counts.

The Germans resented the whole treaty, partly because it registered their defeat in a war which for four years they had appeared to be winning, and partly because it imposed on them a criminal status which they felt to be unjust. They denounced Versailles as a dictated and illegitimate treaty. One German delegate to the Peace Conference predicted that as a result 'the German Nationalist movement will inevitably gain strength, and a leader, as yet undiscovered, would be found to head a great popular uprising.'[4] That leader proved to be Adolf Hitler. But long before Hitler's rise to power, the peace settlement imposed a special status on Germany and created a deep division in western Europe which had not been present before 1914.

The situation in eastern Europe was far worse. Everything was transformed, and in some areas chaos took over. No fewer than nine new or revived states came into being: from north to south, Finland, Estonia, Latvia, Lithuania, Poland, Czechoslovakia, Austria, Hungary and the Kingdom of the Serbs, Croats and Slovenes (later Yugoslavia). Boundaries were drawn and redrawn. In Russia the Bolsheviks proclaimed the dictatorship of the proletariat at home and encouraged revolution abroad. The foundations were shaken in a way not seen in western Europe, marking a long-lasting cleavage in the continent. The peacemakers tried to establish the bases of a new order amid this chaos, though often questions of boundaries and forms of government were settled on the spot, and frequently by force.

Austria and Hungary reappeared as new states, the diminished successors of the former partners in the Austro-Hungarian Empire. Austria became a small country of about 6.5 million people, of whom just over 2 million lived in Vienna. It seemed that hardly anyone actually wanted to be Austrian – unofficial plebiscites showed that most people wanted union with Germany, though the people of the Vorarlberg province wanted to join Switzerland. But union with Germany was explicitly ruled out by the Treaty of Versailles; so the Austrians, like it or not, had to settle down to their new identity and somehow make a living. Hungary's problems were even greater. Bela Kun led a revolution, which imposed a Bolshevik regime for just over three months, until it was overthrown by a Romanian invasion. Admiral Horthy (formerly an officer in the Habsburg Navy) assumed the title of regent, claiming to be a caretaker for the deposed Habsburg monarch, and restored order. After these internal troubles there came the Treaty of Trianon (June 1920), by which the victorious Allies imposed the cession of about two-thirds of the former territory of Hungary. Nearly 3 million Hungarians now lived outside the country: some 1.6 million in Romania, 720,000 in Czechoslovakia, and 500,000 in Yugoslavia.[5] These losses of territory and population aroused deep resentment in Hungary, and the revision of the treaty became the main (almost the sole) objective of Hungarian foreign policy.

The new state of Czechoslovakia reproduced something of the character, and the difficulties, of the old Habsburg Empire. Within its long, narrow territory lived five nationalities: 7.5 million Czechs, 3.2 million Germans, 2.3

million Slovaks, 720,000 Hungarians and 569,000 Ruthenes.[6] To add to their other anxieties, Czech governments were haunted by fears of a Habsburg restoration in Austria or Hungary – so much so that some Czech politicians seemed more afraid of the ghosts of the Habsburgs than the reality of Hitler. In many ways Czechoslovakia held the key to the stability of central Europe, and yet the country was itself profoundly unstable.

Poland was a revived state, with a long and tortured history. The country had been wiped off the map at the end of the eighteenth century, partitioned between Russia, Prussia and Austria; but the Polish people had clung tenaciously to their language, religion and national identity. Polish independence was proclaimed on 11 November 1918, but the country had no recognized borders and little practical unity after a three-way division for over a century. Some of the Poles pitched their territorial claims high – one of their leaders, Roman Dmowski, told the peacemakers in Paris that Poland regarded the frontiers before the first partition in 1772 *as a starting point*. In the event, the Treaty of Versailles fixed Poland's border with Germany; but in the east, where the peacemakers' writ did not run, the frontiers were settled by force (see below, p. 83).

In the Balkans, Romania was the major territorial winner, emerging with more than double its pre-war area and population; but as a result of these very gains it was surrounded by hostile neighbours in Hungary, Bulgaria and Russia, which all hoped to recover lost ground. Yugoslavia (the Kingdom of the Serbs, Croats and Slovenes until the new name was formally adopted in 1929) was a new country comprising five principal nationalities (Serbs, Croats, Slovenes, Bosnians and Montenegrins) and three religions (Orthodox, Catholic and Muslim). Bulgaria had joined the German side during the war, and paid the penalty by losing territory to Romania and Greece.

The settlement with the Ottoman Empire seemed the least pressing of the tasks faced by the peacemakers, and the Treaty of Sèvres was not concluded until August 1920. The terms were severe. The Straits were to be controlled by an international commission. Italy and France were to receive large spheres of influence in southern Anatolia; Greece was to occupy Smyrna and its hinterland; Armenia was to be independent. But imposing these terms was another matter. The Ottoman Empire was at the point of death, but in a new form Turkey was very much alive. Mustafa Kemal, the hero of Gallipoli in 1915, had set up a new government in Ankara and organized a new army. He rejected the Treaty of Sèvres, which Britain, France and Italy no longer had the will or the strength to impose. The Greeks, on the other hand, were willing to enforce the treaty, and make more gains for themselves in the process. A Greek army advanced into Anatolia, to within 50 miles of Ankara; but in August–September 1921 they were defeated on the Sakarya river – a decisive battle, now almost forgotten in western Europe. During the next 12 months the Greeks were driven back to the coast. The Turks occupied Smyrna (now Izmir) in September 1922. Many Greeks were massacred, and about a million were driven out of Anatolia, where they had lived for centuries. For the Greeks, this was 'the Great Catastrophe'; for the Turks, it was a victory which saved their country.

Russia remained a vast territory in a state of confusion. A Bolshevik government was established in Petrograd (later Leningrad), and Lenin had embarked on the task of building socialism – a venture watched with hope and admiration by some outsiders, and with increasing alarm by others. In 1919 its success remained uncertain. White Russian forces, led by Yudenich in the Baltic area, Kolchak in Siberia and Denikin in the south, opposed the Bolsheviks. Fighting flared up and died down over vast areas. In Ukraine, no fewer than 11 different armies were operating at different times, and the capital, Kiev, changed hands 15 times in 1919–20.[7] Allied forces from five different countries (Britain, France, Japan, the USA and Canada) intervened round the periphery of Russia between 1918 and 1920, with different purposes and little success; but for the Bolsheviks their actions were proof that the capitalist powers wanted to strangle the proletarian revolution in its infancy – which was what they had expected.

In these widespread struggles across the old Russian Empire, the Bolsheviks mostly came out on top, defeating the various White armies and conquering Ukraine, the Caucasus and Transcaspia. But they lost one decisive battle, against the Poles at Warsaw in August 1920. If the Red Army had succeeded in pressing on through Poland to Germany, the Bolsheviks might have triggered revolution in central Europe. In the event, the Polish victory drove the Russians back, saved Europe from a Bolshevik invasion, and established the Polish frontier well to the east, by the Treaty of Riga in 1921.

This new frontier became in effect the frontier of Europe, from which the new Bolshevik Russia was excluded. This was partly a matter of self-exclusion. The Bolsheviks cut themselves off as far as possible from the capitalist world, which they regarded – with much justification – as profoundly hostile. Trade with other countries was controlled by the government, and the shadowy but perilous movement of ideas was tightly guarded against. On the other side, European states excluded Bolshevik Russia, which was not invited to the Paris Peace Conference and was not a member of the League of Nations until 1934. Clemenceau spoke of putting a cordon sanitaire around Russia. Even formal diplomatic recognition came only slowly, and in some cases not at all – Switzerland and the Netherlands still had no diplomatic relations with the Soviet Union in 1939. Yet by a strange paradox the great outsider was present everywhere in Europe. Communist parties were established (sometimes clandestinely) in every country, and were controlled from Moscow by the Communist International. For communists, and many of their fellow-travellers, Bolshevik Russia was 'the great light in the East', which would eventually illuminate the whole continent. In this way the long-standing ambiguity of relations between Russia and Europe remained, even in this period of exclusion.

DIVISION AND DISRUPTION

The new Europe was thus deeply divided. There was the split between victors and vanquished, which stood out most obviously in the treatment of Germany as not merely a defeated enemy but as an outcast, held responsible for the war and disarmed. There was also the linked, but by no means identical, division between the 'revisionist' countries, which wanted to change the settlement reached in 1919–21, and those which wanted to maintain it. Germany was determined to change almost all the crucial elements of the Versailles Treaty – to get rid of reparations, evade disarmament, change the frontier with Poland, achieve union with Austria, and remove the stigma of war guilt. Hungary, though on a smaller scale, was equally set on retrieving at least some of the losses imposed by the Treaty of Trianon. Italy had been on the winning side in the war, but was a revisionist power because it was aggrieved at being denied some of its promised gains. These three countries formed a band across the middle of Europe, and proved more vigorous in their pursuit of change than the status quo powers were in preventing it. Of those powers, France had most at stake in upholding the peace settlement, but for a long time lacked the will to do so. Britain soon lost faith in the settlement it had helped to design, and came to accept much of the German case against the injustice and harshness of the Versailles Treaty. On these crucial political questions, Europe was fragile and divided. The stability and cohesion of the European state system before 1914 had vanished.

At the same time, the First World War left a legacy of severe economic disruption. The battle zones in north-east France and Flanders presented a scene of devastation. All over Europe industry, agriculture and transport systems had worked for four years under intense pressure, so that men, machines and land were all exhausted and worn out. The continent was subject to threats of famine and disease, which had previously seemed to be things of the past, and the great influenza epidemic of 1918–19 evoked dreadful comparisons with the Black Death.

Europe's financial and monetary structures had suffered gravely. France and Britain had sold foreign investments to pay for their wartime imports, especially from the USA. The French lost the whole of their pre-war investments in Russia as a result of the Bolshevik Revolution. Germany lost nearly all its foreign investments either during the war or at the peace. All the belligerents had incurred massive burdens of foreign debt – for example, Britain had borrowed heavily from the USA, while France and Italy had borrowed from both Britain and the USA.[8] Germany incurred the debt of reparations under the Treaty of Versailles. Internal government debts also increased enormously during the war, the costs of which were met largely by borrowing. Inflation flourished everywhere, as prices rose and the value of money fell. In Britain, which came out better than most countries, retail prices more than doubled between 1914 and 1918. Neutral countries suffered in the same way as belligerents. The cost of living in Denmark doubled between

1914 and 1919; and the situation in Spain was similar. The impact of inflation on generations which had grown accustomed to stable prices and a reliable currency was enormous, and was as much psychological as economic. The lost landmark of a stable currency proved much harder to restore than the ruins of towns and villages.

By contrast, some of the economic fruits and advantages of the war went to non-Europeans. The USA became a creditor country for the first time, and the American economy thrived on the demands of war. American firms moved into British and German preserves in Latin America. Japan took advantage of wartime conditions to extend its economic influence in China and to break into the Indian market.

After the war, economic conditions remained difficult, and in some countries disastrous. Trade within Europe, so vigorous before 1914, was disrupted by the fragmentation of the continent – for example, the former customs union of the Austro-Hungarian Empire was divided into seven different states, each with its own tariffs. In some of the new countries of eastern Europe, farming was thrown into confusion by the break-up of large estates in the course of land reform. Inflation continued into the years of peace. The most terrible case was that of Germany, where inflation was already rife between 1919 and 1922. Then in 1923 the French occupied the

5 Hyper-inflation in Germany: children playing with banknotes as building bricks, 1923 © akg-images

Ruhr to enforce reparations payments, and the German government financed passive resistance to the occupation by simply printing money, with disastrous consequences. Taking the retail price index in 1913 as a factor of 1, the index stood in January 1923 at 2783, and by December 1923 at 1,261,000,000,000 – an unimaginable figure, meaning that the currency was worth nothing at all.[9] A pay packet lost its value even before a worker got home. People with savings, insurance policies or a fixed income lost their assets completely. This was by far the worst case of inflation, but other countries (notably Austria, Hungary and Poland) also suffered badly.

War and economic disruption were accompanied by social dislocation, which swept away many of the similar characteristics which had prevailed over much of Europe before 1914. The landed aristocracy suffered heavily, and sometimes fatally. In Russia the aristocracy virtually disappeared in the revolution: killed, driven into exile, or reduced to poverty and anonymity. In parts of eastern Europe large landowners suffered heavy losses as new governments undertook land reform and distributed some of the big estates among the peasants. In Yugoslavia, for example, legislation introduced in 1919 fixed the maximum landholding at 30 hectares, and over the next few years many estates were broken up to the benefit of some 650,000 smallholders. In Romania, large estates in Transylvania and Bessarabia (recently annexed from Hungary and Russia, respectively) were broken up and redistributed.[10] In Prussia the Junkers kept their lands, but lost much of their influence and prestige after the fall of the monarchy and the drastic reduction in the army. Even in Britain, spared from revolution or foreign conquest, new levels of taxation and a changed social climate caused many landowners to sell their estates. In politics, the appointment of Baldwin rather than Lord Curzon as prime minister in 1923 marked the stage at which it became impossible for the head of government to be a member of the House of Lords. In Ireland, rebellion, civil war and partition brought the decline of the Anglo-Irish aristocracy and gentry. In all, though in very different ways, the war and its immediate consequences were a disaster for the European aristocracy, which had been so prominent before 1914, and so marked a factor in the coherence of the continent.

The bourgeoisie also suffered heavily. In Russia the old bourgeoisie, never strong, was effectively wiped out, though it was later replaced by a new class of party managers, technicians and administrators. Everywhere inflation eroded, and sometimes destroyed, the wealth of the bourgeoisie. In Germany, the great inflation of 1923 meant that all resources that were tied to the mark simply vanished; the professions did better than rentiers, but even doctors or lawyers could not keep up with the collapse of the currency. In many countries, inflation was accompanied by the undermining of certain values that held middle-class society together – respectability, the value of work, the importance of savings. It is true that in western Europe much was saved. French bourgeois families held on to their property. The *cartel des gauches*, the left-wing coalition that won the French election of 1924, proved far from revolutionary, and Poincaré, who was the embodiment of the bourgeoisie in his policies and even his appearance, conducted a successful defence of the franc. In Britain, Ramsay MacDonald's Labour government of 1924 was cautiously moderate, and Stanley Baldwin, the leader of the Conservative Party, was thoroughly reassuring to the middle classes. The General Strike of 1926 was alarming, but did not last long. In Italy, Mussolini and the Fascists did much to protect property and industry.[11] Even so, the utter solidity of the European bourgeoisie before 1914 could not be restored.

WINDS OF CHANGE

The position of industrial workers was in some ways improved during the war, when wages increased and trade unions were often taken into partnership with governments and employers to organize war production. But at the same time the unions had to accept 'dilution', the relaxation of the lines of demarcation which had protected the skilled trades against infiltration by the less skilled. This tendency was reinforced by the growth of mass production methods, assembly lines and time-and-motion studies, summed up at the time as Taylorism, from its ancestry in the USA.

The war saw a marked change in the employment of women, both in terms of numbers and of the work they undertook. In Germany, Britain and France large numbers of women undertook war work, to replace men serving in the armies – in France, by 1918, about a quarter of the 1.5 million munitions workers were women. But the largest growth in women's employment arose in the tertiary sector, in offices, banks and services; so that the secretary or clerk rather than the munitions worker was the most typical (though not the most noticeable) woman worker in the war years. Recruitment to both categories came in part from those in domestic service, where numbers fell sharply during the war. In industry, these changes proved mainly temporary, because after the war factory jobs reverted to men, by common consent and a natural deference to those returning from war service; but the share of women in office work and services continued to increase.[12]

There was a strong impression, during and immediately after the war, that these changes in women's employment had been accompanied by a marked change in attitudes. Women had had their own money to spend, with the independence that came with earning wages. The large numbers whose husbands had gone to war had assumed responsibilities as heads of households and decision makers. There was a widespread relaxation of social constraints – women wore shorter skirts, smoked cigarettes and went out more freely. The lasting effects of these changes were uncertain, and by no means easy to measure. Long afterwards, some women remembered with pleasure that they had been 'let out of the cage', proud of their work and in some cases of their uniforms. Others simply went back with relief to being housewives and mothers. Doubtless many fell into both categories at different

6 Women at work in wartime: a woman munition worker during the First World War © Imperial War Museum

times; just as men regarded women's roles in wartime with a mixture of alarm and admiration.[13]

The end of the war coincided with the attainment of votes for women in a number of European countries. Women gained the vote in Russia in 1917, when it was introduced by the provisional government after the February Revolution. In 1918 women were enfranchised in Austria and Britain, though in the latter only those aged 30 years and older. Czechoslovakia, Germany, the Netherlands, Poland and Sweden followed in 1919, and Belgium in 1920. This list included two neutral countries, the Netherlands and Sweden, showing that the change was not simply a matter of women gaining the vote as a reward for their war effort; indeed, this was probably not a decisive element in any case. In France, where women had played a large part in the war effort, they did not receive the vote. The Chamber of Deputies passed a suffrage bill in 1919, but it was rejected by the Senate (after long delays) in 1922, partly out of fear that women voters would be anti-Republican and partly out of a deep-seated opposition to change in an essentially conservative political class. Women remained unable to vote in a considerable number of other countries, of very different kinds: Spain, Portugal, Italy, Switzerland, Hungary, the Balkan states and the Baltic republics of Estonia, Latvia and Lithuania. The political effects of enfranchisement were by no means clear-cut. In Britain, there was an assumption that most women tended to be conservative; but in Scandinavia, women's suffrage was part of a steady move towards socialism and the welfare state. Italy did not introduce votes for women, and took to Fascism; Germany did, and eventually went Nazi. In Spain, the Republic granted votes to women in 1932, but Franco's regime withdrew them again after the Civil War. But despite these differences and uncertainties, it seems clear, as Richard Evans concludes, that feminism in its pre-1914 form had run its course by the 1930s. The achievement of the vote in itself inevitably diluted the women's movement, because women voters turned to the political parties to promote their interests. Even where women did not secure the vote, the centre of attention moved elsewhere in the political and economic changes of the 1920s and 1930s. The feminist movement which had characterized parts of Europe before 1914 broke up or lapsed across much of the continent.[14]

The European empires overseas were much changed by the war. The German colonies were divided up among the victors, with territories going to Britain, France, Belgium, South Africa, Australia and New Zealand. The Ottoman Empire was broken up, and its former territories in the Middle East were placed under British or French control. In deference to President Wilson's views on self-determination, the former German and Ottoman territories were not simply annexed by the victorious powers, but were allotted to the states concerned as mandates under the League of Nations, with a view to their being led towards independence over a shorter or longer period of time. At the time, this did not seem to matter very much. The British and French empires emerged from the war larger than before; and in a striking development the former colonies of Australia, New Zealand and South Africa secured their own mandates, and so became imperial powers in their own right – a second generation of empire.

This was one of several ways in which the idea of empire received a new impulse from the war. The British military effort was imperial almost from start to finish, notably in the massive and heroic contribution by the Dominions in France, at Gallipoli and in the Middle East. Indian troops served in France and Mesopotamia. In politics, an Imperial War Cabinet met in London for long periods in 1917 and 1918. The Dominions and India were separately represented at the Peace Conference and became individual members of the League of Nations. France used large numbers of troops from North and West Africa on the western front; and Clemenceau welcomed regiments of black infantrymen in emotional terms. After the war the imperial idea found spectacular expression in the British Empire Exhibition at Wembley in 1924 (which left as its memorial the Wembley Stadium). In 1930 France celebrated with much ceremony the centenary of the conquest of Algiers, and in 1931 a vast Colonial Exhibition was held at Vincennes, including a full-size reproduction of the temple of Angkor Wat in French Indochina. Empires seemed to be at their apogee, and the European grip on the rest of the world appeared to have survived the war intact.

The reality was rather different. The efforts of the British Dominions in war and peace encouraged a rapid growth in their independence, which was given legal recognition by the Statute of Westminster in 1931. The experiences of Indian troops in France and Mesopotamia were often disillusioning and sometimes disastrous, and demands for Indian independence increased as the war came to an end. The French colonial troops suffered heavily on the western front, with the fate of the Senegalese infantry attacking on the Chemin des Dames in a snowstorm just one desperate episode among many. In the Middle East, nationalism developed rapidly during the war, sometimes with British encouragement, as a means of undermining Ottoman rule. In Iraq and Syria the new British and French mandates could only be imposed by force. In Egypt, the *Wafd* nationalist movement demanded independence from the British, and obtained at least a form of it in 1922. In Palestine, the British found themselves faced with the rival forces of Zionism and Arab nationalism, and became trapped in a hornets' nest from which there was no escape. Even the mandate system itself, which the imperial powers had regarded largely as a disguise for colonial rule, proved to have its problems, as the Mandates Commission undertook its enquiries and made reports. Empires were wider than ever before, but in many places they were less secure.

RECOVERY

In all these ways, Europe was badly shaken, and its former coherence broken up, by the war and its consequences. It suffered revolutions, the disruption of self-determination, economic difficulties, social disruption and the weakening of empires. Yet there were also many signs of Europe's survival, recovery and perhaps restoration.

This was true even of the bloodletting and the casualties of war. These were grievous, leaving a sense of catastrophe which endures to this day. European military war deaths numbered at least 8 million, and probably over 9 million. About 7 million more were permanently disabled by their wounds. At least another 4 million, and perhaps as many as 8 million, were killed in the Russian civil wars of 1918–20. In addition, there was a deficit in births, estimated at perhaps 15 million, caused by the absence of vast numbers of men from their homes.[15] The tragedy of these losses remains so powerful that it comes as a shock to read an observation by an economic historian: 'Military casualties were quite small in relative terms.' Put in these detached 'relative terms', military fatalities amounted to 15 per cent of all those mobilized, only 8 per cent of male workers, and a mere 2 per cent of the whole European population.[16] In most countries, population losses were soon made up. Only France suffered a permanent deficit and faced the spectre of the 'hollow years', as the diminished generation born during the war passed through half-empty schoolrooms to make up the thin ranks of conscripts reaching military age in the 1930s. Other countries mourned their dead, but could fill their places.

There was no comfort for the bereaved in this sort of arithmetic. Yet it was true that the European population survived the war and continued to increase. Even in the years from 1910 to 1920, which spanned the period of war, Europe outside Russia increased in population from about 316 million to 321.8 million.[17] In the next 20 years there was steady growth, so that Europe outside the Soviet Union numbered 378.8 million in 1940. Adding estimated figures for the Soviet Union, that total became about 537.8 million.[18] As a proportion of the world population, the European population was estimated at 25 per cent before the war, 24 per cent in 1920, and 23 per cent in 1940 – still a large share for what was in area the smallest continent.[19]

One reason for the rising European population was increased life expectancy, from somewhere between 30 and 50 years in 1910 to over 60 in parts of Europe by 1940. Infant mortality declined over most of the continent, offering a better chance of survival at the start of life.[20] This was part of a demographic transformation which was affecting most of Europe (though with marked differences between countries, and even within them), characterized by a fall in the birth rate and a higher expectation of life. This transition had long been under way in France, where the birth rate per 1000 inhabitants fell from 22.3 in 1891–95 to 18.8 in 1911–13. It later extended to other areas of north-west Europe and later to parts of the Mediterranean, the Balkans and eastern Europe, arising mainly from an improvement in social and economic conditions, and from changing attitudes to children and the family. The eventual result of a falling birth rate and increasing life expectancy, if they continued to prevail, was certain to be an ageing population, but as yet this was only a distant prospect. Even in France the proportion of the population aged 65 or over was 8.4 per cent in 1911, and still only 9.3 per cent in 1931. In Sweden, where the trend was also advanced, the proportion over 65 was 8.5 per cent in 1910, and 9 per cent in 1930.[21]

Another cause of the growth of the European population was a decline in emigration. In 1921 and 1924 the USA introduced legislation drastically reducing the numbers of immigrants; and with the onset of the great economic depression from 1929 immigration to the USA almost ceased. What had been the principal destination for European emigrants was thus progressively shut off. At the same time some of the major sources of emigration were also closed down. Before 1914 European governments had not opposed emigration, often regarding it as a useful safety valve. But in the 1920s and 1930s some important countries took a different line. The Soviet Union prohibited emigration in 1926. Fascist Italy in the 1920s and 1930s and Nazi Germany in the 1930s discouraged it; though in practice the number of Italian emigrants remained high in the 1920s.

The upshot of these changes was that between 1920 and 1929 emigration from Europe amounted to a total of about 5 million, and in the 1930s it fell to about 1 million.[22] Some European countries actually became recipients of immigrants in significant numbers. In the 1920s France received 1.95 million immigrants, mostly from other European countries, but also from North Africa – the census of 1931 showed a North African population of 102,000. In Britain in the 1930s there was a surplus of 650,000 immigrants over emigrants, coming mostly from Ireland and the British Empire, including Africans, Indians and West Indians.[23] Greece underwent a movement of immigration of a drastic type in the early 1920s, when about 1.3 million Greeks were driven out of Anatolia by the Turks, or were transferred under the terms of the Treaty of Lausanne (1923).[24]

A number of governments made a deliberate effort to increase their populations. In Italy, Mussolini aimed at a population of 60 million by 1950, from only 38 million in 1921; and he devoted much propaganda and some financial incentives to that end. Nazi Germany also encouraged childbearing by propaganda and family allowances, with some success; it was notable that when Austria and Czechoslovakia were taken over by Germany in 1938 and 1939 respectively, numbers of births increased. The Soviet Union made abortion illegal in 1936. French governments placed legal bans on contraceptive devices and abortions, and pursued a strong propaganda policy to encourage births, with little noticeable effect; a new family code, with financial payments to large families, was introduced in 1939.[25]

For these various reasons, the population of Europe continued to increase, in spite of the casualties of war. Lower birth rates and improved life expectancy signified an ageing population in the long run, but meanwhile were signs of a healthier population. The fall in emigration meant that vigorous and enterprising people, who might previously have gone overseas, stayed at home, with beneficial effects for the economy. The peoples of Europe survived the bloodletting of the First World War and its consequent conflicts more successfully than might have been expected, and continued to grow in number – in itself a sign of vigour in the old continent.

In rather a similar way, Europe made a recovery from the economic disasters of the war and its aftermath. In Germany the great inflation of 1923 was so calamitous that it became a turning point. At the end of that year, a new Reichsmark, with the backing of foreign (mainly American) loans, was introduced to replace the old currency, at the rate of 1 new mark to 1 million millions of the old. This registered the disappearance of the old currency and brought a fresh start. At about the same time there was a general attempt to stabilize European currencies. Britain adopted the gold exchange standard and set the exchange rate between sterling and the dollar at its pre-1914 level. Switzerland, the Netherlands, Denmark, Norway and Sweden took a similar course. In 1928 France adopted the gold exchange standard, though at only one-fifth of the pre-1914 value of the franc. A number of other countries also stabilized their currencies, albeit at levels well below pre-war values – for example, Italy at 25 per cent and Belgium at 14.3 per cent.[26] These measures were later condemned by economists as being over-rigid and unsustainable, but at the time they represented a vital and largely successful attempt to restore confidence in the value of money.

Stabilization of currencies was accompanied by new arrangements for the payment of reparations by Germany. In 1924 the Dawes Plan, devised by a committee chaired by an American banker, Charles G. Dawes, linked the stabilization of the German currency with a plan for the payment of reparations on a rising scale; and for the next five years Germany made its payments regularly. This was accompanied by and contributed to a general recovery in European trade and industrial production. In France, the index of industrial production passed the 1913 level in 1924, and in Germany passed the same mark in 1926. Trade between France and Germany increased rapidly.[27] Eastern Europe was still in difficulties, but in general the new countries were settling down, and industrial production increased in Hungary, Czechoslovakia, Poland and Romania. This economic recovery was partly dependent on American loans, especially to Germany; and Europe proved vulnerable when the American stock market crash of 1929 cut off the flow of lending. But from 1924 to 1929 the European economy showed encouraging signs of recovery from the shock of war and the ill effects of the peace.

Europe also showed signs of recovering at least some of the political coherence which it had known before 1914, by the widespread adoption of parliamentary institutions, the recovery of socialism and the development of aspects of political Catholicism.

Immediately after the war, it seemed for a time that parliamentary democracy had come into its own. Parliamentary governments in Britain, France and Italy, supported by that great transatlantic democracy the USA, had won the war, while the autocratic empires in Germany, Austria-Hungary and Russia had collapsed. Democratic constitutions were adopted everywhere in the new Europe. In Germany, the constitution of the Weimar Republic went almost to excess in its democratic methods, including an extreme form of proportional representation. The Austrian constitution set up a parliamentary government with universal suffrage. In Hungary, the regent, Admiral Horthy, governed under an adapted form of the late nineteenth-century Hungarian constitution, with a parliament elected on limited manhood suffrage. In Poland, the constitution adopted in 1921 was modelled on that of the French Third Republic and reproduced some of its faults, notably a series of unstable governments. The new Baltic states (Estonia, Latvia and Lithuania) all established parliamentary institutions, with manhood suffrage and proportional representation. All three soon produced a multiplicity of parties and short-lived ministries – in 1925 there were 26 parties represented in the Latvian parliament, and the country had 16 governments between 1920 and 1934. Most of the Balkan countries established or maintained parliamentary constitutions. Spain was ruled by a constitutional monarchy, though the Cortes was often suspended, and there were 10 governments from November 1918 to September 1923. Portugal had introduced manhood suffrage when it became a republic in 1910, but the new regime proved chronically unstable, with 9 presidents and no fewer than 44 governments between 1910 and 1926. With parliamentary institutions also operating in Britain, France, the Low Countries, Scandinavia and Italy, it appeared that Europe had opted en bloc for parliamentary democracy. In

1920, out of a total of 27 sovereign states in Europe (excluding Russia), all possessed parliamentary institutions; though many were already bearing the seeds of their own decay.[28]

Before 1914 socialism had been a rising political force in Europe, and the Second Socialist International a thriving European institution. The war had split socialist parties and the Bolshevik Revolution in Russia divided them further, between supporters and opponents of Lenin's venture. Even so, after the war social democracy recovered its strength and established an influential position in many countries. Socialist parties were agreed on their broad objectives: nationalization of industry and banking; social welfare and better working conditions; internationalism and antimilitarism, often veering towards pacifism. These aims gained widespread support.[29] In Germany, the Social Democrats were strong enough to take part in coalition governments between 1918 and 1920, and again in 1928, and could still secure 20 per cent of the vote in 1932, in the last election before Hitler came to power. In Austria, the socialist vote in the 1920s ranged between 36 and 42 per cent. In Britain, the Labour Party achieved 29 per cent of the vote in 1922, and 30.6 per cent in 1931; and Labour twice formed minority governments, in 1924 and 1929–31. In France, the Socialist Party suffered severely from communist rivalry. The party split in December 1920, when a large majority of the delegates to the Party Congress opted to form a Communist Party; and even the socialist newspaper, *L'Humanité*, went to the communists. But despite these difficulties, the socialists consistently won 18–20 per cent of the vote in French elections, and in 1936 Léon Blum became the first socialist premier, at the head of a Popular Front government.

Socialist parties were particularly strong in Scandinavia, where they regularly secured 30–40 per cent of the vote in these various countries. In Sweden they formed three minority governments in the 1920s and gained a parliamentary majority in 1932. By that time the Swedish Social Democrats had dropped nationalization of the means of production from their programme, and opted to combine private enterprise with a comprehensive welfare state, including index-linked pensions and paid holidays. Socialists in Denmark and Norway followed similar paths, joining coalition governments and developing welfare systems financed by high taxation. At the time, these developments in Scandinavia seemed unimportant by comparison with the great tides of ideology and war which were sweeping over the rest of Europe; but in the long run the Scandinavian countries were to provide an example and inspiration for most of western Europe.

The prestige of the Vatican had suffered during the war, when Pope Benedict XV had in principle refused to take sides, but in practice gained the reputation of sympathizing with the Central Powers. After the war, the Pope mended his fences with the victors by a number of conciliatory gestures. In 1919 he moved quickly to appoint a papal nuncio to the new state of Poland. In 1920 he canonized Joan of Arc, as a mark of respect to French patriotism, and the French government responded by sending a representative to the ceremony of canonization. In Italy, he dropped the long-standing Vatican policy of forbidding Catholics to take part in political life, and instead offered support to a new Catholic party, the *Partito Popolare*.

His successor, Pius XI (1922–39), intensified this policy, concluding concordats with eight European states (in chronological order, Latvia, Poland, Romania, Lithuania, Italy, Austria, Germany and Yugoslavia). By the concordats with Italy in 1929 and Germany in 1933 the Vatican came to terms with two of the principal totalitarian regimes of the time, with very different degrees of success – considerable in Italy, negligible in Germany (see below, p. 110). Towards the third totalitarian power, the Soviet Union, and its ideology, Communism, Pius XI maintained an unyielding opposition, condemning Communism as 'intrinsically hostile to religion in any form whatever'.[30] He accompanied opposition to Communism by denunciations of capitalism for its greed and worship of material possessions. Nor did he have much sympathy for democratic politics – as Eamonn Duffy nicely puts it, 'He had not a liberal bone in his body'.[31]

At the same time, he developed his own political and social theory in the encyclical *Quadragesimo Anno* (1931), outlining the 'corporatist' concept that all those working in the same professions, trades or industries should cooperate in a Christian spirit instead of struggling against one another in a class war. This concept was already current in Europe, in part through earlier Vatican thinking during the papacy of Leo XIII. The corporatist idea had already been adopted (at least on paper) by the Fascist regime in Italy; and it had a strong appeal as a means of controlling the economic and political problems of the 1930s. Pius XI's version was taken up in Austria, where the concordat signed in May 1933 was incorporated in the new constitution adopted in 1934, which declared Austria to be a Christian German state, and set up a federal assembly made up of bodies representing the professions and the regions. In Portugal, the regime set up by Salazar (see below, p. 118) was largely modelled on Catholic social doctrine, with a new constitution (1933) including a Chamber of Corporations. More generally, the ideas set out in *Quadragesimo Anno* became diffused among Catholic intellectuals throughout western Europe, with results which emerged only slowly in post-1945 European social models.

The positive contribution of the Vatican to European politics between the wars was limited. Catholic influence on the regimes of Portugal and Austria did not amount to much in the perspective of the continent as a whole. The close relations between the Vatican and Fascist Italy, the ambiguous consequences of the concordat with Nazi Germany and Pius XI's unrelenting hostility towards Communism all came to count heavily against the reputation of the papacy. Yet in the long term the influence of Catholic social thought was to increase, and Catholic statesmen (Schuman, Adenauer, De Gasperi) were to make vital contributions to the emergence of a new Europe after the Second

World War. Rather in the same way as European social democracy, the Vatican was sowing seeds which were to come to fruition much later.

INTERNATIONAL RELATIONS

Another element in the cohesion of Europe before 1914 had been its system of international relations, which was largely destroyed by the war. The old diplomacy was discredited because it had failed to prevent war in 1914 and had been too secretive in its methods. The grouping of European states into alliances and ententes was also believed to have precipitated the great conflict.

When the war was over, statesmen set out to replace the old international system with a new one. A new and more 'democratic' diplomacy was attempted, based on President Wilson's slogan of 'open covenants openly arrived at'. This got off to a bad start at the Paris Peace Conference, where even Wilson made sure that armed guards were posted to make sure that no one intruded on the discussions of the peacemakers – as Arthur Balfour, the British Foreign Secretary, noted with some amusement, but without surprise. The outcome was a modification rather than a replacement of the old diplomacy, with most governments preferring secrecy and using publicity only when it suited them.

There was a more far-reaching attempt to replace the old system of alliances and alignments with the new League of Nations. In principle this was a worldwide, not a European, organization, and its prominent place in the peace settlement owed more to President Wilson than to European statesmen. But when the USA repudiated Wilson and refused to join the League, it became predominantly European in character, and especially in its leadership. The Council, which was the League's guiding body, was largely European in membership. At the end of the 1920s there were five permanent members (Britain, France, Germany, Italy and Japan); two semi-permanent (Poland and Spain); and seven non-permanent, drawn from various groups (one from the Little Entente in south-eastern Europe, one from the European neutrals – in effect, Scandinavia, one from the British Commonwealth, three from Latin America and one from Asia). The Council thus resembled the old Concert of Europe, with the addition of some middle-sized and smaller countries, which had an opportunity to exercise influence in a way impossible before 1914. Beneš of Czechoslovakia and Branting of Sweden, for example, gained high reputations at Geneva.

The League achieved some striking successes in its early years. In 1922 the new Austrian Republic was in a state of financial and economic ruin, with a worthless currency and little prospect of recovery. A League committee made up of representatives from Britain, France, Italy and Czechoslovakia, along with the chancellor of Austria, produced a plan which comprised a renewed guarantee of Austrian independence, the raising of loans for Austria on the European stock markets and an undertaking by the Austrian government to balance its budget by the end of 1924. These measures created a new confidence, and achieved a lasting economic recovery. Individual states could not have produced such a result. Britain would never have acted alone; France and Italy would have distrusted one another; the Austrians would have resented intervention by Czechoslovakia, which had recently been part of the Habsburg Empire. Only the League could do the trick – and indeed it was a sort of trick, depending above all on the creation of confidence. In 1924 the League applied a similar formula to restore the Hungarian currency and finances. In 1926 the Council of the League also managed to settle a border dispute between Bulgaria and Greece, which in view of the recent history of territorial conflicts in the Balkans had seemed to threaten war.

The League also had its failures. It proved unable to resolve the dispute between Poland and Lithuania over Vilna (or Vilnius, or Wilno, according to nationality and language), which was in fact settled by force on the spot, in favour of Poland. In the Corfu incident of 1923, the League's ruling was more in favour of Italy, which had bombarded and occupied the Greek island, than of the Greeks who had suffered the attack. But in both cases the issues were complicated; and in the case of Corfu a certain indulgence towards Italy as a great power seemed natural. It was more important that the League had settled down as a valuable forum for the conduct of international affairs. Germany was admitted as a member in 1926, and at once became a permanent member of the Council; so the League was no longer a 'League of victors'. By 1928 every European state was a member (except the USSR, which was only doubtfully European, except in the geographical sense). Nearly every foreign minister made a point of attending its sessions. The League was still young, but there seemed a good chance that Europe had found a workable successor to the pre-1914 states system.

The stability of western Europe was also enhanced by the Treaty of Locarno in 1925 – though this was negotiated outside the League, and to some degree weakened its position. The treaty was limited in its geographical scope, confirming the new western boundaries of Germany and the demilitarized zone in the Rhineland, previously imposed by the Treaty of Versailles, on a freely negotiated basis. Britain and Italy acted as outside guarantors of the Franco–German and Belgian–German frontiers, contributing to a sense of security in western Europe. (Eastern Europe, with its more difficult problems, was left aside.) Above all, the 'spirit of Locarno' promised Franco–German reconciliation. The French and German foreign ministers, Briand and Stresemann, worked together and even rather liked one another. A whole network of links grew up. In 1926 French and German industrialists, with others from Belgium and Luxembourg, formed an iron and steel cartel to regulate production and prices. The cartel's chairman, Emil Mayrisch, hoped that these arrangements would lay the foundations for European economic union, and indeed they bear some resemblance to the European Coal and Steel Community set up in 1951. Businessmen, politicians and writers formed an influential Franco–German Committee. *L'Action Catholique de la Jeunesse*

Française made contacts with German Catholics. Ex-servicemen from both countries arranged meetings with their former enemies. It was a time of hope in Franco–German relations, and of promise for Europe.

The shock of the First World War, followed by the hopeful vistas of the 1920s, produced an intensified form of European internationalism. The breakdown of the pre-1914 system had been so drastic, and the effects of the war so terrible, that there emerged a conscious effort to promote a European cohesion that had previously been taken for granted, and to give it an institutional shape. Visionary proposals were put forward. Count Coudenhove-Kalergi, descended from an old aristocratic family in the Habsburg Empire, and himself of wide cosmopolitan outlook, published in 1923 a book entitled *Pan-Europe*, arguing for the establishment by stages of a federal union of Europe. His proposals excluded Bolshevik Russia, which he regarded as hostile to his ideals, and also Britain, which he saw as the centre of a separate group of states, the British Empire and Commonwealth – both of which represented significant limitations to Pan-Europe. He founded a journal, *Pan-Europa*, published in Vienna, where in 1926 he held a Pan-European Congress, attracting a large attendance and receiving warm messages from many European politicians, including the French foreign minister, Aristide Briand.

Briand himself called for a form of European union in a speech at the League of Nations in September 1929, proposing a sort of federal bond between the peoples of Europe. His words were opaque, as was not unknown for Briand; but he made it clear enough that he wanted to start with economic links, and later move on to political arrangements. He also made it plain that he did not intend to infringe upon state sovereignty. His speech received a warm welcome, and the delegates from 27 European members of the League invited him to prepare a formal proposal. Briand did so in May 1930, this time proposing to reverse the order of approach and start with politics, with a federation based on moral union, to be embodied in a European Conference, a permanent Political Committee and a Secretariat. Economic union would follow later, consequent upon the security which would ensue from political union. The response of European governments was mixed. The British adopted an attitude nicely described as 'caution, but cordial caution', and would contemplate nothing which would damage their relations with the Dominions.[32] Germany disliked any proposal which might confirm its eastern frontiers. Italy would accept European cooperation, but not European unity, which was incompatible with Fascist ideas about the predominance of the state. Briand's proposal was referred to a committee, and finally vanished in the economic and political crises from 1931 onwards.

These visions of European unity were to a considerable degree born of fear rather than hope. Coudenhove was afraid that Europe was becoming ever more fragmented, and so losing its influence in the world. Briand was trying to fend off political insecurity and economic disaster. Their proposals came to nothing at the time, though in retrospect they have come to appear as harbingers of later and greater events.

Europe survived the First World War, and began to recover some of the vigour and cohesion which it had enjoyed before 1914. Its population continued to increase; its economy recovered; political movements spanned the frontiers of states; the Scandinavian Social Democratic parties developed comprehensive forms of social welfare which were later to set a pattern for much of the continent; and in international affairs the League of Nations offered a new state system, effectively European in character, to replace that which had collapsed in 1914. In all these ways, encouraging signs of a coherent Europe emerged and it was possible for visionaries like Coudenhove and Briand to envisage turning coherence into unity. But these elements were fragile. The European economy was partially dependent on the USA and vulnerable to events outside European control. There were grave divisions in European politics and ideologies. The League was a grand structure based on new and weak foundations. Europe had survived, but was still on the sick list.

6

DANGERS AND DISASTERS, 1929–1939

ECONOMIC DISASTER

Europe in the 1920s had survived the worst effects of the Great War and was showing signs of recovering some of the prosperity, confidence and coherence which it had known before 1914. But in the ten years between 1929 and 1939 the continent suffered three massive blows. Europe underwent an economic crisis so severe and prolonged that it is still referred to as 'the great depression'. Conflicting ideological systems – communism, Fascism, Nazism and liberal democracy – competed for the allegiance of individuals and for predominance over the continent. In international affairs, a series of crises ended in the outbreak in 1939 of a war which by 1941 came to involve almost the whole continent, and much of the rest of the world as well. In the course of a disastrous decade, Europe was again brought to ruin, amid the collapse of all hopes of cohesion, or even cooperation.

The great depression showed that, for a time at any rate, the economic fate of Europe was subject to events in the USA. In the 1920s, several European countries had become dependent on American loans, and suffered accordingly when the supply dried up. In the space of three years American foreign lending was almost halved, from $1336 million in 1927 to $790 million in 1929, with grave effects, especially in Germany.[1] Then in 1929 a long boom in the American economy came to an end. In October the New York stock market collapsed in the Great Crash. There followed a drastic loss of business confidence, a sharp fall in investment and an abrupt reduction in American foreign trade.

Europe felt the consequences at once, with the agricultural countries of eastern Europe among the first sufferers. In 1929, even before the stock market crash, cereal prices had been falling as a result of overproduction. The American depression brought prices down even further, with no recovery until after 1932. All over eastern Europe farmers could not find an export market for their crops, or else sold for only a poor return. They were reduced to subsistence farming or local trading, with effects which spread out among all those who were indirectly dependent on agriculture – shopkeepers, the professions and all providers of services. In turn, government revenue from taxes fell, forcing reductions in expenditure.

The failure of the American economy brought with it a dramatic collapse in international trade. The total value of the imports of 75 countries (that is, almost the whole world), calculated in US dollars, fell by about two-thirds over four years, from almost $3000 million in January 1929 to just under $1000 million in January 1933.[2] The consequences of this collapse were felt all over Europe. Industrial production fell, profits vanished, share prices fell and demand for services dwindled. Banks and other creditors found it impossible to secure repayment of loans or even payments of interest. Banks themselves had often borrowed and were pressed for repayment. In May 1931 the Credit-Anstalt Bank in Austria, an apparently solid and reputable institution, failed to meet its obligations, and confidence was shaken all over eastern and central Europe. In June 1931 the Reichsbank in Germany suffered a run on gold as many of its customers sought the security of precious metal. In July the Darmstaedter National Bank had to close. Several countries were forced to declare emergency 'bank holidays' to stop the withdrawal of funds. Governments prevented the movement of capital to other countries by imposing exchange controls and suspending payments to foreign creditors. The collapse of credit was disastrous, because much of the economy depended on credit and ceased to function when it dried up. Moreover, as banks failed and customers demanded gold, one government after another took its currency off the gold exchange standard, so that the confidence in national currencies, which had been so painfully restored in the mid-1920s, collapsed.

The most obvious consequence of these economic disasters lay in the rising tide of unemployment that spread across Europe. In 1929 there were 1.9 million unemployed in Germany; in 1932 there were nearly 5.6 million. The corresponding figures for Britain were 1.2 million and 2.7 million; in Italy 301,000 and 1 million.[3] These figures were averages for the year, and in Germany the average figure for 1932 concealed a high point of no fewer than 6 million (30.1 per cent of the workforce) unemployed in May. Unemployment on this massive scale was probably decisive in bringing Hitler to power, as many Germans turned to dictatorship to save themselves from disaster. Parliamentary democracies in Britain, France and the Low Countries survived the depression, but suffered a loss of public confidence as they struggled to cope with unemployment; while in Italy the Fascist dictatorship did not save the country from trebling its numbers of unemployed. There seemed no generally applicable political answer to the problem.

SELF-SUFFICIENCY

In June–July 1933 a World Economic Conference met in London to find a way out of the depression by means of an international agreement on exchange rates and trading conditions. This conference was abruptly torpedoed by President Roosevelt's refusal to hold the dollar–sterling exchange rate steady at least while the conference was in session, preferring instead to retain complete freedom to devalue the dollar. In these circumstances, a permanent agreement on exchange rates was obviously impossible, and the conference quickly broke up. The USA had demonstrated its economic power over Europe and Roosevelt later devalued the dollar when he saw fit.

The result of this failure was an economic and financial free-for-all, dominated by fear and immediate self-interest. Europe, and other parts of the world, rapidly divided into three currency groups. First, there were countries which abandoned the gold standard and devalued their currencies to help their exports and preserve their gold reserves. Britain took this course in 1931, followed by a number of countries in central Europe. Second, there was the Gold Bloc, made up of countries which kept their currencies on the gold standard and maintained free exchange of currency. This group was made up of France, Belgium, the Netherlands, Switzerland and Luxembourg, with Italy partly in (by adhering to the gold standard) and partly out (by not practising free exchange of currency). The bloc began to disintegrate when Belgium devalued in 1935, and France, Switzerland, the Netherlands and Italy all devalued in 1936. Third, there were countries which practised strict exchange control and regulation of foreign trade, principally the Soviet Union, which had always employed such methods, and Nazi Germany, which combined exchange controls with a system of bilateral trade agreements with smaller countries (Hungary, Yugoslavia and Romania), which worked in Germany's favour.

At the same time, almost all European countries attempted some form of self-sufficiency. The mainly agrarian countries of eastern Europe, which suffered badly from the fall in agricultural prices, could not afford to pay for imports and fell back on their own resources, manufacturing goods they had previously imported, even if they were expensive.

The great powers took to self-sufficiency on a larger scale. In 1932 Britain introduced high import tariffs (20 per cent on manufactured goods), and at the Ottawa Conference (July–August 1932) adopted a policy of imperial preference, importing foodstuffs from the Dominions in return for preference for British manufactured goods in Dominion markets. The result was a marked shift in the direction of British trade, so that 50 per cent of British exports went to the Empire-Commonwealth and 40 per cent of imports came from it between 1935 and 1939.[4] Britain also exercised effective control over the oilfields in Iraq and Iran, which secured supplies of fuel from within British spheres of influence, and paid for in sterling.

France, which was much less dependent on foreign trade than most European countries, did not feel the worst effects of the depression until 1935. But keeping the franc on the gold standard meant that French exports to countries outside the Gold Bloc became increasingly expensive and fell away, making it difficult to pay for imports. The French therefore limited imports by means of quotas and adopted imperial preference on stricter lines than the British. Between 1930 and 1936 the French Empire took on average 50 per cent of French exports, and France achieved a high degree of self-sufficiency in many products.[5]

In Italy, Mussolini attempted a degree of self-sufficiency for which the Italian economy was ill-suited. High import duties were imposed, accompanied by a system of import licences to eliminate non-essential purchases. Mussolini launched a 'battle for grain', which succeeded in making Italy self-sufficient in wheat, but only by diminishing other crops and importing large quantities of fertilizers, which was self-defeating in the long run. He also turned to bilateral trade agreements with Germany (in 1934 and 1937), by which Italy imported industrial goods and coal from Germany, and paid for them in part by sending agricultural workers to Germany – an astonishing acceptance of a subordinate role as a mere provider of labour.

Germany sought self-sufficiency without the advantage of an empire. Under the New Plan devised by the economics minister, Hjalmar Schacht, in 1934, all imports had to be licensed by the government, which gave preference to food and raw materials. As far as possible, imports were bought only from countries which were willing to take German goods in return, and any foreign exchange involved was to remain under German control. By these means, Germany built up an economic sphere of influence in central and south-eastern Europe, where Hungary, Romania, Yugoslavia and Greece provided foodstuffs, minerals and oil on terms favourable to Germany. These were valuable arrangements, but proved inadequate as the German economy recovered, with unemployment falling to 2.1 per cent in 1938. This was partly due to a large-scale programme of rearmament, which itself required vast quantities of raw materials. The government increased domestic production of iron ore. Programmes to manufacture synthetic oil and rubber were begun in 1936, and eventually produced remarkable results, but in the short run synthetics were extremely expensive and themselves required imported materials. The Soviet Union, under its own system of government planning and control of all foreign trade, secured a high degree of self-sufficiency, though still importing machinery and technology.[6]

Complete self-sufficiency was beyond any country's grasp, but these various attempts achieved substantial successes. For most countries, 1932 proved the lowest point of the depression. After that, recovery was strong in Germany, Sweden and Finland – curiously, one dictatorship and two parliamentary democracies, though of course their circumstances were very different. Britain recovered more slowly, with unemployment falling from about 3 million at the end of 1932 to 1.7 million at the beginning of 1937. France's worst point came in 1935, with the lowest level for foreign trade and the highest for unemployment. In general, the economic indicators of industrial production, employment and prices moved upwards between 1934 and 1937, demonstrating a recovery that was largely based on home markets rather than exports, and showing that self-sufficiency was working, up to a point. The advantage of the new system became plain in 1937, when the USA fell into renewed depression, but without causing the same disastrous consequences in Europe as in 1929–32. Europe, by its policies of self-sufficiency, had largely protected itself against a recession in the American economy, and recovered control of its own economic destiny. There was a cost to be paid for this success within Europe, where by the late 1930s there were a number of self-contained economies competing with one another.

OTHER SOLUTIONS

The great depression of the early 1930s left a profound mark on the European psyche, with memories which lasted far longer than the economic effects themselves. In Britain, the march of the unemployed from Jarrow to London remains one of the defining images of the period, though it actually took place in 1936, when the trough of the depression was past, and total unemployment was down by 1 million since 1932. That scarcely mattered in Jarrow, where two-thirds of workmen were still unemployed and likely to remain so; and it has not mattered since. The wounds left by the depression years could not be healed while memories remained alive, and immense efforts were devoted,

7   The Great Depression: the Jarrow Crusade of the unemployed, marching to London, 1936
© Hulton-Deutsch Collection/Corbis

almost for the rest of the century, to ensuring that the experience was not repeated.

The first answer, as we have seen, was self-sufficiency, which achieved real, if limited, success. In western Europe, the most influential long-term response was provided by J.M. Keynes in his *General Theory of Employment, Interest and Money*, published in 1936, arguing that the main cause of the depression lay in weak demand, and therefore that governments should stimulate demand by public spending, even at the cost of budget deficits and inflation. In the 1930s this prescription was not widely followed, because most governments, worried by the prospect of inflation, preferred to stick to the tried and trusted formula of a balanced budget. A notable exception was Sweden, where in 1938 the government, trade unions and employers' organizations agreed on a policy of high public spending and increased wages. This came at a favourable moment, when demand for Sweden's two principal products, iron ore and timber, was growing as a result of rearmament and a housing boom in Europe – a combination of policy and circumstances which produced a reduction of Swedish unemployment in 1939, apparently demonstrating the virtues of Keynes's theories. Much later, after the Second World War, the European Economic Community was to adopt a mixture of self-sufficiency and Keynesian economics as a successful formula for economic growth.

A third answer was offered by the Soviet Union – a planned economy, designed to eliminate the vagaries and troubles of capitalism by state control of agriculture, industry and foreign trade. This was the Soviet prescription in the 1930s, and after 1945 the whole Soviet bloc, including eastern Europe and most of the Balkans, was to follow the same course. The great economic depression thus cast a long shadow, and continued to exercise a divisive effect long after the depression itself was over.

The economic divisions of Europe were real but not spectacular. Import quotas and exchange rates did not make striking headlines or vivid footage for the newsreels. Ideologies, on the other hand, provided drama in plenty, and Europe between the wars, and above all in the 1930s, was a battleground of rival ideologies – organized systems of ideas, amounting to secular religions, with their beliefs, ceremonies and icons.[7]

Communist Russia, Fascist Italy and Nazi Germany were ideologically based states of a kind previously unknown in Europe, even in revolutionary France or Calvinist Geneva. Each had its own idea to explain the past and the present: Communism asserted the primacy of class; Fascism claimed the predominance of the state; Nazism was based on the concept of race. They were also embodied by men – Lenin and Stalin, Mussolini and Hitler – giving them a popular appeal which no abstract idea alone could possibly exert. They used the power of propaganda to a degree unknown before, though propaganda itself is as old as history. Mussolini's appearances on a balcony in Rome; Hitler's Nuremberg rallies (brilliantly filmed by Leni Riefenstahl in *The*

Triumph of the Will); the parades in Moscow on May Day and the anniversary of the revolution – all were marvellously fitted to the mass media of the time and appealed powerfully to the popular imagination. All three regimes were modern and vigorous, confident that they represented the wave of the future. They offered hope to an ageing and weary continent, to a degree which is difficult to recapture now that all three have run their course and been discarded. Each claimed to offer salvation to Europe, and to provide the basis for a new European order, in contrast to the inadequacy of liberal democracy and capitalism, which were failing to deal with the problems of the day. They proposed instead a totalitarian solution, though only Mussolini liked to use the word.

Totalitarianism, despite the complexities of scholarly debate, may be simply defined as a regime in which the state claims to control the whole of existence, allowing no other focus of loyalty in either public or private life. Totalitarian regimes displayed four main characteristics: an ideology serving as a secular religion; the dominance of a single political party, with a leader who was accorded the status of a superman – the cult of personality; the complete subordination of the individual to the state, whether by indoctrination or coercion (or both); and control by the state over the economy.[8] The Soviet Union, Fascist Italy and Nazi Germany all displayed these characteristics, albeit in different degrees. Fascist Italy made strong totalitarian claims (Mussolini spoke in 1925 of 'our ferocious totalitarian will'), but was weaker in practice, making compromises with the Church, the monarchy and the armed forces. Nazi Germany stopped short of totalitarianism by retaining private property and controlling industry without nationalizing it. The Soviet Union went furthest in totalitarian practice, nationalizing industry, collectivizing agriculture, eliminating most forms of private property and attempting total control over all forms of expression. But even the Soviet Union fell short: there were cracks in the system; people found their own sources of news; and even in the Gulag Solzhenitsyn remained his own man.

Each of the three movements was based in one country, but they all had European-wide aspirations and attracted support across the continent. They aimed to recreate Europe in their own image, and yet they divided Europe between their conflicting ideologies.

COMMUNISM

Of the three great totalitarian regimes, Communism came first in point of time. Lenin and the Bolsheviks seized power in Russia in October 1917, and set up a new kind of state, whose constitution (promulgated in July 1918) claimed to establish 'the dictatorship of the urban and rural proletariat and the poorest.'[9] At first, the Bolsheviks believed that they were the vanguard of a European revolution, but that revolution never came. Instead, the Soviet Union had to build socialism in one country, under the rule of Stalin, perhaps the most formidable of the great dictators.

The main economic pillars of socialism in one country were collectivization of agriculture, accomplished with extraordinary speed and brutality between 1929 and 1934; and rapid industrialization, forced through in a series of five-year plans, which were all declared to be resounding successes. The dark political side of the process lay in the systematic and large-scale use of repression and terror, which began under Lenin and reached its appalling apogee in Stalin's purges in the 1930s. Carefully kept figures showed that the prison camps of the Gulag Archipelago contained 1,371,195 inmates in 1939.[10] The positive side of the regime could be seen in new schools and apartment blocks, and the Moscow underground – clean, efficient and free; as well as in the attainment of a vast industrialized society. In 1936 a gleaming new front was fitted to the whole edifice when the Congress of Soviets adopted a new constitution, which claimed to guarantee freedom of speech, the press, assembly and conscience, as well as the inviolability of the person – claims which stood in stark contrast to the realities of the purges and the prison camps.

This brave new world being created in the Soviet Union was largely cut off from the rest of Europe. The regime took as its capital Moscow, the old capital of Ivan the Terrible, rather than St Petersburg/Leningrad, the city which Peter the Great had built to look out westwards. The country and its people lived in virtual isolation, with strict controls on travel and communication.

Yet in spite of this isolation, the Soviet regime sent cracks and divisive effects throughout Europe. Communist parties were set up in every European country, though sometimes only clandestinely and outside the law. The appeal of communism transcended national boundaries and the loyalties of class or upbringing. In Britain, the Soviet agents recruited at Cambridge (Philby, Maclean, Blunt, Burgess) were by most standards privileged in their own society; that the Cambridge of the 1930s provided the Soviet Union with such devoted followers was a remarkable phenomenon, 'symbolic of the force of the Communist idea in the twentieth century'.[11]

As well as a hard core of devoted communists, the Soviet Union also attracted a wider following of fellow-travellers and sympathizers. Sidney and Beatrice Webb visited the country and wrote a thick volume entitled *Soviet Russia: A New Civilisation?*; and in a revised edition they removed the question mark. John Strachey, later a member of Attlee's government after the Second World War, wrote in 1935 that 'to travel from the capitalist world into Soviet territory is to pass from death to birth.'[12] Edouard Herriot, an experienced French politician and former premier, found during a visit in 1933 that unemployment had ceased to exist in Russia. Stalin exercised a magnetic attraction on those who met him, who found him self-effacing, unassuming and yet a true leader. The tributes on his fiftieth birthday (21 December 1929) came from many outside the ranks of Party members.

There was doubtless a good measure of gullibility and self-deception in this admiration of the Soviet Union; but also much genuine sympathy and enthusiasm. The concept of equality, the professed ideal of communism, had widespread appeal. On a more material plane, the Soviets appeared to have discovered how to defeat the economic depression, when capitalist countries were struggling in vain with the curse of unemployment. The Soviet Union became 'the Great Light in the East', shining across Europe; and the appeal of communism was so strong (though only among a minority) that it divided countries, split families and severed friendships. The historian John Roberts was not exaggerating when he wrote that communism 'split Europeans culturally and politically as they had not been since the Reformation.'[13]

There has survived a strange inheritance from this division, which still affects us today: the contrast in the impressions left by the Nazi death camps and the Gulag. Norman Davies has observed that 'If space in history books were allotted in proportion to human suffering, then Vorkuta would warrant one of the longest chapters.'[14] More people perished in the Soviet camps at Vorkuta than at Auschwitz, yet the name of Vorkuta is scarcely known, while that of Auschwitz is indelibly etched on the European mind. This remarkable phenomenon is a lasting remnant of the ideological division of Europe, though the ideologies and the divisions have long passed away.

FASCISM

Fascism was chronologically the second of the great totalitarian movements. It arose in Italy in the aftermath of the First World War, in reaction against the apparent failures of parliamentary government. The war had brought heavy casualties, social strains and high inflation, with little reward, in that Italy did not secure all the gains promised by the Allies when the country had entered the war in 1915. Peace was followed by economic depression, strikes and the occupation of factories in northern Italy. It also brought a reaction by Italian nationalists against the peace terms. Gabriele d'Annunzio (poet, airman and ardent nationalist) occupied the city of Fiume with a force of volunteers in September 1919, and held it until December 1920, with no one daring to remove him. Parliament was in a state of constant crisis and there were five different governments between 1919 and 1921, none of them able to get to grips with the country's problems.

These circumstances presented an opportunity for Mussolini, who had founded the Fascist movement in Milan in March 1919. He came to power in October 1922, by a mixture of force and constitutional means. The Fascist blackshirt militia had beaten up socialists in the streets, seized control of provincial towns and entered the capital in what they called the March on Rome – though in fact most travelled by train. The constitutional forms were observed, in that Mussolini formed a government at the king's invitation; included Liberals and Catholics in his first Cabinet; and presented his ministry to the Chamber and Senate. Parliament voted him full powers to carry out reforms, by comfortable majorities. Mussolini was the Fascist leader – Il Duce – but he also came to office as prime minister in a monarchical and parliamentary state.

This was a useful tactical combination, but it was as the Fascist leader that Mussolini made his mark on Italy and Europe. Fascism made sweeping claims as a new political movement, setting out (like the Bolsheviks) to create a new kind of state. Fascism was *against* communism, liberalism and conservatism – a comprehensive list of enemies.[15] They were *for* a new totalitarian state, not based on traditional authority but on the 'leadership principle', with Mussolini as the leader. Mussolini wrote that 'The keystone of Fascist doctrine is the conception of the State, of its essence, of its task, of its ends. For Fascism the State is an absolute before which individuals and groups are relative.' Giovanni Gentile, a prominent Fascist political philosopher, repeated the claim, with even more emphasis: '...for the Fascist, everything is in the State, and nothing human or spiritual exists, much less has value, outside the State. In this sense Fascism is totalitarian, and the Fascist State...interprets, develops and gives strength to the whole life of the people.'[16] These claims were revolutionary, not conservative. Il Duce was to be a new kind of leader, with more than a touch of the superman about him. Under his leadership, Fascism promised unity, as against the division enshrined in parliamentary democracy, with its concept of government and opposition; and it promised dynamism, in contrast to the weakness and inertia of the old political parties. Fascism introduced its own drama and style: mass meetings and parades, uniforms and symbols, songs and ceremonies, and a cult of youth and violence. The *appearance* of Fascism was probably more important for its success in Italy than its principles, and did more to define its character.

The reality of Fascism fell some way short of its claims. The regime was in practice far from totalitarian. The monarchy remained in being, with a constitutional provision (set down specifically in December 1925) that the king retained the power to dismiss the head of government – which he finally did, to Mussolini's astonishment, in 1943. The army was allowed considerable freedom in its internal arrangements, and notably in promotions. Above all, Mussolini concluded the Lateran Treaty with the Vatican in 1929, acknowledging the separate and in some ways privileged position of the Church in Italy. (Gentile, who was serious about totalitarianism, opposed the Lateran Treaty.)

Mussolini's Italy fell well short of Stalin's Russia or Hitler's Germany in its machinery of repression. The staff of the OVRA, the secret police, in 1940 was 375, a tiny number compared with the Gestapo or NKVD. Between 1929 and 1943, the Special Tribunal imposed 42 death sentences for political crimes, of which only 31 were carried out. Some tens of thousands were sent into internal exile (in the south of Italy or on islands) or put under some form of house arrest or other surveillance.[17] Compared to the Gulag or the Nazi camps, this was small-scale repression.

For some time, it was by no means clear what the new regime signified and what its impact would be. Giolitti, who had made an art of political management before 1914, remarked in 1921 that the Fascists were like fireworks: 'they'll make a great deal of noise but only leave smoke behind'. Cardinal Gasparri, Secretary of State at the Vatican, predicted in 1923 that Fascism would last about 20 years and be followed by a return to a parliamentary fixer like Giolitti – a remarkably accurate forecast.[18] Outside Italy, the new regime was accepted and even welcomed, in marked contrast to the widespread hostility to the Bolshevik government in Russia. In Britain, Lord Rothermere, Winston Churchill and the editorial writers in *The Times* (among others) regarded Mussolini as a man who had saved Italy from disorder and perhaps even revolution. Mussolini was welcomed to London in 1925 to sign the Treaty of Locarno, a ceremony which he attended dressed in a frock coat, not a uniform. Austen Chamberlain, while Foreign Secretary between 1924 and 1929, met Mussolini privately five times. No European government broke off diplomatic relations with the new regime.

Mussolini declared that Fascism was not for export, but in practice he tried to promote it in other countries. A government press office distributed Fascist propaganda, and it seems almost certain that money was sent to the Nazi Party in Germany. In December 1934 an International Fascist Congress met at Montreux, attended by parties from 15 countries (though not Germany). This proved short-lived, and its so-called Permanent Committee only met twice; but links with individual parties continued. Italian money was supplied to the *Heimwehr* in Austria, the Rexists in Belgium and the British Union of Fascists. In France, support was given to the *Francistes* and to Déat and his dissident socialists; and in Spain to José Antonio Primo de Rivera, son of the former dictator and head of the Falange. Perhaps more importantly, Mussolini was admired by aspiring Fascists and by many more who were growing disillusioned with parliamentary democracy – a state of mind common to much of Europe in the late 1920s and 1930s (see below, pp. 117–8).

The appeal of Fascism was widespread. At the same time, *opposition* to Fascism became international in character. Anti-Fascist Italians in exile gathered in Spain and France to organize resistance to Mussolini. It was in Paris in 1936 that Carlo Rosselli, the leader of the Italian Action Party, wrote: 'Beware! A European conflict is developing. We have reached the moment when the two opposed worlds, the world of freedom and the world of authoritarianism, are about to find themselves face to face.'[19] That conflict was already under way. In August 1935, at its Seventh Congress, the Communist International reversed its previous policy of treating the Social Democrats as its main enemy, and instead took up the cause of left-wing union – the Popular Front against Fascism. Communists, socialists and even bourgeois liberals were all to be drawn into the struggle. Fascism in this context was used as a blanket term, to include both Italian Fascism and German Nazism; and this usage by its enemies gave the word a new and wider currency. To this day, Fascism rather than Nazism is the name attached to right-wing movements by their detractors.

In 1936 anti-Fascism found a battleground and an inspiration in the Spanish Civil War. In retrospect, this conflict appears complex and deeply Spanish in its nature. At the time, it seemed simple and European: democracy was at war with Fascism. Fascist Italy and Nazi Germany both intervened on the side of the Nationalist rebels. On the other side, the Soviet Union supported the Republican government. The International Brigades, organized by the Comintern, reached a total of 25–35,000 men and created a modern legend of left-wing heroism. Spain was the battleground, but Fascism was the enemy, and the fate of Europe was at stake. The Spanish Civil War fixed the image of the international struggle against Fascism for generations to come, to the end of the twentieth century and beyond. The standing of Fascism as the favourite demonizing word of the European left was firmly established.

NAZISM

The third of the great totalitarian ideologies of the interwar period in Europe was Nazism. German Nazism and Italian Fascism are often lumped together under the general label of Fascism, for obvious reasons. Mussolini and Hitler used the same title, Duce and Fuehrer. They had common enemies. The two regimes presented the same appearance: uniforms, mass rallies, marching columns and even the goose-step (though Mussolini called it the *passo romano* when he adopted it in 1937). The name 'Rome–Berlin Axis' asserted the common ground between the two countries, and the grandly named Pact of Steel brought them into a formal alliance in 1939.

Though plausible, this conflation is misleading. In vital respects the two movements were very different. They had different origins and divergent characters. Nazism was rooted in the racial theories of the nineteenth century, especially the supremacy of the Aryan race and anti-Semitism. Fascism had no racial theory, and Mussolini's views on the subject were limited to the belief that Europeans were superior to other peoples, and especially to blacks. Originally, he had nothing against Jews, who were admitted to membership of the Fascist Party. In 1926 he received Chaim Weizmann, the Zionist leader, and expressed sympathy for the creation of a Jewish state, declaring that Jerusalem should not become an Arab capital. It was only as late as 1938, under strong German influence, that Mussolini introduced anti-Semitic legislation. Moreover, the two movements behaved very differently in applying the principle of totalitarianism. Mussolini used the word, but in practice made compromises, notably with the Church and the monarchy. It appears that Hitler did not use the word (though Goebbels did), but in practice he came much nearer to controlling the whole of society. The repression practised in Germany was more intense, and the death toll in the Nazi camps far greater, than anything in Italy. The two regimes were different, and Nazism must be examined separately.

The key to Nazism lay in Hitler's world outlook, made up of an extreme form of nationalism and racialism, incorporating anti-Semitism; the demand for living space for the German people; and the concept of life as a perpetual struggle, based on social Darwinism. These ideas overlapped and reinforced one another, and are to be found throughout Hitler's writings and conversations, and not least in what he did – actions speak louder than words.[20]

Hitler claimed that the Aryan race was the true founder and transmitter of culture, with an overriding right to self-preservation and predominance over other races. He did not trouble to define the Aryan race, though it had been much debated by anthropologists in the nineteenth century. Hitler believed that the Germans were Aryans, along with other similar peoples, for example the Dutch. Some anthropologists maintained that Aryanism could be defined by scientific measurement, and the Germans spent much time and effort trying to compile a register of 'correct' physical characteristics. At the opposite pole to the Aryan stood the Jew, representing the lowest race. Anti-Semitism permeated Hitler's writing and speeches, and the extermination of European Jews in the Final Solution was eventually to dominate much of Nazi policy during the Second World War. Between 5 and 6 million Jews perished in the Nazi death camps. Almost to the end of the war, the Germans continued to transport Jews across Europe to be slaughtered, when they could have used the rolling stock for the war effort and the SS guards from the camps on the battlefields. The place of anti-Semitism in Hitler's thought is the subject of earnest debate, but its place in his *actions* is only too apparent. But the racial war was not limited to the Jews. The Slavs too were racial enemies and suffered heavily under German occupation in Poland and the Soviet Union. So were the gypsies, whose ordeal is often forgotten.

Living space (*Lebensraum*) meant primarily land to feed and settle a growing German population, to be secured by conquest in the east. Hitler wrote in his *Secret Book* of the need for 'a clear, far-seeing territorial policy', to provide 'sufficient living space for the next hundred years'. In his first address to German military leaders on 3 February 1933 he spoke of his eventual aim: 'the conquest of new living-space in the east and its ruthless Germanisation.'[21] In turn, the idea of living space was linked to Hitler's interpretation of social Darwinism, which translated the ideas of the life and death of species and the survival of the fittest into terms of states and peoples. The German people had to prove its fitness by constant struggle.

Since the Second World War, Hitler has become the embodiment of evil, a yardstick against which all other tyrants are measured. To liken someone to Hitler is the worst condemnation in the vocabulary of politics. In these circumstances, it is difficult to go back in time and understand what it was that gave Hitler and Nazism their attraction – indeed, it is almost impossible to admit that they had any attraction at all. But to understand the impact of Nazism, that is what we must try to do.

The Nazi Party achieved remarkable political success in Germany. In the Reichstag elections of 1928 the Nazis secured only 810,000 votes. In 1930 they received 6,410,000, becoming the second largest party in terms of votes (after the Social Democrats). In July 1932 they scored 13,746,000 and became the leading party in the country. They lost ground in another election in November 1932, but still won 11,277,000 votes and remained the leading party, more than 4 million ahead of the Social Democrats.[22] It is true that some of these votes were gained by intimidation and violence, and also that even at their highest point in July 1932 the Nazis attained no more than 37.4 per cent of the vote;[23] but however the figures may be interpreted, they still showed an astonishing electoral success. The Nazis were offering the German electors something they wanted, which the other parties did not provide.

What they offered was a combination of revolution and security. Weimar Germany had long presented the spectacle of a republic almost without republicans. Very few Germans were actually convinced of its merits, so that the Weimar regime had become hollow, and even conservatives were ready for a revolution to replace it. But it would have to be a revolution that promised security, and not least a sound currency. Successive governments had produced no answer to the depression, and unemployment figures had risen at a terrifying rate, from 2.4 million in March 1930 to a peak of 6 million in May 1932. The Nazis proclaimed that they could conquer unemployment, restore the economy *and* preserve the value of the mark. They were as good as their word. Hitler came to power in January 1933 and the annual unemployment figures fell: 4.8 million in 1933, 2.7 million in 1934, 2.1 million in 1935, 1.6 million in 1936. They then went below 1 million, and by 1938 were a mere 429,000, or about 2 per cent of the workforce. For comparison, the British unemployment figure in 1938 (in a population about two-thirds the size of Germany's) was 1.8 million, or 13 per cent of the workforce.[24]

With hindsight, this achievement appears less striking. German unemployment was declining before Hitler came to power. Previous governments, headed by Papen and Schleicher, had already begun to increase government spending, embark on public works and encourage credit – policies which Hitler did not change when he took office. Hitler did not apply ideological solutions to unemployment, and did not put Nazis in charge of economic affairs; in fact he recalled Hjalmar Schacht, the 'man who saved the mark' after the collapse of 1923, as President of the Reichsbank. Hitler's own contribution was psychological. Economic recovery stemmed to a large degree from *confidence*, and in 1933 Hitler radiated confidence. He said that he would conquer unemployment, and he did.

At the same time he restored Germany's position as a great power. He embarked on large-scale rearmament and reintroduced conscription in March 1935. (This helped to reduce the unemployment figures – by 1938 there were 730,000 men in the army instead of on the labour market.) In six years, from 1933 to 1939, Germany moved from being one of the weakest military powers in Europe to being one of the strongest. Political successes followed, one after another. In January 1935 a plebiscite in the Saar region produced an overwhelming vote for reunion with Germany. In June 1935 a naval agreement was signed with Britain, something which Hitler's predecessors before 1914 had failed to achieve. In March 1936 German troops occupied the demilitarized zone in the Rhineland, restoring German control over the country's own territory. In March 1938 union with Austria was achieved, without a shot being fired and with German troops being greeted by welcoming crowds. In September 1938 Germany occupied the Sudeten areas of Czechoslovakia, and in March 1939 the Germans took over the rest of the country (except for the Ruthenian tip, which they handed over to Hungary in an almost condescending gesture). No one in German history, not even Frederick the Great or Bismarck, had achieved so much in so short a time. It is a commonplace that nothing succeeds like success, and for a nation which had gone through the trauma of defeat in 1918, the destruction of its currency in 1923 and mass unemployment in the early 1930s, success on the scale achieved by Hitler up to 1939 was overwhelming.

There was a price for this success. Germany was subjected to a dictatorship of a brutal and arbitrary kind. All political parties except the Nazi Party were suppressed. Trade unions were absorbed into the Nazi Labour Front. The press was censored and books by Jewish or anti-Nazi writers were burned in the streets. The first concentration camp was set up at Dachau in 1933. Within a year there were some 30,000 Germans imprisoned in the camps, which in 1934 came under the exclusive control of the SS, the *Schutzstaffel*, a sinister body recruited on racial criteria and destined to become the single most powerful organization in Nazi Germany.

Persecution of the Jews increased steadily. As early as April 1933 Jews were purged from the civil service. The Nuremberg Laws, introduced in 1935 and later extended, defined 'full Jews' and 'half Jews', supposedly on racial grounds. Marriages between Jews and non-Jews were forbidden, as well as any sexual relations between Aryans and Jews. In 1938 Jews were excluded from all professions and from entering university education. Even Jewish businesses, previously tolerated for the sake of their profits, were closed down or Aryanized. On 9 November 1938 Jews were attacked, synagogues set on fire and shop windows smashed all across Germany. More Jews were herded into the concentration camps. Later, under the cover of war, the Final Solution, the extermination of the Jews, was to be undertaken; but even before the war the extreme brutality of Nazi anti-Semitism was already evident.

The successes of Nazi Germany attracted support and sympathy across much of Europe. Nazi or neo-Nazi parties arose in Austria, Hungary (the Arrow Cross), Romania (the Iron Guard), the Netherlands (the *National-Socialistische Beweging*), Belgium (the later stages of the Rexist movement) and Norway (the *Nasjonal Samling*, led by Vidkun Quisling). In Britain, Oswald Mosley's British Union of Fascists, despite its name and the financial support it drew from Mussolini, was closer to Nazism than Fascism by virtue (if that is the right word) of its anti-Semitism. In France, Doriot's *Parti Populaire Français* became primarily Nazi in character. These parties gained little support at the polls in established democratic countries – Quisling averaged 2 per cent of the vote in the elections of 1933 and 1936.[25] But they formed a core round which support could gather in the heady period of Nazi victory in 1940–41, when there was a strong temptation to join the winning side.

As well as outright supporters of Nazism there were sympathizers – the 'fellow travellers of the Right', in Richard Griffiths's striking phrase. There were many who admired Hitler for his success in reviving Germany's prosperity and self-confidence, in marked contrast to the inertia of the democracies. Others found in Nazi Germany a welcome barrier against Communist Russia. Some shared Hitler's anti-Semitism, while others refused to take it seriously. A stream of visitors called on Hitler, and (for example) Lloyd George, George Lansbury, the Duke of Windsor and C.B. Fry all found something to admire. Lloyd George, after meeting Hitler in September 1936, wrote that he was 'unquestionably a great leader', who had 'effected a remarkable improvement in the working conditions of both men and women'.[26] The more extreme, like Unity Mitford, were completely bewitched and raved about Hitler's eyes.

Some admired Hitler. Others were repelled. The most obvious and vocal opponents of Nazism were to be found among socialists and communists; but just as communism divided the left, so Nazism divided the right, where some of its most determined opponents were found. In Germany itself, the most significant opposition to the Nazis arose among conservatives and army officers. In Austria the right-wing governments led by Dollfuss and Schuschnigg outlawed the Nazi Party. In Hungary Horthy opposed the Arrow Cross. During the Second World War two of the most implacable foes of Nazi Germany were Churchill and de Gaulle, both men of right-wing views.[27]

Nazism created ideological rifts all over Europe. At the same time, Germany presented the political and military challenge of a dynamic and aggressive force in the centre of Europe. Those very successes which were so welcome in German eyes represented a growing threat to the rest of Europe. By the middle of 1939 Germany was the strongest power on the continent. In 1938 and 1939 two independent countries, Austria and Czechoslovakia, were wiped from the map, and others seemed certain to follow. The British and French had tried appeasement for some six years, without success – indeed, the German appetite grew as it was fed. But eventually Nazi methods of deception and intimidation brought about a revulsion. It became clear to the British and French governments and their peoples that the advance of German power would have to be resisted, if necessary by war. Hitler had been given the benefit of the doubt for long enough; he could no longer be trusted; and he would have to be stopped. Nazism and its leader had created a fatal division in Europe.

DIVISION, DICTATORSHIP AND DEMOCRACY

The emergence of these three totalitarian regimes within a few years says much about the state of Europe at that time. Together they marked a profound reaction against European political traditions, which seemed incapable of dealing with the problems of the continent. It was as though three revolutions had broken out almost at the same time. Yet each represented an aspect of those same European political traditions. Soviet Communism was based on Marxism, which was a European political philosophy of the nineteenth century. Nazism drew on racial theories and social Darwinism from the same period. Italian Fascism was a mixture of nineteenth-century nationalism and the Futurism of the early twentieth century. Of the three, it seems that Italian Fascism might just have been accommodated into a cohesive Europe. At home, Mussolini managed to coexist with the Church and the monarchy. Abroad, Italy did not have the power to dominate Europe. Nazi Germany was a different matter. Hitler's totalitarian claims were more far-reaching, and German power was far stronger than that of Italy. Europe could not accommodate Hitler: it could only resist him or be dominated by him. Stalin's Russia seemed to fall between the two. Europe was well accustomed to Marxism as a theory, and many socialist parties adopted Marxist principles up to a point. But on the other hand communist parties behaved as agents of a foreign power in their own countries; and those who understood the full horror of Stalinist terror knew that the practice of Communism, as distinct from its theory, could never be absorbed into European politics or civilization.

The totalitarian movements were opposed to one another. Fascism and Nazism were both opposed to Communism and vice versa. They were able to make agreements with one another, most spectacularly in the Nazi–Soviet Pact of August 1939; but these were merely temporary truces in a fundamental conflict. Again, Fascism and Nazism, though they had much in common, were to some degree hostile to one another. Even the controlled Italian press criticized and made fun of Nazi racial theories, while Nazis distrusted the Italians as poor soldiers and of impure race. So there was a deep divide between right and left, but also a lesser one between Fascism and Nazism.

The rise of these three totalitarian regimes was accompanied by a swing against parliamentary government over much of Europe. We have observed that in 1920 as many as 27 European states outside Russia were parliamentary democracies. By the beginning of 1938, only 12 remained – Britain, France, the Scandinavian states of Norway, Sweden, Denmark and Finland, Belgium, the Netherlands, Luxembourg, Ireland, Switzerland and Czechoslovakia. The others had all become dictatorships of one kind or another. Fascist Italy and Nazi Germany were by no means typical of what was a mixed bag of different authoritarian regimes. In Poland, Marshal Pilsudski took over in 1926, after six years of rapidly changing governments, and imposed a limited form of dictatorship. He was a soldier and a patriot, not an ideologue. Parliament continued to meet and to include different political parties; elections were held. The Baltic states all adopted one-party dictatorial regimes: Lithuania in 1926, Estonia in 1933 and Latvia in 1934. In Latvia, the president, Paets, took the title of Leader (Vadonis), like Mussolini and Hitler, but in fact he established only a limited dictatorship to deal with the problems of a country which had managed to produce no fewer than 26 political parties from a population of just over 1,100,000.

In central Europe, Admiral Horthy extended his powers as regent of Hungary, but retained parliamentary forms and allowed opposition parties (including the Social Democrats) to continue. In Austria, Dollfuss set up a Catholic and corporatist dictatorship in 1933–34. The Balkan states took to various forms of monarchical dictatorship. King Alexander of Yugoslavia dissolved parliament in 1929 and assumed wide powers under a new constitution in 1931. King Boris of Bulgaria set up a royal dictatorship in 1935. In Romania, King Carol dissolved all political parties in 1938 and set up a new constitution with some corporatist elements. King George II of Greece appointed Metaxas, a retired general, as prime minister in 1936; Metaxas went on to suspend parliament and set up an authoritarian government. In Albania, King Zog ruled as a rather rudimentary absolute monarch.

In Iberia, Portugal became a one-party state in 1933, with a National Assembly elected on a single list, and a Corporative Chamber representing different sections of society. These elements resembled Fascist Italy, but Salazar, the Portuguese dictator, could scarcely have been more different from Mussolini. He never wore uniform, held mass rallies or sought the limelight. He had all the personal charisma of a professor of economics, pursuing the prudent aims of balancing the budget and stabilizing the currency. Spain produced two dictators, both generals. Primo de Rivera carried out a *coup d'état* in 1923, and for a while tried to run the country by putting his fellow-generals in charge of everything, with only limited success. At the end of 1929 he did something very rare among dictators and resigned, without even naming a successor. Later, in the Spanish Civil War of 1936–39, General Franco defeated the Republican government, with much help from Fascist Italy and Nazi Germany; but the regime which he established was only partially Fascist in character, and was principally a conservative dictatorship supported by the army, the Church, monarchists and landowners.

A Europe of parliaments in about 1920 thus became a Europe of dictators by 1938. The remaining parliamentary democracies were mostly small states – the Scandinavian states, the Low Countries, Switzerland and Ireland; all well established in their political traditions, but without significant military power. The two great democratic powers in Europe were France and Britain.

In the 1930s France was in a state of decay, perhaps even decadence. The casualties of the Great War had taken the life out of the country, especially among the peasants, still regarded as the backbone of French society. The gap left by the deficit of births during the war – a lost generation of unborn children – moved inexorably through French society. A deep revulsion against war dominated French sentiment, with paralysing effects on foreign policy, which could scarcely even contemplate a serious war. Government economic policy in the 1930s was to keep the franc on the gold standard and balance the budget by cutting expenditure – even civil service salaries and payments to ex-servicemen. Governments themselves were merely temporary. There were three changes of government in 1932, four in 1933, two in 1934 and two in 1935 – a total of eleven in four years. In these circumstances political opinion veered towards the extremes. Right-wing groups (conservative, Fascist or Nazi) grew in strength. On 6 February 1934 right-wing rioters in Paris threatened to storm the National Assembly and throw the deputies into the Seine. A left-wing reaction followed, and when the Popular Front won the elections in 1936 there was a wave of strikes, demonstrations and factory occupations, which alarmed investors and provoked a flight of capital abroad. In foreign policy, France seemed condemned to watch the inexorable growth of German power without moving a muscle (or a soldier) to stop it. France, once the standard-bearer of modern democracy, had fallen into weakness and despair.

Britain was in rather better shape. Governments were stable, with large majorities in the House of Commons. There was little movement to political extremes. The Communist Party won only one seat in the general election of 1935, and Oswald Mosley's British Union of Fascists made little headway. The stability of British institutions was not in doubt. Moreover, governments achieved some real successes. The economy as a whole recovered; unemployment declined, though leaving some areas still in deep recession; and rearmament began in the mid-1930s. But there still remained an *impression* that ministers were unable to cope, especially in contrast with the dynamism of Nazi Germany. The reputation of the 1930s as 'a low dishonest decade' remained firmly established for many years.[28] Even when the government pursued an energetic policy, as it did in some aspects of foreign affairs, these energies were directed to the appeasement of Germany, and to a lesser degree Italy, in a fruitless attempt to conciliate enemies who could not be bought off and who despised those trying to woo them. When Chamberlain and Halifax (Prime Minister and Foreign Secretary respectively) visited Rome in January 1939, Mussolini remarked scornfully: 'These...are the tired sons of a long line of rich men, and they will lose their empire'. Hitler told a meeting of senior officers on 22 August 1939 that 'our enemies are small fry. I saw them at Munich.'[29]

In the event, reports of the demise of British parliamentary democracy proved premature; and France was eventually able to survive military defeat and the collapse of the Third Republic, and revive its fortunes after the Second World War. But at the end of the 1930s the liberal democracies seemed to be in steep decline, while the totalitarian regimes were on the rise. If any form of European unity was to survive the conflict of ideologies, it seemed likely to be a continent dominated by Nazi Germany.

That domination was prevented only by war. In 1919, when 'never again' was the heartfelt resolution of so many, it had seemed impossible that Europe should again go to war; but in 1939 the conflict came about with a dreadful, unavoidable certainty. Under Hitler's leadership, Germany embarked on a course of aggression destined to lead to the domination of Europe (and possibly the world), which was bound to be opposed at some stage. The motives behind this astonishing drive were partly personal, in Hitler's impatient determination to go to war while he was still in the prime of life; partly ideological, in the pursuit of domination over lesser races; and partly economic, in the drive for more resources and more territory. Whatever the make-up of this deadly mixture, the effects were plain enough. German power and territorial gains advanced at increasing speed: rearmament, the Rhineland, Austria, the Sudetenland, Czechoslovakia. At some point this advance was certain to be resisted by another great power. The only questions were at what point, and which power?

THE ROAD TO WAR

The most likely opponents were France and Britain, the victors of 1918, with much to lose if Germany dominated Europe. It remains a striking feature of the 1930s that in fact the French and British acquiesced for so long in the advance of German power, until the point had been reached when it could only be resisted at the cost of a major war. The policy of appeasement, which meant making one-sided concessions to Germany in the hope of achieving a secure peace, was understandable and defensible up to a point. There was a deep and natural revulsion against war after the calamities of 1914–18, which produced a profound desire for peace in both France and Britain. This never meant peace at any price, as is often said; but at any rate peace at some substantial price, often (it must be said) paid in other countries' territory. Again, resistance to Germany would mean large-scale rearmament, and neither France nor Britain wished to make the necessary financial and economic effort. Indeed, both believed that another war would mean economic ruin, which proved to be true enough. There was a widespread hope that Hitler, when in office, would shed the dangerous views of his younger years and become a sensible and moderate statesman with whom one could do business. Moreover, a moderate Hitler would be a powerful bastion against communism.

Such reasoning made much sense, and it took a long time for the British and French to realize that it was based on the false premise that Hitler was a man with limited aims, who would settle for a compromise. When it became clear that this was not the case, and that he was set on the domination of Europe, and perhaps the world, the previously appeasing leaders of Britain and France, Chamberlain and Daladier, resolved to oppose him. In this they were supported by their peoples, who accepted the coming of war with a reluctant but resolute determination. The previously influential peace movements in both countries remained almost silent in September 1939. To all but the most absolute pacifists, the necessity for war was plain. The war of 1914 has long appeared as a tragic mystery. The coming of war in 1939 was a tragedy, but there was no mystery about it. Hitler's Germany had gone too far and would have to be stopped.

In eastern Europe, the Soviet Union made its own attempt at appeasement, by making the Nazi–Soviet Pact of August 1939. Stalin was a tougher negotiator than Chamberlain or Daladier. He made sure that, when Germany gained territory and spheres of influence at the cost of Poland and the Baltic states, so did the Soviet Union. Even so, Stalin made the same mistake as the Western appeasers in thinking that Hitler was amenable to compromise. He was not, as Stalin was to discover when Germany attacked the Soviet Union on 22 June 1941.

The other aggressor power, Fascist Italy, played a smaller, but not insignificant, part in the coming of war. The Italian conquests of Ethiopia in 1935–36 and Albania in 1939 seemed less dangerous than those made by Germany. Ethiopia, after all, was in Africa, and Albania was the smallest and most obscure country in the Balkans. By contrast with Germany, Italy simply did not have the military or economic strength to threaten the rest of Europe. The significance of Italy, therefore, was that of a small-scale disturber of the peace, and the junior partner in the Rome–Berlin Axis – an accessory in the aggression that was afflicting Europe, but not the prime mover. Even so, the fact that the Axis dominated the centre of Europe, from north to south, added to the general sense of threat and contributed to the impression that war was inevitable.

It is striking that, despite the disasters that the Second World War brought upon Europe, there has remained a widespread conviction that it was a necessary conflict, and in a true sense a 'just war'. There have been some advocates in Britain and France who argue that it would have been better to accept German domination in Europe in 1939, or to come to terms with Hitler in 1940 or 1941, but they have gained little support. There has been none of the sense of futility which has clung to the events of 1914–18. The Second World War simply could not be avoided. One of the merits that must be conceded to the appeasers is that they had made every effort to avoid it, without success. It was necessary for Europe to risk destroying itself, rather than be destroyed, with utter certainty, by Nazi conquest and domination.

In the period between the two great wars, Europe survived, and still showed some signs of the unity which had marked the years before 1914. But the survival was precarious and the unity limited. In the 1930s the destructive and divisive forces of economic depression, ideological conflict and a crisis in liberal democracy tore the continent apart. Then came war to complete the destruction. The attempts to find a European identity and unity which had emerged after 1918 collapsed, leaving little by way of achievement behind them. The divisions of Europe proved deeper than its unity. There was to follow a war even more disastrous, though more necessary, than the Great War of 1914–18.

PART FOUR

THE SECOND WORLD WAR, 1939–1945

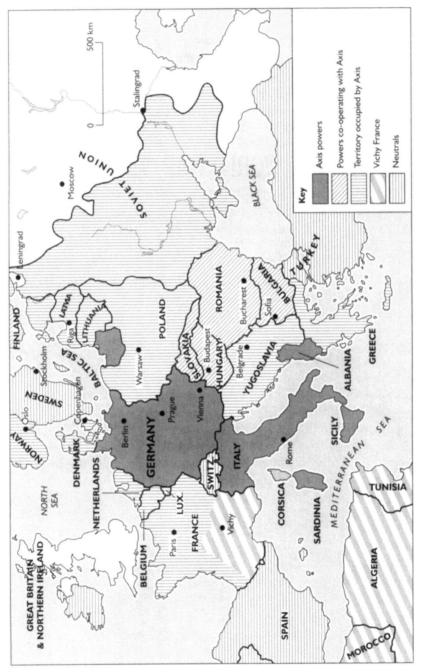

Key

Axis powers

Powers co-operating with Axis

Territory occupied by Axis

Vichy France

Neutrals

GREAT BRITAIN & NORTHERN IRELAND

NORTH SEA

NETHERLANDS

BELGIUM

LUX.

FRANCE

Paris

Vichy

SWITZ.

SPAIN

CORSICA

SARDINIA

MEDITERRANEAN SEA

ALGERIA

MOROCCO

TUNISIA

SICILY

ITALY

Rome

GERMANY

Berlin

Prague

Vienna

DENMARK

Copenhagen

NORWAY

Oslo

Stockholm

SWEDEN

BALTIC SEA

FINLAND

Leningrad

Riga

LATVIA

LITHUANIA

Warsaw

POLAND

SLOVAKIA

Budapest

HUNGARY

Belgrade

YUGOSLAVIA

ALBANIA

GREECE

ROMANIA

Bucharest

BULGARIA

Sofia

TURKEY

BLACK SEA

SOVIET UNION

Moscow

Stalingrad

0   500 km

3   Hitler's Europe, 1942

7

THE INITIAL TRIUMPHS OF GERMANY, 1939–1942

THE PHONEY WAR AND EUROPEAN UNION

The Second World War had far-reaching consequences for Europe, which swung dramatically between the opposite poles of near-unity and utter division. It witnessed a remarkable upsurge of schemes for European union, first during the 'phoney war' of late 1939 to early 1940, and later among the European resistance movements in 1943–45. Nazi Germany came near to imposing its own form of European unity by military conquest. On the other hand, the war fatally damaged European primacy in Asia, the Middle East and Africa, and so removed what had earlier been a key element in European identity and cohesion – the sense of dominance over other parts of the world. Finally the war ended with Europe divided between east and west, along the line of the Iron Curtain, which was to dominate the fate of the continent for over 40 years. All this took place within an astonishing six years.

In eastern Europe the war opened with the German invasion of Poland on 1 September, which was rapidly successful. On 19 September, the Soviet Union joined in by attacking Poland from the east, and by early October Poland had been partitioned between Germany and the USSR. The occupying powers rapidly embarked on a series of deportations and massacres, which were to afflict the Polish people throughout the war. In the face of defeat, the Polish government, and parts of the armed forces, refused to surrender, but left the country and continued the war, first from France and then from Britain. Many of the Polish people, inspired by their long history, began to organize clandestine resistance to their occupiers. The Polish campaign was brief, but it displayed omens of what was to follow for Europe as a whole. It was to be a war to the death.

In complete contrast to the blitzkrieg in Poland, western Europe witnessed at first only a *sitzkrieg* – a stationary war, or, in the phrase of the time, a phoney war. France and Britain were content mainly to stand on the defensive while preparing for a long war. Germany meanwhile made successive plans for an offensive in the west, only to be repeatedly frustrated by the weather. It was a curious period of inactivity, which lasted until April 1940 and offered an opportunity for reflection and speculation, which had some striking results.

The phoney war witnessed a remarkable flowering of plans for the future unity of Europe, especially in Britain, where they might not have been expected to flourish. The quiescence of the phoney war on the military fronts went alongside a vigorous press discussion of war aims, supposedly in order to inspire public opinion, to win the support of neutral countries (especially the USA) and to appeal to the German people by showing that they would be offered reasonable terms. In this discussion of war aims, various ideas of European union or federation took a prominent part. Harold Nicolson, an MP and writer, found in the course of a speaking tour of Britain in November 1939 a widespread desire among his audiences to escape into 'the lush meadow of wishful thinking', which before the war had meant collective security and now meant federalism.[1]

Much of the debate was led by Federal Union, an organization founded in 1939 under the chairmanship of Sir William Beveridge, which attained a membership of some 10,000 by the end of the year. Federal Union published a stream of books, pamphlets and newspaper articles, arguing that national sovereignty was the root cause of war, which could only be eradicated by the creation of a federal government with authority over national governments. These proposals usually envisaged a federation of west European states, including Germany; though sometimes the countries of the British Commonwealth were added for good measure.[2] Outside the ranks of Federal Union, a broad current of opinion concurred that something had gone badly wrong in international affairs between the wars, and that a cure had to be found for 'inflamed nationalism'. In November 1939 Clement Attlee, the leader of the Labour Party, made a speech on war aims which was later published as a pamphlet, *Labour's Peace Aims*. He advocated, in rather general terms, the acceptance of the rule of law in international affairs, and argued that international anarchy must be replaced by an international authority superior to individual states. 'Europe must federate or perish', he declared in a ringing sentence, on which he did not elaborate.[3] This proclamation did not become a permanent part of official Labour policy, but that it was made at all was a sign of the unusual circumstances and atmosphere of the time.

It was common ground in all these discussions that unity should first be developed between Britain and France, thus forming the basis for a wider European union. Early in 1940 the British and French governments took up this idea and considered proposals for continuing after the war the institutions which they had devised for wartime cooperation, notably the Supreme War Council and joint committees for economic affairs. The two

Ministries of Information promoted the idea of Britain and France forming a single unit in post-war Europe. The Education Ministries set up joint bodies to improve language teaching and cultural exchanges. A postage stamp was designed for use in both countries. In Britain, in April 1940, the Political Intelligence Department at the Foreign Office drew up a draft Act of Perpetual Association between Britain and France, which was considered (somewhat sceptically) by a Cabinet Committee. R.A. Butler, then a junior minister at the Foreign Office, advocated the creation of a Europe 'within the fortress of civilisation, that is, this side of the Maginot Line' – a narrow but reasonable definition at that time.[4]

Some of these proposals were implausible hothouse growths, flourishing in the strange and unreal atmosphere generated by the phoney war. For example, in 1939 it was impractical to consider Germany, as it then existed under the Nazis, as a part of a European federation. In any case, the whole mass of speculation and discussion was suddenly swept away by the German victory in France in May and June 1940. (On one occasion, this was almost literally true: a meeting of the British and French education ministers in Paris was hastily cancelled because of the rapid advance of the German armies.) It is true that the military crisis produced a last spectacular bid for Anglo-French unity, in the shape of the proposal for union between Britain and France which was dramatically put forward by the British War Cabinet on 16 June. In fact this was a sudden reaction to events rather than a continuation of the earlier proposals. The British were making a last desperate attempt to

8   Steel helmets, cocked hats and a wig: perhaps the last ultra-formal proclamation of war, London, 3 September 1939 © CORBIS

9   Hitler's Europe: the Fuehrer in Paris on a one-day visit to savour his victory, 23 June 1940
© Bettmann/Corbis

keep France in the war, not proposing some far-reaching scheme for European union. The French Cabinet for its part dismissed it as an irrelevance, or as an attempt to reduce France to the status of a British Dominion. Events were driving the two countries apart, not bringing them together.

These slightly unreal and exotic discussions of European union during the phoney war were swept away by the onset of the real war. Yet they deserve to be remembered. Those who took part in them formed a group of intellectuals and publicists whose significance was greater than their numbers. There was a considerable body of opinion which was convinced that the European political system had broken down, that the League of Nations had failed to produce a replacement and that to preserve the peace of Europe in the future something new must be attempted, probably involving some form of federal union. These ideas never entirely disappeared during the war, but continued to ferment and develop, until they re-emerged in rather different forms when the war was over.

BRITAIN STANDS ALONE

The strange inactivity of the phoney war came to a shattering end in the spring of 1940. In April the Germans invaded Denmark and Norway. On 10

May they launched an offensive in the west. They overran the Low Countries, drove the British Expeditionary Force out of France and defeated the French armies, all in less than six weeks. The French government asked for an armistice during the night of 16–17 June. In an astonishingly short space of time Hitler's Germany achieved more than the kaiser's Germany had done during the whole of the 1914–18 war. By the end of June 1940 Germany dominated western, central and northern Europe. Italy entered the war as Germany's ally, and Spain under Franco became a close associate of the Axis powers, though stopping short of a declaration of war. At the same time, the Soviet Union maintained active cooperation with Germany under the terms of the non-aggression pact of August 1939 and the treaty of friendship in September.

Britain stood out against this massive German onslaught, alone but not entirely alone. Churchill, in one of his early speeches as prime minister, declared that Britain would fight on, 'if necessary for years, if necessary alone'. The cartoonist Low, in one of his most striking drawings, depicted a British Tommy shaking his fist at a stormy sea and a sky darkened by enemy aircraft and saying grimly: 'Very well, alone!'[5] This impression of an island fortress, embattled in lonely defiance against a German-dominated Europe, took deep root in British national consciousness. The long-standing ambiguity of Britain's relationship with Europe was for a time resolved as Britain stood firmly and proudly outside a Europe under German domination.

Yet in crucial ways Britain was not alone. In June 1940 a Canadian division was present in Britain, and an Australian division was on its way. A New Zealand brigade was actually stationed at Dover, in the front line against a likely invasion. Fighter pilots from all over the Commonwealth played a vital part in the aerial Battle of Britain. In addition to this inspiring physical presence, the governments of all the Dominions offered Britain their moral support. The Commonwealth rallied in the hour of greatest danger, leaving a long-lived memory of reassuring solidarity.

Britain also provided a refuge – indeed a home – for a number of European governments which did not surrender to the Germans but instead left their countries and continued the struggle in exile. In 1940 the governments of Poland, Norway and the Netherlands were established in London, together with other bodies representing Belgium, Luxembourg and Free France. Their armed forces, however small, took part in the defence of Britain – Polish fighter pilots, for example, were prominent in the Battle of Britain. Britain thus became the rallying point for European resistance against Nazi Germany, offering refuge, material support and, above all, hope. Pitt's words in 1805 were often recalled in 1940, with striking aptness: 'England has saved herself by her exertions, and will, as I trust, save Europe by her example.' As far as the British were concerned they would bring that salvation from outside Europe, and it was because they were outside that they could provide a rallying point for resistance.

Pitt's words were inspiring, but they were only partly true. Britain alone could not save Europe. Churchill believed that Britain could survive in 1940, but he also knew perfectly well that if survival was to be turned into victory his country would need an ally, and he was in no doubt that this must be the USA. He set out to build up an alliance with the USA to replace that with France which had long been the mainstay of British strategy and policy, and to a remarkable degree he succeeded. He worked hard to develop a personal friendship with President Roosevelt, first by means of a frequent correspondence, and than in several long and intimate meetings. As the war went on, the British and Americans coordinated their strategy through the machinery of the Combined Chiefs of Staff, meeting in Washington every week, and through integrated military commands which achieved an unprecedented degree of cooperation. British economic needs were met by the remarkable system of Lend-Lease, which was immensely generous on the part of the USA and yet also led inexorably to a British economic dependence on America. While all this was going on, a whole generation of British politicians, civil servants and senior officers grew into the habit of working with the Americans in all kinds of ways. The wartime Anglo-American alliance, despite the friction which inevitably dogs any such enterprise, achieved a remarkable degree of closeness.

Britain also formed a difficult yet effective wartime alliance with the Soviet Union. When Hitler invaded the USSR on 22 June 1941 Churchill at once set aside his anticommunist sentiments and offered Russia all the support that Britain could spare from her limited resources. Eden, the Foreign Secretary, visited Moscow in December 1941; the two governments concluded a treaty of mutual assistance in May 1942; and Churchill went to Moscow to meet Stalin in August 1942. Churchill also conducted a personal correspondence with Stalin, though with nothing like the same friendliness and intimacy that he achieved with Roosevelt.

There thus developed a triple alliance between Britain, the USA and the Soviet Union, which Churchill liked to call the Grand Alliance, recalling the diplomatic achievements of his great ancestor the Duke of Marlborough. Britain was the weakest of the three powers in population and material resources, but Churchill worked hard to maximize his influence. He undertook immense journeys to visit Roosevelt and Stalin, and took a full part in the three-power conferences at Teheran (1943), Yalta and Potsdam (1945), though in practice his leverage diminished as the war went on and British power weakened in relation to that of the USA and the USSR.

The cumulative effect of these events on Britain's relations with continental Europe was immense. Britain stood almost alone against Nazi Germany in 1940, supported by the Commonwealth and by European governments in exile which were dependent on British support. From 1941 to 1945 Britain played a crucial role in the Grand Alliance, which eventually defeated Germany and produced the outlines of a post-war settlement. The upshot of all this seemed perfectly clear. Britain stood outside Europe and appeared destined to continue its role as a world and imperial power. In cold calculations of power and economic strength this was an over-optimistic assessment. In 1945 Britain was exhausted by six years of war, by the loss of gold and foreign currency reserves, by the concentration of industry on the war effort and, not least, by the physical effects of increasingly severe food rationing, which did not cease when the war came to an end. But psychologically the self-confidence generated by the heroic stand of 1940 and Britain's wartime role remained strong. The country had done great deeds, and had done them outside Europe. Not for the first time, Britain's role had been to save Europe by providing a rallying point against a tyrant. The fault line between Britain and continental Europe, always present, became wider during the war years.

THE NEW ORDER

The German victories of 1940, and British resistance to them, thus confirmed Britain's position outside Europe. But those same victories also opened the way to a new unity for continental Europe. Hitler's Europe was on the march. In 1940 Germany dominated western and northern Europe. Then in April and May 1941 the Germans conquered Yugoslavia and Greece, extending their control over the Balkans. On 22 June 1941 they attacked the Soviet Union and achieved astonishing successes, capturing Kiev, surrounding Leningrad and coming within 20 miles of Moscow. They were then brought to a halt and suffered terribly in the Russian winter; but in 1942 they resumed their offensive, reaching the River Volga at Stalingrad and advancing far into the Caucasus. Moreover, at the end of 1941 and in early 1942 Japan entered the war in the Pacific and South East Asia, inflicting not merely defeat but humiliation on the British, Dutch and Americans. The victory of the Axis in Europe and Japan in Asia seemed assured.

The early successes of German arms came as a surprise even to the Germans themselves. The Nazis had talked a good deal about a New Order in Europe, but they had no plans ready when Europe suddenly fell into their hands. Neither the military high command, nor government ministries, nor Hitler himself knew exactly what to do with the gains they had achieved so suddenly. Even so, between mid-1940 and mid-1942 the outlines of Hitler's Europe became discernible.

At the centre lay the new German empire. In the east, Germany annexed Danzig and the provinces which between the wars had formed the north and west of Poland, which were ruthlessly Germanized. The rest of German-occupied Poland was designated as the Government-General of Poland, where Hans Frank ruled what was in effect an SS state, used (among other things) as a dumping ground for Poles and Jews and as a source of slave labour. In the west, Alsace and Lorraine were governed by German gauleiters, though they were not formally annexed as yet.

Other areas were dealt with piecemeal. Slovakia became a German protectorate, with its own government, but under close German control. Denmark was occupied, but retained its own government until August 1943. The Netherlands and Norway were governed by Reich Commissioners, and with their presumed Aryan populations were thought suitable for eventual inclusion within Germany. Parts of conquered Soviet territory were designated as the *Reichcommissariats* of the Ostland and Ukraine, and intended for future colonization, with schemes for German settlements among a native population reduced to a subservient labour force. Hitler seems to have regarded this, at least on occasion, as the expansion of Europe, saying in September 1941 that 'the border between Europe and Asia is not the Urals but the place where the settlements of Germanic types of people stop and pure Slavdom begins. It is our task to push this border as far as possible to the east, and if necessary beyond the Urals.'[6]

Hitler's Europe was improvised and unsystematic; but it had powerful binding forces in the German Army, the SS and the Gestapo, even though these organizations were sometimes in dispute with one another. Moreover, Hitler's Europe provided a vast economic zone, to be used for German advantage. Officials in the German Economics Ministry in 1940 envisaged a Europe subordinated to Germany by means of bilateral trade arrangements, the use of the Reichsmark as the principal currency for international commercial transactions and the appointment of German officials to key economic posts in other countries. There was to be an inner ring of small states in western Europe and the Danube valley, very closely tied to Germany; a middle group, including Switzerland, Sweden and Finland, less tightly bound to Germany, but still firmly associated; and an outer ring, including France, Britain, Italy and perhaps even (at this stage in mid-1940) Russia, not belonging to the German bloc, but in close relations with it. At the same time, German industrialists represented in the *Reichsgruppe Industrie* also produced schemes for the economic organization of Europe in which the advanced economies of western Europe and Scandinavia would be subordinated to Germany, suppressing competition for German industry and providing safe markets for German exports.

In practice, the economic organization of German-dominated Europe, like the political organization, was improvised. Some occupied territories were run at a handsome profit. France was compelled to pay for the German occupation at the rate of 20 million Reichmarks per day, with the mark overvalued by about 50 per cent against the French franc. The Germans also secured a large part of French industrial and agricultural production for their own purposes, either without payment or at prices they fixed for themselves. Norway also paid heavily for the privilege of being occupied, and supplied Germany with hydroelectric power at cheap rates; though the German army of occupation was so large that the whole operation was probably unprofitable. In the east, the cereal-growing areas of Ukraine and the cattle lands of Poland were intended to play an important part in the economic New Order, but in practice the German occupation of these territories reduced them to ruin, with the Slav populations being deported, reduced to slave labour or sometimes simply exterminated, without regard to production. So sometimes occupation paid the Germans well, and sometimes proved a disaster, even for the occupiers.

Other countries were compelled to subordinate their economies to German needs. Romania, as a German ally, was required to diminish its own industrial production and concentrate on supplying Germany with oil and cereals. Sweden, though remaining neutral and never coming under German occupation, was virtually surrounded by a German-occupied Norway and a German ally in Finland, and therefore had little choice but to export much of its iron ore on German terms. From mid-1940 to the autumn of 1944 Swedish external trade was overwhelmingly with German-occupied Europe. Switzerland too, while remaining neutral and determined to defend its own territory, was constrained to accept certain German financial demands, using Swiss currency to allow Germany to purchase specialized imports.

The main principle of the economic New Order in Europe amounted to the subordination of the European economy to German needs, but at the same time the Germans took a good deal of trouble to present their economic purposes as being of a higher character than mere self-interest. As early as July 1940 Seyss-Inquart, the Reich Commissioner for the Netherlands, said:

> The new Europe of solidarity and co-operation among all its people, a Europe without unemployment, economic and monetary crises, a Europe of planning and the division of labour, having at its disposal the most modern production techniques and a continent-wide system of trade and communications developed on a joint basis, will find an assured foundation and rapidly increasing prosperity once national economic barriers are removed.[7]

A weekly propaganda magazine launched in October 1941 was entitled *The New Europe: A Magazine of Struggle against the English-American World and Historical View* – a remarkable title at a time when the German attack on the Soviet Union was well under way but the USA was still neutral. The Berlin Union of Businessmen and Industrialists held a conference in 1942 on economic aspects of the new Europe, including lectures on agriculture, industry and currency matters, as well as one entitled 'The Development towards the European Economic Community'. These were all covers for German exploitation, but the wrapping round the parcel could be made to look quite attractive.[8]

SUPPORT FOR THE NEW ORDER

In fact, the New Order attracted a good deal of support. Germany had allies, notably Italy, which entered the war in June 1940, intending to fight what

Mussolini called a 'parallel war', with Italy operating in the Mediterranean and Germany to the north of the Alps. This tidy scheme did not work out. The Italians got into difficulties in Greece and North Africa, and had to be rescued by the Germans. In 1941–42 Italy committed large numbers of troops on the eastern front, where they suffered heavy casualties. Other German allies were Finland, Hungary and Romania, which all joined in the war against the Soviet Union, for reasons of their own as well as under German pressure – Finland, for example, sought to reverse its defeat in the Winter War of 1939–40.

In 1940 Spain seemed another likely ally for the Germans. Franco was convinced that an Axis victory was certain and intended to enter the war when the circumstances were right; but he was cautious enough to wait, and the condition of Spain after the Civil War discouraged rash adventures. In the event Franco confined himself to non-belligerency in a form favourable to Germany. In 1941 he sent the Spanish Blue Division, 18,000-strong, to the Russian front, where it fought with great courage and suffered heavy losses.

Germany also found many collaborators, among governments and peoples. There were people in occupied Europe who, without being Nazis or Fascists, thought that the pre-war European order had failed and must be replaced; and that a German-led unified Europe would be better than the old regime. This was an even more attractive proposition for those who thought that, with time and diplomatic skill, the rougher aspects of German domination could be softened. There were others whose anticommunist sentiments were so strong that they were glad to join forces with Nazi Germany against the Soviet Union.

In France, military defeat in June 1940 was followed in July by the abdication of the Republic and the establishment of a new *Etat Français* under Marshal Pétain. Pétain met Hitler at Montoire in October 1940 and announced on the radio that he had accepted the principle of collaboration with Germany. He left the word undefined, but the basis of his policy was the belief (amounting at the time to a certainty) that Germany had won the war, and that the only future for France lay in a new Europe under German control. Pierre Laval became the most persistent advocate of this policy, in the belief that by clever diplomacy he could save something for France, even in disaster. In the event, Vichy France did not declare war on Britain or sign a treaty with Germany, but this was due as much to German indifference as to French reluctance. The Vichy government remained committed to the principle of collaboration.

Less conspicuously, a Danish coalition government formed after the German occupation pursued a policy of reluctant collaboration, joining the Anti-Comintern Pact in 1941 and permitting the recruitment of Danish workers for German industry. The foreign minister, Erik Scavenius, made a favourable reference to 'the New Order in Europe' in a Berlin newspaper as early as July 1940. (It should be added that the situation changed radically in 1943, when Denmark was placed under direct German rule and the Danes succeeded in saving almost all the Jews in the country by organizing their escape to Sweden.)

France and Denmark represented two significant traditions in European democracy: France was the home of the Revolution and the Rights of Man; Denmark represented the sober good sense of Scandinavian self-government. By collaborating with Nazi Germany they succumbed to superior force, but they also accepted a new political order. In France, in particular, it appeared that history had delivered a damning verdict on the old order of the Third Republic. The same sentiment was shared by many individuals. Throughout Europe there were 'ideological traitors' – people who wished for the defeat of their own state and were prepared to work and even fight for its enemies. There were Russians and Ukrainians and Cossacks who preferred the defeat of the Soviet Union to the victory of Stalin; Frenchmen and Belgians and Dutchmen who were willing to fight for Germany out of sympathy for Nazism or hatred of Communism.

Indeed the most extreme form of support for Hitler's Europe was shown by those who volunteered to fight in the war against Bolshevism. In 1941 the Germans were surprised by the offers to join up which came from all over Europe, and hastily had to devise a system to deal with them. Volunteers were at first organized according to their racial origins, with those regarded as Aryan (Finns, Swedes, Norwegians, Dutch, Flemish and Swiss) being attached to the *Waffen SS*, and others (French, Walloons, Spanish and Croats) being allotted to the *Wehrmacht*. These distinctions were later abandoned and, eventually, at the beginning of 1945, out of a total of 38 *Waffen SS* divisions, 13 were made up of non-German volunteers: two Hungarian, two Russian, two Croat, two Lithuanian, and one each Estonian, Galician, Ruthenian, Albanian and Italian. As late as February 1945 a French *Waffen SS* division, called the Charlemagne Division, was formed, bringing the total to 14. These formations varied greatly in strength and rarely attained the full establishment of a German division; but the degree of commitment required to volunteer for the eastern front was high, and by 1944–45 no one could be accused of merely wanting to join the winning side.[9]

Hitler's Europe may have been improvised rather than planned, but it had a strong framework and established an economic system geared to German needs. In its early stages it presented the attraction of a new and dynamic force when liberal Europe was in decay. For certain individuals, its anticommunist credentials commanded a conviction strong enough to volunteer to fight on the eastern front. In the event, it was short-lived. It rose by military conquest and fell by military defeat. Moreover, its most deliberate deed was the extermination of between 5 and 6 million Jews, an act so appalling that it has stained the names of Hitler as a man and Nazism as an ideology to an unequalled degree.[10] Yet Hitler's Europe made its mark, however briefly, and cannot be disregarded or struck from the historical record of attempts at European unification. It was almost certainly the last attempt to unite the continent through the domination of a single European power.[11] Europeans remain awed and dismayed by the degree of its success, and thankful that it failed. Since that failure, they have sought other paths to union.

The opening phase of the Second World War in Europe thus confirmed and widened one of the divisions in Europe: the separation of Britain from the continent. It also witnessed the formidable but short-lived success of Hitler's Europe. The final phase of the war was to see the partitioning and the apparently fatal weakening of the continent.

8

THE ALLIED VICTORY AND THE DIVISION OF EUROPE, 1942–1945

ALLIED VICTORIES AND A DIVIDED EUROPE

In the middle of 1942 it seemed that Europe might well be united under the domination of Hitler's Germany, in a form of unity imposed by conquest, and prepared to face the rest of the world from a position of military strength. In fact, the next three years of war saw the continent divided between West and East, under the sway of the USA and Soviet Union respectively, and so gravely weakened that for a time it almost lost control of its own fate.

For most of 1942 it did not seem likely that the tide of war was about to turn. In Asia and the Pacific the Japanese had swept all before them. In Russia the German armies stood on the Volga, and in North Africa they came within 60 miles of Cairo. But behind the scenes the production figures for war material told a different story. In 1942 the USA, the Soviet Union and Britain together produced about 105,000 aircraft; Germany produced 15,400. In the same year American, Soviet and British tank production totalled 54,700; German production was 9400. The populations and manpower resources of the Allies far exceeded those of Germany. It is true that overwhelming material force does not necessarily guarantee victory, as the Americans were to find out much later in Vietnam; but in Europe from the end of 1942 onwards the Allied superiority in material and numbers was applied ruthlessly and effectively.

On the eastern front, the Soviet Union gained a decisive victory at Stalingrad at the beginning of 1943, and then won the greatest tank battle of the war at Kursk in July. Thereafter the Red Army advanced relentlessly, though at immense cost. They drove the Germans out of Soviet territory, and then in 1944–45 they occupied the whole of eastern and much of central Europe, including the great capital cities of Warsaw, Budapest, Prague and Vienna. Finally, in May 1945 the Red Army entered Berlin and hoisted the Red Flag over the Reichstag, a scene which was re-enacted for the film-makers and provided one of the symbolic images of the war. These victories, and the sacrifice of life which accompanied them, conferred immense prestige on the Red Army, on the Soviet regime and on Stalin. By the end of the war the Soviet Union had established a physical grip on eastern Europe and a psychological hold on the imagination of many people in western Europe.

The Western Allies took a lesser but still vital part in the defeat of Germany. They won the battle of the Atlantic against the German U-boats. They achieved mastery of the air, overwhelming the German air force and bombing cities and industries in a campaign the effects of which have often been underestimated. On land, the British and Americans won the war in North Africa in 1942–43. They invaded Italy and forced the Italians to surrender in 1943, thus breaking the Rome–Berlin Axis. In 1944 American, British and Canadian forces invaded Normandy and liberated France and the Low Countries. In 1945 the Western Allies advanced into Germany, though they made no attempt to reach Berlin, which was left for the Soviets to capture.

These Allied victories brought about a double division of Europe: military and political. In the assault on Germany, most of western Europe (France, the Low Countries, Italy and the Western part of Germany) was occupied by the armies of the Western Allies – the USA, Britain, Canada and France – while most of eastern and central Europe was occupied by the Red Army. There thus

10 The Red Army in Berlin: the Soviet flag raised over the Reichstag building, May 1945
© Yevgeny Khaldei/Corbis

took place a military division of Europe, in which the principal military powers were the Soviet Union and the USA. The Red Army engaged the mass of the German forces on land, inflicting and enduring the sort of immense losses which had been seen on the western front in 1914–18. The USA provided overwhelming material superiority in the west, and eventually deployed manpower on a scale which the British could not match – though it was not until June 1944 that the Americans actually had more troops in action against Germany than the British. When American and Soviet soldiers met at Torgau on the River Elbe on 25 April 1945, they shook hands in the midst of a continent which their two armies dominated. Europe was in effect controlled by two powers, neither of which, by geography, culture and population, was more than partially European.

At the same time, a series of diplomatic agreements between the principal Allied powers brought about a political division of Europe. In October 1943 a Three-Power Conference in Moscow (the USSR, the USA and Britain) set up a European Advisory Commission to devise plans to deal with Germany after the war. By September 1944 the Commission had agreed on the division of Germany into three zones of occupation, with a Soviet zone in the east and two zones for the USA and Britain in the west. The boundary recommended by the Advisory Commission eventually became the frontier between East and West Germany, and the line which came to be called the Iron Curtain. (The Commission also provided for the division of Berlin into separate occupation zones, which later played a crucial role in the division of Europe.) Soon afterwards, in October 1944, Churchill and Stalin met in Moscow and concluded the so-called Percentages Agreement, by which the Soviet Union was to exercise a predominant influence in Romania, Bulgaria and Hungary, while Britain was to secure a similar influence in Greece. Later still, at the Three-Power Conference in Yalta in February 1945, the Americans and British accepted in practice that the Soviet Union would play a controlling part in Poland, by agreeing that the Soviet-nominated Lublin government should form the basis for a new Polish government.

In these ways, a military division of Europe emerged de facto, while a political division was devised by agreement; and in practice these two forms of division followed much the same lines and involved the same areas. Military and political events went hand in hand, and as early as 1944 were producing different results in the two areas, west and east, as was shown vividly by events in France and Poland.

In August 1944 French Resistance forces launched a rising to liberate Paris. General Eisenhower, the American Supreme Commander of the Allied forces in France, despatched a French armoured division (under General Leclerc) and an American infantry division to assist the rising and occupy Paris, thus allowing the French to take a prominent part in liberating their own capital, which was of immense symbolic importance to them. Events in Poland at much the same time stood in sharp contrast. In August 1944 the Polish

Resistance launched a rising to liberate Warsaw. The Red Army, already close to the city, halted in its advance and made no move to assist the rising. This pause may have had sound military reasons; but Stalin also refused (except on one occasion) to allow American or British aircraft to use Soviet landing grounds to supply the insurgents by air. As a result, the Germans virtually wiped out the Polish Home Army and destroyed Warsaw, which the Soviets later occupied at their leisure.

Such was the plight of Europe at the time. The Americans and Soviets held the fate of France and Poland in their hands. The Americans permitted the French to take a prominent (though by no means a decisive) part in liberating their own capital. Later, President Roosevelt, despite his long-established hostility to General de Gaulle and the Free French, recognized de Gaulle's administration as the provisional government of France. Stalin, on the contrary, allowed the Germans to crush the Polish Home Army and then imposed on Poland a Soviet-controlled government of his own choosing.

The Americans and Soviets were thus in the process of dividing Europe between them, in very different ways. Each country represented not only a centre of power but a creed and a way of life. The USA was the standard-bearer of liberal democracy, individual liberty and capitalism. The Soviet Union was the world's first socialist state, dedicated to building Communism at home and extending it abroad whenever possible. Each of these two powers began to fashion a part of Europe in its own image. The frontier between these two spheres and ways of life was to become a great divide, which soon acquired the ominous name of the Iron Curtain. It was Goebbels, the Nazi minister of propaganda, who first used this phrase, in an article in *Das Reich* in February 1945, where he wrote that if the Germans were to lay down their arms the whole of east and south-east Europe would be occupied by the Soviets. 'In front of these territories…an iron curtain would come down at once behind which the mass slaughter of the people would take place.' On 12 May 1945, presumably unaware of Goebbels's use of the phrase, Churchill wrote in a telegram to Truman (who had become president on the death of Roosevelt in April): 'An iron curtain is drawn down upon their [the Russians'] front. We do not know what is going on behind.'[1] It was some time before the Iron Curtain took material form in the shape of barbed wire and minefields, but already in 1945 the division of Europe between East and West was beginning.

DESTRUCTION AND THE COLLAPSE OF EMPIRE

The continent which had been fought over and was being partitioned was also grievously weakened, in itself and in relation to the rest of the world. Material destruction was greater than in the war of 1914–18, due to the extent of the land fighting and the weight of bombing from the air. Parts of the Soviet Union had been fought over several times as the battle line swayed to and fro. Warsaw had been largely destroyed and Budapest heavily damaged in the battles of December 1944 to February 1945. Parts of many German cities were reduced to rubble by aerial bombardment. Across the continent, houses had been destroyed in vast numbers – 10 million is a widely accepted round figure. Transport was almost at a standstill, except for military purposes. Rolling stock had been destroyed or worn out by constant use; marshalling yards and railway junctions had been bombed repeatedly. Ports had been damaged and sometimes blocked for long periods – the Germans held out in ports along the French Atlantic coast long after the rest of the country had been liberated. Industrial production had suffered severely: in the summer of 1945, production stood at about half the pre-war levels everywhere except in Britain and some neutral countries, and was down to less than a quarter of pre-war figures in Germany, Austria and Italy. Agricultural production had increased during the war in Britain and Denmark, but had fallen everywhere else, sometimes drastically. There had been heavy loss of livestock all over eastern Europe, and everywhere the land was impoverished by over-cultivation and lack of fertilizers. There were food shortages over much of the continent, and in some places actual famine – in the winter of 1944–45 the people of the northern Netherlands, still under German occupation, were actually starving to death.[2]

Europe was a ruined continent, and behind the immediate damage there loomed a long-term economic problem. The continent was in desperate need of imports, to feed the people, rebuild houses and factories, and restore the land. These imports would have to come from outside the continent, and above all from the USA, but there was hardly a country in Europe that had the means to pay for them. The need for foreign exchange, and above all for US dollars, was to become the dominant economic issue of the immediate post-war years.

Ruin was accompanied by death, on an appalling scale. The casualties of the Second World War in Europe ('war-related deaths', in the careful yet chilling language of demographic historians) are difficult to establish accurately, but are grievously heavy by any estimate. A generally accepted total is about 40 million dead in Europe as a whole, including the Soviet Union – roughly three times as many as in the Great War of 1914–18, and including a higher proportion of civilians than in the previous conflict. Losses were particularly high in the Soviet Union, Germany and Poland. Figures for the Soviet Union published in 1990 put the total dead at about 26 million. German casualties have been estimated variously at between 4.5 and 6.5 million. Poland suffered between 4.1 and 5.8 million deaths. Among the smaller countries of eastern Europe, Hungary lost 430,000; Romania 460,000; Czechoslovakia 415,000; Greece 425,000; and Yugoslavia a grim 1.5 million.

In western Europe, French casualties were remarkably high for a country which largely ceased hostilities between 1940 and 1944: about 600,000 dead, of whom 316,000 were civilians. Britain suffered just over 300,000 dead, including 52,000 civilians – strikingly, until 1942 civilian casualties exceeded military. The Italian dead numbered 458,000. All these three countries suffered markedly fewer casualties than in the Great War, and escaped more lightly than Germany and most countries in eastern Europe.[3]

Destruction and death were accompanied by movements of peoples on a vast scale. In the early part of the war, Hitler concluded treaties securing the movement of German-speaking populations from the Baltic states, eastern Poland and Bessarabia to Germany. The Soviet Union deported large numbers of people from eastern Poland and the Baltic States in 1939–40, and later transported large numbers of its own citizens (for example, the Volga Germans and Crimean Tartars) from their homelands to Siberia. At the end of the war there were vast migrations, with millions of Germans fleeing westwards to escape from the advancing Red Army, while others were driven out from the Sudetenland in Czechoslovakia and from the territories taken over by Poland. Prisoners and slave labourers were released, often with nowhere to go. At the end of the war there were at least 16 million refugees in western Europe, and perhaps as many as 30 million. Most of them never returned to their homes. This represented an uprooting of peoples unlike anything seen in Europe since the Dark Ages.[4]

Europe was also profoundly shaken morally and psychologically. The Allied troops invading Germany in 1945 were appalled by the horrors they discovered in the concentration camps, and the shock was rapidly transmitted to a stunned public by newsreels and photographs. The German armies had inflicted terrible atrocities during their invasion of the Soviet Union, and in 1945 the Soviets took their revenge; the advance of the Red Army into Germany was accompanied by rape and savagery on an appalling scale. During the war, Soviet prisoners of war captured by the Germans were allowed to die in droves, while German prisoners of war in the Soviet Union also died in vast numbers. All the belligerents in the war, often for compelling reasons or out of sheer necessity, disregarded the laws and customs of war which had been painfully developed over the centuries. Bombardment from the air could observe no distinction between combatant and civilian, and in any case many civilians were engaged in war work. Resistance movements by their very nature meant that civilians became combatants; and the resistance fighters themselves sometimes performed acts which in another context might have been regarded as forms of terrorism. The Warsaw Rising of 1944 involved a whole city and its people. By the end of the war Europe faced the breakdown of its own civilization.

Almost inevitably, this tortured and weakened continent lost most of the control which it had earlier established over other parts of the world. The shocks began with the defeat of France in 1940, which weakened the hold of the French on their empire. In North Africa they rode the blow successfully, at any rate for a couple of years; but in the Middle East, French influence in Syria and Lebanon was first undermined by the defeat of 1940 and then fatally weakened by the British invasion of the territories in 1941. In the Far

East, the Japanese established bases in northern Indochina in 1940, and moved into the south in July 1941.

The most damaging blows to the European empires came with the Japanese entry into the war in December 1941. Within a few months they drove the British out of Malaya, Singapore and most of Burma, and the Dutch out of the Netherlands East Indies. They tightened their grip on French Indochina, though leaving a shadowy French administration in place. They threatened to invade India, where the British were already in difficulties. Under the slogan of 'Asia for the Asians', they encouraged nationalist movements in the areas they occupied. It was true that 'Asia for the Asians' tended in practice to mean 'Asia for the Japanese', but that made little difference in the long run. European predominance in East Asia had long relied as much on prestige as on military strength. The Japanese victories swept both away.

The turn of the tide in favour of the Allies during the second part of the war often confirmed or even hastened the decline of empire. In North Africa, the Anglo–American landings in November 1942 did more damage to the French than the German victory of 1940. President Roosevelt visited the Sultan of Morocco in January 1943, and encouraged him to expect American help in ending the French protectorate. In Tunisia a brief German occupation at the end of 1942 and early 1943 broke the continuity of French control. Indeed the Germans actually released a prominent nationalist leader, Habib Bourgiba, from prison in France and allowed him to return to Tunisia. Throughout North Africa, the prolonged presence of American troops had an unsettling effect and weakened French control. On the very day of victory in Europe, 8 May 1945, there was a rising against the French at Sétif, in Algeria, which was repressed at the time but proved to be the prelude to the later war of independence.

In the Middle East, the struggle between the British and French in Syria and Lebanon continued until 1945, ending finally in French defeat; they abandoned their mandate in 1946. The British position in its turn was undermined by the wartime growth of Arab nationalism, and above all by Zionism. The appalling massacre of the Jews in Nazi Europe made the case for a Jewish state unanswerable in the view of international opinion at the time. The British could no longer hold their ground in Palestine, and announced in 1947 that they would leave the country the following year.

In the Far East, the imperial powers returned to their possessions in 1945, but in most cases were unable to re-establish their authority fully. The speed of their retreat varied a good deal. The British left India and Burma in 1947, but held on in Malaya, defeating a communist insurrection in the 1950s before granting independence in 1957. Sri Lanka did not become independent until 1972. Hong Kong remained a British colony until 1997. The Dutch fought for four years to restore their hold on the East Indies, before giving up the struggle and recognizing the independence of Indonesia in 1949. The French waged war for ten years to regain their control of Indochina, until they were finally defeated at Dien Bien Phu in 1954 and withdrew in 1955. But almost everywhere, sooner or later, the effects of the Second World War worked themselves out, and the long-established European predominance in East Asia came to an end.

There were exceptions to this weakening of empire. The Russian (later Soviet) hold on the Caucasus and Central Asia, established overland during the eighteenth and nineteenth centuries while other European powers were gaining territories across the sea, remained intact. (Stalin made sure of his grip by taking drastic preventive action against the Tartars and the Chechens.) Portugal, the weakest of the imperial powers, was to retain its African colonies for 30 years after the Second World War ended. Generally speaking, European rule survived longer in Africa south of the Sahara than in the Middle East and Asia. But even so, the Second World War marked the end of European supremacy over other continents, which had been so strong at the start of the century, and which had formed a significant element in European identity and self-consciousness.

RESISTANCE

In this catalogue of European calamities there were some unexpected signs of hope and stirrings of life. The resistance movements which arose in every country under German occupation, and even inside Nazi Germany itself, were signs of renewed courage, determination and self-respect. It is true that resistance groups alone could achieve little by way of military success, especially against determined and ruthless occupying forces; but the moral and psychological force of resistance infused new life into what had previously seemed exhausted countries and peoples. It was significant that many of the political leaders who emerged in western Europe after the war had been active in the resistance, bringing a new outlook and a shared experience to bear on their countries' problems.

The motive power of resistance lay in a revived and often intense patriotism, and yet at the same time many resistance groups took the view that the nation state had failed, and advocated the creation of some form of European union or federation when the war was over. As early as June 1941 two Italian opponents of Mussolini, Ernesto Rossi and Altiero Spinelli, who were interned on the island of Ventotene, drew up a manifesto proposing a European federation. Released from their captivity after the fall of Mussolini, these two anti-Fascists formed the *Movimento Federalista Europeo*; after the war, Spinelli became secretary of the Federalist Movement, and cooperated with De Gasperi, Monnet, Spaak and Adenauer in working for European union.

In France in 1943 several clandestine newspapers (for example, *Combat, Franc-Tireur, Résistance, Le Populaire*), and some distinguished writers, notably Albert Camus, advocated some form of union in Europe after the war. Camus wrote, in one of his *Letters to a German Friend*:

During all the time when we were obstinately and silently serving our country, we never lost sight of an idea and a hope, forever present in us – the idea and hope of Europe. To be sure, we have not mentioned Europe for five years. But this is because you talked too much of it. And then, too, we were not speaking the same language: our Europe is not yours.[5]

In fact the French did indeed speak about Europe, and in 1944 *Mouvement National de la Résistance* drafted a far-reaching proposal for a European federal state, with the right to control economic and commercial activities, conduct foreign policy and have command of a European army.

In July 1944 a number of resistance leaders from various countries met in Geneva and adopted a *Déclaration des Résistances européennes*, claiming that only a federal union could reconstruct Europe and, moreover, allow the German people to participate peacefully in the life of the continent – a strikingly generous outlook in the circumstances of the time. The declaration went on to propose the establishment of a European government, with an army and a court of justice. The resistance movements never achieved any unity across Europe – or even within their own countries – but even so they succeeded in reviving a sense of common European feeling, which persisted when the war ended and was one of the streams which fed the later movement for European unity.

Another sign of life appeared in an upturn in the birth rates in several European countries during the war. This remarkable, and at first sight unlikely, change occurred in countries whose circumstances were very different. It took place in France, which was defeated and occupied; and also in Britain, which was not. It occurred in neutral countries as far apart as Portugal, Switzerland and Sweden. We cannot tell what lay behind these increases in the birth rate, which contrasted with steady decreases during the interwar years. The presence of foreign armies (whether of occupation, like the Germans in France, or as allies, like the Americans in Britain) doubtless had some influence; so did the fact that most of the British Army remained at home from 1940 to 1944. But that tells us nothing about the neutral countries. At any rate these upturns formed a striking coincidence, and offered evidence of vitality and hope among some European peoples at a time when hope seemed lost for so many.[6]

The Second World War left Europe ruined and divided. The crippling of the European economy, amounting in some areas to near-destruction, meant that the continent had to struggle for life, and European predominance in the world economy, already much weakened, came to an end. Western Europe came to rely on the USA, while eastern Europe fell under the domination of the Soviet Union. The European populations suffered grievous losses, which upturns in the birth rate in some countries did little to offset. As for European unity, the strongest move in that direction was the brief imposition of Hitler's Europe, which created a form of union unwelcome to most of the continent and hideously cruel in some of its aspects. The hopeful schemes for European federation produced by the resistance movements were aspirations which by their very nature lacked substance, and might have remained no more than pipe dreams. By 1945 the harsh reality was that Europe was divided into East and West, into zones dependent on the USA and the Soviet Union, a division which was becoming sharper and deeper with every month that passed. At the end of the Second World War, the curtain fell on a gravely weakened and bitterly divided Europe.

PART FIVE

THE GREAT DIVIDE: WEST AND EAST, 1945–1989

ICELAND

SWEDEN

NORWAY

FINLAND

Helsinki

GREAT BRITAIN &
NORTHERN IRELAND

Oslo   Stockholm

NORTH
SEA

DENMARK

IRELAND

Dublin

NETHER-
LANDS

Copenhagen

SOVIET UNION

London

GERMAN
DEMOCRATIC
REPUBLIC

POLAND

Warsaw

Berlin

ATLANTIC
OCEAN

BELGIUM

FEDERAL
GERMAN
REPUBLIC

CZECHOSLOVAKIA

Paris

LUX.

FRANCE

SWITZ.

AUSTRIA   HUNGARY   ROMANIA

ITALY

Bucharest

YUGOSLAVIA

PORTUGAL

Madrid

CORSICA

Rome

BULGARIA

Sofia

TURKEY

SPAIN

SARDINIA

GREECE

Tangier

Algiers

SICILY

ALBANIA

Athens

MEDITERRANEAN SEA

CRETE

Key

Divide between Eastern &
Western Europe

0   500 Km

Tripoli

EGYPT

4   Cold War Europe, 1945

9

WESTERN EUROPE, 1945-1961

FRAGMENTATION

In the years following the Second World War Europe was divided in a fashion unique in the modern history of the continent. The Iron Curtain cut the continent in two, along a line which ran, not where Churchill famously put it, from Stettin in the Baltic to Trieste in the Adriatic, but to the west of that, dividing Germany on a line dropping south from Lübeck. Moreover, the predominant powers on either side of the divide were fundamentally non-European: the USA, far away across the Atlantic, though with a people of mainly European origin, and the Soviet Union, a state which was only very partially European in its history, geography and character. The continent which had controlled most of the world before 1914 was now in the hands – almost at the mercy – of alien powers.

This fracturing of the continent was sharper and more severe than anything seen in recent years – indeed in centuries. There were two Europes, each under the aegis of a superpower which exercised predominance in the Soviet case and powerful influence in the American. The ideological struggles for the soul of Europe which had developed after 1917 and which took violent form in the 1930s and early 1940s now assumed a new and rigid shape as a Soviet-dominated, communist eastern Europe faced an American-led liberal-democratic western Europe – a division which came to seem increasingly final and immoveable as time went on. Moreover, even within each Europe there was much diversity, so that the continent was fragmented as well as divided.

This division came about within a very few years. It began with the division of Germany. In 1945 the victorious Allies intended to administer Germany as a whole, with the commanders-in-chief of the occupying forces making up a Control Council. In practice, the country became divided, politically and economically, before the end of 1946. The Soviet occupation authorities set up their own political system, based on a forced amalgamation between the

Communist Party and the Social Democrats in a new Socialist Unity Party, set up in April 1946 and in practice controlled by the Communists. In the Western zones, the Americans and British encouraged the establishment of a range of political parties. The Communists attempted an amalgamation with the Social Democrats, but were rebuffed. Berlin, under the joint occupation of the Allied powers, became divided in the same way. (For some time, the French, who controlled their own occupation zone, were much more reluctant to let the Germans undertake political activities, but that did not affect the main issue.)

Meanwhile, Germany was also divided economically. The Soviet Union, to exact revenge and also to recoup some of its vast material losses, set out to secure reparations from current production in their own zone, and by removing machinery and even whole factories from all four zones, as had been agreed at the Allied conference in Potsdam in July 1945. By 1946 the Americans and British were following a very different policy. Their zones were densely populated and mainly industrial in their economy, requiring imports of food and raw materials; and the occupying powers found themselves having to feed the population at their own expense – indeed in July 1946 the British government introduced bread rationing at home in order to send wheat to Germany. The Americans and British therefore argued that current industrial production in their zones, such as it was, should be used to pay for feeding the German people. In May 1946 the American commander-in-chief, General Clay, stopped the despatch of any reparations from the American to the Soviet zone, and in July the American and British zones were merged for purposes of economic administration into the so-called 'Bizonia'. On 5 September 1946, in a speech made in Stuttgart, the American Secretary of State, Byrnes, declared that Germany should be allowed to export enough goods to pay its own way and to assist the economic recovery of Europe as a whole – a policy which made much sense, but was not what the Allies had agreed in 1945. The French dissented from the new policy and continued to take reparations from current production. For some time, therefore, the economic division of Germany was not between east and west, but between the USSR and France on the one hand, and the USA and Britain on the other – that is, those who had been occupied by the Germans and those who had not. It was not until April 1947, when a meeting of foreign ministers from the four Allied powers in Moscow failed to agree on a German peace treaty, that the French concluded that they could no longer stand out. They joined Bizonia and changed their reparations policy, so that by June 1947 the division of Germany on an east–west basis was finally established, on lines which were to persist until 1990.

THE MARSHALL PLAN AND NATO

During the Moscow Conference of Foreign Ministers (10 March–24 April 1947), the American Secretary of State George Marshall became convinced that Stalin intended to let events in Europe drift until the continent disintegrated, and then exploit the ensuing chaos to Soviet advantage. Western Europe was already in the throes of an economic and political crisis. Countries desperately needed imports from America, but had no dollars to pay for them. Food rationing in Britain was more stringent than in wartime. In France the daily bread ration was reduced to 250 grammes on 1 May 1947. People were exhausted after six years of war, and peace had brought little relief. In France and Italy governments were unstable and communist parties strong, and there were acute fears of communist insurrection. It now appears that the underlying facts of the economic situation were less grave than they seemed, but at the time the sense of crisis in western Europe was very real.[1] Marshall himself was convinced of the danger. Speaking on the radio in the USA, he said: 'The patient is sinking while the doctors deliberate. So I believe that action cannot await compromise through exhaustion.'[2]

Within a few weeks Marshall went on to outline the great concept which bears his name: the Marshall Plan. The USA offered economic aid to countries in Europe, on condition that the recipient states coordinated their economic efforts and did what they could to help themselves. The Americans declined to accept piecemeal requests or to supply assistance that the Europeans could provide for themselves. The offer was made to the whole of Europe, East as well as West. (The one exception was Spain, which under Franco's rule was at the time still excluded from international society.) Britain and France welcomed the proposal at once and set about organizing a European conference to put it into practice. The Soviet Union at first temporized, but on 2 July 1947 Molotov declared that the concept of a coordinated programme was incompatible with economic independence and national sovereignty. The east European states (Bulgaria, Romania, Yugoslavia, Albania, Hungary, Czechoslovakia, Poland and Finland) all declined to attend the conference, even though at one stage Poland and Czechoslovakia had formally accepted the invitation and Hungary had seemed ready to join them. The conference to discuss Marshall's proposal which opened in Paris on 12 July 1947 therefore comprised 16 states: Belgium, Canada, Denmark, France, Greece, Iceland, Ireland, Italy, Luxembourg, the Netherlands, Norway, Portugal, Sweden, Switzerland, Turkey and the United Kingdom.[3]

These events brought about a profound economic division in Europe. Eastern Europe, under Soviet leadership and control, pursued its own economic course, for reasons which from Stalin's point of view were unimpeachable. If the Soviet Union and the countries of eastern Europe had accepted Marshall aid, they would have necessarily accepted economic coordination, and thus been open to economic influence from western Europe and the USA. The Soviet zone of control built up since 1945 would certainly have been endangered, and might well have crumbled away. As Molotov commented long afterwards, 'The imperialists were drawing us into their company, but as subordinates.'[4]

Meanwhile the states which agreed to accept Marshall aid set out to make the best use of it. They established in April 1948 the Organization for European Economic Cooperation (OEEC), to administer the American aid and to coordinate the assistance they provided to one another. The OEEC's headquarters were established in Paris, and its first Secretary General was a French official, Robert Marjolin.

The total aid provided under the Marshall Plan from 1948 to 1952 amounted to nearly 13 billion US dollars, of which rather over 9 billion dollars were in gifts and the rest in loans. The largest recipients were the United Kingdom (24.4 per cent), France (20.3 per cent), Italy (11 per cent) and West Germany (10.1 per cent). The actual sums involved were not enormous, amounting to only a small proportion of the gross national product of the recipient countries – 2.4 per cent for Britain, 6.5 per cent for France in the first year of operation. Results were sometimes slow in coming. French unemployment actually increased between 1948 and 1950, while unemployment in Italy (which was much higher) went down only slightly. The political effects were not always evident. The Americans hoped that Marshall aid would diminish the appeal of communism, but in fact support for the Communist Parties in France and Italy remained strong. Despite all this, Marshall aid achieved a great deal. It allowed European countries to pay in dollars for vital imports – in 1949, as much as 42 per cent of French imports were financed by Marshall aid. It permitted investment which would otherwise have been impossible, and gave some leeway for resources to be used for consumer goods rather than being reserved for foreign exchange. Above all, its main effects were psychological: the participating countries came to believe that there was a way out of their difficulties. A popular Greek film, *Welcome Mr Marshall!*, hit the nail on the head.[5]

The Marshall Plan thus provided the confidence and some of the resources for economic recovery in western Europe. It did not provide military security. In February 1948 the communists suddenly took power in Czechoslovakia, arousing fears of internal subversion and external Soviet attack throughout western Europe. In June 1948 the Soviets imposed a blockade of West Berlin, arousing fears of an attack on West Germany and western Europe. In March 1948 five west European countries (Britain, France, Belgium, the Netherlands and Luxembourg) combined for self-defence in the Brussels Treaty, which was little more than a gesture, because they simply did not have the military strength to defeat a Soviet attack. For that they needed the Americans, and the British and French set themselves to bring the USA into an alliance. They were slow to respond – entangling alliances were contrary to the whole tradition of American foreign policy; and it was only after long and difficult negotiations that the North Atlantic Treaty was concluded on 4 April 1949. Its original 12 signatories were: the USA, Canada, Belgium, Denmark, France, Iceland, Italy, Luxembourg, the Netherlands, Norway, Portugal and the United Kingdom. Greece and Turkey joined in 1952, and West Germany in

1955. The key article of the treaty declared that an armed attack on any of the member states would be considered an attack on all, and to back this up the member states agreed in December 1950 to set up an integrated defence organization, under an American supreme commander. Thus came into being the North Atlantic Treaty Organization (NATO), which was to become a long-standing feature of international politics. At first NATO did not have much military strength on the ground, and (as with the Marshall Plan) its main importance was psychological. Under the cover of NATO, with at least some American troops on the ground and the American atomic (later nuclear) bombs as a powerful deterrent in the background, the states of western Europe recovered their nerve. The fears of 1947 and 1948, when it appeared that everything might dissolve into subversion, chaos or war, were dispelled. The economic division of Europe brought about by the Marshall Plan was thus followed by a military division, established by NATO, and confirmed when in 1955 the Soviet Union responded by setting up the Warsaw Pact, whose members were: the USSR, Albania, Bulgaria, Czechoslovakia, East Germany, Hungary, Poland and Romania, with a joint military command always headed by a Soviet marshal.

The influence of the USA was decisive in both cases. The Marshall Plan arose from an American initiative taken up in western Europe. NATO, on the other hand, came about because Britain and France took the initiative, and drew the USA somewhat reluctantly into a military commitment. But in neither case could western Europe have acted alone. American resources provided Marshall aid. American military power made up the backbone of NATO. The new western Europe, deeply divided from the east, was heavily dependent on the USA.

ECONOMIC RECOVERY

The west European countries turned this dependence to their own advantage. Marshall aid proved the start of a new period of prosperity. American military protection provided defence at a good deal less than full cost – Germany in particular undertook no defence expenditure until 1955, and could devote all its resources to economic development and social security.

But at the same time the west European countries achieved much by their own efforts. The West German economics minister in the 1950s, Ludwig Erhard, disliked the term 'economic miracle' to describe the achievements of his country, on the grounds that the German people had worked hard for their success. There was indeed a new outlook, in West Germany and western Europe as a whole. The years of war and post-war privation generated a demand for food, clothing, houses, and goods and services of all kinds. People were anxious to spend, if they had the money, which marked the beginning of a remarkable change in west European society. Families and individuals who would previously have *saved* if they had spare cash, now set out to *spend* it; and they even began to borrow in order to spend. This new impulse was strengthened by the development of the welfare state, in the shape of unemployment benefits, pensions and improved health services (none of them new, but greatly extended after 1945). The presence of this safety net took some of the risk out of spending. Governments provided state investment and evolved a mixed economy, in which state control was combined with private enterprise. Trade unions and employers often worked with governments and with one another, notably in West Germany, where trade union leaders became a part of management and did much to restrain wages and improve productivity.

The result of all these elements was a remarkable surge in production and prosperity, with France, Italy and, above all, West Germany showing strong economic growth throughout the 1950s. The average annual growth rate in gross domestic product (GDP) from 1949 to 1960 was 4.5 per cent in France, 5 per cent in Italy, and 7.4 per cent in West Germany; though Britain lagged behind at 2.4 per cent. The Scandinavian countries, the Low Countries and Switzerland also showed strong growth; and even Portugal, a comparatively poor country, increased its GDP by about one-third between 1953 and 1960.[6] In all respects West Germany was the star of the show. Productivity was high. Unemployment fell from 1,870,000 in 1950 (8 per cent of the workforce) to a mere 270,000 (1 per cent) in 1960. Inflation diminished from 7.7 per cent in 1951 to 1.4 per cent in 1960. National economic growth was translated into individual prosperity – West Germans owned 515,000 private cars in 1950, and a prodigious 4,066,000 in 1960.[7] Everywhere this booming economy was accompanied by a new flexibility. Production of plastics and electrical goods increased, and services such as advertising, retailing and insurance flourished; so that when the older industries such as coal and steel faltered, there were resources available to make up the losses. The new economic growth seemed guaranteed and immune from the threat of recession. Confidence was in the air.

POLITICS

In politics, the picture was more mixed but still favourable on balance, especially by comparison with the extremism and instability of the interwar years. In Britain the Labour Party led by Clement Attlee won a massive majority in the general election of 1945, lost most of it in 1950 and gave way in 1951 to Conservative governments – under Churchill, Eden and Macmillan – which held office through the rest of the 1950s. Despite this swing of the political pendulum, British politics settled into a steady centre-left consensus. The Labour governments extended and remodelled the welfare state, with the National Health Service as its key element. Railways, the coal mines and the steel industry were nationalized, and the government imposed a large measure of economic planning. When the Conservatives returned to power they accepted the bulk of these changes, limiting their denationalization measures to steel and road haulage. The financial and economic policies of the two main parties were so similar that journalists called them 'Butskellism', running together the names of the Conservative and Labour Chancellors of the Exchequer, Butler and Gaitskell. A consensual foreign policy was firmly established, with Bevin for Labour and Eden for the Conservatives working along the same lines, supporting NATO and maintaining Britain's role as a world power. Britain had a threefold basis for its reputation: its record in the Second World War; its stable and successful political system; and its venture into social change under the Attlee Government. British prestige stood high.

The most striking success story was that of West Germany. After the failure of the Weimar Republic, the violent extremism of the Nazi regime and the ultimate disasters of the Second World War, the West Germans rapidly achieved a remarkable degree of stability. The Federal German Republic was founded in 1949, under the guidance of the Western Allies, and its first chancellor, Konrad Adenauer, held office until 1963. The new constitution (the Basic Law) struck a balance between the powers of the provinces (*Länder*) and the federal government. The voting system avoided the errors of the Weimar Republic, which had carried proportional representation to extremes; and the parliamentary system encouraged stable governments. Adenauer himself was opposed to centralization and was happy to establish the federal capital in Bonn, a minor provincial city which looked towards the west. He was also an extremely shrewd international statesman, setting out to anchor West Germany in western Europe – 'the most European nation among the Europeans' – and also to create a firm alliance with the USA.[8] The new Germany emerged as a solidly democratic state, with stable governments and a people who now tended towards pacifism rather than militarism. West Germany also possessed, partly on British initiative, a modern trade union movement, and introduced legislation requiring a majority of 75 per cent in a secret ballot before any strike action – something which was to give German industry an edge over the British for many years to come. By the end of the 1950s the Federal Republic was fully accepted as a partner in western Europe, a member of the European Coal and Steel Community and the European Economic Community (see below, pp. 159–62). Even more strikingly, Germany became a member of NATO in 1955, and a new German Army took its share in the defence of the West.

The politics of France and Italy presented a marked contrast to the stability of Britain and West Germany. In France, the Fourth Republic set up in 1946 was an almost exact copy of the Third, which had collapsed in 1940, and reproduced most of its weaknesses. Three main political parties (the Christian Democrats, the Socialists and the Communists) balanced one another, producing political deadlock; and in 1951 the intervention of a newly formed Gaullist party complicated the situation still further. Governments followed one another in rapid succession – no fewer than 20 between December 1946 and May 1958, when the Fourth Republic finally collapsed.

The situation in Italy was similar. Two left-wing parties, the Communists and Socialists, which for some time worked together, were roughly balanced by the right-wing Christian Democrats. In the legislative elections of 1946 the Christian Democrats won 207 seats, the Socialists 115 and the Communists 104; and a multiparty coalition government took office. In 1948 the Christian Democrats won a substantial victory over a Communist–Socialist alliance (305 seats to 183) and went on to form a series of short-lived governments, averaging one a year. There was more continuity than these figures might indicate – for example, Alcide de Gasperi remained prime minister for almost eight successive years (1945–53); but even so, the best that Italian politics could contrive was deadlock tempered by volatility.

Behind these contrasts, west European politics (not just in the 'big four', but also in the smaller countries) showed some common characteristics. Christian democracy, drawing on ideas set out half a century earlier by Pope Leo XIII, emerged as a strong political movement in several countries – France, West Germany, Italy, Belgium, the Netherlands and Austria. The political leadership of Robert Schuman, Konrad Adenauer and Alcide de Gasperi, and the cooperation between them, was a powerful cohesive force, and contributed much to the movement towards west European unity which we will consider below (see pp. 159–62). At the same time, socialist parties established themselves in government, sometimes alone (Attlee's Labour Government in Britain, and Erlander's administration in Sweden), but more often in coalitions. In Austria Christian Democrats and Socialists actually worked together in coalition governments from 1945 to 1966, after shooting at one another in the 1930s. In most countries, right and left were agreed on developing the welfare state and on government management of the economy. The pattern of a mixed economy, high taxation and comprehensive social security, long established in the Scandinavian countries, now took root over most of western Europe.

WOMEN IN SOCIETY AND POLITICS

There was another common factor among the west European democracies: a further change in the position of women in society and politics. During the Second World War women made new strides towards equality, though sometimes in unwelcome ways. In Britain, conscription and direction of labour were extended to women by legislation in 1941 and 1943. By 1943 nearly 38 per cent of the workforce were women (7.75 million, as against just over 5 million in 1939). The women's services recruited 470,000 members, though not for combat duties except for a few in the Special Operations Executive. In Germany, the government never used its powers to conscript women, but even so the proportion of women in the workforce grew steadily from 37 per cent in 1939 to nearly 52 per cent in 1944. In occupied countries, and in northern Italy after 1943, women took active roles (including armed combat) in resistance movements. The war projected women into a variety of experiences, from the comparative freedom of life in the services and some forms of war work, to the restrictions and monotony of domestic life in wartime. After the war, something of a reaction set in, with a reversion to home life and 'femininity' which was widely welcomed by women and men alike, and sometimes became a sort of 'mid-20th century cult of domesticity'.[9]

In politics, women achieved the franchise in France in 1944 and Italy in 1946; though in Switzerland they waited until 1971 and in Spain until 1975. In most west European countries they therefore made up rather over half the electorate, though under the secret ballot it was not easy to tell exactly how they voted. The evidence of opinion polls and surveys indicated that they tended to vote more on the right than the left, moderate conservative rather than socialist; and this may have contributed to the stabilization of west European politics in the late 1940s and 1950s.[10]

EUROPEAN INTEGRATION

In foreign policy, most countries in western Europe were committed to NATO and supported the USA in the cold war against the Soviet Union and Communism. The cold war gave western Europe a common enemy and a strong sense of its own identity, embodied in parliamentary democracy, the rule of law, individual freedom, a free market and a mixed economy under the supervision of interventionist governments.

There were exceptions. Some countries followed their traditions of neutrality, so that Switzerland, Sweden and Ireland remained outside NATO, though they accepted Marshall aid. France and Italy had strong Communist parties, solidly in favour of the Soviet Union, winning up to 25 per cent of the vote in France and about 20 per cent in Italy. In France there was also a strong current of neutralism – for example, Beuve-Méry, the influential editor of *Le Monde*, sometimes claimed that the Americans and the Soviets were equally dangerous. There was also a good deal of plain anti-Americanism, which flourished among disparate groups: supporters of the French Empire who resented American anticolonialism; Gaullists who were determined to reassert French greatness; and intellectuals who condemned American 'chewing-gum imperialism' and 'Coca-Colonisation'. Such sentiments were present in one form or another in most west European countries, though least so in West Germany, which was closest to the Soviet danger and recognized most clearly its reliance on American protection. There thus developed a significant dichotomy between governments which were solidly pro-NATO and a majority of opinion which was broadly pro-American, on the one hand, and a section of opinion which was in different degrees anti-American on the other. This was to prove a consistent characteristic in west European politics.

Shortly after the war ended the perennial question of European political unity was reopened. On 19 September 1946 Winston Churchill, then out of office but still a towering political figure, made a speech at Zurich, appealing for the establishment of 'a kind of United States of Europe', and declaring that

'The first step in the re-creation of the European family must be a partnership between France and Germany' – a startling assertion at the time. He went on at once to say that Britain should not take part in such a venture, but offer support and encouragement from outside. Despite this reservation, the greatest European statesman of the age had thrown his immense prestige behind the 'European idea', which had flourished among resistance movements during the war, but then lost its impetus amid the demands of reconstruction.[11]

Churchill's speech struck a responsive chord throughout western Europe. In December 1947 a number of organizations concerned with European unity, representing all shades of opinion, from simple cooperation to federal union, agreed to call a Congress of Europe, which met at The Hague in May 1948, with Churchill as its honorary president. Several hundred delegates from 26 European countries attended, along with observers from the USA and Canada. The Congress agreed on a series of recommendations, including: the creation of an economic and political union, which would include Germany; the gradual removal of trade barriers as a prelude to economic union; the preparation of a Charter of Human Rights, to be implemented by a European Supreme Court; and the creation of a European Consultative Council to bring about the progressive integration of Europe.

Most of these proposals, which seemed visionary at the time, eventually came about. Meanwhile, the immediate result of the Congress was the establishment of the Council of Europe in 1949, with ten founder members: Belgium, Denmark, France, Ireland, Italy, Luxembourg, the Netherlands, Norway, Sweden and the United Kingdom. Greece and Turkey joined later in 1949 (Turkey being a special case which will be examined later). Later adherents were: Iceland (1950), West Germany (1951), Austria (1956) and Cyprus (1961). A further seven states joined up to 1989, and another 12 up to 1995.[12] The Council of Europe laid much emphasis on ideas and principles. The first Article of its founding document referred to 'the ideals and principles which are their [the members'] common heritage'; and membership was limited to European states which accepted the rule of law and recognized human rights. In 1950 the Council drew up a Convention for the Protection of Human Rights and Fundamental Freedoms, with a Court of Human Rights to implement its provisions. As time went on, and European integration took increasingly economic and bureaucratic forms, the Council's concern with values as distinct from economic arrangements became a significant element in European identity. The Council of Europe also kept alive a wide (if vague) vision of Europe, with a membership of 16 states in the 1950s, when a more tightly knit organization was emerging as a Europe of only six members.

This so-called Europe of the Six began in 1950 with the Schuman Plan, the joint brainchild of Jean Monnet and Robert Schuman. Monnet had become an international figure as a coordinator of French and British economic policy during the two World Wars, and in 1946 became the head of the French

Commissariat du Plan, a prime source of ideas in French economic planning. He was a convinced internationalist, and also quite determined that France should take the lead in internationalism – a highly significant combination. He believed that only individuals could set an idea in motion, but only institutions could ensure its permanence. In 1950 his idea was European federation, and the institution that he proposed was a single authority, independent of governments, to control French and German coal and steel production. While Monnet worked on this idea in the background, Robert Schuman, the French foreign minister, took the lead in public. Schuman was, in the events of his own life, almost an epitome of Franco–German relations. He was a Lorrainer when Lorraine was part of Germany; he attended German universities and served in the German Army in 1914. In 1919 he was elected to the French Chamber of Deputies, and after the Second World War became a leading member of the French Christian Democratic Party. He was a practising Catholic, deeply rooted in Christian European culture – 'the defender of a certain kind of western European civilisation', in the words of his most distinguished biographer.[13]

On 9 May 1950 Schuman made what proved to be a historic speech, proposing nothing less than Franco–German reconciliation by means of 'immediate action at a limited but decisive point', by placing French and German production of coal and steel under a common High Authority whose decisions would be binding on both countries. Two points stood out in Schuman's speech. He intended to lay 'the first concrete foundations of a European federation', which was necessary for the preservation of peace; and he was concerned above all with Franco–German relations – Germany was the only foreign country mentioned by name, several times over. The proposal was open to other countries which were willing to accept its fundamental principles; but Germany was essential to its whole nature.

Other countries soon joined: Italy, Belgium, the Netherlands and Luxembourg. The British government did not, refusing to accept the principle of a supranational High Authority. At that stage, Britain was opposed to any fusion of sovereignty (in Schuman's words) or surrender of sovereignty (as it appeared to the British). The proposal for a European Coal and Steel Community therefore went ahead with six members, led by France and Germany. The 'Europe of the Six' had begun. Its immediate consequences were slow to come about and slight in their effect. The High Authority began to operate only in August 1952, and levied a small tax on the selling price of coal, iron and steel on 1 January 1953. As late as 1959 France refused to allow the High Authority to take decisions which might lead to the closure of French coal mines. But the true importance of the Schuman Plan was symbolic and proved more significant than any amount of prosaic fact.

For some time this was by no means obvious. The next move towards European integration, a plan for a European Defence Community and a European Army, proved a miserable failure. It began in autumn 1950 under

American pressure to rearm West Germany, rather than as a genuine west European initiative. The French, reluctant to accept a German Army, but unable to resist American demands, proposed a European Army as a compromise. After nearly four years of tortuous negotiations, the scheme was killed off by the French National Assembly, thus receiving its death blow from the country which had proposed it. The question of how to achieve German rearmament (which proved to be nowhere near as urgent as the Americans had claimed in 1950) was eventually resolved by conventional diplomacy. Anthony Eden, the British Foreign Secretary, proposed an arrangement under which West Germany should become a member of NATO and establish an army under NATO command, and Britain soothed any remaining fears of German rearmament by undertaking to maintain a British force in West Germany. The problem was thus quickly resolved by intergovernment cooperation, whereas the tortuous proposals of the supranationalists had consumed four years to no purpose. European integration seemed to be an idea whose time had passed.

Events turned out otherwise. Politicians in the Benelux countries (notably Beyen from the Netherlands and Spaak from Belgium) proposed a new movement towards a common market. Jean Monnet founded an Action Committee for the United States of Europe, comprising members from all six of the ECSC countries and from a wide range of political parties, which proved an influential lobby for integration. In 1955 the three Benelux governments (Belgium, the Netherlands and Luxembourg) proposed that the six ECSC countries should come together to form a common market, and also to integrate their policies on atomic and nuclear energy. From this initiative there emerged a conference of the Six at Messina in June 1955, which agreed in principle to set up a European Economic Community and a European Atomic Energy Community, and established a committee under the chairmanship of Spaak (the Belgian foreign minister and a convinced integrationist) to work out the details. Britain was invited to the Messina conference, but declined to attend; the British were also invited to join the Spaak committee, but sent only an official from the Board of Trade.

The Spaak committee deliberated for a year, and then recommended to a meeting of the foreign ministers of the Six at Venice (29–30 May 1956) the· acceptance of the two main proposals from the Messina Conference: to set up a European Economic Community, with institutions on the same lines as the existing Coal and Steel Community; and a European Atomic Energy Community, to coordinate various aspects of the non-military use of nuclear energy. The British declined to accept these proposals and took no further part in these events.

The foreign ministers of the Six accepted the Spaak recommendations and their governments negotiated two treaties, which were signed in Rome on 25 March 1957, setting up a European Economic Community (EEC) and a European Atomic Energy Community (Euratom). It is the EEC agreement which has become known as the Treaty of Rome and has influenced the history of Europe ever since.

THE TREATY OF ROME

The purpose of the treaty was set out in the preamble: 'to lay the foundations of an ever closer union among the European peoples' – a phrase which was carefully left undefined. The treaty provided for the gradual abolition of all customs duties and other trade barriers between the member states, and the introduction of a common external tariff on imports from other countries. There was to be free circulation of goods, services, capital and persons within the EEC; and social welfare policies were to be harmonized so as to prevent unfair competition. On the insistence of France, the signatories undertook to introduce a Common Agricultural Policy (CAP), whose objectives were to be: to improve the productivity of agriculture; to secure a fair standard of living for the agricultural community; to stabilize markets; to secure the availability of food supplies; and to secure reasonable food prices for consumers. The details of this policy were left to be worked out in the future. The Community was to have power to conclude treaties on matters over which the EEC exercised control; for example, the EEC would act as a

11   The signing of the treaty establishing the European Economic Community, Rome, 25 March 1957 © Bettmann/Corbis

whole in negotiations with the GATT organization (the General Agreement on Tariffs and Trade).

Following the precedent of the ECSC, the treaty established four Community institutions: a Council of Ministers, to decide on policy; a Commission, to carry out decisions made by the Council and also to make proposals for legislation; an Assembly, for purposes of consultation only, made up of delegates nominated by the various parliaments of the member states; and a Court of Justice, to interpret the terms of the treaty and rule on disputes between member states. The Council of Ministers was essentially an intergovernmental body, making the EEC less supranational in character than the ECSC. But in the course of time the Commission and the Court of Justice assumed growing importance. The Commission proposed policies and legislation, taking the initiative in devising the Common Agricultural Policy, and in developing the far-reaching concept of harmonization of social policies, which encroached increasingly upon the domestic affairs of member states. As for the Court of Justice, test cases in 1962 and 1964 established that, in the event of a conflict between EEC law and national law, the former should prevail, leading to a far-reaching transfer of authority from individual states to the EEC.[14]

Certain features stood out in the Treaty of Rome: the common external tariff; the proposed Common Agricultural Policy; the harmonization of social policies; and the establishment of permanent institutions, including a court whose rulings prevailed over national law. In these ways the EEC became more than a customs union or common market, because its institutions had some of the powers of a state; yet it was less than a state, because those powers were limited. The result was a polity of a type not previously known. What it would become in the future no one knew.

DIVISION AND THE COLLAPSE OF EMPIRE

The signatories of the Treaty of Rome aspired to ever closer union among the European peoples, but in fact the immediate consequence of the establishment of the EEC was the further division of Europe. Britain was at that stage opposed to the EEC, and in late 1956 tried to undermine the whole project by proposing a free trade area which would comprise all 16 European members of the Organization for European Economic Cooperation. This proposal for a simple free trade area would exclude a common external tariff; would apply only to industrial products, not to agriculture; and there was to be no supranational element, but only cooperation between governments. The British proposal thus cut out all the elements which the creators of the EEC thought vital. If carried through, it would have dissolved the EEC in a free trade area 'like a lump of sugar in an English cup of tea', as one of its opponents observed.[15] In particular, it would have removed the key elements which safeguarded French interests: the common external tariff and the Common Agricultural Policy. After long negotiations, France (by this time under the leadership of General de Gaulle) declared on 6 November 1958 that the British proposals were unacceptable, a position rapidly endorsed by the other five members of the EEC.

The British were left with the remnants of their proposal, which emerged as a free trade area confined to west European countries other than the Six. The European Free Trade Association (EFTA) was established by the Treaty of Stockholm (4 January 1960), with seven members: Austria, Britain, Denmark, Norway, Portugal, Sweden and Switzerland. The treaty was a simple affair, providing for the progressive reduction of customs duties on trade between the member states in industrial goods, but not in agricultural products or fish. It established no institutions, except a small secretariat in Geneva, and laid down that all decisions required the unanimous agreement of all the member states. It achieved its modest aim of free trade in industrial goods between its members by 1967.

The result was further division within western Europe, which by 1960 comprised three distinct (though sometimes overlapping) groups. First, there was an Atlantic Europe, working closely with the USA, with the Organization for European Economic Cooperation as its economic basis and NATO as its military backbone. Second, there was the EEC, which despite its narrow basis of only six states laid claim to a far-reaching European vocation. Third, there was EFTA, a group of mostly small countries which existed largely in order to be a rival to the EEC.

This did not complete the tale of disunity in western Europe. Two countries stood in isolation, though for very different reasons. Switzerland was one of the most respectable of European countries; Spain under Franco was an outcast.

Switzerland was a country without a common language or religion. In 1962, 74 per cent of the Swiss spoke German, 21 per cent French, 4 per cent Italian, and 1 per cent Romansch; Catholics and Protestants were not far from equality in numbers, at 48 and 44 per cent, respectively. It had little geographical unity, and almost no natural resources, except its mountains and lakes; and its prosperity was achieved by specialized industries, banking and tourism. As a Swiss historian observed wryly, no one would set out to establish a state on such a basis – it was 'contrary to common sense'.[16] In fact, the country was deeply rooted in history and tradition, and worked admirably. There was a long-established balance of power between the communes, the cantons and the Confederation, and all important decisions were taken by a referendum of all citizens. Compulsory military service gave the army a vital role in national consciousness, contributing to a sense of identity which prevailed over differences of language, religion and geography. Some critics found Switzerland dull and the Swiss self-satisfied; but after all they had much to be satisfied about. They had produced a multilingual country, based on local autonomy and respect for the wishes of its own people.[17] The Swiss felt little need of international organizations. They accepted Marshall aid, but joined neither NATO nor the EEC; they only joined the Council of Europe, which committed them to little, as late as 1963. Switzerland stood alone, and was so distinctive as to be an almost impossible model for others to follow.

Spain was very different. Franco's dictatorship was regarded as a survival of Hitler's Europe and treated as an outlaw. In the winter of 1944–45 French Resistance groups, inspired by Spanish exiles who had fought alongside them against the Germans, talked of carrying the war across the Pyrenees to liberate Spain. The Allied powers drew the line at this and settled instead for ostracism. They withdrew their ambassadors from Madrid, putting Spain into diplomatic isolation. Spain was excluded from the United Nations, from Marshall aid and from the North Atlantic Treaty; the United Nations imposed economic sanctions on Spain in 1946. This treatment was far more severe than that extended to Salazar's dictatorial regime in Portugal, which received Marshall aid and became a founder member of NATO, despite its lack of democratic credentials. The difference arose from the intense emotional and political impact of the Spanish Civil War, which was still a vivid memory in the late 1940s, and also from the degree to which Franco had favoured the Axis side during the Second World War, when Portugal had contrived to be more even-handed, and had (under pressure) allowed the Allies to use bases in the Azores. Spain only began to emerge from its isolation in 1953, when the United Nations lifted sanctions and the USA established military bases in the country in return for economic aid. Even so, west European countries, closer to the scene than the USA and more deeply moved by recent history, kept Spain at arm's length – some people would not visit the country, even when it became a tourist centre, as long as Franco remained in power.

There was another transformation in the situation of western Europe at this time: decolonization and the end of empire. In the age of imperialism European states had controlled large parts of Asia and almost the whole of Africa. In the two decades following the end of the Second World War that domination came to an end.

The British began their retreat early, leaving India in 1947 – the biggest single break with the imperial past, achieved with remarkable speed, but at immense cost in lives when the country was partitioned between India and Pakistan. In Palestine the British found themselves unable to cope with the double enmity of Zionists and Arab nationalists, and left in 1948, leaving war and chaos behind. In the late 1950s and early 1960s British governments hastened to grant independence to colonies in Africa: Ghana in 1957, Nigeria in 1960, Sierra Leone and Tanganyika in 1961, Kenya and Zanzibar in 1963, and Malawi and Zambia in 1964. (Southern Rhodesia, later Zimbabwe, remained a difficult problem for many years to come.) In Malaya, the British fought a successful war against communist insurgents and granted independence in 1957 on terms advantageous to themselves. It was an extraordinarily rapid end to the largest of the European empires, and the British congratulated themselves that in the main they had achieved an orderly transfer of power; though in fact there were disasters in India and Palestine, and constitutional governments in Africa proved short-lived. Britain also contrived to preserve the Commonwealth (which in 1945 comprised only Australia, Canada, New Zealand and South Africa). India set a vital example by joining the Commonwealth as a Republic in 1950, and it then became customary for former colonies to join the Commonwealth when they attained independence. The result was an amorphous but tenacious body, which did much to ease the transition from empire and retained a powerful attraction for sections of British opinion for many years.

By contrast, the French made an immense effort to hold on to their empire. In Indochina they fought a long war, ending in 1954 with a crushing defeat at Dien Bien Phu, one of the decisive battles of modern history, demonstrating to all the world that a European army could be defeated in a pitched battle. In North Africa, the French abandoned their protectorates in Morocco and Tunisia in 1954–56, in a reasonably orderly fashion, but faced an insuperable problem in Algeria. The French occupation of the country went back to 1830; in French law the three departments of Algeria formed part of France; and the country was home to a European population of about a million, mostly settled there for generations. Successive French governments proclaimed that they would on no account give up what was a part of France, and backed up their words with force. In a war lasting eight years (1954–62) the French engaged vast numbers of troops (400,000 at the end of 1956) and won individual battles (for example, an assault on the Algerian quarter of the city of Algiers in 1957), but they could not win the war. The political stresses of the conflict brought down the Fourth Republic in 1958. General de Gaulle returned to power and eventually brought the war to an end, by what amounted to a French surrender in 1962. Algeria became independent and at once expelled about a million Europeans, who were offered a stark choice between the suitcase and the coffin. They packed their suitcases and moved to France, where they were absorbed with a degree of success which has been largely forgotten, but deserves to be remembered.

De Gaulle also moved swiftly to anticipate nationalist movements in French colonies in black Africa. Guinea became independent in 1958, followed in 1960 by no fewer than 13 countries: Cameroon, the Central African Republic, Chad, Dahomey, Gabon, Ivory Coast, Madagascar, Mali, Mauritania, Niger, Senegal, Togo and Upper Volta. The transition was achieved smoothly and most of the new states signed treaties with France, received French economic aid, retained cultural and linguistic ties with France, and in some cases allowed French troops to remain in the country.

Of the lesser European colonial powers, the Dutch fought for four years to retain at least a part of their control over the East Indies. Finally, wearying of a war they could not win and under heavy pressure from the USA (then in its anticolonialist mode), the Dutch accepted the independence of Indonesia at the end of 1949. Belgium, holding a vast colonial territory in the Belgian Congo, made almost no preparations for a transfer of power until 1960, and then suddenly granted independence to a bewildered country in six months. Almost at once the new state collapsed into chaos. Two of its wealthiest provinces seceded; military coups followed one after another; the United Nations intervened with little success. It was one of the most disastrous episodes of decolonization in Africa; yet it appeared to do Belgium little harm, even in terms of prestige. Finally, Portugal, the weakest among the European colonial powers in economic and military terms, managed to retain its African colonies (Angola and Mozambique) longer than any of the others, until 1975, mostly by an act of will. Under the dictatorship of Salazar, Portugal was determined to remain a colonial power, and succeeded in doing so.

This transformation came about partly as a result of a change in the military balance. In the nineteenth and early twentieth centuries, European armies, even when small in number, had been almost constantly victorious – exceptions like the British defeat at Isandlwhana and the Italian debacle at Adowa stood out just because they were so rare. After 1945 this position was reversed. Even large European armies failed to win colonial wars – the French in Indochina and Algeria, the British in Cyprus and Kenya. For these military failures there were military causes. Asian and African forces were better led and better equipped than before, and sometimes received crucial aid from other countries – it was Chinese heavy artillery that crushed the French at Dien Bien Phu. But deeper forces were also at work. The nationalist leaders after 1945 were a new breed, very different in motivation and will power from the Indian princes or African rulers of earlier times. Some were communists, imbued with the discipline and certainty of their faith. The Europeans, on the contrary, had largely lost their imperial certainties. Opposition to imperialism, mainly on the left, had increased in the early part of the twentieth century, and became predominant after 1945 as a left-wing political consensus took shape over most of western Europe. (It is striking that Portugal, under a right-wing dictatorship, held on to its colonies longest.) Colonial wars exacted a cost in political division and bitterness which became impossible to sustain. Moreover, in the nineteenth century imperialism had been practised and supported by every significant power in the world – even the USA became an openly imperial power during the war against Spain in 1898. After the Second World War this changed utterly. The two greatest powers in the world, the USA and the Soviet Union, proclaimed themselves to be anticolonialist, even though in practice each maintained an empire. The United Nations Organization, within a few years of its creation, began to throw its psychological and propaganda weight against colonialism. By 1960 the UN included a majority of former colonies and anticolonial states of the Soviet bloc. That year, the Soviet Union sponsored a resolution in the General Assembly, declaring that 'All peoples have the right of self-determination', and that inadequate political or economic preparation must not serve as a pretext to delay independence. This resolution was passed *without a single contrary vote*, and with only nine abstentions, demonstrating the moral authority of the new consensus; though an attempt to fix the very next year, 1961, as the latest date for universal independence was defeated.[18]

Colonial wars thus proved expensive to wage, difficult to win, divisive at home and abhorrent to world opinion. It is not surprising that most of the imperial powers gave up sooner rather than later. This shared experience brought some of them together. France, Belgium and the Netherlands threw themselves into their new European venture as a substitute for empire. Belgium, at the same time that it was failing utterly to prepare the Congo for independence, was playing a leading part in setting up the EEC. France managed to preserve links between its old empire and the new Europe by insisting on an advantageous form of association with the EEC for its former African colonies, in the Yaoundé Convention of 1963. Britain followed a different course, finding its own substitute for empire in the Commonwealth, which exerted a strong and persistent attraction in opposition to the EEC. So the common experience of decolonization produced a new cause of division, taking Britain in one direction and the members of the Six in another.

Only once did Britain and France combine to try to check their imperial decline and launch a counter-attack against their nationalist enemies, in the Suez expedition of November 1956. At that time, Britain and France had a common enemy in Egypt. The British felt that Colonel Nasser, the ruler of Egypt, was the spider at the centre of a web of intrigue against them in the Middle East. The French thought they could win the war in Algeria by cutting off the aid which Egypt was providing for the rebels. In 1956 Nasser threw down a new challenge to both countries by nationalizing the Suez Canal Company and taking control of the canal. Together the British and French governments planned a military attack to occupy the Canal Zone and overthrow Nasser. Israel was brought into the operation, in an elaborate scheme by which Israeli forces would occupy the Sinai peninsula and Britain and France would seize the Canal Zone, ostensibly to protect it from attack by both Israel and Egypt. The Israeli attack went ahead on 29 October, and British and French forces captured Port Said and a stretch of the Canal on 5–6 November. Their success was short-lived. The superpowers intervened at once. The Soviet Union threatened Britain and France with rocket attacks. The USA refused to provide a loan to Britain, to save the exchange value of the pound and protect the British gold and dollar reserves, unless the British and French halted their attack immediately. There was vocal opposition from developing countries, notably from the Indian Prime Minister Pandit Nehru, whose prestige at the time was high. The British government (though not the French) was also in difficulty from domestic opposition. The British yielded to these pressures and accepted a ceasefire, leaving the French with no choice but to follow them. The two countries withdrew their forces from Egypt before the end of the year.

The two strongest imperial powers of western Europe, Britain and France, were thus defeated by a combination of pressure from the superpowers, opposition from the Third World and (in Britain's case) a divided public opinion. Instead of reasserting their strength, they had exposed their weakness. The two countries drew opposite conclusions from the Suez episode. The British government concluded that it must restore good relations with the USA and never again act against American wishes in any great matter – a policy which was followed by all succeeding governments for the rest of the century. The French, on the contrary, blamed the Americans for their failure at Suez, and concluded that their future lay in building an integrated western Europe. It so happened that on 6 November 1956, at the very time when the French premier, Guy Mollet, was constrained to agree to a ceasefire in Egypt, he was in conference with Chancellor Adenauer of West Germany on matters relating to the proposed European Economic Community. 'Europe will be your revenge', said Adenauer.[19] It was a symbolic moment. 'Europe' provided a new vision to replace the imperial mission of France, and offered a way for France to counterbalance the weight of the superpowers in the world. So the Suez operation, which began as a show of Franco–British unity, ended with the two countries drawing widely different conclusions from the failure of their joint venture, and confirming the existing opposition between them on the future of western Europe. By the start of the 1960s, the European imperial powers no longer ruled the world. If anyone did, it was the USA, under some challenge from the Soviet Union.

Western Europe shared several common characteristics between 1945 and 1961. The economic and military influence of the USA was all-pervading. Almost every country enjoyed economic growth and a wide-ranging welfare state. The imperial states lost their empires. But there was much to divide them. Spain and Portugal were governed by dictatorships, left over from the 1930s and at odds with the parliamentary democracies of other states. Britain remained semi-detached from continental Europe, looking outwards towards the Commonwealth and the USA and opposed to the movement for European integration. Even those who aspired towards a United States of Europe had only achieved by 1961 a European Economic Community of six countries; and a movement which was intended to unite Europe had so far acted as a divisive force even within western Europe. Western Europe had much to hold it together, but was far from being a cohesive whole. But whatever its divisions, it had one characteristic which no one would dispute: it was not eastern Europe.

10

EASTERN EUROPE, 1945-1961

THE SOVIET ZONE

In the period after the Second World War the Soviet Union stood largely alone, outside Europe except in a geographical sense, in what Pieter Geyl described as 'an attitude of bitter and dogmatic aloofness'.[1] The Soviet Union cut itself off from the rest of eastern Europe as well as from the West. It is not sufficiently recognized or emphasized that there were two Iron Curtains, not one. Because the Soviet government tried to shut off its peoples from outside contact, even with other communist countries, the western frontier of the Soviet Union was in some respects more impassable than the borderline which divided East from West in Germany.[2] Yet at the same time the Soviet Union also dominated a large part of eastern Europe, imposing its own order and pattern upon it, and dividing it apparently fatally and finally from western Europe.

The Soviet zone in eastern Europe eventually comprised Poland, Romania, Bulgaria, Hungary, Czechoslovakia and the German Democratic Republic (East Germany). Within this group, countries reached the same destination – communist rule – by different routes and at different speeds. In Poland, Stalin always insisted on a 'friendly' government, which meant one run by communists who were themselves controlled by the Soviet Union. The crucial factor in bringing this about was the presence of Soviet troops – Wladyslaw Gomulka, an independent-minded Polish communist leader, told the Central Committee of the Party in May 1945 that without the Red Army the communists could not have defeated 'the reactionaries'.[3] Even so, members of non-communist parties (notably Mikolajczyk, the leader of the Peasant Party and the last premier of the wartime government in exile) remained as ministers until January 1947, when the communist-dominated Democratic Bloc won a rigged election with 80 per cent of the vote. An interim communist constitution was introduced in February 1947, and a permanent constitution in July 1952.

In Romania, a National Democratic Front controlled by the communists won an election with an 80 per cent majority in November 1946, and a communist constitution was introduced in April 1948. In Bulgaria, the Communist Party and its allies formed a Fatherland Front bloc, and won an election (against a real opposition) in October 1946. A new constitution was then established in December 1946; and in 1949 the Fatherland Front won 99.8 per cent of the votes cast in an election. Hungary was a different matter. Elections in November 1945 resulted in a 57 per cent vote (2.7 million) for the Smallholders Party, and only 17 per cent (800,000) for the communists. In the subsequent coalition government the communists took over the Ministry of the Interior, and with it control of the police, and pursued 'salami tactics', cutting away their opponents slice by slice. At another election in 1947 the communists emerged as the largest single party, with just over 1 million votes; but 2 million votes still went to the Smallholders, Social Democrats and National Peasants. In 1948 the Social Democrats were compelled to merge with the Communist Party in a unified People's Front. In an election in May 1949 only candidates from the People's Front were allowed to stand, and they gained nearly 96 per cent of the vote. It was a great change from the 17 per cent of 1945, achieved by stages.[4]

Czechoslovakia was different again. There were no Soviet troops stationed in the country. There was a strong tradition of parliamentary democracy dating from the period between the wars. The president, Eduard Beneš, was determined to follow a pro-Soviet foreign policy, and at the same time to establish his country as a political bridge between the Soviet Union and the West. In 1945 the communists had taken a prominent part in resistance against the Germans in the last stages of the war, and joined a coalition government. In an election in May 1946 the Communist Party won 38 per cent of the vote and emerged as the largest single party, with 2.7 million votes and 114 seats in a chamber of 300. The communist leader, Klement Gottwald, became prime minister in a genuine coalition government, with Jan Masaryk (the son of the founder of Czechoslovakia and a figure respected throughout the Western world) as foreign minister. The country was still so open towards the West that in 1947 the government (including the communist members) was prepared to accept Marshall aid, but the Soviet Union stepped in and forbade it. This marked a significant shift towards Soviet control – Masaryk said that he went to Moscow as foreign minister of an independent state, but returned as 'a lackey of the Soviet Government'.[5] In February 1948 the communists took over the government, in what was not strictly a *coup d'état*, because the constitutional forms were observed. The non-communist ministers played into their hands, by resigning in the hope of forcing Beneš to form a new government without the communists. Beneš himself was still convinced of Soviet moderation, and observed the constitutional rules which allowed Gottwald to form a new government. Even so, the takeover was decisive. After the change of government, Jan Masaryk's dead body was found beneath a window in the Foreign Ministry building. Whether he was murdered or committed suicide was uncertain, but either way it was an ominous event. If he was murdered, it showed that the communists would stop at nothing; if he had committed suicide, it showed that he had despaired of his country. In May 1948 elections were held at which only a single list of National Front (that is, communist-dominated) candidates were allowed to stand. Some 6.4 million voted for the National Front; almost 1 million contrived to vote against. In June a new constitution was introduced; and in 1954 a new electoral law allowed only one candidate to stand for each constituency.[6]

In East Germany, which in 1945 was simply the Soviet-occupied zone in Germany, the Communist and Social Democratic Parties were merged under Soviet pressure into a single Socialist Unity Party in 1946. After the Berlin blockade and the formation of the Federal Republic in West Germany, the German Democratic Republic was established in the East, with Otto Grotewohl as communist prime minister and a new constitution on the communist model.

These six countries settled down as the Soviet zone in eastern Europe, displaying common characteristics which we will examine later. Meanwhile, two other countries in south-eastern Europe became communist without falling under Soviet domination: Yugoslavia and Albania.

YUGOSLAVIA AND ALBANIA

In Yugoslavia, Tito's communist Partisans had liberated much of the country by their own efforts, with some help from the British and later from the Soviets. Tito's post-war government was thus communist, but independent-minded, and set about its own programme of nationalization of industry, land reform in the distribution of farms to peasants and ex-soldiers and a start on agricultural cooperatives, and then in April 1947 a Yugoslavian five-year plan. In 1947 Tito also took a number of initiatives in foreign policy, proposing a plan for a Yugoslav–Albanian federation, sending help to the Greek communists in their rebellion against the government, and visiting neighbouring countries to expound the Yugoslav line in politics. In Albania, a Communist Party had been founded only recently (in 1941), but its leader, Enver Hoxha, formed a government in 1945, and organized elections in which only the communist Democratic Front was allowed to put forward candidates, who won 93 per cent of the vote. A communist constitution was introduced as early as March 1946. Hoxha was to remain in control for a remarkable 41 years, pursuing a highly individual course; but at this early stage Albania was largely under the influence of Yugoslavia, its powerful communist neighbour.

It was in Yugoslavia that a serious breach among the communist countries began. In September 1947 Stalin set up the Communist Information Bureau (Cominform), comprising the Communist Parties of the Soviet Union, the east European countries, and France and Italy in the west, to secure ideological conformity under Soviet control. The headquarters of the new organization was established in Belgrade, as a sign of confidence in the Yugoslav Communist Party; though there was no doubt that Stalin and the Soviet Communist Party were to be in charge. In the event, as we have seen, Tito was already striking out along his own paths, at home and in foreign policy. In August 1947, just before the founding of Cominform, he had concluded a treaty with Bulgaria without consulting Stalin first; and at the end of 1947 he negotiated a customs union between Yugoslavia, Albania, Bulgaria and Romania, which might have been the start of a Balkan federation. At the start of 1948 Stalin decided to restore order and assert his authority. In February he summoned Yugoslav and Bulgarian delegations to Moscow and instructed them not to take any foreign policy initiatives without his permission. If there were to be a Balkan federation, it must be under his control. He accused the Yugoslav Communist Party of deviations from Marxism-Leninism, of exaggerating the importance of guerrilla warfare during the Second World War and of hostility towards the Soviet Union. The Yugoslavs accepted some of these criticisms, but stuck to what they regarded as their own achievements in liberating their country and bringing about their own revolution. In June 1948 Stalin ordered the expulsion of the Yugoslav Party from the Cominform (though putting up the Romanian leader Gheorghiu-Dej to denounce Tito at the Cominform conference which carried out the order). The Soviet Union cut off economic assistance to Yugoslavia and directed a propaganda barrage against Tito, who was accused among other things of being a fascist hireling of the USA.

Yet Tito survived. Stalin prepared a military attack, but did not launch it. Yugoslavia embarked in 1949 on its own road to socialism, introducing workers' councils and self-management in industry in place of Soviet-style central control. Tito also pursued a particularly severe form of collectivization of agriculture, to show that he took his socialism seriously, even to the point of provoking risings in the countryside. He also accepted American economic assistance, without compromising his communism; though he did give up his aid to the Greek communists. Yugoslavia lived through the anathemas and the economic sanctions and lived to tell the tale as an independent communist state outside the Soviet zone.

The breach with Tito led to drastic purges in communist parties throughout the Soviet zone, ordered by Moscow and sometimes directly carried out in detail by Soviet agents. Nothing demonstrated more clearly, and indeed horrifically, the separation between eastern and western Europe than the communist show trials and purges of 1949–53. A different world was put on display. At first, the hunt was for associates of Tito, but the net spread to all who had acted independently, in the Spanish Civil War or in resistance movements, even if they were loyal and devoted communists. In 1949 Stalin turned against Jews and Zionists, and a further range of accusations was opened. Even a brief roll-call will bring the nature of these events back to mind.

The purges began in Albania in 1949, where Koci Xoxe was dismissed as minister of the interior and then put on trial as a supporter of close relations with Tito; he was executed in June. In Bulgaria, Traicho Kostov, a prominent communist and member of the government, was arrested early in 1949 and put on trial in December. At his trial, which was being broadcast, he retracted a part of his confession and denied having contacts with Tito and the British during the Second World War. He was executed on 16 December. In Hungary Laszlo Rajk, a long-serving communist and at one stage minister of the interior, was put on trial in September 1949, on charges of treachery to the communists in Spain during the Civil War, acting as an informer for Horthy's government in Hungary, spying for the Americans and collaborating with Tito. He admitted his guilt and was executed – along with others – on 15 October. In Czechoslovakia, Rudolf Slansky, the general secretary of the Communist Party, was arrested in November 1951 and tried with others in November 1952 on charges of being 'Trotskyist-Zionist-Titoist-bourgeois-nationalist traitors, spies and saboteurs, enemies of the Czechoslovak nation, of its people's democratic order, and of socialism' – the full panoply of the accusation is worth setting out.[7] All confessed, and Slansky and ten others were executed. In other countries the purges were markedly less severe. In Poland, Gomulka was denounced as a right-wing deviationist and arrested, but escaped with his life, and there were no show trials. In Romania, three prominent communists (Luca, Georgescu and Anna Pauker) were executed. In East Germany, purges did not begin until 1950, and were comparatively mild – some were directed against communist officials who had been in Spain during the Civil War. All the prominent communists who were brought to trial confessed their guilt, and some even professed to welcome their own execution. It was a throwback to the Soviet show trials of the 1930s. Everywhere the purge of the communist leadership was only a part of a much wider purge of rank-and-file party members – in Poland, membership fell by about a quarter between 1948 and 1952. There were also wide-ranging 'social purges', with arrests reaching into the hundreds of thousands in order to strike terror into the population at large; as well as trials of non-communists – Cardinal Mindszenty in Hungary, and evangelical clergymen in Bulgaria.[8]

The establishment of complete communist rule and Soviet domination came at different speeds and by different routes in the various countries of the Soviet zone. (Yugoslavia and Albania established communist regimes, but escaped from the Soviet zone.) It has been rightly pointed out that these countries remained diverse in nature, and were not 'Soviet clones'.[9] But there remained a pattern of Soviet domination, in the threefold form of ideological conformity, economic organization and force.

SOVIET IDEOLOGY AND ORGANIZATION

Ideology was for public purposes the cement of the whole structure. At the end of the Second World War communism was an attractive creed. The Soviet Union enjoyed the prestige conferred by victory over Nazi Germany, which had been won by the regime as well as by force – it was, after all, the *Red Army* that had fought its way into Berlin in 1945. In almost every country there were communists of the old guard who had survived Nazi persecution, and sometimes even Soviet prison camps, with their faith intact; and these veterans were now reinforced by a younger generation which welcomed communism as a change from the old order, whether that was a parliamentary democracy or one of the right-wing dictatorships which had flourished in eastern Europe in the 1930s and early 1940s. It is worth remembering in simple terms that 'some people believed in Stalinism' – and in Stalin.[10] There was much support for communism among intellectuals, sometimes out of genuine Marxist conviction and sometimes out of self-interest, or indeed both at once. Soviet culture became the model to follow, sometimes in ways whose very absurdity attests to their significance – for example, the Union of Czech and Slovak composers solemnly embarked in 1948 on a musical five-year plan; and Romanian experts in linguistics set out to prove that their language, though apparently Romance in character, was in fact Slavonic.[11] All forms of association, whether cultural, sports, youth or other matters, came under political control; and many forms of social organization were disbanded. In Hungary, where there had been an estimated 13–14,000 clubs and associations in the 1930s, there were only about a thousand in 1950.[12] History was rewritten to conform to the new circumstances, as in the striking example of the massacre of Polish officers at Katyn. In fact, this massacre was carried out by the NKVD in April 1940, but the responsibility was transferred by the Soviet government, propaganda and historical writing to the Germans when they invaded the USSR in 1941. The history of this episode assumed a symbolic importance, so that when the Polish government (though still communist) finally asserted the truth about Katyn in public in March 1989 it was in effect a declaration of independence. For many communists, ideological conformity sprang from conviction; but as we have seen, Stalin and the Soviet Union imposed it at will by purges, show trials and executions. In the long run, this was largely counterproductive. By the end of the purges of 1948–53, faith and idealism had been replaced by fear, which was doubtless effective, but was a very different cement for society.

The economic uniformity of the Soviet zone began out of necessity at the end of the Second World War, when over much of eastern Europe the Soviet Union was the only source of supplies and the only market for such exports as could be produced – for example, coal from Poland. In the following years the Soviet Union systematically established its economic control. The Council for Mutual Economic Assistance (COMECON) was founded in January 1949 as the opposite number to the OECD in western Europe, and operated in its early years very much in favour of the Soviet Union.[13] COMECON currencies were not convertible outside the area, and the east European states found it difficult to obtain hard currency; even the so-called 'transferable rouble' used by COMECON countries was in fact *not* convertible, and its nominal exchange rate with the US dollar was fictional. The foreign trade of the countries of the Soviet zone, both exports and imports, was carried on very largely with the USSR and on Soviet terms. In the 1950s and 1960s the balance of advantage was substantially on the Soviet side; though the situation was to change in the 1970s, when Soviet prices (notably for oil) as fixed by COMECON became favourable for the countries of eastern Europe.[14]

The main elements of the Soviet economic system were adopted by the states of the Soviet zone, with some limited degree of flexibility, but with no option as to the total pattern. Foreign trade was a state monopoly, with all external payments controlled by the government; this was imposed at varying dates between 1948 and 1952. The economy was centrally controlled through State Planning Commissions, which were set up in Bulgaria in 1947, Romania in 1948, Czechoslovakia, Hungary and Poland in 1949, and East Germany in 1950. Industry and services were nationalized at dates between 1947 and 1949, except in East Germany, where it came about much later. Agriculture was collectivized, beginning in 1948 (in East Germany it did not start until 1952); but it was carried out in different ways, and in Poland it was never completed.[15] In these centralized command economies priority was given, following the Soviet model set in the 1930s, to rapid industrialization, and especially to the development of heavy industry. This was a political as well as an economic choice, because it was expected that industrial workers would automatically become communist supporters. This proved to be an error, on two counts: economically, the growth areas in the future proved to be in light industry, services and administration; while politically, many industrial workers turned against communism, as they were to do in Poland, where resistance to communist rule arose in the 1980s in the shipyards at Gdansk.

This regime produced substantial economic growth, though from a desperately low base at the end of the war, which made figures for percentage growth misleadingly impressive; moreover all official production figures were unreliable, because officials had to show that norms were being met and plans fulfilled. For what it is worth, it has been estimated that domestic output in the USSR and the east European states taken together grew at an average rate of 7 per cent per year between 1950 and 1970.[16] These gains were made at a high cost. The whole system emphasized quantity rather than quality, and also the production of only a limited range of goods – quantity rather than variety. When prices were fixed centrally there was no attention to cost-effectiveness in any particular factory or operation, and the whole system of centralized planning led to waste and corruption. Investment for the future took priority over making products available for purchase, so that economic growth was not translated into goods in the shops. Constant shortages were virtually built into the system, and the consumer boom which took place in western Europe in the 1950s had no parallel in the East.

Ideological conformity and economic organization were important elements in the Soviet zone; but behind them lay the ultimate weight of force. Soviet troops were stationed in large numbers in Poland, Hungary and East Germany from 1945 to the early 1990s, and in Romania from 1945 to 1958. Czechoslovakia had no Soviet garrison until 1968, but was almost surrounded by countries that did, and had a frontier with the USSR which Soviet troops could cross at will. This military presence was not usually the most prominent feature of the Soviet system, but in the last resort it was the most important. In the period between 1945 and 1961, Soviet control was threatened in East Germany in 1953 and Hungary in 1956. The troops and tanks moved in and order was restored. The same thing was to happen again in Czechoslovakia in 1968. But in 1989, under Gorbachev's leadership, the Soviet government refused to use force to sustain communist regimes. The troops remained in their barracks and the tanks stayed off the streets, and the whole system collapsed. When the chips were down, it rested on force.

THE FOUNDATIONS ARE SHAKEN

That collapse lay well in the future. But even in 1953 a new era began in the Soviet Union and its zone in eastern Europe. Stalin died in March 1953, lamented by communists and their sympathizers throughout Europe, and revealing a curious unity in emotion across the continent, mainly though not solely on the left in politics. There followed a series of shocks to the Soviet system: a revolt in the German Democratic Republic in 1953; a speech by Khrushchev denouncing some elements of Stalinism in 1956; a rising in Hungary in 1956 which almost became a revolution; and a crisis in East Germany in 1961 which ended with the building of the Berlin Wall. These events shook the Soviet zone in eastern Europe, but ended by confirming its separation from the West.

In 1953 there occurred a brief but portentous set of events in the German Democratic Republic. In May the East German communist leader, Walter Ulbricht, announced that 'production norms' for workers were to be increased by 10 per cent at the end of June, without any increase in wages; at the same time there were to be price increases for a number of goods. This at once aroused serious opposition, which in turn caused concern in Moscow. The Soviet leaders, still feeling their way after Stalin's death, were divided as to what to do. Beria, supported by Malenkov, was prepared to abandon socialism in the GDR, arguing that for the security of the Soviet Union it would be enough for East Germany to be simply a 'peaceful country' – and this despite Beria's well-founded reputation as a ruthless head of the secret police. Molotov, the foreign minister, disagreed completely, arguing that to abandon socialism in East Germany would undermine the communist cause all over Europe, and would eventually lead other east European states to defect to the West and to capitalism – which was very much what was to happen, though in different circumstances, in 1989. Khrushchev supported Molotov, and Beria gave way. The Soviet government would maintain socialism in East Germany. But the Soviets also intervened to compel the East German government to make a number of concessions – to allow the manufacture of more consumer goods, to allow ration cards to those who had been deprived of them and generally to improve living standards in the future. What they did not do was to change the new production norms, which remained in effect, according to an announcement in the press on 16 June. Construction workers in East Berlin went on strike on 16 June, and on 17 June there occurred the astonishing event of widespread strikes and demonstrations by workers against a communist government. Beria was sent from Moscow to deal with a crisis which he had sought to avoid. Soviet tanks and troops came out on the streets of East Berlin and other towns during the afternoon of 17 June, and order was restored by the evening. This was the first open use of force by the Soviet Union to sustain a communist government in eastern Europe. According to official East German figures, 21 demonstrators were killed; the true figure was certainly higher. There were large numbers of arrests, followed by some death sentences and long terms of imprisonment. The next year the East German government made a number of economic concessions, and the Soviets put an end to reparation payments and cancelled other East German debts. The East German economy gradually improved, and the state itself (a very recent creation) began to settle down. The crisis passed, and this first crack in the communist structure in eastern Europe was repaired. The possibility (though only a slender one) that East Germany might have slipped out of the Soviet system, and so changed the division of Europe along the Iron Curtain, was firmly closed.

The foundations of Soviet authority were next shaken in Moscow itself. On 25 February 1956 the Twentieth Congress of the Communist Party of the Soviet Union met in secret session to hear an astonishing speech by Nikita Khrushchev, the general secretary of the Party – the post held by Stalin for so long, and from which he had ruled the Soviet Union with an iron hand. Khrushchev actually denounced Stalin's cult of personality – an unheard-of act of daring. He criticized the purges of the 1930s, though only to some degree, because he himself had been involved in them. He accused Stalin of endangering the country by failing to foresee the German attack in 1941. He extended an olive branch to Yugoslavia and opened the way for reconciliation with Tito; and in that context he crucially acknowledged that countries might take different roads to socialism. Shortly afterwards, in April 1956, he gave an earnest of his good intentions by dissolving the Cominform.

The first country to take up Khrushchev's proposition of different roads to socialism was Poland, under the leadership of Gomulka, who had survived his arrest and returned as first secretary of the Polish Communist Party. He took the bold step of dismissing the Soviet Marshal Rokossovsky, who had long held the key post of minister of defence in the Polish government, and so controlled the armed forces. In face of this, Khrushchev ostentatiously made preparations for military intervention in Poland, but then flew to Warsaw (19 October) and proposed a compromise. Gomulka was to retain his leadership and Khrushchev did not insist on the reinstatement of Rokossovsky. On the other side, Gomulka undertook to maintain the existing forms of socialism in Poland, and to reaffirm Polish membership of the Warsaw Pact, thus removing the danger of Polish neutrality. In effect, Khrushchev maintained the essentials of the Soviet position, notably on the Warsaw Pact; while yielding on Rokossovsky's dismissal and allowing Gomulka to keep his position. It was a compromise, but in the Soviets' favour.

Events in Poland were followed closely in Hungary, where the Soviet Union had recently intervened sharply in the country's internal affairs, leaving no doubt as to who was in charge. In 1955 the Soviets had dismissed Imre Nagy, who had a reputation as a reformer, as leader of the Hungarian Communist Party, and replaced him with Mátyás Rákosi, a strict Stalinist. Then in July 1956 they removed Rakosi, installing instead Ernö Gerö, who had long been an associate of Rakosi and was therefore simply an arbitrary replacement. A Hungarian road to socialism was not on offer, unless it ran through Moscow.

In October 1956, under the impulse of events in Poland, discontent grew in Hungary, led by intellectuals, students and some factory workers. A meeting at the Technological University in Budapest on 22 October produced a set of demands: the restoration of Imre Nagy as prime minister; the withdrawal of Soviet troops from Hungary; free elections and freedom of the press; and economic reform. They also made symbolic demands: the removal of the statue of Stalin which stood in the centre of Budapest; the restoration of Kossuth's coat of arms as a national emblem; and the laying of a wreath at the statue of a Polish general who had fought with Kossuth against the Russians in 1849 – striking invocations of history that illuminated the national character of the protest movement. On 23 October a mass of demonstrators marched to the statue of the Polish general and laid their wreath; many of them then went on to the statue of Stalin and tore it down.

The Soviet government responded to these events by moving troops into Budapest and sending in large reinforcements from outside Hungary. But they also agreed to the dismissal of Gerö and the appointment of Nagy as prime minister. This mixture of force and conciliation failed to work. There was heavy fighting in Budapest between insurgents and the Soviet forces; and Nagy urged the Soviet government to make more concessions. The Hungarian Army mostly went over to the side of the rebels, and soldiers got rid of their communist insignia. On 30 October Nagy announced the end of one-party rule, and appointed a member of the Smallholders' Party to his government. On 31 October he declared that Hungary would withdraw from the Warsaw Pact and assume a neutral status, on the model adopted by Austria in 1955.

These two steps proved fatal. It was highly unlikely that the Soviet government would have accepted the abandonment of single-party rule, which was the guiding principle of communism; and it was completely impossible for them to accept Hungarian neutrality and withdrawal from the Warsaw Pact, which threatened to break up the whole Soviet zone in eastern

12 Budapest, 1956: Soviet tanks knocked out in the streets - but they won in the end
© akg-images / Erich Lessing

Europe. On 31 October Soviet troops had withdrawn from Budapest; but during the night of 3–4 November they returned in overwhelming force, including some 6000 tanks. Despite this, the insurgents fought on in the capital and in the countryside for as long as ten days, and sporadic resistance went on until the end of November.

The intense drama and violence of these events was unlike anything seen in western Europe, and again emphasized the division of the continent. The passions which guided the insurgents were, as a leading scholar has highlighted, 'first and foremost national', at a time when nationalism was in decline in western Europe.[17] The Soviet Union re-established its domination of Hungary by force, and by so doing issued a warning to all the countries in the Soviet zone: the fundamental interests of communism and Soviet security would be defended. At the same time, the Americans did not intervene, and thus made it clear that they would not challenge Soviet predominance in eastern Europe except by words. As a one-time head of the CIA said later, 'President Eisenhower decided that it was tough on the Hungarians, but they weren't worth World War Three'.[18]

EAST AND WEST

The Soviets reasserted their control, and the Americans accepted it. Europe remained divided. Yet in the long run the effects of the Hungarian rising were corrosive. Soviet control in Hungary, and by extension in other east European countries, was shown to depend basically upon force. The element of attraction, and even idealism, which was strong in 1945, largely vanished in Hungary and diminished elsewhere. Something like 200,000 Hungarians left their country and took refuge in the West, bearing their own stories of the events. Among communist supporters in western Europe doubt began to spread. Many left the Party, and among some of those who remained the realization grew (though often with painful slowness) that the Workers' Fatherland was in fact a tyranny.

In eastern Europe, life settled down after the disturbances of 1956. Khrushchev made economic concessions to Poland, cancelling debts and providing grain on credit. Numbers of Soviet troops stationed in the country were reduced. In Hungary, the ruler imposed by the Soviets, János Kádár, gradually allowed a degree of flexibility in the regime, for example by giving extra scope for private plots in agriculture, and by diminishing the severity of the criminal code.

Even so, Khrushchev remained nervous about the stability of the Soviet zone. To remove one likely cause of trouble, he set out to squeeze the Western powers out of West Berlin. In November 1958 he deliberately initiated a Berlin crisis by challenging the Western powers' right of access to the city; but in a manner characteristic of his own waywardness he did not follow this through, and allowed a number of so-called deadlines to pass. By 1961 it was not the Western powers but the communist regime in East Germany that was under pressure. The population of the country was draining away to the West through the gap in the Iron Curtain provided by West Berlin. In 1960 nearly 200,000 people left East Germany, and in the first six months of 1961 more than 100,000 followed.[19] Many were young, or members of the professions – engineers or doctors. To stem this debilitating outflow, the East German leader Ulbricht asked Khrushchev for economic aid in food, hard currency or even gold. Failing this, Ulbricht proposed on 31 July 1961 the last clumsy resort of building a barrier to keep people in their own country. Khrushchev agreed, and action followed swiftly. Overnight, on 12/13 August 1961, East Berlin was cut off from West Berlin by barbed-wire barriers. Over the next few weeks these obstacles were replaced by a concrete wall with watchtowers, surrounding West Berlin and cutting it off from East Germany.

This was a self-inflicted wound to Soviet and East German prestige, because nothing could disguise the fact that the wall was built to imprison the East Germans in their own country. And yet the wall was at least in part a success. It ended the exodus to West Germany and stabilized the East German state, which began to strengthen its economy and improve its living standards, though not to the levels that characterized West Germany. The wall also allowed Khrushchev to give up his attempt to squeeze the Western powers out of Berlin, which was no longer necessary.

The barrier of the Berlin Wall set in concrete the division between the two parts of Berlin, and confirmed the division of Germany and Europe. The two parts of the continent were strikingly different. Western Europe was in the course of rapid economic growth; the East was managing only modest improvement. The West was enjoying political and personal liberty, veering towards licence; the East was subjected to dictatorship, purges and censorship. By 1961 the two were physically, materially and morally separated from one another by a great gulf which seemed destined to be permanent.

11

THE DEVELOPMENT OF WESTERN EUROPE, 1961–1989

THE ECONOMY

In the 1950s, western Europe was divided, to the point of being fragmented. The European Economic Community was at odds with the European Free Trade Area; Franco's Spain and Salazar's Portugal stood out as right-wing dictatorships against the parliamentary democracies in most of western Europe; and decolonization divided the former imperial powers. During the next three decades, of the 1960s, 1970s and 1980s, this situation changed markedly, and western Europe came together, as something like a coherent whole, displaying a clutch of similar characteristics across the half-continent. It was a striking development.

In economic affairs, the boom of the 1950s continued into the 1960s. Between 1961 and 1970, 12 countries right across western Europe (Belgium, Denmark, France, West Germany, Greece, Ireland, Italy, Luxembourg, the Netherlands, Portugal, Spain and the United Kingdom – which were to make up the EEC by 1986) showed an average growth rate in their GDP of 4.8 per cent per year, and an almost identical average growth rate in industrial production of 4.9 per cent per year.[1] Steadily rising prosperity had come to be taken for granted, after a boom which had lasted for some 20 years. But booms come to an end, and there were already signs that heavy industry (coal, iron and steel) was falling into decline. In the event, a perhaps unavoidable slackening in economic activity coincided with a sudden and unexpected blow from outside – the 'oil shock' at the end of 1973.

In the 1960s all the Western industrialized countries had grown accustomed to cheap oil as the main fuel used in their flourishing economies. Aircraft, diesel locomotives, oil-burning ships, the ever-growing production of plastics – all consumed vast quantities of oil. The private car using cheap petrol had become a commonplace of everyday life. At the beginning of October 1973 the price of oil stood at a mere three US dollars per barrel.

Then the long-standing Arab–Israeli dispute suddenly broke out into large-scale fighting in the Yom Kippur or October War (6–25 October 1973). During this conflict, the oil-producing Arab countries decided to use the oil weapon to strike against Israel's supporters. Six Persian Gulf states raised the price of their oil by stages to $11.65 by the end of December, thus almost quadrupling the price in three months; and at the same time they cut back substantially on their production. Other non-Arab members of the Organization of Petroleum Exporting Countries (OPEC) also increased their prices, even though they had no interest in the Arab–Israeli conflict. The immediate effect was a fit of panic among the oil-consuming countries, and even when the panic subsided western Europe had to adjust to a tripling of the price of oil. Economic growth slowed down sharply. Unemployment more than doubled across the whole of western Europe, from 2.5 per cent of the workforce in 1970 to 5.4 per cent in 1980. Inflation ran high in almost every country from 1973 to the end of the decade. In 1975 it reached double figures in several countries: France, 11.8 per cent; Italy, 17 per cent; and Britain, an alarming 24.2 per cent; even in West Germany, with its solid currency, the inflation rate was 6 per cent.[2] Economists coined a new word, 'stagflation', to denote the unexpected new phenomenon of stagnation combined with inflation.

In 1979 there was an Islamic revolution in Iran, and in 1980 war broke out between Iran and Iraq, both major oil producers. These two events sent oil prices up again, reaching a high point of $34 per barrel in 1981; though after that they declined again sharply, coming down to $11 in 1986. Under the impact of this second oil shock, west European growth rates fell again. Between 1981 and 1990, the annual average growth of GDP in the 12 countries listed above was only 2.3 per cent; the increase in industrial production was even lower, at 1.7 per cent per year. Inflation declined, as governments applied severe controls on the monetary supply and imposed high interest rates. Unemployment, on the other hand, increased, with percentages reaching double figures in a number of countries.[3]

At the same time there was a substantial shift in the nature of employment. The numbers of people employed in agriculture declined sharply as large-scale farming increased, and peasant farming was diminishing even in countries where it had flourished previously. The former staple industries of coal-mining, steel manufacture and shipbuilding diminished, sometimes to vanishing point, in face of competition from countries on the Pacific Rim, where costs were lower and quality often higher than the Europeans could manage. This led to a progressive erosion of the old manual working class, and a rapid increase in the so-called tertiary sector – administration, commerce and the provision of services. What had previously been regarded as an appendage to the 'productive' sectors of agriculture and manufacturing became by far the most important sector of the economy, and the principal area of growth and innovation.[4]

These economic changes revealed the alarming dependence of western Europe on events and forces outside its own control. Wars between Arab states and Israel, and between Iraq and Iran, and the power of oil producers to increase the price of their product threw the countries of western Europe into confusion and crisis. The days when Europe dominated the world economy were long gone, and the prosperous and well-organized countries of western Europe were at the mercy of distant countries where their influence counted for little. Even so, it is worth recalling that even amid these difficulties the countries of western Europe did not actually fall into economic decline – their economies simply grew at a rate of just over 2 per cent instead of nearly 5 per cent. Even in adversity, western Europe continued to prosper.

THE POLITICAL AND SOCIAL SCENE

In political and social affairs, the countries of western Europe also tended to move together. One such case was the wave of student unrest which broke across much of western Europe in 1968–69. This movement actually began in America, with student opposition to the war in Vietnam, but in crossing the Atlantic it acquired some specifically European aspects. In France, where student agitation reached its peak in May 1968, the protesters attacked an immense range of targets: the physical and intellectual state of the universities; the rigidity of French secondary education; and above all the materialism and conformity of modern society. The vague yet sweeping nature of the protesters' demands was caught in the slogan *L'imagination au pouvoir*. In retrospect, much of this seems hollow. Many of the students who protested against materialism came from prosperous families and could return to the thoroughly material comforts of their own homes when they felt inclined. Even at the time, the clear-sighted Raymond Aron found little of substance in *La révolution introuvable*. Yet the attraction of the events of 1968 to those who took part, and to others who came later and regretted that they had not been on the barricades, has been pervasive and long-lived. The generation of 1968 has left its mark, and continues to do so as the '68-ers' have grown older and attained positions of authority. The events of 1968, however shallow they were in some respects, left a profound inheritance in the self-doubt which came to affect Western society. François Furet, who lived through that time, put it thus: 'Self-doubt has led to a characteristic of modern democracy probably unique in universal history: the infinite capacity to produce offspring who detest the social and political regime into which they were born...' An American historian has written succinctly of 'a generation that had lost faith in its own culture.'[5] The wave of student unrest itself passed as quickly as it had arisen, and in France produced an overwhelming reaction in a sweeping victory for the right-wing Gaullists in elections in June 1968, only a month after the peak of the crisis. But the self-doubt and disillusion lasted much longer, and penetrated deeply into west European society.

One legacy of 1968 was the emergence, over most of western Europe, of 'Green' or environmentalist movements, demanding the protection of the environment from the pollution caused by industry, nuclear power, intensive farming and the internal combustion engine. Like student unrest, this phenomenon was not confined to western Europe. Greenpeace, the main campaigning organization, was set up in the USA in 1971, and one of the first Green political parties was founded in New Zealand in 1972. But the movement scored its most significant political successes in western Europe, and particularly in West Germany, where the Greens elected members to the Bundestag in 1983. Green parties also did relatively well in elections to the European Parliament in 1989, when turnout was low and enthusiastic parties could score successes out of proportion to their numbers. Indeed, the effect of the whole movement was greater than a simple counting of votes would indicate, so that environmental issues were taken up by mainstream political parties in most countries. The material success of western Europe produced a reaction that could only have appeared in a society with ample wealth to spare.

There also arose in the 1960s and 1970s a new wave of the feminist movement, with a new name, women's liberation. Like environmentalism, this was not specifically a west European affair. The vanguard of feminism, and some of its more extreme manifestations, were to be found in the USA. Even so, the effect of the movement was felt across most of western Europe as a widespread, though not uniform, phenomenon. Its most solid achievements took the form of legislation to secure parity of treatment between the sexes: equality of opportunity in employment, equal pay for equal work, even-handed treatment in laws regarding marriage, divorce and property-holding. In the United Kingdom, for example, an Equal Pay Act was passed in 1970; the Sex Discrimination Act of 1975 established equal rights in employment, and set up an Equal Opportunities Commission to impose that principle; the Employment Protection Act of 1975 secured women's right to maternity leave without endangering their jobs. The aspirations embodied in such laws were not always realized, and female high-flyers sometimes met a glass ceiling, an invisible barrier which they could not cross; even so, the principles were of crucial importance. In France, legislation in 1965 extended civil rights for married women by freeing them from their husbands' supervision in various ways; but equality in the administration of family property and resources was introduced only in 1985. Civil marriage was introduced in Italy in 1970, Portugal in 1975, Spain in 1981 and Greece in 1982; equality of rights to administer family property followed in the same countries in the same order between 1975 and 1983.

Feminist organizations also concentrated much effort on the issue of abortion, expressed as a woman's right to choose whether or not to bear a child. The first aim was the legalization of abortion itself, secured in Britain by an act of 1967, in West Germany in 1974, and in France and Italy in 1975 – in each case under various restrictions as to the period of pregnancy.

Abortion remained an emotional and difficult issue in politics, the law and medical ethics.

The franchise was by this time open to women across western Europe, and had been so in several countries for half a century or more; but political life remained dominated by men. The proportion of women members in west European parliaments was low. Around 1990, the Scandinavian countries (Finland, Norway, Sweden and Denmark) returned between 33 and 39 per cent of women members to their parliaments; the percentages in the Netherlands, Iceland, Austria and Germany were in the twenties. The United Kingdom just reached 10 per cent. Belgium, Italy, Ireland, Portugal, France and Greece were in single figures.[6] Margaret Thatcher, the British prime minister from 1979 to 1990, was at the time unique as a woman attaining the highest political office; though as a Conservative her success was unwelcome to many feminists, whose political sympathies lay on the left.

Much of western Europe also shared a powerful current of political violence. In the United Kingdom, there was intermittent civil war in Northern Ireland between Republicans and Unionists, Catholics and Protestants, from 1971 onwards. On the British mainland, the Irish Republican Army (IRA) maintained a campaign of bombing attacks, of which the most spectacular was an explosion at a Brighton hotel in October 1984, which was intended to kill the prime minister, Margaret Thatcher, and in fact did kill five people and wounded many more. In Spain, the Basque separatist movement ETA (*Euzkadi ta Azkatasuna* – 'Basque homeland and liberty') made repeated attacks on police, government officials and politicians, and succeeded in killing the prime minister, Carrero Blanco, in December 1973. That was under Franco's rule; but ETA kept up its attacks against the subsequent democratic regime, which extended a large degree of autonomy to the Basque region. In West Germany the Red Army Faction (the Baader–Meinhof gang) claimed to be the leaders of a revolution to overthrow the whole West German regime, on the grounds that it was materialistic, corrupt and tainted with Nazism. The group began its attacks with a bomb in the American Army headquarters in Frankfurt in 1972, and in 1977 succeeded in killing the federal minister of justice, the chairman of the Dresdner Bank and the president of the Federation of German Industry – a triple blow against law and capitalism. The principal leaders were arrested as early as 1972, but bombings continued throughout the 1970s and 1980s. Italy suffered a similar and even more dangerous revolutionary campaign, carried out by the Red Brigades against politicians, officials, judges and industrialists. Their most spectacular coup, in 1978, was the kidnapping and subsequent murder of Aldo Moro, the leader of the Christian Democrats and a former prime minister. They killed about 400 people between 1969 and 1981, and at times seemed to reduce the Italian government to impotence.

None of these groups – the IRA, ETA, the Red Army Faction and the Red Brigades – was large in number; but they often supported one another, and their causes, whether nationalism or left-wing revolution of an anarchist kind, attracted some sympathy from those who accepted their idealist claims. There was also a reaction in liberal public opinion, not so much against the violent conspirators as against governments which took harsh measures to oppose them. On the whole, governments and peoples withstood the assaults of extremists successfully; yet the impression gained ground that there was a crisis of authority in western Europe.

This sense of crisis was reinforced by developments in that ancient and usually authoritarian institution, the Roman Catholic Church. Pope John XXIII was elected in 1958 at the age of 77, in the general expectation that he would be a caretaker, not an activist. Instead he summoned a Second Vatican Council. The First Council, in 1869–70, had been a conservative body, notable for its introduction of the doctrine of Papal Infallibility. The Second Council, on the contrary, proved revolutionary. Its keynote was modernization, bringing the Church up to date: revising the liturgy; giving up the Latin mass in favour of the vernacular; and introducing a new element of collegiality in the government of the Church. The consequent wave of change was attractive to some Catholics but profoundly disorienting for others, who lost old landmarks without finding new ones. The Church, which had long been a bastion of certainty and permanence, was suddenly plunged into doubt and flux. What had been a symbol of authority became involved in a crisis of authority.[7] The ensuing uncertainty lasted throughout the reign of the next Pope, Paul VI (1963–78), and beyond. Strictly speaking, this was a worldwide, not a European, crisis – of the 2800 bishops who attended the Vatican Council, less than half were from Europe; but its effects were felt with particular force in Europe.

THE EEC AND POLITICAL CRISIS

While all this was going on, the European Economic Community maintained what one of its historians has called 'a tenacious shuffle in the direction of greater integration'.[8] One of the first objectives of the Treaty of Rome of 1957 was the removal of customs duties between the member states (at that time France, West Germany, Italy, Belgium, the Netherlands and Luxembourg). This was completed by July 1968, when a Common External Tariff between the EEC and other states also came into force. This was some 18 months ahead of schedule, and offered a striking contrast between the student upheavals of 1968 and the steady march of EEC measures, quite unaffected by riots, barricades and appeals to bring imagination to power.

The Treaty of Rome also set out the principle of a Common Agricultural Policy (CAP), a measure of crucial importance to France, whose agriculture was competitive within the Six but not in relation to other farming countries in the rest of the world. The actual terms of the CAP, finally accepted in January 1962, were complicated in detail but simple in essence. There was to be a common market for agricultural produce, in which producers were to receive a single price for a given commodity (for example wheat, whether grown in the vast fields of the Beauce in France or on a small farm in Germany); these common prices were to be fixed annually within the EEC. A system of Community preference was established, making it cheaper for the consumer within the EEC to buy Community produce rather than imports – for example, French rather than American wheat. What was called *solidarité financière* ensured that agricultural prices were maintained at a high level by payments for surplus production and subsidies for exports. Funds for these purposes were to be provided by the Agricultural Guidance and Guarantee Fund, financed partly by levies on agricultural imports into the EEC from outside, and partly by direct payments by member states. The import levies were paid mainly by countries (notably West Germany) which imported large quantities of agricultural produce from outside the EEC. The Germans therefore paid more into the Guarantee Fund than they received from it, while the French received more than they paid in.

These arrangements resulted in high food prices within the EEC – a French historian has estimated that in the first ten years of the CAP's operation EEC prices were between 50 and 100 per cent higher than world prices.[9] There was also much surplus production, purchased and stocked by the EEC in what became notorious as beef and butter mountains and wine lakes. On the positive side, the CAP resulted in the modernization of agriculture; stable prices, even though at a high level; and something close to self-sufficiency in foodstuffs within the EEC, which was thus largely insulated from swings in world prices. France was the largest single beneficiary, but the Netherlands also did well when income from the CAP was calculated per head of population; and small-scale German wheat farmers were able to grow crops in circumstances which would otherwise have been impossible.

The EEC thus secured two of its first economic objectives. At the same time, it passed through two sharp political crises. The first arose out of the British application to join the EEC, which got under way in July 1961, after the British government had become impressed by the economic progress and vigour displayed by the Community. Long and difficult negotiations brought agreement on commercial details within sight by the end of 1962. But at that stage, at a press conference in Paris on 14 January 1963, General de Gaulle, the president of France, decisively and even scornfully rejected the British application in a remarkable *coup de théâtre*. At first this seemed to threaten a crisis in the EEC, because some of the member states (notably the Netherlands) had supported British entry and resented de Gaulle's high-handed and unilateral action. In the event, the resentment passed quickly and the Community emerged stronger than before. On 22 January 1963, only eight days after de Gaulle's press conference, Adenauer and de Gaulle signed in Paris a treaty of cooperation between their two countries. Despite occasional difficulties, the 'Franco–German couple' became the driving force of the EEC for decades to come. As Adenauer said to Willy Brandt, the German Social Democrat leader, shortly after signing the Treaty of Paris: 'Look, what is

Europe? First and foremost, France and us. And things are going well. If the British make a third, there's no certainty that they'll continue to do so.'[10] Few have cared to be so blunt.

France plunged the EEC into another dispute in 1965–66. Under the terms of the Treaty of Rome, the EEC Council of Ministers was to act on a majority vote rather than unanimously on a number of issues with effect from 1 January 1966; and it was widely understood that the president of the European Commission, Walter Hallstein, intended to make these changes the occasion for an increase in supranational action and in the authority of the Commission. De Gaulle refused to accept these new arrangements, and from June 1965 France ceased to attend EEC meetings (except for the Committee on the Common Agricultural Policy, which was presumably too important to neglect). In a forthright press conference, de Gaulle declared that France wanted a 'reasonable' Community, not one run by 'some technocratic body of elders, stateless and irresponsible'.[11] The French policy of 'the empty chair' effectively brought the EEC to a halt, because all important decisions required unanimous support.

In January 1966 a meeting of the foreign ministers of the Six devised a way out of the impasse. They agreed that when issues very important to one or more member states were involved, the Council should try to reach unanimous decisions within a reasonable time. The French delegation continued to insist that in such cases discussion should continue until unanimity was reached; while the other delegations disagreed. But it was agreed that this divergence should not prevent the Community's work being resumed. The concept of majority voting was thus maintained in principle, but the French reserved the right to veto or obstruct any decision by the Council of Ministers which affected their vital interests. This was politely called 'the Luxembourg compromise', but it meant in practice that the French had got their way, and by implication other member states could also exercise a veto. This was not wholly unwelcome to the other five EEC members. Robert Marjolin observed in his memoirs that the other governments 'did not want the majority vote any more than the French did and they sacrificed it to the French with no great pain, and some even with secret relief'.[12] In the event, the Community almost certainly benefited from a further period of having to reach agreement by discussion and compromise, even at the cost of some delays, because it was through the habit of cooperation that the members developed their cohesion. In the same way, it was probably advantageous to the Community that British entry was rejected in 1963, and the Six gained further time in which to settle down and establish their institutions.

THE EXPANSION OF THE EEC

In the 1970s and 1980s the EEC developed in a number of ways: by enlargement; by changing its institutions and workings; and by altering its character.

In 1971 the accession of Britain to the Community was finally agreed upon, to take effect in 1973. Harold Macmillan, as Conservative prime minister, had made the first attempt at entry in 1961–62, motivated by the hope that the British economy would benefit; a conviction that the old Commonwealth links were growing ever more slender; and a vague but strong belief that Britain could no longer remain isolated from the force represented by the EEC. At that stage, the British application (as we have seen) was dramatically rejected by de Gaulle. In 1966–67 Harold Wilson, as Labour prime minister, was somewhat reluctantly converted by the same arguments. The two main British political parties thus came into agreement on the issue; and the Liberals had long been 'European' out of conviction. De Gaulle was still opposed, and Wilson's attempt followed Macmillan's into failure. Finally, in 1971, Edward Heath (who was one of the few convinced advocates of European integration in British politics, and who had little interest in the 'special relationship' with the USA) reached an agreement with President Pompidou of France, and the details fell into place. Wilson still had second thoughts when he returned to office in 1974. He appeased the doubters in his own party by renegotiating the terms of British accession, and then held a referendum on whether Britain should remain a member. The renegotiation proved to be cosmetic rather than fundamental. The referendum produced a result which was decisive in terms of votes (two-thirds voted yes), but oddly ineffectual in its effects on public opinion (see below, p. 195).

Ireland and Denmark joined at the same time, bringing the membership of the EEC to nine. The Norwegian government signed a treaty of accession, but the electorate rejected it in a referendum. Three more states joined in the 1980s: Greece in 1981, and Spain and Portugal in 1986. These countries differed from earlier members, being markedly poorer in income per head of population, and none was strong industrially. Moreover all three had recently been governed by authoritarian regimes. In Greece, the military rule of the Colonels had been comparatively short-lived, from 1967 to 1974. In Spain, Franco's dictatorship extended from the end of the Civil War in 1939 to his death in 1975. In Portugal, Salazar headed an authoritarian government from 1932 to 1970, and after his death a period of uncertainty and military coups persisted until 1976, when a stable parliamentary regime was finally established.

All three countries treated accession to the EEC as an immediate priority after emerging from dictatorship. In Greece, Prime Minister Konstantinos Karamanlis had negotiated associate status with the EEC before the military coup in 1967; and during the rule of the Colonels the EEC kept that agreement in suspense rather than cancelling it. When the military regime fell in 1974, Karamanlis returned to office and at once applied for full membership, primarily for political reasons, seeking the prestige that membership would confer on his new government. Economically, Greek industry (such as it was) was unprepared for competition within the EEC; agriculture was backward, but could hope for subsidies under the Common Agricultural Policy. France gave strong support to the Greek application, and a treaty of accession was concluded in 1979, leading to membership on 1 January 1981.

In Spain, Franco's death on 22 November 1975 marked the end of an era – in a curious sense it could be seen as the end of the 1930s. Yet the country was already changing during the last year of Franco's rule, under the impact of growing prosperity, mass tourism and greater social freedom. King Juan Carlos managed the transition from the old regime to a parliamentary government with remarkable skill and courage, persuading former supporters of Franco to accept from the Crown changes which they would have rejected under a Republic. In 1977 the Spanish Communist Party was legalized by a right-wing prime minister; and in 1981 the king defeated a military coup – with officers threatening parliament at gunpoint – by sheer moral authority. As a part of the process of adjustment, Spain applied for accession to the EEC as early as 1977, seeking the prestige and acceptance into political society that membership would confer. The application made painfully slow progress, partly because the EEC itself was preoccupied with other matters, and partly because the French wanted safeguards against competition from Spanish agriculture. Spain finally became a member of the EEC in 1987, symbolically rejoining the political life of western Europe after more than 40 years of isolation. Spain was already conforming to west European patterns in other respects. In the 1960s, roughly 1 in 100 Spaniards owned a car; by the mid-1980s it was 1 in 10.

Portugal under Salazar had been less isolated from western Europe than Spain under Franco, receiving Marshall aid and being a member of NATO and the European Free Trade Area. During the country's difficult transition to parliamentary democracy, west European leaders offered crucial moral support. In 1974, a particularly dangerous year, Helmut Schmidt (the chancellor of West Germany), James Callaghan (the British Foreign Secretary), Olaf Palme (prime minister of Sweden) and François Mitterrand (the leader of the French Socialist Party, then in opposition) all visited Portugal to encourage its nascent democracy. In 1976 Portugal was admitted to the Council of Europe, which, as a later foreign minister explained, may have seemed banal to some but was of key psychological importance to the Portuguese.[13] Portugal applied for membership of the EEC in March 1977, shortly before Spain, primarily in search of political acceptance and support; economically, the hope of grants from the EEC Regional Fund was counterbalanced by the risks to Portugal's backward agriculture. Portuguese entry was delayed by being tied to that of Spain, but was eventually achieved in 1986. The anxiety of these three new recruits to join the EEC was a sign of the prestige as well as the prosperity which the Community had attained.

EUROPEAN UNION

This enlargement of the EEC to 12 members meant that western Europe itself became less divided than it had been in the late 1950s and early 1960s.

Moreover, the EEC which the new members were joining was constantly changing in the direction of further integration. In December 1974 the heads of government of the EEC, who already held frequent meetings, decided to formalize these conferences under the name of the European Council, to meet three times a year. At the same time, they agreed that the European Parliament, previously nominated by the various national legislatures, should be directly elected; and the first elections were held in June 1979. These changes took the EEC another step towards providing itself with the institutions of a state, with an executive council and an elected parliament.

The EEC also moved tentatively towards monetary union. In 1969 a sharp devaluation of the French franc and a revaluation upwards of the West German mark had perturbed the common market within the EEC and the Common Agricultural Policy, which were both affected by fluctuations in exchange rates. In 1970 a report by Pierre Werner, the prime minister of Luxembourg, proposed that the EEC should move towards monetary union, and possibly a single currency. The members first set out to keep their currencies within set limits, not varying more than 2.25 per cent up or down in relation to one another. This device was commonly known as 'the snake'; and in 1972 it was followed by another scheme, oddly called 'the snake in the tunnel', which was intended to relate the relevant European currencies to the value of the American dollar. These mechanisms failed to work. High inflation and other problems following from the oil shock of 1973 made it impossible to hold currencies within the defined limits, and by 1974 the scheme had broken down. At the end of 1977 Roy Jenkins, then President of the European Commission, revived the idea of monetary union, and the Council of Ministers in July 1978 agreed on a new European Monetary System. This was based on the same principle as the snake, in that participating currencies should move no more than 2.25 per cent up or down from a fixed value; but with the addition of a new unit of account, the European Currency Unit (ECU), with a value determined by a grouping (or basket) of currencies, in which the German mark was the predominant element. The enthusiasts for the new system intended the ECU, which came into being in March 1979, to be a prototype for a European currency, but in the meantime the new Exchange Rate Mechanism (ERM) worked mainly through the cooperation of West Germany and France. Britain took part in the negotiations which set up the new system, but did not join it until October 1990, in a move which rapidly proved disastrous – but that is another story.

In December 1985 the European Council, meeting in Luxembourg, adopted the terms of the Single European Act, designed to complete the single market which the Treaty of Rome had aimed to create. The economic aspect of this Act was designed to remove barriers to free trade within the EEC (in services as well as goods); to harmonize rates of indirect taxation and excise duties; and to align different technical standards and measurements. (These processes were immensely detailed – a paper drawn up to prepare for the Act listed 300 separate issues needing to be cleared up in order to achieve the single market.) The second aspect was political in character, introducing qualified majority voting in the European Council for measures to promote the single market, which could be very extensive; increasing the influence of the European Parliament in decision making; and by its preamble committing member states to transforming their relations into a European Union.[14] It thus looked back to the Treaty of Rome, seeking to complete the work which was still unfinished after 30 years; and looked forward to the establishment of a political union.

What sort of union was it to be? Opinions differed on a comparatively simple matter like the nature of the single market. The British prime minister, Margaret Thatcher, when she committed her country to the Single European Act, believed that its purpose was to set up a free market economy; but most of the other members, with strong traditions of state intervention, were aiming at a social market economy, with strong controls over commerce, industry and conditions of employment.[15] Moreover, individual countries within the EEC had different opinions and emotions about the underlying concept of a federal European union – a United States of Europe, which Monnet had long ago aspired to.

Italy was one of the most enthusiastic advocates of closer union, for historical and political reasons. There could be no question of Italy losing its identity in a united Europe, because a true Italian identity had never existed. A nationalist had said to Cavour at the end of 1860: 'We have made Italy; now we must make Italians' – but this had never fully come about. Italy had remained deeply divided, with its separate regions more important and self-conscious than the state, so that the idea of an entity made up of Europe and regions was perfectly acceptable. As an Italian writer put it forcibly in 1999, Italy was ready to be European; and Italy in its diversity would contribute to a diverse Europe.[16] Belgium, again for historical reasons, was in a similar position. The country was a comparatively recent creation, divided between French and Flemish speakers, well accustomed to the compromises of a federal political structure and ready to welcome a federal Europe.

There were two countries, France and West Germany, which prided themselves on providing the locomotive of European integration. From the time of Adenauer onwards, the West Germans had seized on the idea of European integration as a means of escape from the heritage of Nazism and the passport to acceptance by their former enemies. Moreover the federal structure of the state, with its careful distribution of power between the federal government and the *Länder* gave the German people a sympathetic appreciation of the workings of federalism. France, with its long history and strong sense of national identity, was at first sight an unlikely partisan of European unification; and yet France had been the originator of the Schuman Plan of 1950, which had begun the whole process of integration. This was partly a matter of psychology – the new vision of Europe replaced the old vision of empire; and partly a matter of practical politics – the French politicians were sure that Europe would promote their interests. There was one crucial point when a particular version of French interests came into conflict with Europe, in an episode which is worth pausing to examine. In 1981 François Mitterrand, newly elected as the socialist president of France, embarked on a left-wing programme of nationalization, high taxation and the redistribution of wealth. The results were disastrous. France ran into a deficit in its balance of payments, and the franc had to be devalued twice, in 1981 and 1982. Mitterrand and his ministers had to choose between their vision of socialism, which demanded something like a siege economy, and their commitment to the EEC, with its single market and European Monetary System. When it came to the point, there was not much choice. France was too far committed to Europe; West Germany held all the economic cards; and Mitterrand's socialist principles proved to be sufficiently flexible to bend. In any case, a siege economy was out of fashion in western Europe by that time. France resumed its role as a leader of west European integration, and Mitterrand went out of his way to rebuild the Franco–German axis, round which the EEC turned.

Among the member states of the EEC, Britain was the least committed to unification. Despite the 'yes' vote in the referendum of 1975, popular enthusiasm for the EEC was at best limited. Public opinion polls in the 12 years from 1974 to 1982 showed that positive approval for British membership ('a good thing') never rose above 37 per cent; disapproval ('a bad thing') ran at about 30 per cent, though declining over the years; while indifference remained in the high twenties.[17] The Labour Party fought the next three general elections (1979, 1983 and 1987) on a platform hostile to the EEC. As prime minister, Margaret Thatcher fought a running battle with the other members of the EEC about the British contribution to the Community Budget, which ended in 1984 with the British securing an annual rebate on their payments. The British also attempted from time to time to reform the Common Agricultural Policy, but met steadfast opposition from the French, for whom the CAP was an essential pillar of the whole European project. Britain also remained outside the Exchange Rate Mechanism (introduced in 1979) until 1990. Britain remained an awkward member of the EEC, with little faith in its integrationist objectives. Neither people nor governments felt that they had done well out of membership, or at any rate not as well as they had hoped.

The character of the Community changed markedly in the 1960s, 1970s and 1980s. In 1962 Walter Hallstein, the first president of the EEC Commission and an advocate of political integration, pointed out some of the EEC's shortcomings. 'The European Community has no emblems, it has no flag, no anthem, it holds no parades and it has no sovereign. It has no instruments of integration which appeal to the senses, to the eye or to the ear.'[18] By the end of the 1980s most of these gaps had been filled. The Community had an emblem and a flag (12 gold stars on a blue ground), which was adopted by all the EEC organizations in 1986, on the initiative of the then president of the

European Parliament, Pierre Pflimlin. It had an anthem, the 'Ode to Joy' theme from Beethoven's *Ninth Symphony*. Parades were still not quite in fashion, but the creation of a mixed Franco–German brigade was proposed in 1987, and in 1994 German tanks paraded down the Champs Elysées as part of a Eurocorps.

There was still no sovereign, and indeed no certainty that one was in the making. In 1975 the European Court of Justice observed that 'it is not yet clear what the expression [European Union] imports'; and that remained the case in 1990.[19] In 1964 a Swiss historian wrote that the analogy between the United States of America and a potential United States of Europe was false. The foundations which had existed in eighteenth-century America were not present in Europe, where there was no sign of 'a common European sense of citizenship and nationality'.[20] An American, writing in 1979, claimed that if all the American settlers had kept their own languages the USA might not exist at all, and if it did it would be very different in its character. Europe could not escape from its diversity of languages, and the EEC was reliant on translators and interpreters. Behind the several languages, he could find 'no European culture in the sense of one that extends beyond national cultures'.[21] Stanley Hoffmann, a scholar who was as much at home in France as in America, offered the crushing comment that 'Europe [i.e. the EEC], when it speaks with one voice, has little to say...'[22]

If these verdicts were anywhere near the truth, the foundations for a United States of Europe were lacking. What the EEC possessed instead, and in plenty, were superstructures. The European Council, made up of heads of government, met three times a year, and sometimes more often. The Council of Ministers met in many different forms according to the subject under discussion (for example, agriculture, economics and finance, industry, education, transport, culture and tourism – the total reached about 20 subjects). Most of the work of these Council meetings was prepared by committees – as many as 150 or more – and a Committee of Permanent Representatives (COREPER in the EEC's habitual abbreviation), which exercised a considerable influence by 'harmonizing' proposals before they came to ministers. The increasing weight of work carried out by these bodies may be illustrated by the number of days taken up by their meetings: in 1968, Council meetings took up 61 working days, and in 1988, 119.5 days. In 1968, committees took up 1253 working days; in 1988 2000.5 days.[23] In 1991 there were no fewer than 80 Council meetings, resulting in 72 directives, 335 regulations and 174 decisions, all of which governed some aspect of life and activity in the member states.[24] Whatever they were called, these bodies in effect made up a government which regulated a considerable part of the affairs of 12 European states; though with the substantial exceptions of defence, foreign policy, taxation, education and much of social policy.

The European Economic Community thus changed markedly in character between 1961 and 1989–90. It comprised 12 members in place of the original 6; had established an elaborate organization and habits of cooperation; and had built up what was called the *acquis communautaire*, a cumulative body of law, practice and custom which formed the gains of the Community over the years of its existence, which were never relinquished and which new members had to accept when they joined.[25] It was building up institutions rather than a foundation in citizenship, but it was creating a form of cohesion and integration among its members of a kind not seen in western Europe before. In a way which was not true at the time of the EEC's foundation in 1957, the European Community had become the potential basis for a wider European entity; though it was as yet uncertain what that entity would prove to be. A book published in 1973 was entitled *Europe: Journey to an Unknown Destination*, and that was still true at the end of the 1980s.[26] But already the destination looked much more like a state than it had done in 1957.

EUROPE AND THE REST OF THE WORLD

Western Europe thus pursued its own internal affairs and attained a new coherence. But it was also defined by its relations with outsiders: the USA, the Soviet Union and Turkey. Relations with the USA raised the question of how far western Europe was an entity in itself, and how far a part of a wider Atlantic (or 'Western') community. Relations with the Soviet Union, and the Soviet zone in eastern Europe, opened the question of the permanence of the division of Europe. Relations with Turkey raised fundamental questions as to the character of Europe itself.

Throughout the 1960s, 1970s and 1980s the USA continued to play the predominant role in the defence of western Europe, maintaining strong conventional forces and providing almost the whole of the nuclear deterrent. (Britain and France were nuclear powers, but only on a small scale.) Only the Americans matched the Soviet Union in total defence expenditure. The figures were remarkable. In 1970 the expenditure of the USA stood at $77.8 billion, and that of the USSR at $72 billion. For comparison, West Germany spent $6.1 billion; France $5 billion; Britain $5.8 billion; and Italy $2.4 billion. Even added together, the expenditure of the four major west European countries did not attain one-third of the American total. At least a part of west European prosperity arose from acceptance of American protection rather than paying the full bill for self-defence.[27]

Dependence sometimes bred resentment, notably in France, where de Gaulle set out in the 1960s to demonstrate his independence. The French nuclear *force de frappe*, though small in numbers, was entirely under French control. De Gaulle withdrew France from the NATO command structure in July 1966 and insisted on the removal of NATO headquarters from Paris. He vehemently opposed American intervention in Vietnam, and in 1966 went to Cambodia and denounced the Americans before an immense crowd in Phnom Penh. His attitudes won him applause in France, where there was a strong current of anti-Americanism; and also struck a chord across much of western Europe, where opposition to the Vietnam war was widespread.

But anti-Americanism had its limits. French intellectuals might denounce the cultural tyranny of blue jeans on the one hand and the political tyranny of the Gulag prison camps on the other, as though they were in some way equivalent; but most of the French wore blue jeans, and came round to a clear-sighted view of Soviet oppression.[28] Moreover, most governments and a solid section of public opinion in western Europe were firmly Atlanticist in their outlook, recognizing that 'the West' (including the USA) was fundamental to their security, prosperity and way of life. Superficially, relations with the USA brought out divisions in western Europe; but fundamentally there were common interests between the two.

In relations between western Europe and the Soviet Union, it appeared that the building of the Berlin Wall in 1961 had put the final barrier in place across the continent. With every year that passed, West Germany became more deeply integrated into western Europe and the Atlantic alliance. Towards the east, the Federal Republic displayed a stern hostility. As early as 1955 the West German foreign minister, Walter Hallstein, had laid down the policy which became known by his name – the Hallstein Doctrine – by which West Germany refused to recognize East Germany, and undertook to break off diplomatic relations with any government which did so. In theory, this resolute stance was intended to display a commitment to the unity of Germany; but in practice it confirmed the division of the country.

This policy began to change under the 'Grand Coalition' government (1966–69), headed by the Christian Democrat Kurt Kiesinger, with the Social Democrat Willy Brandt as foreign minister. In 1967 the Federal Republic established diplomatic relations with Romania and Yugoslavia, even though those countries recognized East Germany, thus departing from the strict application of the Hallstein Doctrine. In 1969 Brandt became chancellor, at the head of a coalition with the Liberals, and embarked on an ambitious *Ostpolitik* (eastern policy), aimed at improving relations with Moscow, accepting the western Polish frontier along the Oder–Neisse line, and ultimately recognizing East Germany.

The circumstances were favourable for Brandt's initiative, because the two great antagonists in the cold war, the USA and the Soviet Union, had moved into a period of détente and were improving their relations. Brandt gained the support of President Nixon for his initiative at the end of 1969, and then began a sort of game of chess, with complicated moves designed to lead to his desired result – which in this case was not checkmate (victory), but stalemate (a draw). He first signed a treaty with the Soviet Union in August 1970, by which the two governments undertook to respect the territorial integrity of all states in Europe within their existing frontiers, specifically including the frontiers between Poland and East Germany and between East and West Germany. A further treaty between West Germany and Poland (December

1970) again accepted the Oder–Neisse line and affirmed that neither state had any territorial claims against the other, signifying that West Germany renounced claims to the territories lost in 1945. The final achievement of *Ostpolitik* was a treaty between West and East Germany, by which the two states recognized one another, affirmed the inviolability of the frontier between them, and declared that the sovereign power of each was limited to its own territory, signifying that West Germany abandoned its claim to represent the whole German people.

This elaborate series of treaties was intended to confirm the status quo in Germany, and therefore more widely the division of Europe, but in fact the results were quite different. The new flexibility of West German policy encouraged flexibility in others. The apparently arid and legalistic change by which the two Germanies recognized one another put the two countries on a different footing, and led to improved relations between them, including a strange and hidden traffic by which East Germany allowed people to leave the country in exchange for payment in West German marks – a secret trade in people which by 1989 reached a total of nearly 250,000 persons in exchange for 3.5 billion marks.[29]

Brandt's *Ostpolitik* paradoxically opened the road to change by recognizing the status quo. The same proved to be true of the Helsinki agreements of 1975, which took the process of détente in the cold war a stage further. The initiative for a general conference on European security and cooperation came from the Soviet Union in 1966, emerging after negotiations of infinite slowness at the Helsinki Conference in July 1975, where 33 European states (including the Soviet Union), plus the USA and Canada, were represented. The Soviet Union's purpose in beginning this vast diplomatic effort was to secure formal international recognition of the post-war boundaries in eastern Europe, and of the existing order in Europe as a whole, a recognition to which the Soviet government attached great importance. In this the Soviets achieved a partial success. The first section of the Helsinki Accords (often referred to as a basket) comprised a declaration of principles, including the inviolability of existing frontiers, the territorial integrity of states, and non-intervention in the internal affairs of other states – which together amounted to the acceptance of the European status quo, and so met the Soviet Union's main objective. It also included a declaration of respect for human rights and fundamental liberties, including freedom of thought, conscience and religious or other convictions. The second section dealt with cooperation in trade, industry, science and technology, tourism and the environment. In the third section the signatories agreed to increase cultural and educational exchanges, and to improve access to information, including newspapers, films and broadcast material. Several of these provisions dismayed the Soviet leaders (who had left the details to the Foreign Ministry), because they might open the way to intervention in the internal affairs of the Soviet Union and loosen the Soviet government's grip on eastern Europe. But on the whole Brezhnev and his colleagues thought the balance was favourable, and they accepted the agreements.

In the event, the doubters were proved right. The Helsinki Accords were published in *Pravda*, giving them wide circulation and the stamp of government approval. Dissidents within the Soviet Union made use of the provisions on access to information to evade censorship, and the government felt unable to risk its reputation abroad by reviving the full weight of Stalinist repression. In east European countries, advocates of human rights (for example, Charter 77 in Czechoslovakia and Solidarity in Poland) claimed the support of the Helsinki agreements for their activities. So it came about that the Soviet Union's move to consolidate the status quo in eastern Europe, and thus make permanent the division of Europe, ended by having a destabilizing effect, contributing to the later collapse of communism and the reunification of the continent.

These developments brought profound changes to Europe; yet at the same time they demonstrated that Europe's fate lay in the hands of others. Brandt's *Ostpolitik* depended for its success on the goodwill of the USA and the support of the Soviet Union. The Helsinki negotiations involved a whole range of states, but the keys to their success or failure lay in Moscow and Washington. Détente affected Europe, but its fate lay largely outside European hands.

The same was true when détente ran into difficulties and the cold war was revived with a new intensity at the end of the 1970s. In 1977 the nuclear arms race between the two superpowers took a new turn when the Soviet Union deployed in eastern Europe a new type of medium-range missile, the SS-20, which could strike targets anywhere in western Europe, but could not reach the USA. The Americans proposed to station missiles of a similar type (Pershings) in western Europe, which meant in practice Britain and West Germany. (France refused to allow any American-controlled weapons on its territory.) Public opinion across western Europe was deeply stirred, and nuclear disarmament movements in Britain and West Germany revived in strength; though they directed their efforts almost entirely against the American, not the Soviet nuclear weapons – a striking example of anti-American sentiment. In the event, the Atlantic alliance prevailed. Margaret Thatcher, the British prime minister, agreed to accept Pershing missiles in Britain, and stood fast against a wave of protests. President Mitterrand of France told the West Germans unambiguously that they should accept the Pershings, using a speech to the West German Bundestag on 20 January 1983 to deliver his message directly. After this intervention, the Christian Democrats won the general election in March, and the new Bundestag voted to accept the missiles in November, despite a remarkable demonstration of public opposition, led by the veteran Willy Brandt and the young leader of the Green Party, Petra Kelly. The cold war could still divide west European opinion.

It could seem almost as dangerous to some west Europeans when the USA and the Soviet Union suddenly came to the verge of a nuclear agreement. At a summit conference held in Reykjavik in October 1986, President Reagan of the USA and Gorbachev, the Soviet leader, almost agreed on a so-called 'zero option', doing away with all strategic nuclear weapons. This scheme quickly broke down, but not before it had alarmed the two west European nuclear powers, Britain and France. Thatcher and Mitterrand met in November, and agreed that they would not submit their own nuclear forces to any limitations laid down by the USA and USSR. At least in principle, the British and French were prepared to oppose the Americans as well as to work with them, as they had done over the Pershing missiles; though it was probably as well that they did not have to work out the consequences of their declaration of nuclear independence.

In any case, the Euro-missile crisis showed that the cold war in Europe was still very much alive, and its strategy was dominated by the two superpowers; while the possible 'zero option' demonstrated that the USA and the USSR might make a nuclear peace over the heads of the west European powers. Even Britain and France, with resolute and experienced leaders such as Thatcher and Mitterrand, could have done little about it.

Relations between western Europe and Turkey were relatively simple in their strategic aspects, but complicated in other respects. Turkey became a member of the North Atlantic alliance in 1952, holding a vital strategic position in the cold war and possessing a strong and reliable army. Membership of west European political institutions was a different matter, raising difficult questions as to how far Turkey was a European state and how Europe saw its own identity. Turkey had become a member of the Council of Europe as early as 1949, joining the other members in declaring its 'devotion to the spiritual and moral values which are the common heritage of their peoples'.[30] The European Economic Community laid down no specific requirement that its members should observe the forms of parliamentary democracy, but in practice that assumption prevailed – when a military dictatorship took over in Greece in 1967, that country's associate membership of the EEC was suspended. Turkey had a chequered record in this respect. Governments were overthrown by military coups in 1960 and 1980. Turkish governments took a strong line against Kurdish separatist revolts, and often acted in breach of west European views on human rights. In 1981 the Council of Europe suspended Turkish membership on this basis, and in 1982 the EEC opened an enquiry on Turkish failure to respect human rights.

Yet despite these problems Turkey repeatedly pressed to open negotiations for membership of the EEC. In 1963, by the Ankara agreement, the EEC accepted Turkey as an associate member. After years of modernization and economic growth, Turkey applied for full membership in 1987. This application was not rejected, but its consideration was repeatedly postponed. Turkey remained a poor country, with high unemployment. The Kurdish question and respect for human rights remained an issue, highlighted in 1989 during a visit by Danielle Mitterrand (the wife of the French president) to Turkish Kurdistan. Also in 1989 the potential problems implicit in religion were brought into the open by the affair of Salman Rushdie's novel *The Satanic Verses*. When this book was published, the Ayatollah Khomeini, the Islamic ruler of Iran, issued a fatwa against Rushdie, condemning his book as blasphemous and calling on zealous Muslims to kill him and his publishers. The states of the European Economic Community unanimously condemned the fatwa and supported Rushdie's right to free expression. Ever since the creation of modern Turkey by Kemal Atatürk, the country has been firmly secular in its government and constitution; but the prime minister in 1989, Turgut Ozal, declared that *The Satanic Verses* was a blasphemous book, and its publication in Turkey was forbidden. The contrast was glaring. Other contentious issues remained in the background: the problem of how the EEC would cope with a rapidly rising Turkish population; and the geographical question of whether the boundaries of Europe should be extended to the headwaters of the Tigris and Euphrates.

In the event, the EEC postponed the question of Turkish membership into the 1990s, and we must pursue it in the next two chapters. The issue left open the question of European identity, in political, religious and geographical terms; and the identity of Turkey itself was still uncertain – part Western and part Eastern, secular in government, but Muslim in population. The question marks remained.

12

EASTERN EUROPE, 1961–1989

THE ECONOMY

Eastern Europe, at least on the surface, had no doubts as to its identity. The countries of the Soviet zone maintained the pattern established earlier, based on ideological uniformity, economic similarity and Soviet military predominance. But within this pattern individual countries developed in different ways, so that there was diversity even within an overall similarity.

The Soviet Union set the tone for the whole Soviet zone. Its military effort remained immense, absorbing some 12–15 per cent of GNP to sustain large conventional forces and a formidable nuclear arsenal stocked with sophisticated ballistic missiles. Soviet ideology was imposed on east European countries more formally than before by the Brezhnev Doctrine of 1968 (see below, p. 206). The Soviet economy continued to give priority to heavy industry, and figures for steel production (though not entirely reliable) showed a strong growth, from 65.3 million tons in 1960 to 148 million tons in 1980.[1] On the other hand, the Soviets were slow to develop the computer, which was to become the key to all forms of production and administration, as well as the symbol of modernity. In 1974 there were estimated to be only 12,500 computers in the USSR, as against 207,000 in the USA; and by 1977 the figures stood at 20,000 and 325,000, respectively.[2] Soviet agriculture was in serious difficulties. In the 1970s the government aimed at self-sufficiency in food production, but failed to achieve it, importing large quantities of cereals, mostly from the USA. In 1975 the Soviet government signed a five-year agreement to import 6 million tons of wheat and corn each year from the USA, partly paid for by borrowing US dollars. Under Brezhnev, the government chose to set meat consumption as an indicator of the standard of living, yet in 1988 meat was rationed in 26 out of 55 regions in the Russian Republic.

The Soviet economy thus presented a strange contrast, producing large quantities of efficient military hardware, but failing to grow enough food. The

USSR could put a man into space, but housewives could not rely on buying simple household objects. Statistics of life expectancy and infant mortality worsened ominously in the 1970s, though they improved in the 1980s.[3]

The countries in the Soviet zone of eastern Europe followed much the same pattern. Heavy industry was given priority in the 1960s and 1970s, and collective agriculture was the norm, except in Poland; though with variations from one country to another. The collective farms were often inefficient, and over most of eastern Europe agricultural output declined in the 1970s and 1980s, bringing food shortages and occasional rationing. In other respects the countries of the Soviet zone benefited from their ties with the USSR. The Soviet Union supplied oil to the COMECON countries at prices which were fixed in advance at the average of the previous five years on the world markets. When the oil shock at the end of 1973 brought a sudden fourfold increase in the price of oil, the COMECON countries were shielded from the immediate effects because the price rise was spread out over five years; and the Soviets kept to their agreements even though they could have earned hard currency by selling their oil elsewhere at world prices. The USSR also imported east European goods, often of poor quality, which would have been difficult to sell anywhere else.

Like the Soviet Union, the COMECON countries borrowed from the USA and western Europe to pay for imports from the West, reaching a total debt of 31.7 billion US dollars in 1977. By 1989, Polish foreign debt alone totalled $41 billion; while that of Hungary reached $17 billion, the highest in eastern Europe per head of population.[4] This state of affairs, which would have been inconceivable a few years earlier, was made politically possible by the détente between East and West in the 1970s. West European governments were willing to extend loans and credits in order to promote their exports in the difficult years after the oil shock. Economic contacts across the Iron Curtain thus developed, in some cases quite strongly – as, for example, between Britain and Poland.

Most east European countries made some attempt at economic reform in the 1970s, making the planning system more flexible and introducing limited doses of a market in some products. There was an increase in GNP and a rise in individual prosperity, though at much lower levels than in western Europe. From about 1970 onwards, televisions, washing machines, refrigerators and family cars became commonplace in Hungary, Czechoslovakia and East Germany. There was a steady movement of population from the countryside to the towns, so that parts of eastern Europe became urban rather than rural in character. Demographically, there was a move towards Western patterns in a decline in the birth rate over most of eastern Europe, but life expectancy declined from the mid-1960s to the 1990s.

THE BREZHNEV DOCTRINE

In 1968 events in Czechoslovakia led to an emphatic reassertion of Soviet control in eastern Europe, and a formal affirmation of ideological unity.

During the previous year there had been internal difficulties within the Czechoslovakian Communist Party; and in December 1967 Brezhnev, the Soviet leader, had attended a Party meeting and declared that the leadership of the Czechoslovak Party was a matter for its own members. The first secretary of the Party, and therefore effectively the ruler of the country, Antonin Novotny, was replaced in January 1968 by Alexander Dubček, who took over as a new broom, determined to bring about reform, though only within the framework of the communist system. Novotny had combined his post as first secretary with that of president of the Republic; and on 21 March he was replaced as president by General Ludvik Svoboda. That day was also the first day of Spring, and Svoboda's name meant 'freedom'. The 'Prague Spring' had begun.

Dubček embarked on a radical programme, though always within limits. He relaxed censorship in March 1968, and abolished it in June, which was unheard of in any communist regime at the time. He called a Special Congress of the Communist Party to meet in September, to consider proposals for self-management and workers' councils in factories, and the setting up of 'interest groups' which might be represented in the communist-controlled National Front. In a striking phrase, Dubček described his aim as 'socialism with a human face', with the unhappy but realistic implication that so far socialism had *lacked* a human face. But at the same time he insisted that he remained committed to socialism, to the directing role of the Communist Party, and to the Warsaw Pact.

Despite this, the Soviet leaders soon concluded that they could not allow Dubček a free hand, which would encourage other countries to follow suit, with potentially dangerous results. For some time they were uncertain how to act, hesitating between the direct use of force and subversion to undermine Dubček's authority. Eventually Soviet leaders called Dubček to a meeting in Czechoslovakia at the end of July, and received a formal undertaking that his government would not permit anyone to undermine the bases of socialism. This was not enough. During the night of 20/21 August a powerful Soviet force, including 7500 tanks, invaded Czechoslovakia, supported by contingents from East Germany, Poland, Hungary and Bulgaria to emphasize the international character of the operation. (Only Romania among the Warsaw Pact states made no contribution.) There was little armed resistance to such overwhelming force; but on the other hand passive resistance was such that the Soviets could find no collaborators of any significance to replace Dubček and form a compliant government. Instead, Dubček was for a time allowed to remain in office, but was compelled to go to Moscow and accept the restoration of strict communist orthodoxy. Censorship was reimposed in September. The special Party Congress never met. Eventually, in April 1969, Dubček was replaced as first secretary by Gustav Husak, and in May 1970 he was expelled from the Party. But in contrast to the east European communist leaders who had been purged by Stalin, Dubček escaped with his life, being relegated to a post in the State Forestry Administration – a sign that in this respect socialism had attained a more human face.

The Soviet government was not content simply to restore the status quo in Czechoslovakia, but chose to redefine its general position by setting out the so-called Brezhnev Doctrine in an article in *Pravda* on 24 September 1968, under the heading: 'Sovereignty and the international obligations of socialist countries'. This laid down that the freedom of non-Soviet socialists to determine their own countries' path of development must be subordinate to the cause of universal Marxism-Leninism. 'Any decision of theirs must damage neither socialism in one country nor the fundamental interests of other socialist countries nor the world-wide workers' movement... This means that every Communist party is responsible not only to its own people but to all socialist countries and to the entire Communist movement.'[5] In short, communist countries must subordinate their independence to the interests of communism as a whole, as defined by the Soviet Union. Separate roads to socialism were out. In a sense there was nothing new in this. After all, the Soviets had crushed the Hungarian rising in 1956. But the Brezhnev Doctrine asserted Soviet domination as a matter of principle, and declared it to be immutable. The division of Europe was re-emphasized and reinforced.

This was accepted in the West with resignation and little ado. At the United Nations, a majority in the Security Council voted in favour of a resolution condemning the Soviet intervention, and calling upon the USSR and the Warsaw Pact countries to withdraw their forces. The Soviet Union vetoed the resolution, and there the matter rested.

Even so, all was not quite as it seemed. The Prague Spring stirred a response in other communist countries, even those which took part in the invasion. Dubček's evocation of 'socialism with a human face' lingered in many minds. Some 20 years later, Mikhail Gorbachev was to raise again the possibility of reforming socialism by means of glasnost, or openness, which recalled Dubček's attempt to do away with censorship. Dubček himself was to emerge from obscurity to take part in the fall of communism in Czechoslovakia. But meanwhile the communist domination of eastern Europe was reaffirmed by Moscow, and quietly accepted in the West.

During the 1970s and 1980s the countries of the Soviet zone developed in rather different ways, though mostly within the limits set by the Brezhnev Doctrine.

Romania took its own line in foreign policy. It was the only Warsaw Pact member to condemn the Soviet invasion of Czechoslovakia. The Romanian dictator, Ceauşescu, visited China at a time of hostility between the Soviet Union and China. Two American presidents, Nixon and Ford, made visits to Bucharest, and Ceauşescu paid no fewer than three return visits to the USA. Romanian athletes took part in the Olympic Games at Los Angeles in 1984, which were boycotted by the Soviet Union. At home, Ceauşescu established his own personality cult, as a sort of mini-Stalin. He completed the Stalinist grand project of a canal between the Danube and the Black Sea. He gave himself the title of 'Conducator', or Leader (or even Il Duce or Fuehrer). His seventieth birthday on 25 January 1988 was publicly celebrated with grandiloquent ceremony, and he awarded himself (for the fourth time) the decoration of Hero of the Socialist Republic of Romania. He set up a tight-knit ruling group by giving jobs to members of his family. All in all, Ceauşescu established a dictatorship more erratic and arbitrary than the others in eastern Europe, and ostentatiously independent from the Soviet Union – which earned him much kudos in the West.

Hungary was more relaxed. In 1961 Kádár, who had been installed by the Soviets after the rising of 1956, declared that 'Whoever is not against us is with us', introducing a flexibility in which some parts of life could work in comparative freedom as long as there was no overt political opposition – for example, literature, music and art were allowed some latitude as long as they steered clear of politics. In 1971, political life itself was marginally opened up by legislation which permitted elections to involve more than one candidate, though all candidates had to be approved by the Patriotic People's Front, that is, the Communist Party. Economic restrictions were relaxed, with some scope for the market and enterprise – there was a saying that 'We are socialists in the morning and capitalists in the afternoon'.[6] There were more consumer goods in the shops than in most of eastern Europe; the collective farm system worked reasonably well; and agricultural production increased during the 1970s.

In Czechoslovakia too there was material progress during the 1970s. Consumer goods were available and car ownership roughly doubled, from 1 car to 17 persons in 1971, to 1 to 8 in 1979. On the other hand, political conditions were severe after the Soviet invasion, with purges among the intelligentsia, the writers' union and university teachers. Yet it was in Czechoslovakia that the first effects of the Helsinki Accords became manifest. On 1 January 1977 a group called Citizens' Initiative (later to become Charter 77) published a demand that the government should respect the individual rights set out in its own laws or in the agreements concluded at Helsinki. Among the original signatories of this demand were the former foreign minister in Dubček's government and the playwright Václav Havel, later to become president of post-communist Czechoslovakia. Charter 77 was never a large movement (with about a thousand adherents in 1980), but it became a constant moral presence in the country, a source of semi-clandestine publications, and a channel of communication with the Western world. It was a considerable achievement with small numbers.

Poland was different again – the largest of the east European states, with a population of about 35 million in 1980, a people intensely patriotic and for the most part deeply Catholic. In October 1978 the world was astonished by the election of a Polish Pope, Karol Wojtyla, John Paul II, who in 1979 returned on a visit to his native land and celebrated mass before crowds numbered in millions. The authorities were almost helpless in the face of such a movement, and their moral position was fatally undermined. The government also faced economic difficulties. In 1980 strikes began in the big shipyards at Gdansk, led by Lech Walesa – a worker, a patriot and a Catholic. Walesa and his fellow-workers founded a new trade union, called Solidarity, independent of the government and the Communist Party, opening up a public breach between the communist regime and the industrial workers it was supposed to represent. Solidarity was thus a threat not only to the Polish government but to the whole Soviet zone, and the Soviet leaders considered military intervention, as in Czechoslovakia in 1968. In the event they found a Polish intermediary capable of imposing an internal solution: General Jaruzelski, a former minister of defence, who became prime minister in 1981. On 13 December that year Jaruzelski suddenly imposed martial law, arrested Walesa and other leading members of Solidarity, and revoked most of the concessions previously granted to the new trade union. Up to a point, martial law worked. The Poles preferred intervention by their own forces to a Soviet invasion, and Jaruzelski himself proved to be a patriot as well as a communist, anxious to do his best for his country. The government dissolved Solidarity in October 1982, and ended martial law in December 1982; but the opposition movement continued underground, and the breach between the Communist Party and the people remained. Pope John Paul visited the country again in 1983, and declared that Poland had a right to independence, and to 'her proper place among the nations of Europe, between East and West'.[7]

Poland was the largest and most difficult of the countries in the Soviet zone. Bulgaria was at the other end of the scale, being the smallest (8.9 million people in 1981) and the most obedient. The Communist Party exercised rigid control, and the country felt a historic sympathy for Russia. In 1963 and in 1973 the president and Party chairman, Todor Zhivkov, actually tried to have Bulgaria incorporated into the USSR as a Soviet Republic, but was rebuffed. No other country in eastern Europe would even have made the attempt.

East Germany after the building of the Berlin Wall proved the most successful economy in the Soviet zone. Large-scale nationalization of industry and other sectors was undertaken in the 1970s, and productivity was good by east European standards. Collective farms were reorganized on a rational basis, dividing arable from livestock. On the other hand, much of this success depended on loans from western Europe and on a growing trade with West Germany – both of which encouraged a form of dependence on the West rather than the East. Moreover, some signs of opposition to the regime began to take shape, notably in the evangelical churches and pacifist groups.

By the mid-1980s Soviet control over its zone in eastern Europe (except for Romania as the odd man out) was in principle firmly established, formally proclaimed in the Brezhnev Doctrine and enforced by the invasion of Czechoslovakia and martial law in Poland. Political stability was assured. The zone had done well during the oil shock, and showed reasonable economic growth until the mid-1970s. But the system was running into increasing difficulties. Economic growth slowed down, and in some cases went into reverse, in the late 1970s. Eastern Europe became an economic burden to the Soviet Union. The military contribution of the Warsaw Pact countries to Soviet security was dubious, because it was not certain that their forces could be relied upon. Ideologically, the countries of eastern Europe were a poor advertisement for communism – 'not a showcase but an eyesore', as one writer put it.[8] Communist leaders in the West found the east European example unattractive. The Italian communist leader, Enrico Berlinguer, wanted to follow his own course, and even the French communists, who remained in some ways the most Stalinist party in western Europe, preached the principle of different roads to socialism. Communist unity was breaking up, unless maintained by Soviet power.

THE COLLAPSE OF SOVIET RULE

The Soviet Union itself was in a paradoxical situation. The Soviet empire and spheres of influence were at their most extensive in the 1980s. The USSR possessed immense military strength, with powerful land forces and a rough parity with the USA in nuclear weapons. The prestige of communism remained high in developing countries and among some west European intellectuals. Yet at the same time the Soviet leadership was ageing and atrophied. Brezhnev was partly incapacitated by illness long before his death in 1982. Andropov was in poor health for most of his short term as general secretary. Chernenko, who took over in 1984, was ineffectual – a man without qualities. The massive military effort was only maintained by spending as much as 14–15 per cent of GNP on the armed forces, as against only 4–6 per cent for the USA. The Soviet Union was under increasing strain.

This was the situation when Chernenko died on 10 March 1985. The very next day the Politburo nominated Mikhail Gorbachev, its youngest member at the age of 54, to take over as general secretary of the Communist Party and ruler of the Soviet Union. This was a sudden change of generations in the Soviet leadership, but apparently not in its character. Gorbachev had risen quickly, but by an orthodox route: a degree in law at Moscow University; service in the local Communist Party; membership of the Central Committee of the Party in 1971, and of the Politburo in 1981. He had for some time been the protégé of Andropov, who was himself a long-serving head of the KGB.

Gorbachev has been well described as 'a Marxist-Leninist believer' and an optimist.[9] Both characteristics were important. As a Marxist-Leninist, he was convinced that the Soviet Union worked well in many respects, but needed reform to revive the stagnant economy, improve agriculture and sharpen up the bureaucracy. As an optimist, he was sure this could be done. The disaster at the Chernobyl nuclear reactor in April 1986 added another element. He became convinced that it must be done quickly. Gorbachev therefore made haste with a double-barrelled programme of reform, under the watchwords of 'perestroika' and 'glasnost'. 'Perestroika' meant restructuring: invigorating the economy by decentralization and the introduction of limited market forces; and, more widely, the renewal of all aspects of Soviet life, social and moral as well as economic. 'Glasnost' meant openness: in the expression of opinion, publication of news about current events, and discussion of Soviet history. Taken together these made up a drastic prescription, which had more dangerous consequences than Gorbachev expected. As he himself put it in retrospect: 'Just like reformers before me, I thought we had a system that could be improved. Instead, I learned that we had a system that needed to be replaced.'[10]

Domestic reform demanded a new foreign policy, to secure a durable peace and reduce the armaments budget. In principle, Gorbachev set out to diminish the role of ideology in foreign relations, by redefining the long-established concept of peaceful coexistence with the capitalist powers, to show that it meant genuine cooperation rather than simply another form of the class struggle. In practice, he moved quickly to meet President Reagan at Geneva in November 1985, the first of four summit meetings which transformed Soviet–American relations. In December 1987 the two leaders actually agreed to *reduce*, rather than merely to limit, their nuclear armaments.

Gorbachev was also prepared to renounce the use of force to maintain Soviet control in eastern Europe. As early as April 1985, at Chernenko's funeral, he told the leaders of the Warsaw Pact countries that in future they must take control of their own domestic affairs. There would be no more Soviet interventions in the manner of Hungary in 1956 and Czechoslovakia in 1968. They did not believe him. They had lived too long in the certainty that they could rely on Soviet troops in the last resort. In some respects they had simply been in power for too long. Zhivkov had been the ruler of Bulgaria since 1954; Kádár of Hungary since 1956; Ceauşescu of Romania since 1965; Husak of Czechoslovakia since 1969; and Honecker of East Germany since 1971. Only General Jaruzelski, who took over in Poland in 1981, was a newcomer; and even he had served for many years as minister of defence, in close cooperation with the Soviet armed forces.[11] The force of habit was inescapable, even if anyone had wanted to escape it. The prospect of surviving without the support of the Soviet Union was unthinkable. But in 1989 the unthinkable happened.

With hindsight, it became possible to see signs of the shape of things to come. In the Soviet Union, Solzhenitsyn and Sakharov were dissidents of such stature that they could be neither ignored nor suppressed. In eastern Europe, the Helsinki Accords of 1975 encouraged dissidents, like Charter 77, to come out into the open. Declining living standards in the 1980s undermined faith in socialism, which after all was supposed to *improve* the lot of the workers, not make it worse. Material contrasts between East and West became increasingly visible. Hungarian visitors, under comparatively lenient travel regulations, made frequent trips to Vienna, while Hungarian newspapers printed the Austrian radio and TV programmes. In East Germany, viewers watched West German television in their own language, and could observe the contrast in prosperity between the two parts of the country. Everywhere there was an inexorable change of generations, through which the original appeal of communism and the wartime prestige of the Soviet Union faded away. Already in 1988 there were danger signals in parts of eastern Europe. In Hungary two non-communist political organizations, the Hungarian Democratic Forum and the Alliance of Free Democrats, were founded and survived. In Czechoslovakia a petition appealing for greater religious freedom attracted a remarkable 400,000 signatures. In September 1988 the Polish government resigned after a vote of no confidence in parliament, an unheard-of event in a communist country, even though it was only followed by another communist government. Even in Bulgaria, where communist rule seemed unshakable, an Association for the Defence of Human Rights became active.

These omens might have been read aright and the collapse of the Soviet empire foreseen; but few did so. There remained a convincing air of permanence and solidity about Soviet power. In 1987 a perceptive and well-informed correspondent for the *New York Times* wrote that 'the east-west division of Europe is unnatural, unhistoric, unacceptable to its people and therefore ultimately unstable. But it cannot be changed or dismantled without provoking great conflict, possibly catastrophic nuclear war.'[12] Over 70 years had passed since the October Revolution in 1917, and 40 years since the Soviet Union took over in eastern Europe. The system had lasted a long time, and seemed destined for a long life yet. What followed was a tale of the unexpected.

Poland took the lead. Solidarity, though legally dissolved, still operated underground, and in February 1989 the Polish government agreed to round-table talks with other organizations to discuss the legalization of the former trade union. In March the government declared in public that the Soviet Union had been responsible for the massacre of Polish officers at Katyn in 1940 – a step of immense symbolic importance. In April the government lifted the ban on Solidarity, granted full legal recognition to the Catholic Church and cancelled the May Day parade – another symbolic act, renouncing a key socialist celebration. In June, parliamentary elections were held, under an unusual new system, in which 65 per cent of the seats were to be reserved for government candidates, provided that they received 50 per cent of the vote, and the other 35 per cent were open to contest. In the event, 160 out of 161 open seats were won by the Solidarity candidates. Meanwhile, in the elections for the Senate, all 100 seats were contested, and Solidarity won 92 of them.[13] It was a triumph for Solidarity and a debacle for the Communists. At the end of the year the new parliament abolished the leading role of the Communist Party and declared the country to be simply 'The Republic of Poland', and no longer the People's Republic.

Meanwhile the rest of eastern Europe was transformed. In Hungary, the government organized a symbolic state funeral for Imre Nagy, the hero of

1956, on 16 June 1989. In July the government followed the Polish example and held round-table discussions with other organizations, which led to a rapid erosion of communist authority. In October the Communist Party renounced the doctrine of the dictatorship of the proletariat, thus removing the justification for its own exclusive exercise of power. The state was renamed the Hungarian Republic. These events in Hungary had unexpected effects in East Germany. Already in 1988 some 9000 East Germans had taken advantage of relaxed border regulations in Hungary to reach the West by taking their holidays in Hungary and then crossing into Austria. In August 1989, at the height of the holiday season, about 6000 East Germans again followed this route, with thousands more following behind. On 10 September the Hungarians simply opened the border with Austria, and on 11 September an astonishing total of 125,000 East Germans crossed from Hungary to Austria, mostly in Trabant cars, which became symbols of this new exodus.

East Germany then became the centre of attention. In September 1989 a number of Lutheran churches became centres for gatherings demonstrating against the regime. In Leipzig the numbers grew to an estimated 150,000 each Monday evening. The East German leader, Honecker, was set in his ways and refused to make concessions, even when Gorbachev went to see him in person (6–7 October) and advised him to introduce reforms. Honecker planned to suppress the Leipzig meetings by force, but was overruled by his own politburo. On 18 October he resigned, and his successor Egon Krenz was simply carried away by the speed of events. Soviet troops in East Germany, some 375,000 in number, stayed in their barracks, with orders not to intervene. The East German government was on its own, and gave up the struggle. On 8 November the politburo resigned in a body – an unprecedented abdication. The next day Krenz announced that East German citizens could present requests to leave the country without specifying reasons, and undertook that authorizations would be granted rapidly. Crowds moved towards the checkpoints, where the frontier guards allowed free passage to West Berlin. During the night of 9/10 November parts of the wall were knocked down and East Berliners simply wandered into the other half of the city. These astonishing scenes were broadcast live on television throughout Europe. In the next few days most of the wall was removed and the East German authorities issued over 7 million visas to their citizens, who swarmed across the border. The effect of these events was enormous. The building of the Berlin Wall in 1961 had confirmed the division of Berlin, Germany and Europe. When the wall came down the division came to an end, and a new era began.

The end of communist rule in other countries came quickly, and mostly without bloodshed. On 10 November Zhivkov was deposed as ruler of Bulgaria, and in December the Communist Party permitted the formation of other political parties; the 'leading role' of the Party was formally abolished in

13   The end of the Berlin Wall, 1989 © Robert Maass/Corbis

January 1990. In Czechoslovakia, a series of massive demonstrations in Prague brought about what was called the velvet revolution. President Husak resigned on 10 December, and on 29 December the Federal Assembly elected Václav Havel as president in his place. Dubček became president of the Assembly – a largely symbolic role, but the symbolism was full of meaning. In Romania there was fighting when troops and security police fired on demonstrators in Bucharest and other cities; but the army gave up the struggle and changed sides. Ceauşescu, who had been confident of success to the last, attempted to escape by helicopter, but he was captured and shot out of hand on Christmas Day.

   The key to all these events lay in a fundamental change in Soviet policy. In the past, the Soviets had maintained their control by force – in East Germany in 1953, Hungary in 1956 and Czechoslovakia in 1968. It is possible that Gorbachev could have prevented, or at any rate delayed, the collapse of communist governments by using force at an early stage – for example, by preventing the Hungarians from opening their frontier with Austria – but he showed no sign of doing so. Instead Gorbachev said repeatedly (three times in four days, 5–8 July 1989) that countries and peoples could decide their own affairs and social systems; and he meant what he said.[14] Early in November 1989, when some of the consequences were already plain, the principal spokesman for the Soviet Foreign Ministry, Gennardy Gerasimov, even made light of the new situation, saying that the Brezhnev Doctrine was dead, and had been succeeded by the Sinatra Doctrine – Hungary and Poland were doing it their way.[15] It was a joke which would have been inconceivable, and probably incomprehensible, in an earlier era.

It is likely that Gorbachev could not have used force even if he had wished. He had gone so far in improving his relations with the Americans that he could not afford to go back to the old days and bring out the tanks. Soviet repression in eastern Europe in 1989 would have destroyed all the work of the summit meetings with Reagan, turned the clock back to the days of confrontation and killed off the chances of perestroika at home. Gorbachev simply could not do it. At that stage, he appears to have believed that he could let eastern Europe go and still maintain the Soviet Union intact; but events were to prove otherwise.

Meanwhile, Gorbachev continued to hope. When he visited Chancellor Kohl at Bonn in June 1989 the two statesmen issued a joint declaration of intent to build 'a Europe of peace and co-operation – the common European home – in which the United States and Canada will also have their place'.[16] The phrase 'common European home' was a flash of inspiration, offering a hopeful vision of the future. It remained to be seen whether the vision would become a reality.

PART SIX

EUROPE IN OUR OWN TIME

13

EAST MEETS WEST? 1990-1999

The cold war which had divided Europe for over 40 years came to an end in 1990, closing in a series of Soviet–American negotiations and summit meetings in late 1989 and early 1990. On 4 June 1990 Gorbachev felt able to assure an enthusiastic audience at Stanford University that 'The Cold War is now behind us.'[1] So the cold war was concluded, as to a large degree it had been waged, by the two superpowers, over the heads of the European countries; and indeed no one but the Americans and Soviets could have brought the long conflict to a close.

But Europe too had its peace conference, which seemed to offer the prospect of a reunited continent. The Conference on Security and Cooperation in Europe, held in Paris on 21 November 1990, was a massive assembly, representing 32 European states, including the Soviet Union and the Holy See, together with the USA and Canada. The participants signed a Charter of Paris for a New Europe, which opened by declaring that 'The era of confrontation and division of Europe has ended', and went on to fill several pages with sections on human rights, democracy and the rule of law, economic liberty and responsibility, culture, security and unity.[2] This 'New Europe' was launched on a tide of good intentions, reflecting the optimism of the time. 'Bliss was it in that dawn to be alive', wrote Wordsworth about the French Revolution 200 years earlier. Poets no longer wrote like that in 1990; but a similar hope was in the air.

It proved a false dawn. Europe was not ready for the unity proclaimed in the Charter of Paris. The shattering changes of 1989–90 left behind a host of difficulties and uncertainties. Gorbachev, who had launched the inspiring phrase about 'a common European home', soon found that his own home-land was crumbling around him. He did not expect the collapse of communist regimes in eastern Europe to extend to the Soviet Union, and still intended to reform the Soviet system while leaving its essential features intact. In fact the system was heading for a threefold crisis – ideological, national and economic.

THE COLLAPSE OF THE SOVIET SYSTEM

In February 1990 Gorbachev prepared a document to be put to the Central Committee of the Communist Party of the Soviet Union, entitled 'Towards a Humane, Democratic Socialism', and he went on to propose the repeal of the article in the constitution which ensured the political monopoly of the Communist Party. This proved fatal. The whole system of government had been totalitarian, and to remove the role of the Communist Party was to destroy the key to the whole system, and with it the confidence that kept everything working. If the Soviet Union did not believe in communism, it had no purpose – 'a total system could only end in total collapse.'[3]

At the same time, the different nationalities within the Soviet Union asserted themselves in a manner which caught Gorbachev completely by surprise. There is every sign that he actually believed that under socialism the nationalities question had been resolved, and he was astonished when nations came forward with demands for independence. This movement had begun as early as 23 August 1989, when something like a million people joined hands in a human chain across the Baltic Republics of Estonia, Latvia and Lithuania to protest against the German–Soviet Pact of 1939 which had led to the absorption of the three countries (then independent) into the Soviet Union. In March 1990 Lithuania and Estonia declared their independence, while the Latvian parliament took the more cautious line of announcing its intention of becoming independent. This was only a prelude. In June and July the whole Soviet Union began to break up. On 12 June the Supreme Soviet of the Russian Republic, by far the biggest Republic in the USSR, declared its 'sovereignty', followed rapidly by Uzbekistan (20 June), Moldova (23 June), Ukraine (16 July) and Belorussia (27 July). The exact meaning of 'sovereignty', as against independence, was uncertain, but such a refined point of semantics could not disguise the fact that the Soviet Union was breaking up. The machinery of the Soviet government remained in being, but increasingly whirred round in a void. On 17 March the government itself held a referendum to ask whether the Union should be maintained. This produced a 76 per cent 'yes' vote, but for the government to submit the continued existence of the Soviet state to a popular vote was in itself an act of weakness in the face of growing national sentiment.

In the midst of these events the Soviet economy was in crisis. In 1990, even official figures showed that the gross national product had diminished for the first time since the end of the Second World War. In 1991 the situation worsened still further. Outside estimates put the decline in GNP at about 17 per cent; the government budget was badly in deficit; inflation rose to about 250 per cent; and the rouble virtually collapsed. The command economy broke down as the commands from the top became contradictory, and

Gorbachev tried to introduce some elements of a market economy with no clear idea of where market forces might lead.

Worse still, economic collapse was also an ideological disaster, bringing the whole crisis full circle. Communists had always claimed to understand the true laws of economics, and the Soviet Union had staked its prestige on economic success; yet it ended in economic failure. One Soviet leader after another had put everyone's money on the wrong horse. A humiliating sign of this failure came in July 1990, when Chancellor Kohl of West Germany visited Gorbachev at Stavropol and secured an agreement on total sovereignty for a reunited Germany, including liberty to join NATO, in return for large West German subsidies for the Soviet economy. Capitalist West Germany was handing out largesse to Communist Russia. In the same month Gorbachev attended a meeting of the G7 (the Group of Seven leading industrialized countries), partly as a welcome guest, but partly to request a programme of aid for the Soviet Union. This came dangerously near to going round with the begging bowl.

In face of these cumulative crises and the progressive collapse of the Soviet state, a group of conspirators, including the head of the KGB and the minister of defence, attempted a *coup d'état* in August 1991, to overthrow Gorbachev and restore the authority of the Communist Party. Gorbachev, who was on holiday in the Crimea, was placed under house arrest, but the coup failed. Gorbachev refused to yield to the demands made on him, and in Moscow Boris Yeltsin, the president of the Russian Republic, led a defiant resistance outside the parliament building. This sounded the death knell of the Communist Party. Gorbachev resigned as general secretary of the Party, the post from which Stalin and his successors had run the country. The Supreme Soviet suspended all the activities of the Party and froze its bank accounts. The Soviet Union itself dissolved during the next few months. On 8 December the presidents of Russia, Ukraine and Belarus met at Minsk and declared that the Soviet Union had ceased to exist. They proposed to replace it by an ill-defined Commonwealth of Independent States, and on 21 December most of the former Soviet Republics agreed, by the Treaty of Alma-Ata, to join this new Commonwealth. (The Baltic States and Georgia refused to take part.) On 25 December 1991 Gorbachev resigned from the post of president of the Soviet Union, which no longer had any functions. Yeltsin moved into the Kremlin as president of Russia. The red flag with the hammer and sickle was lowered, and the new Russian flag was raised in its stead. Formally, the Soviet Union ceased to exist at midnight on 31 December 1991/1 January 1992.

It was an event the like of which had not been seen since the fall of empires in 1917–18. The Soviet Union had been one of the two superpowers in the world; its disappearance left only one, the USA. The Soviet Union had offered a new model for the state, for economics and for society. For many people, the appeal of communism had been akin to that of religion, and the disappearance of the USSR meant much more than the vanishing of a state. Moreover, the Soviet Union had also tried to impose its own form of unity on eastern Europe (and, as many feared, perhaps on the West as well), by means of force, repression and ideological uniformity. The collapse of the Soviet Union meant the end of that attempt and opened a new phase in the story of European unity and division.

THE NEW RUSSIA

The Russians now had to create a new state, a new economy and a new set of political principles, starting in the midst of chaos. It was an uphill struggle. The economy continued to decline, with a diminishing GNP and an ever-weakening rouble. In 1994 the International Monetary Fund agreed to make Russia a loan of $1500 million, on condition that the government brought down inflation, reduced public expenditure and improved its methods of tax collecting – requirements that treated Russia as a beginner among states, not a great power. In fact, the government had to default on its domestic debt in 1998, and devalue the already weak rouble still further. Taxes went uncollected and the government met its budget deficit by printing money, which only led to more inflation.

Economic decline was accompanied by political uncertainty, with the one feeding off the other. President Yeltsin proved an erratic leader, prone to ill health, vodka and uncertain judgement. Disillusion with the new regime set in, arousing nostalgia for old times and the former certainties. The communists gained striking successes in elections to the Duma in December 1995, winning 22 per cent of the vote and just over one-third of the seats. Yeltsin suddenly resigned in 1999, and was replaced as president by Vladimir Putin, a former KGB man, who took an authoritarian line which was welcome to many Russians. Throughout the 1990s, Russia remained absorbed in its own internal problems, and was effectively detached from the rest of continental Europe. Indeed, it was even less a part of Europe (except in a geographical sense) than in the period when the USSR had controlled its own zone in eastern Europe.

THE FATE OF THE FORMER SOVIET ZONE

While Russia was struggling with economic failure and political uncertainty, the fate of the former Soviet zone in eastern Europe slowly became clearer. The formal structures of the old regime, the Warsaw Pact and COMECON, were quickly dismantled. The Warsaw Pact was dissolved on 1 July 1991, despite Soviet attempts to preserve some of the political aspects of the treaty. Russian troops left East Germany, Czechoslovakia, Hungary, Poland and the Baltic states during the next three years. COMECON was formally dissolved on 28 June 1991, and its east European members suffered sharply as a result, because under the COMECON system the Soviet Union had bought their exports, which were hard to sell elsewhere, and also supplied them with oil at below world prices. The end of COMECON was doubtless inevitable, but it brought some unwelcome consequences.

Politically, the countries of the former Soviet zone found themselves in a strange sort of no-man's-land. They had undergone a revolution, in a short space of time and in extraordinary circumstances. Except in Romania, there had been almost no bloodshed. The former rulers, who had held the jobs and enjoyed the privileges of the old regime, abdicated without a struggle, in a silent confession of failure. Yet it was a revolution without a creed or a clear purpose. The communist regimes had produced in their citizens an almost total scepticism – practically no one believed in anything, but almost everyone knew how to survive and work the system. When communism vanished, the scepticism and the instinct for survival remained, but for a time there was no firm positive impulse.[4] The countries of eastern Europe remained separated from the West, but now by a different sort of division. The Iron Curtain had vanished, but there remained a line of separation between an active, bustling, prosperous western Europe and an area of confusion and economic backwardness in the East. The dividing line was no longer obvious to the eye, but it was none the less real for that.

The countries of eastern Europe faced a host of common, or at any rate similar, problems. They had to shift from a command economy to a free market, or perhaps some mixture of the two, involving the privatization of industry, commerce and agriculture. They faced uncertainty as to legal titles to property after large-scale confiscation and collectivization under the communist regimes. In politics they struggled to establish stable governments under parliamentary democracy where there had been one-party states for some 40 years. Almost inevitably disillusion set in, and people grumbled that things had been better under communism. In nearly every country problems of nationality and ethnic minorities, shelved or suppressed under communism, came to the surface. Czechoslovakia was split between Czechs and Slovaks at the end of 1992, and broke into two states. The new Slovakia then had to deal with its own Hungarian minority. Romania too had a Hungarian minority, in Transylvania. Hungary itself included no substantial minorities, but its foreign policy had to be largely concerned with the fate of Hungarians outside its borders. Nations and nationalism were very much alive.

All the countries in the former Soviet zone sought answers to their problems by means of entry to NATO and the European Union, thus aspiring to a formal unification between East and West. They had lost one set of landmarks and associations, and sought psychological reassurance by replacing them with others. Russia still loomed large to the east, and NATO offered security against a possible revival of Russian power, as well as a link with the USA, which was the world's strongest military power and the embodiment of successful capitalism. The European Union, with its long record of economic success, held out the prospect of prosperity to countries which were unhappily aware of their comparative poverty. Politicians who knew about survival in the Soviet system were not afraid of the complications and bureaucracy of the EU. Certainly isolation did not seem a workable option, and so the new governments of eastern Europe set out to become 'Western' (in the shape of NATO) and 'European' (in the shape of the EU) at the same time; with results that we will see in due course.

POLAND

Poland, the largest and most influential country in the former Soviet zone, deserves particular attention in itself *and* as an illustration of many of the economic and political difficulties of eastern Europe as a whole.[5] On the economy, the Polish government tried the bold course of changing to a market system in one fell swoop – the 'Big Bang' was the current term, borrowed from the capitalist West. Early in 1990 price controls and most government subsidies were abolished, but wage controls were retained, which proved a recipe for chaos. Prices rose rapidly (by as much as 600 per cent in some cases) and the purchasing power of wages fell. Unemployment, which in principle had not existed under communism, rose to about 1.3 million (8 per cent of the workforce) in 1990, and continued to rise in subsequent years. In 1992 it was considered something of a success that inflation was only 43 per cent. Not until 1995 did the Polish economy begin to show growth; and even then unemployment remained high and inflation ran at over 20 per cent.

As for politics, the Polish constitution was revised in 1990, abolishing censorship and the state monopoly of the mass media. An election for a new president in November–December 1990 was won by Lech Walesa, the leader of Solidarity and hero of the anticommunist struggle in the 1980s, who took almost three-quarters of the second-round vote; though on a turnout of only 53.4 per cent. Released from the communist straitjacket, Polish politics then plunged into almost infinite diversity. In parliamentary elections in 1991, no fewer than 67 parties took part, of which 29 won at least 1 seat; but people were beginning to lose interest, and only 43 per cent of voters turned out. Governments followed one another in quick succession. In July 1992 Hanna Suchocka had the distinction of becoming the first woman prime minister of Poland; but also had the doubtful privilege of forming the fifth government in two and a half years since the end of communist rule. One government after another struggled with the country's economic problems, closing unprofitable coal mines and proposing to end state subsidies for coal-mining by the year 2000. A political reaction set in and ex-communists scored an electoral victory in 1993. But the pendulum swung back, and the Solidarity Electoral Alliance (made up of no fewer than 36 separate parties) made a comeback in 1997 on a programme supporting private property, Christianity and family values – a striking combination for a recently communist country.

The foreign policy of successive governments, whatever their political persuasion, was to join the European Union and NATO. With active support from Germany, Poland secured associate status in the EU in 1994. In 1997 the country came within sight of achieving the double, with NATO agreeing that Poland should join the alliance in 1999, and the EU formally accepting Polish candidacy for full membership, with a good expectation of success – though only if Polish agriculture and industry could adapt to some harsh conditions.

OTHER EAST EUROPEAN COUNTRIES

Most other countries in eastern Europe went through similar difficulties. Hungary, Romania, Bulgaria, and the three Baltic states (Estonia, Latvia and Lithuania) struggled with the problems of changing to a market economy. They suffered severe inflation and high unemployment. They found themselves with steel plants and coal mines whose products were no longer needed, but which it was politically dangerous to close. They had little private capital for investment, and could offer potential Western investors inadequate security or incentives. Their peoples had grown accustomed to levels of social welfare which could no longer be maintained. Nearly all countries faced problems of nationality, suppressed but never removed under the communist regimes. The position of the large Hungarian minority in Transylvania was an obvious example; and the Baltic states faced the problem in even more extreme forms. These countries had been annexed by the Soviet Union in 1940, and after the war had been Soviet Republics, not satellite states. The Soviet forces stationed there had been on their own territory, and even when they withdrew they left behind large numbers of retired soldiers, civilian staff and their dependants, as well as many Russians and others who had moved in over many years. In 1992 it was estimated that the population of Latvia was only 52 per cent Latvian and 34 per cent Russian. Estonia comprised 62 per cent Estonians and 30 per cent Russians. (Lithuania was much better placed, with only 9 per cent Russians.)[6]

The fate of two countries stands out from the rest, and deserves particular attention: Czechoslovakia and Yugoslavia, which both split up in the 1990s, but in completely different ways. Czechoslovakia divided into two states in a remarkably orderly fashion; Yugoslavia dissolved into chaos and civil strife.

CZECHOSLOVAKIA

Post-communist Czechoslovakia started with some notable advantages. It had functioned as a stable parliamentary democracy between the wars. Under communism the country had made an outstanding mark when Dubček made his daring attempt at reform in 1968. Later, Charter 77 had been a rallying point for opposition to communism, with a reputation far outside the borders of its own country. In 1989 Czechoslovakia produced its own velvet revolution, and Václav Havel was probably the most distinguished figure in east European political life. In 1990 the country took eagerly to the new political and cultural conditions, with flourishing political parties and a plethora of new journals, films and plays (after all, it is rare for a country to have a playwright as its president). Economically, the country had a strong industrial base. It suffered when the Soviet Union reduced its cheap oil exports and ceased to buy Czechoslovakian products; but Czechoslovakia was quickly admitted to membership of the International Monetary Fund and received loans to ease the transition to a new economic system.

The country's deepest problem, which had haunted it ever since its foundation, was its division on lines of nationality. The name Czechoslovakia claimed a unity between Czechs and Slovaks which had never been fully achieved, and after the fall of communism Slovak separatism increased in strength. In 1991 the preparation of a new constitution reached deadlock on the question of relations between the federal Czechoslovak government and the separate Czech and Slovak Republics. After elections in June 1992, the respective Czech and Slovak premiers, Václav Klaus and Vladimir Meciar, agreed to form a federal government with the sole purpose of dividing the country. This was accomplished by agreement, and the joint assets and organizations were split up with reasonable smoothness. It was a partition carried out from above, and neither the Czech nor the Slovak leaders chose to put the issue to a referendum, preferring to avoid publicizing questions which they managed to deal with in an administrative and technical manner. Czechoslovakia ceased to exist at the end of 1992, and was replaced by the Czech Republic and Slovakia – a separation which testified to the persistent influence of nationalism, and yet was carried out in a manner which was a tribute to the caution and restraint of the two new states.

After separation the Czech Republic achieved for some years a political stability and economic progress rare in eastern Europe. Klaus's coalition government lasted until November 1997; and the Czech economy managed a modest but steady growth rate, reaching 4 per cent in 1995, with low unemployment and a successful programme of privatization of former state companies. In 1997 the country struck its first economic crisis, causing the fall of Klaus's government; the president then appointed the governor of the National Bank as prime minister, to restore confidence in the economy. In foreign policy, the Czech Republic, like Poland, aimed at joining the European Union and NATO, and scored a double success in 1997, when NATO invited the Czechs to join the alliance in 1999, and the EU formally accepted the Czech candidacy for membership.

Slovakia, by contrast, found political stability hard to achieve. There were three elections and three different governments in 1994. The economy, which was largely dependent on agriculture, achieved only low growth, and unemployment ran at about 13 per cent of the workforce in 1995 and 1996. The Slovaks had achieved their own national independence, but at once faced the problem of a Hungarian minority which made up about 11 per cent of the population. The government took a tough line, insisting on Slovak as the only official language, to be used for all public business. This caused trouble for Slovakia in its aspiration to join the European Union, which urged the Slovaks to relax their language laws, but without success. As a result, the EU placed Slovakia on a slower track towards membership than the Czech Republic. But Slovakia remained undeterred, and kept its sights on joining both the EU and NATO.

YUGOSLAVIA

By contrast with the orderly partition of Czechoslovakia, Yugoslavia disintegrated amid civil war and so-called ethnic cleansing, a euphemism for massacre and deportation. Militant nationalism, which had largely died away in western Europe and was at any rate contained in most of eastern Europe, took command in Yugoslavia, bringing conflict and disaster in its wake.[7]

In 1990 Yugoslavia was a federation, made up of six republics: Serbia, Croatia, Bosnia, Slovenia, Montenegro and Macedonia; plus two autonomous provinces of Serbia: Kosovo and Voivodina. Of the republics, Serbia was the largest, with nearly 10 million people; Montenegro was the smallest, with about 650,000; and Slovenia was the wealthiest. Serbia and Slovenia were largely homogeneous in their populations; the others were all mixed, with Bosnia as the most extreme case, with a population made up of Muslims (about 44 per cent), Serbs (31 per cent) and Croats (17 per cent).

The movement towards a break-up of Yugoslavia began in Slovenia and Croatia, which held referendums on independence early in 1991 and formally declared their independence on 25 and 26 June 1991, respectively. Slovenia achieved rapid success. The country was prosperous, homogeneous in population, and militarily prepared to defend itself. A half-hearted Serbian attempt at invasion was beaten off, and the Slovenes made good their secession. Croatia was in a very different position. The country included a substantial Serbian population, which effectively controlled about one-third of the country and opposed the declaration of independence. Civil war began, with both sides consolidating their hold on their parts of the country by bouts of ethnic cleansing. The Serbian government in Belgrade intervened on the side of the Serbs; and at one stage Serbian warships bombarded the ancient and beautiful port of Dubrovnik – an action which gained the Serbs a reputation for barbarism from which they never recovered in the West; though in general terms the balance of brutality between Serbs and Croats was fairly even. After heavy fighting and much destruction, United Nations mediation secured a ceasefire at the end of 1991, leaving the Croatians with effective independence in about two-thirds of the country, and the Serbs in control of the remainder.

Meanwhile, the break-up of Yugoslavia continued. In September 1991 a referendum in Macedonia produced an overwhelming vote for independence. In 1992 the government of Bosnia under Alija Izetbegovic (a Muslim) declared independence; but the Bosnian Serbs broke away and set up their own separate Republic of Srpska. By the end of the year the Bosnian Serbs held a large part of the territory of Bosnia, from which they drove out Muslims and

Croats, who retaliated in kind in other parts of the country. The fighting continued, with some intermissions, for another three years, with heavy casualties and many atrocities against civilians (notably the massacre of some 8000 Muslims at Srebrenica in July 1995). Vast numbers of refugees, reckoned at over 1.5 million from a population in 1990 of no more than 4.5 million, fled or were driven from their homes. It was a conflict more terrible than anything seen in Europe since the end of the Second World War.

These events inevitably became matters of international concern. The former Yugoslavia had frontiers with three members of the European Union (Italy, Austria and Greece). Refugees from the fighting fled into neighbouring countries, and then onwards across Europe. Massacres, perhaps amounting to genocide, evoked cries that 'something must be done'.

Such events could not be ignored; and politicians who were seeking to develop a common foreign policy for the European Union even welcomed the opportunity to show what they could do. In June 1991 Jacques Poos, the foreign minister of Luxembourg (which held the presidency of the EU at the time) declared grandly: 'This is the hour of Europe. It is not the hour of the Americans.'[8] He was soon proved wrong. A three-man team from the EU (the foreign ministers of Luxembourg, Italy and the Netherlands) visited Yugoslavia several times, securing only empty promises of a ceasefire. The EU agreed on an arms embargo, to little effect. The EU foreign ministers convened a peace conference at The Hague, under the chairmanship of Lord Carrington (a former British Foreign Secretary), which achieved no success. On 23 December 1991 Germany, instead of observing an EU agreement to act together, went ahead and recognized the independence of Slovenia and Croatia. Austria soon followed. If this was 'the hour of Europe', then the EU missed the bus.

Instead, the initiative passed to the United Nations, and effectively to the USA. In 1992 the task of mediation was taken up by Lord Owen (another former British Foreign Secretary) and Cyrus Vance (a former US Secretary of State), acting on behalf of the UN Security Council. Owen and Vance proposed a complicated plan for the partition of Bosnia into no fewer than 10 autonomous cantons, which was rejected by the Bosnian Serbs. The Security Council despatched a United Nations Protection Force (under the ungainly acronym of UNPROFOR) to Bosnia, not to impose a settlement or a ceasefire, but only to administer humanitarian aid to the population and to protect 'safe areas' where civilians could take refuge. In the latter task the UN force failed sadly, and one of the worst massacres took place in a so-called safe area.

Eventually, in 1995, the Americans lost patience, and intervened against the Serbs. They armed and trained Croatian forces, and bombarded Serbian troops and other targets from the air. Under this assault, the Serbs agreed to a ceasefire, which was generally observed; and the USA convened a peace conference in Dayton, Ohio, held at a US Air Force base, as a pointed reminder of the force which had brought the conference about. The meeting, under

American chairmanship, was attended by the presidents of Serbia, Croatia and Bosnia, as well as representatives from Britain, France, Germany and Russia. They reached an agreement by which Bosnia was recognized as a sovereign state, but was divided into two autonomous parts: Bosnia-Herzegovina, with a population mostly made up of Muslims and Croats; and a Serb Republic of Srpska. This complicated arrangement maintained the unity of Bosnia in principle, while accepting its division for most practical purposes. A NATO force of some 60,000 troops (including 20,000 Americans) was to enforce the agreement – recognition that the fragile settlement could only be maintained by external compulsion.[9]

The disintegration of Yugoslavia was by no means 'the hour of Europe'. By the time of the Dayton agreement, the crisis had lasted a full five years, and its partial resolution had only been achieved by the military and diplomatic intervention of the USA. The contribution of the European Union had been slight.

As an uneasy peace was established in Bosnia, a further conflict developed in Kosovo, where a large majority of Albanians (85–90 per cent, according to one source) lived under Serbian rule. The Serbs, for their part, regarded Kosovo as vital to their national identity, because it had been the scene of a disastrous battle against the Ottoman Turks in 1389, and remained hallowed ground. In 1996 an Albanian revolt against Serb rule broke out, led by the Kosovo Liberation Army (KLA). By 1998 the KLA, with help from Albania, had established control over large parts of the countryside, while the Serbs held the towns and main roads. There were atrocities on both sides, and the Serbs drove some 200,000 Albanians out of their parts of the province. Eventually outside powers, led by the USA, intervened. In February 1999 NATO convened a conference at Rambouillet in France, under American chairmanship and attended by representatives from Serbia and the Kosovo Albanians. The conference devised a proposal for an autonomous administration in Kosovo, including both Serbs and Albanians, which was accepted by the KLA but rejected by the Serbs, who also refused to admit a NATO peacekeeping force into the territory they controlled in Kosovo.

NATO, under American leadership and with prominent support from Britain and France, took the Serbian rejection as a cause for armed intervention, claiming that they must prevent ethnic cleansing and preserve the human rights of the people of Kosovo. On 24 March 1999 NATO forces began to bombard Serbia from the air, aiming at military targets but inevitably hitting others as well. On the same day, the leaders of the European Union meeting in Berlin supported these attacks, declaring that they could not tolerate a humanitarian disaster on their own borders, nor allow the majority of Kosovars to be deprived of their rights. The result was an extraordinary sort of war, fought by one side almost without risk and without casualties. Some American aircraft flew from bases in the USA, dropped their bombs from a safe height, and returned home. But on the receiving end of this bombardment casualties and damage were heavy. In Kosovo itself the situation actually worsened, as the Serbs continued to drive out Albanians from territory they controlled, and refugees fled from the war zone in large numbers.

Eventually, in June 1999, the Serbian government under Milosevic gave up the unequal struggle and accepted NATO terms. Kosovo was to be granted autonomy, but still remained under Serbian sovereignty; an international peacekeeping force was to be deployed in the province; and refugees were to return to their homes. On these terms, the NATO bombardment ceased on 10 June. Within a short time, a large force of NATO troops from the USA, Britain, France, Germany and Italy moved into Kosovo. The return of refugees to their homes, on the other hand, proved much more difficult; and indeed many had no homes to return to.

The results of this strange war were an odd mixture. The USA and NATO had bombed Serbia into submission and could claim a victory. But the Serbs, under Milosevic, could also claim a sort of success, because Kosovo remained legally part of Serbia. Against this, the Albanian majority in Kosovo had gained autonomous status, and could hope to achieve independence at some future time. Only the European Union could claim nothing, and the humanitarian disaster in Kosovo, which the EU leaders had said they could not tolerate, had in fact come about.

By the end of 1999 the disintegration of Yugoslavia was complete. Slovenia had come out of it best, and had settled into a reasonably stable and prosperous existence. The government applied to join the European Union in 1997, and in 1998 was permitted to open formal negotiations for entry. Croatia was slowly recovering from its civil war, and the drastic methods of ethnic cleansing had finally resulted in a largely homogeneous population, including 80 per cent Croats and only 5 per cent Serbs. Bosnia was held together on paper by a complicated federal constitution, and in practice by a NATO administrator (a governor in all but name) and NATO troops. Serbia had suffered heavily during the NATO bombardments, and was patching up the damage as best it could. In the south, Macedonia had established its independence, but included an Albanian minority which made up nearly a quarter of the population and was hard to assimilate. The only international body to make an impact on the situation, for good or ill, was NATO, which for most purposes meant the USA.

These events demonstrated a grave weakness in the European Union, which had been unable to intervene effectively in the Yugoslavian crises. Moreover, one of the assumptions on which the EU was based – the declining force of nationalism – manifestly did not hold true in Yugoslavia, where nationalism was very much alive. Nations asserted their right to independence and took up arms to achieve it. Violence and atrocities flourished. The Americans and NATO used their own forms of violence in order to restore peace – of a sort. Conditions reminiscent of the Second World War prevailed over large areas.

The contrast between the supranational and peaceable character of the European Union and the nationalist struggles of ex-Yugoslavia could scarcely have been sharper.

ALBANIA

Much the same was true with regard to Albania, which sometimes scarcely functioned as a viable state. Albania had long been a communist country, though outside the Soviet sphere; and after the upheavals of 1989 it retained the title of 'People's Republic' until April 1991, when a new constitution was introduced. Governments followed one another in quick succession, and new political parties came and went without much basis in the country. By 1997 Albania was in a state of anarchy, with parts of the country outside government control; on occasion prisons were opened and their inmates simply walked out. The country became a centre of crime, and a starting point for illegal migration to Italy and other parts of western Europe. Albania was geographically in Europe, but politically and socially apart from it, and a greater irritant to other countries than might have been expected from its population of about 3 million.

THE EUROPEAN UNION

We have already seen that among these sometimes confused and chaotic events all the countries of the former Soviet zone, plus the Baltic states which had actually been part of the Soviet Union, and Slovenia which had been part of Yugoslavia, set out to join NATO and the European Union. Their attempts achieved little by way of immediate reward in the 1990s. In 1999 three countries were admitted, after long negotiations, to membership of NATO: the Czech Republic, Hungary and Poland. None actually secured membership of the European Union, though several had made real progress on an arduous obstacle course towards admission (see below, p. 233). But none of them, even the least favoured candidates such as Romania or Bulgaria, ever stopped trying. All persisted, with a determination which showed the importance of the objective. To join the European Union was the central aim of their foreign policy, and of much domestic policy as well.

What was this organization which others were so determined to join? There is often much in a name. Up to 1991 the organization was still called the European Economic Community (EEC), a title going back to its founding document, the Treaty of Rome, signed in 1957. In December 1991 the member states agreed to drop the word 'Economic', modifying the exclusive emphasis on economic integration and shortening the name to European Community (EC). The Maastricht Treaty, which was formally signed on 7 February 1992 and came into force on 1 November 1993, changed the name again, to European Union (EU), a more resonant title than 'Community' though retaining an element of ambiguity, even vagueness. Some expert observers maintained that the newly named Union represented only a closer form of cooperation between its members, while leaving the ultimate objective of the organization uncertain – still 'a journey to an unknown destination' (see above, p. 197); while others argued that the change marked a decisive move towards the creation of a united European state, of which some elements were already in existence and others were coming into being.[10]

The Treaty of Maastricht, which introduced the new name of 'European Union', initiated three major changes: the acceptance of a programme for economic and monetary union, whose final stage was to be the adoption of a single currency; agreement on common social policies; and a proposal to evolve a common foreign and security policy some time in the future. Britain and Denmark reserved the right to opt out of economic and monetary union; and Britain also opted out of the agreement on social policy. The British were also wary of the proposal for a common foreign and security policy, and sought to preserve their close political and military links with the USA.

THE EUROPEAN ECONOMY

Despite these reservations, the Maastricht Treaty represented 'an unprecedented voluntary cession of national sovereignty'.[11] This was most obviously true of the programme for economic and monetary union, which required the acceptance of 'convergence criteria' relating to budget deficits, public debt, inflation and interest rates. Governments thus accepted an eventual loss of control over their monetary policy; and agreed to abandon the important symbol of sovereignty and identity represented by a national currency. In the event, this plan ran into difficulties almost at once. The Exchange Rate Mechanism (ERM), which was set up as a step towards monetary union, broke down in September 1992, when sterling was forced out of the ERM by heavy speculation against the pound – a severe blow to the British government, which had claimed to be committed to the Mechanism up to the very hour of abandoning it. Italy too claimed that the ERM was vital to its interests, but was compelled to devalue the lira. Spain and Portugal remained in the ERM in principle, but in practice had to devalue; and in January 1993 Ireland followed. At the end of July France was in effect compelled to devalue the franc; and at the beginning of August 1993 the ERM had to allow a 15 per cent margin of variation between its member currencies, rendering it almost pointless.

These events might well have undermined the whole scheme for monetary union, but in fact they proved only a setback, not a death blow. The states which were committed to the project held to their course and were joined by new supporters. Three new countries joined the EU in January 1995; among them, Austria and Finland agreed to adopt the single currency, though Sweden did not. A European summit meeting in Madrid in December 1995 agreed on a name for the new currency – the euro. Exchange rates between national currencies and the euro were to be fixed on 1 January 1999, and euro banknotes and coins were to be issued on 1 January 2002. It was true that some countries were adaptable (not to say shifty) in the methods they adopted to meet the convergence criteria set down at Maastricht. For example, the French treated the pension fund assets of France Telecom as state revenue in order to bring down their budget deficit to the necessary level. Italy introduced a 'Euro-tax', which was in fact a loan because it was to be set against tax in future years. But by whatever means the process went ahead. The euro was introduced, according to plan, on 1 January 1999, and the currencies of 11 countries were fixed in relation to it, losing any separate existence or value of their own. The 11 founder states were: Austria, Belgium, Finland, France, Germany, Ireland, Italy, Luxembourg, the Netherlands, Portugal and Spain. Britain, Denmark and Sweden chose not to adopt the currency; Greece did not qualify at once, but managed to do so by 2001.

The introduction of the euro had far-reaching consequences. It removed key instruments of financial and economic policy (notably the setting of interest rates) from national control, and transferred them to the newly established European Central Bank (ECB). It also marked a symbolic change. As the first president of the ECB, Wim Duisenberg, went out of his way to emphasize, a currency was not simply a medium of exchange: 'A currency is also part of the identity of a people. It reflects what they have in common, now and in the future.'[12] The euro was also a remarkable testimony to the continuity and persistence of EEC policy. As early as 1971, the Luxembourg prime minister, Pierre Werner, had proposed the establishment of economic and monetary union by 1980. His timescale had proved to be well astray, but the objective had finally been reached; and when the new currency came into being, the president of the European Commission, Jacques Santer, marked the occasion by presenting Werner with a copy of the European Union's *Journal Officiel*, dated 31 December 1998, listing the fixed exchange rates of the euro with the national currencies which it replaced.

MEMBERSHIP CRITERIA

The concept of a common foreign and security policy outlined in the Treaty of Maastricht proved for some time an empty aspiration. During the 1990s, the EU faced a great foreign policy issue on its doorstep, in the break-up of Yugoslavia. As we have seen already (see above, pp. 226–9), the EU attempted a united intervention, but without success, and the initiative quickly passed to NATO and, above all, to the USA, the only country with the will and the military power to take effective action. Whether this failure would prove a fatal blow to the concept of a common foreign policy or only a temporary setback (as the collapse of the ERM had been for the single currency) remained to be seen.

The new circumstances created by the Treaty of Maastricht, and the requests for membership from the east European states, impelled the EU to reconsider its own character and identity. In June 1993 the EU leaders, meeting at Copenhagen, set out three criteria for states seeking to open negotiations for membership. These were: the possession of stable democratic institutions, and an established respect for the rule of law, human rights and the rights of ethnic minorities; the existence of a functioning market economy, capable of meeting economic conditions within the EU; and the ability to accept all the obligations involved in political, economic and monetary union.[13]

These criteria raised serious questions. They defined the European Union in economic terms, but also as 'a community of values' (democracy, human rights, the rights of minorities). In fact, these values were not specifically European, or exclusive to the EU. The USA, Canada, Australia and New Zealand had been functioning democracies for far longer than some members of the EU. Switzerland and Norway, which remained outside the EU, were admirable examples of civic virtue. In many ways, it was more accurate to speak of 'Western values' than to claim 'European values' peculiar to the states of the EU. Moreover, the insistence on stable democratic institutions imposed a criterion that was at once rigid yet vague, and might well present problems in its application. Were member states never to change their regimes? What would happen if a democratic choice produced a government which other EU states found undemocratic – or simply did not like? In 1958 France had changed its regime from the Fourth Republic to the Fifth, and de Gaulle had introduced a strong presidency, arousing mistaken fears in some quarters that he was aiming at some form of dictatorship. At that time, the EEC was in its formative stages and no difficulty arose; but how would similar events be dealt with under the Copenhagen criteria? A question of this type, though in a milder form, was in fact to arise in Austria in 2000 (see below, pp. 245–6).

There was another difficulty in that the democratic credentials of the EU itself were open to question. Elections for the European Parliament in June 1994, the first since the Maastricht Treaty, showed a total turnout in all member states of only 56.5 per cent, even though in some countries voting was compulsory. In the Netherlands, long a leader in the move towards European integration, turnout was only 35.6 per cent. In the next elections in 1999, total turnout fell below 50 per cent, with the Netherlands down to 30 per cent.[14] Moreover, public opinion polls revealed little sense of a European, as against national, consciousness, without which even a high electoral turnout would not signify a real democratic commitment to the EU. At the end of 1997 only 5 per cent of those polled across the EU felt European without qualification, and 6 per cent European plus their own nationality; the vast majority retained their own national identity.[15] An elite was pressing ahead with European integration, but the mass of the population was some way behind. If the EU were to be classified as a regime, it was more of an oligarchy than a democracy, and probably more of a bureaucracy than either.

EUROPEAN UNION: EAST AND WEST

During the 1990s the European Union suffered an economic setback, and ceased to deliver the buoyant economic growth which had characterized its earlier years. Growth rates fell to 2 or 3 per cent in most years (with the notable exception of Ireland, which spurted ahead at 9 or 10 per cent per year). Unemployment in the EU rose to 18 million in 1993, and 19 million (about 11 per cent of the total workforce) in 1997.[16]

Partly because of this comparative economic stagnation, the countries of the EU provided only limited economic assistance to the countries of eastern Europe as they emerged from communism. The EC introduced a programme of aid, encouragingly called 'Phare' ('lighthouse'), in 1989, but allocated only small sums of money to it. The European Bank for Reconstruction and Development, under the presidency of Jacques Attali, spent more on its new buildings in London than it provided in aid or loans. West European investors were wary of conditions in the East, where titles to property and the ownership of companies were often difficult to establish. Industrial goods manufactured in eastern Europe were often of poor quality, and did not find ready markets in the West. The European Union in its loftier moments claimed to represent 'Europe' as a whole; but in its down-to-earth mode it looked after its own interests.

In these circumstances, there was something of a mismatch between the eagerness of the east European states to join the EU and the guarded response of the EU itself. The leaders of the member states, meeting at Essen in 1994, laid down that applicants had to prepare their economies, banking systems and legal arrangements for the transition, as well as meeting the Copenhagen criteria with regard to democracy and human rights. The EU might claim to be moving with all deliberate speed to accept the new candidates, but the emphasis was more on deliberation than on speed. In 1998 the European Commission divided the east European applicants into an 'A list' (the Czech Republic, Estonia, Hungary, Poland and Slovenia) and a 'B list' of weaker aspirants (Bulgaria, Latvia, Lithuania, Romania and Slovakia). In 1999 this distinction was abandoned, and the EU leaders agreed at a meeting in Helsinki that applications should be considered on their individual merits.

On the whole, the EU was slow and cautious in its attitude to the east European countries which were knocking on its doors. The Council of Europe on the other hand, founded many years before in 1949, was a different kind of body and offered a different approach. It required a concurrence of values, in that membership was open to European states which accepted the rule of law, human rights and fundamental freedoms; but had no programme of economic integration or supranational administration. The Council's geographical definition of Europe was given a wide interpretation when Turkey was admitted as a member in 1949, and in the 1990s the Council took as its scope a vast area, accepting countries which the EU did not even contemplate as members at that time. Albania, Moldova and Ukraine were admitted in 1995, and Russia in 1996. By the end of 1996 only six countries in geographical Europe were not yet members – Armenia, Azerbaijan, Belarus, Bosnia, Georgia and Yugoslavia; and of these, the admission of Armenia,

Azerbaijan and Georgia was well under way, leaving only three outside (where they still remained in 2000). This flexibility was achieved at the cost of a lack of rigour in how the Council's principles were applied – could it really be said, for example, that the rule of law prevailed in Albania in 1995? But at any rate, the east European countries could find a way to assert their European identity in a looser association than that provided by the European Union.

GERMANY

East met West most immediately in Germany. The Iron Curtain had divided Germany, physically and psychologically; and on a wider scale the division of Germany had symbolized the division of Europe. In the 1990s Germany presented a test case, to see how far and how quickly those divisions could be overcome.

The political unification of Germany came about with astonishing speed. Chancellor Helmut Kohl of West Germany seized the initiative between November 1989 and February 1990. He secured Gorbachev's consent to rapid unification, and to the newly united Germany remaining a member of NATO and the European Economic Community. He made a grand and costly gesture of welcome to the East Germans by promising to accept the weak East German mark as equal to the Deutschmark, one of the strongest currencies in western Europe. In March 1990 elections were held in East Germany, with Kohl and other politicians from West Germany campaigning as though they were at home. On a massive turnout of 93 per cent, parties linked to the West won an overwhelming victory. The Christian Democrats and their allies won 48 per cent of the vote and 192 of the 400 seats; the Social Democrats 22 per cent and 88 seats.[17] On 18 May a State Treaty was signed between the two Germanies, by which the two countries were to be united by the absorption of the East into the West. East Germany accepted the West German political system, and East German wages, pensions and savings (up to a certain amount) were to be converted to Deutschmarks at a rate of one to one. At midnight on 2/3 October 1990 the German Democratic Republic ceased to exist, and a united Germany with a population of over 78 million came into being.

The European Economic Community as a body had very little to do with these events – a remarkable demonstration of how it could be ignored in a political crisis. But many members were dismayed by the rapid reunification of Germany, and sought to bind the new state yet more tightly into an integrated Europe. A meeting of EEC leaders in Dublin in May 1990, in the midst of the dash to German unification, agreed that the Community should make a new move towards political union; and so set in train the process which led to the Maastricht Treaty. This move was welcomed in Germany, where politicians had long been committed to European integration to a degree not fully shared even by the French, and certainly not by the British. German political leaders, and to a large extent the German people, had undergone a revulsion against nationalism after the experience of Nazism and defeat in the Second World War. They were also well accustomed to the workings of their own federal state, and ready to welcome a federal structure for the EEC. (The hostile British reaction against the word 'federalism' was almost unintelligible to Germans, to whom federalism meant protection *against* the central government, not subjection to it.) In December 1992 the Basic Law under which Germany had been unified was amended so as to commit Germany to the realization of a united Europe. The commander of the German Army, General Naumann, declared that he looked forward to the day when German soldiers could take an oath to the European flag.[18] So it came about that most members of the EEC pressed on towards closer union out of a residual fear of German power, while the Germans themselves pursued the same aim out of conviction. Either way, German unification gave an extra impulse to greater unity in the EEC.

Yet Germany itself remained divided. Separate development under radically different regimes for over 40 years could not vanish overnight, or even over several years. Psychologically, the legacy of the communist security police, the Stasi, with its network of informers, left a shadow over the former East Germany. The Western political parties found it hard to put down roots in the East, where the ex-communists, under their new name of the Party of Democratic Socialism, recovered after their defeat in 1990. Economically, the two parts of the country remained very different. Privatization of state-owned companies in the East moved slowly, with many problems as to the legal ownership of property and assets. Productivity in the East was lower than in the West. The rate of unemployment in the East was roughly double that in the West for the first half of the 1990s, even though the figures in the East were kept artificially low by short-time working, early retirement and other devices. The West remained richer than the East. In 1995 it was estimated that the financial assets of the average household in the former West Germany amounted to 137,000 DM; in the former East Germany the equivalent figure was only 40,000 DM.[19] In these circumstances, disillusion set in on both sides of the line. West Germans wearied of pouring money into the East. East Germans grumbled at their comparative poverty, and sometimes regretted the old days when there had been 'no unemployment under communism'.

OTHER UNION MEMBERS AND THE CONCEPT OF UNITY

Alongside Germany stood France, the initiator and prime mover of the movement towards European integration, from the launch of the Schuman Plan in 1950 onwards. The 'Franco–German couple' had long provided the motive force of the EEC, and the alliance with Germany had become the main element in French foreign policy. This alliance was shaken in 1990, when Mitterrand found that he was consigned to the sidelines as Kohl dashed ahead to achieve German unification. In 1992 the French government's assumptions about the state of their own public opinion were belied when a referendum on the Maastricht Treaty produced an intense debate and a very close result: 51.05 per cent 'yes', 48.95 per cent 'no'.[20] French opinion on European integration proved to be more divided than had previously been assumed.

But despite these difficulties, French policy stayed on course. Franco–German relations recovered from the shock of German unification and remained close during the 1990s. Public opinion accepted the next stage in European integration, monetary union and the single currency, without much ado. The main political parties on both left and right were in favour of adopting the euro; though the National Front on the right and the Communist Party on the left were against it. When the change came, most people took it in their stride – though they grumbled about rising prices. On the other hand, there were limits to the French devotion to integration. French governments talked a good deal about common European defence and foreign policies, but they showed no sign of giving up control of their nuclear weapons or abandoning their independent policy in Africa.

Italy was committed to European integration in principle, and the Italian government took its turn at the presidency of the EEC in 1990 as an advocate of federalism. But in 1994 right-wing parties (*Forza Italia* and the Northern League) gained a majority in the Chamber of Deputies, and Silvio Berlusconi became prime minister in a nationalist coalition government. Some members of the European Parliament were dismayed at Berlusconi's victory, and passed a resolution opposing the inclusion of 'fascists' in the governments of member states of the EU. (This was an occasion when the enthusiasm of the EU for democracy wavered, when democracy produced unwelcome results.) Berlusconi denied that his Cabinet included any fascists; and in any case the balance swung again in 1996, when the left-wing 'Olive Tree' coalition gained a majority, and Romano Prodi, a committed 'European', became prime minister. Italy was determined to adopt the euro and successfully met the required criteria, though only with the aid of some fiscal sleight of hand.

Spain remained strongly committed to the European Union, which was not only financially advantageous, but was linked in the public mind to the end of dictatorship and the country's return to the mainstream of west European political life. Spain was a prominent founder member of the single currency. Portugal shared the same sense of rejoining a European fellowship, and also did rather well from EU subsidies during its first decade of membership. Afterwards there was some disillusionment, but no serious change of mind.

Greek attitudes to the EU were intriguingly inconsistent. Greek governments claimed to be good Europeans, and Greek agriculture did well out of European subsidies – sometimes for an exaggerated production of olive oil. Greece failed to meet the conditions to be a founder member of the single currency, but still managed to adopt the euro only two years later than the others. On the other hand, Greek national feeling remained strong. In the long-running dispute in Cyprus between the Greek and Turkish populations, the government supported its fellow-Greeks, whatever line the EU chose to take. When the former Yugoslav Republic of Macedonia became independent in 1992, Greece resolutely opposed recognition of the new state as long as it used the name 'Macedonia', which the Greeks claimed belonged exclusively to their own province of that name. For a time the other EU states accepted the Greek claim; but even when they changed their minds and recognized Macedonia at the end of 1993 the Greeks stood their ground, and even imposed a trade embargo against Macedonia, contrary to a ruling by the European Commission. A compromise was reached in 1995, when the Macedonian government stated publicly that their country's name implied no territorial claim against Greece, and the Greeks gave up their trade embargo. The Greeks had made their point, and demonstrated that on some issues they were Greek first and European second.

Britain and Denmark were in some ways the most reluctant members of the EU. The British government opted out of the single currency at Maastricht, and rejected the Social Chapter of the treaty, which was eventually signed as a separate agreement between the other 11 member states. Even with these modifications, the treaty had a difficult passage through Parliament in 1992–93, with the majority in favour falling as low as three on one vote. The Labour Government elected in 1997 was more sympathetic to the EU than its predecessor, and the new prime minister, Tony Blair, was a convinced 'European'. The new government accepted the common social policies from which its predecessor had opted out, and was in principle in favour of adopting the euro when the time was right. But it appears that some ministers, notably Gordon Brown, the Chancellor of the Exchequer, had doubts about the euro, and the 'right time' was not found. In any case, the government was never sure that it would win a referendum on the issue.

In Denmark parliament ratified the Treaty of Maastricht (with the Danish opt-out from monetary union) in May 1992 by an overwhelming majority of 130 votes to 25; and the treaty was also supported by most of the press, industrial and commercial opinion, and the trade unions. But in a referendum on 2 June the treaty was defeated by 50.7 per cent to 49.3 per cent, on a high turnout of 82.9 per cent – a narrow margin, but one that revealed a significant gap between the elites and the electorate. The Danish government then asked the EU for further reassurances, for example on the question of a possible common defence policy, and another referendum in May 1993 accepted the treaty by 56.8 to 43.2 per cent, again on a high turnout.[21] Nonetheless, the Danes had made their point, and were to do so again when the government attempted to adopt the euro (see below, p. 248).

Three new members joined the EU in January 1995: Austria, Finland and Sweden. Austria had resumed its independent existence in 1955, with the end of the Allied occupation; and at the same time adopted a status of neutrality under a special constitutional law. When Austria applied to join the EEC in July 1989, the government and public opinion were determined to preserve this neutral status, which was carefully defined: Austria was to have no military alliances; to permit no foreign military bases on its soil; and to take no part in any armed hostilities. In negotiations between Austria and the European Union, it was agreed that membership of the EU would not infringe these conditions; and with this assurance the Austrian government accepted entry, which was endorsed in a referendum in June 1994, with a yes vote of 66 per cent on a high turnout of 81 per cent.[22] The government then took severe measures to allow the country to qualify for monetary union and the single currency, reducing public expenditure and raising taxes. Public opinion became disillusioned, and in 1999 the right-wing Freedom Party, led by Jörg Haider, which was strongly opposed to the EU, did well in parliamentary elections. Haider was widely accused of sympathizing with Nazism, and his political success later led to a dispute between the EU and Austria (see below, pp. 245–6).

Finland had managed, for over 40 years after the end of the Second World War, to maintain a skilful balancing act between the Soviet Union and the West. At home the Finns practised parliamentary government and a mixed economy; abroad, they accepted Soviet-imposed limitations on their foreign policy, rejecting Marshall aid in 1948, and later making no attempt to join the EEC. When the Soviet Union ceased to exist at the end of 1991, this situation changed dramatically. The new Russian government signed a Treaty of Friendship with Finland in January 1992, and made no further objection to Finnish membership of the European Union. The Finns had no hesitation in applying for membership in March 1992, on both economic and political grounds. The government agreed terms, and a referendum in October 1994 endorsed membership by a substantial majority (57 per cent to 43). Finland acceded to the European Union in January 1995.[23] In contrast to Austria, there was no subsequent disillusion. The government pressed ahead to accept monetary union and adopt the euro, with steady public support.

Sweden was more cautious. The Swedish government applied for membership of the European Union in July 1991, mainly for economic reasons. A referendum in November 1994 produced a narrow majority in favour of entry, and Sweden joined the EU in January 1995. But public support then diminished. The government at first intended to accept monetary union rapidly and adopt the euro as a founder member, but later hesitated, and in 1997 undertook to hold a referendum on the issue. This did not take place until 2003, when it showed a clear majority against the euro (see below, pp. 248–9). Sweden thus joined Britain and Denmark as members of the EU which remained outside the single currency.

At this stage, the European Union had attained a substantial, and indeed remarkable, measure of unity. Eleven member states had given up their currencies in favour of the euro, sometimes at considerable cost – the Germans, in particular, had given up the Deutschmark, the symbol of their prosperity and financial stability. The Greeks, who sometimes took their own political line, were determined to adopt the euro, and were soon to succeed in doing so. A significant fault line ran between this group and Britain, Denmark and Sweden, where public opinion ran contrary to the pro-EU attitudes of their governments, especially on the issue of the single currency. In these circumstances there was some talk of formally acknowledging a 'two-speed Europe', which would reflect these differences of commitment. On the other hand, this would run contrary to the character of the European Union, which tended strongly towards rigidity in its institutions and legislation. There remained an unresolved tension within the EU, which in the late 1990s was preparing to accept new members, but had not yet achieved complete unity within itself.

NORWAY AND SWITZERLAND

Two west European countries remained outside the European Union: Norway and Switzerland. The Norwegian government had negotiated terms for entry to the European Economic Community as early as 1972, only to see the proposal rejected in a referendum. A later government applied again in 1992, and signed a treaty of accession in 1994; but the electorate again rejected membership, by a majority of 52.2 per cent to 47.8.[24] In Switzerland the government moved cautiously towards membership of the EU in 1992, agreeing to join the European Economic Area (a combination for certain purposes of the European Union and the European Free Trade Association), and also applying for Swiss membership of the EU itself. The Swiss parliament accepted entry to the European Economic Area by comfortable majorities in both houses; but in December 1992 a referendum rejected entry, by a narrow majority in the popular vote, and by 16 cantons to 7. (A majority of cantons as well as a majority of votes was necessary for success.) Since this limited proposal failed, the Swiss government did not pursue its application to join the EU.[25]

Norway and Switzerland are small in population, but of considerable significance because they are undoubtedly European in character and civilization, and display in robust form the values which the European Union claims to uphold. Both have unimpeachable democratic credentials and a long-standing respect for the rule of law. Both countries are wealthy, with a GDP per head higher (in several cases much higher) than any EU member except Luxembourg. Switzerland has a tradition of independence going back to the thirteenth century, and a more recent but much valued status of neutrality. Norway experienced an unhappy union with Sweden in the nineteenth century, and became independent only in 1905 – a memory which still colours Norwegian attitudes towards another union. After the experience of the Second World War, Norway abandoned its policy of neutrality and became a founder member of NATO; but the Norwegians drew a clear distinction between a defensive alliance and the far-reaching commitments of the European Union.

TURKEY

Throughout the 1990s the European Union remained hesitant on the crucial issue of what to do about Turkey. Turkish governments, despite earlier prevarications and rebuffs by the EU, persisted in their requests for membership, and could show evidence of increasing prosperity, modernity and European outlook. The Turkish economy showed strong growth, and the tourist trade boomed. In 1993 Tansu Ciller became Turkey's first woman prime minister, a sign of modernity not yet attained by most EU countries. On the other hand, Kurdish nationalists continued their insurrection, and in response the Turks used methods which offended EU sensitivities about human rights. In 1999 the leader of the Kurdish Workers' Party (PKK), Abdullah Öcalan, was tried and sentenced to death, which ran counter to the EU's rule that the abolition of the death penalty was an essential condition for membership. Behind these problems lay wider issues of geography, the size and vigour of the Turkish population, and religion (Turkey was a secular state, but overwhelmingly Muslim in its population).

So Turkish governments kept knocking on the EU's door, but the EU hesitated to open it. In 1990 the EU leaders decided against even considering Turkey's application until 1993 at the earliest; and then the Turkish case was postponed among the various applications from eastern Europe. In December 1997 the EU did not even include Turkey among the states which were being considered for entry, and instead invited the Turks to a conference to discuss the conditions on which Turkey might become a candidate – specifically, respect for human rights and the rights of minorities. Not surprisingly, the Turks refused this proposal; but they were not deterred and they eventually achieved a measure of success. An EU summit meeting at Helsinki in December 1999 agreed to accept Turkey as a candidate, 'destined to join the Union on the basis of the same criteria applied to other candidate states'.[26] This change in principle was not yet accompanied by setting a date for the start of negotiations, and opinion on Turkish membership remained divided (see below, pp. 259–62). The deeper questions which the Turkish application presented for the identity of the European Union were left not so much unanswered as unasked.

EAST MEETS WEST?

The 1990s were a decade when East tried to meet West, without quite managing to do so. The Iron Curtain vanished, but Europe remained divided. On one simple measurement, western Europe was richer than the East. Measured roughly in GDP per head in US dollars in 1993, Switzerland stood at $35,050; Sweden $25,110; Germany, $23,650; France, $20,380; the United Kingdom, $16,550. Even among the poorest countries in the West, GDP per head in Portugal stood at $7600, and in Greece at $6340. Against this, in the former Soviet zone the richest countries were the Czech Republic at $2500 per head and Hungary at $2250; the poorest were Romania at $1390 and Bulgaria at $1225. In 1999 the gap remained wide. Switzerland stood at $40,080 per head; Sweden at $25,620; Germany at $25,850; France at $24,950; the UK at $21,400; Portugal at $10,690; Greece at $11,650. The Czech Republic had moved ahead to $5040 per head, and Hungary to $4510; but Romania was stuck at $1390 and Bulgaria at $1230.[27] The contrast was stark, and even the most thriving countries in the East remained well behind the poorest in the West.

There were also marked political and psychological distinctions. In the West it seemed that the nation state was in decline – no longer a focus of loyalty, for which people were willing to fight and die, but merely 'a large-scale provider of services'.[28] All over western Europe, people were becoming more mobile, taking jobs and buying houses in other countries, with a consequent blurring of national lines. In the East, on the contrary, nationalism and the nation state were very much alive. Czechoslovakia split into two countries on national lines. Hungary struggled to protect its Hungarian-speaking minorities in neighbouring countries. Yugoslavia broke into fragments based on nationality, and sometimes on religion, in a way that west European governments failed to grasp – it was striking that in 1991 the EU and its member states maintained their support for a united Yugoslavia, even after Slovenia and Croatia had declared their independence on the basis of convincing referendums – and even though the EU claimed in principle to uphold the rights of national minorities.

There is in this situation a curious and perplexing paradox. Nations and nationalism were alive and vigorous in eastern Europe, and yet the countries of that area (or at any rate their governments) set themselves with great determination to join the European Union, which involved at least some limitation of national independence and identity. How, or indeed whether, this paradox can be resolved remains to be seen.

An American historian, William Hitchcock, has written: 'Evermore, historians will look back on 1989 as the real starting-point of the common, united Europe'.[29] This is surely true. But the starting point proved to be a long way from the finishing post. East was East and West was West, and they did not quite manage to meet in the 1990s. Russia and most of the successor states of the former USSR went their own way. The countries of the former Soviet zone in eastern Europe (plus the three Baltic states) all wanted formal union with the West, and persistently sought to join NATO and the European Union, but they were held back by their own difficulties and by the caution of NATO and EU leaders. In the West, the European Union developed closer forms of integration as the Maastricht Treaty took effect, yet even the EU remained divided between the eager and the reluctant advocates of unity. A common, united Europe had not yet come into existence.

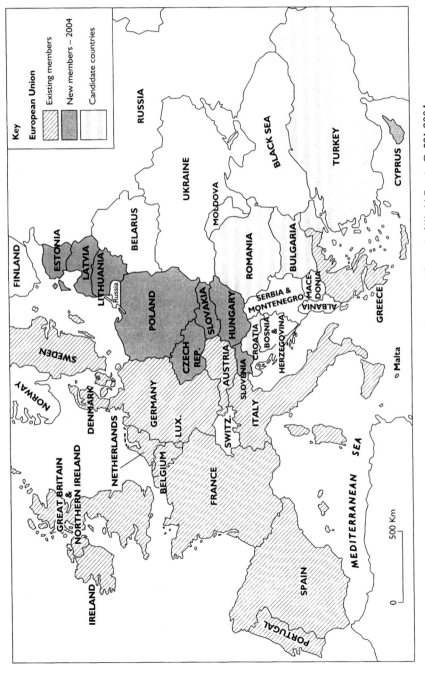

Key

European Union

Existing members

New members – 2004

Candidate countries

RUSSIA

FINLAND

ESTONIA

LATVIA

LITHUANIA

Russia

BELARUS

UKRAINE

MOLDOVA

ROMANIA

BLACK SEA

BULGARIA

TURKEY

SERBIA & MONTENEGRO

MACE DONIA

ALBANIA

GREECE

CYPRUS

POLAND

SLOVAKIA

HUNGARY

CZECH REP.

AUSTRIA

SLOVENIA

CROATIA

BOSNIA & HERZEGOVINA

ITALY

SWITZ.

GERMANY

LUX.

SWEDEN

NORWAY

DENMARK

NETHERLANDS

BELGIUM

FRANCE

GREAT BRITAIN & NORTHERN IRELAND

IRELAND

SPAIN

PORTUGAL

MEDITERRANEAN SEA

Malta

0   500 Km

5   Membership of the European Union, 2004. Reprinted from *The Annual Register: A Record of World Events* © CSA 2004.

14

A NEW EUROPE? BUT WHAT EUROPE?
2000–2004

THE EUROPEAN UNION

What is Europe? In 1900 there was a geographical Europe, from the Atlantic to the Urals and from the North Cape to the Mediterranean. Historical Europe looked rather different, with doubtful areas – Britain and Russia were partly European and partly not; the Balkans were a sort of no-man's-land, aspiring to be European, with only partial success. Turkey retained a sizeable area in geographical Europe, but in other respects was generally agreed to be outside. The degree of unity and coherence that Europe (including the doubtful territories) possessed was taken for granted. There was a sense of being European, shared strongly by aristocrats, the bourgeoisie and the internationally conscious working class; and reinforced by the consciousness of European predominance in the world. At the beginning of the twenty-first century, parts of this situation remained. Continental Europe was the same shape. Britain was still to some degree hesitant about its place in Europe; Russia was largely outside; the Balkans were still a doubtful zone. Turkey was on the margin, but figuratively speaking in motion, becoming more in than out. But there were two profound changes. First, European predominance in the world had ended; and second, the concept of being European was no longer taken for granted, but was defined by institutions and specific criteria. To be European was in common parlance to be within the European Union, belonging to a set of institutions and accepting a growing body of laws and practices best known by the French term *acquis communautaire*. Geographical Europe was divided into the European Union, which was often regarded as the true Europe, and the rest.

The primary answer to the question 'What is Europe?' at the start of the twenty-first century is therefore 'The European Union'. But this leads at once to another question: 'What is the European Union and what is it intended to become?' The EU dominates all discussion of European identity, and yet its own identity remains uncertain. It is certainly an economic union, and it claims also to be a community of values. It possesses some of the characteristics of a state, but not others; and its nature is constantly in flux, changing like a chameleon in slow motion.

Indeed, the European Union has sometimes been not just in flux but in crisis. Its movements have assumed a roller-coaster character, with striking developments towards closer union (the introduction of the euro, the acceptance of ten new members and agreement on a constitution by all member governments) accompanied by powerful evidence of dissent in public opinion on all these matters, and of popular disillusion with many aspects of the EU. Many of these events may appear dry, and full of arcane institutional detail; but all in all the story is a dramatic one, and we cannot foresee the end. Perhaps we should fasten our seatbelts.

ORIGINS AND AIMS OF THE UNION

The European Union had its relatively prosaic origins in the European Economic Community, and it retains important economic elements. It provides a single market for trade and permits freedom of movement for all individuals, who are called for this purpose European citizens. Since 1 January 2002, 12 of its members have used a single currency, the euro, with identical banknotes and interchangeable coins. This is at once a practical expression of economic unity and a symbol of a more far-reaching aspiration to political unity. It is true that the foundations of the single currency are in danger of being undermined, as the major west European countries – France, Germany and Italy – have disregarded the rules set up by the Stability and Growth Pact, by which national budget deficits were not to exceed 3 per cent of GDP, nor the public debt to exceed 60 per cent of GDP. Repeated attempts by the Council of Economic and Finance Ministers to agree on a reform of the Pact failed, and finally, in March 2005, an EU summit meeting accepted a relaxation of the rules so far-reaching as to call into question the whole Pact. There were to be no sanctions for breaches of the rules if a state was suffering a recession or persistent low growth in its economy; and whole categories of expenditure were excluded from calculations of budget deficits, including education, research, defence, foreign aid and anything contributing to European unification, which allowed Germany to discount the continuing costs of unification.[1] But despite these difficulties, the European Union could still claim major economic achievements.

The European Union also seeks to transcend its economic aspects and to represent a community of values, which were set out in the Copenhagen criteria of 1993 (see above, pp. 231–2) and elaborated in detail in the Charter of Fundamental Rights of the European Union, adopted at an intergovernmental conference in Nice on 7 December 2000. The preamble to this Charter asserted:

The peoples of Europe, in creating an ever closer union among them, are resolved to share a peaceful future based on common values. Conscious of its spiritual and moral heritage, the Union is founded on the indivisible, universal values of human dignity, freedom, equality and solidarity; it is based on the principles of democracy and the rule of law. It places the individual at the heart of its activities, by establishing the citizenship of the Union and by creating an area of freedom, security and justice.

The document then goes on to enlarge, in a series of chapters, on the themes of dignity (including a total rejection of the death penalty), freedom, equality, solidarity (setting out workers' rights), citizens' rights and justice.[2]

These principles had already been shown, in the course of 2000, to present some difficulties. In October 1999 parliamentary elections in Austria brought down the so-called grand coalition between the Social Democrats and the conservative People's Party, which had ruled the country for nearly 50 years. In place of its old alliance with the socialists, the People's Party turned to the right-wing Freedom Party to form a new coalition government. The leader of the Freedom Party was Jörg Haider, who had allegedly made speeches favourable to Nazism. Haider himself did not take office in the new government, but the reputation of his party brought immediate denunciation from the European Union. On 1 February 2000 the Portuguese government, which held the presidency of the EU at the time, declared that if the Freedom Party were included in the Austrian government, Austria would be placed in a sort of diplomatic quarantine, with ministerial contacts reduced to the lowest level and Austrian ambassadors denied access to members of EU governments. This policy was strongly supported by France (due to be the next holder of the EU presidency), and accepted with varying degrees of enthusiasm by the other member states. (The European Commission, on the other hand, took its own line and continued to work with the Austrians as usual.)

In face of this boycott, the Austrians protested that they had held a fully democratic election and formed a government according to correct constitutional procedures. They asked that the Freedom Party should be judged by its actions in government, rather than by speeches in the past; and they issued a formal assurance of their commitment to human rights and European values. None of this cut any ice, and the EU governments kept Austria in diplomatic isolation. The result was an impasse, until the EU sought a way out at the end of June by appointing a three-man committee to visit Austria and report on the situation. The committee reported on 8 September, arguing smoothly but implausibly that the sanctions imposed on Austria had been effective so far, but that if they were continued they would become counterproductive. They concluded that the Austrian government was upholding European democratic values; and that the Freedom Party was a right-wing populist party with extremist characteristics – which was doubtless true, but did not advance matters very far. This report allowed the

EU to remove its sanctions on 12 September, without any changes in the Austrian government; though the French wanted to maintain the quarantine, to Austria's lasting resentment.

The whole episode seemed faintly absurd, but it raised serious issues. The normal processes of democracy had produced in Austria a government including a party of which other countries in the EU disapproved. What then was to become of democracy? Would any country be isolated if an election produced what others believed to be the 'wrong' result? The Austrian affair passed without such questions being pressed, but they might well recur in the future.[3]

EXPANSION AND ORGANIZATION OF THE EU

The European Union thus defined itself in economic terms and as a 'community of values'. It was also faced with circumstances that required its reorganization. In 1999 the EU had decided in principle on the admission of new members from eastern Europe and the Mediterranean, though as yet without fixing the exact number or the dates of entry. At the end of 2002 the EU leaders, meeting at Copenhagen, agreed to admit ten new members in May 2004: from eastern Europe, the Czech Republic, Estonia, Hungary, Latvia, Lithuania, Poland, Slovakia and Slovenia; and in the Mediterranean, Cyprus and Malta. It followed therefore that the institutions of the European Union, originally designed for the six founder members of the EEC, and adapted to accommodate 15, would shortly have to cope with 25 member states, with possibly more to follow. These changes presented practical questions of organization, and also deeper issues of principle.

The practical questions were detailed, and sometimes arcane in nature. The European Commission had so far been made up by each member state nominating at least one member, and the larger states nominating two. In 2000, with a total of 15 member states, Britain, France, Germany, Italy and Spain appointed two commissioners each, and the other ten countries one each. With an increase in the number of members, should every state continue to nominate at least one commissioner, and should the larger states still nominate two? Another question related to the method of voting in the Council of Ministers, in which votes were allocated in some relation (though not in strict proportion) to population, with provision for minority votes which could block measures in certain circumstances.

These practical matters were discussed at a difficult European summit meeting in Nice in December 2000, which resulted in a treaty that pleased almost no one but was reluctantly accepted by all. On the make-up of the European Commission it was agreed that each member state should nominate one commissioner, and that from 2005 the larger states would lose their double representation. On the issue of voting in the Council of Ministers, it was agreed that Britain, France, Germany and Italy should retain equal voting weights, with 29 votes each, even though Germany had a population of 82 million and the others 57–59 million. Spain was to have 27 votes, and other countries smaller voting weights in rough relation to population. The position of the larger states was strengthened by a provision that a measure could be blocked by a vote by countries representing 62 per cent of the total population of the EU; which could mean Germany plus two other large countries. On the other hand, the position of smaller countries was safeguarded by permitting a simple majority of member states, whatever their population or voting weight, to reject any proposal. The result of these arrangements was to make voting more complicated than before, and also more prone to deadlock, because any three large states or a substantial group of smaller ones could block any measure.[4]

These detailed and cumbersome provisions did nothing to resolve the deeper issue of principle which faced the European Union: what sort of body was the EU to become? Three ideas were currently in play: a federal state; a Europe of homelands, based on cooperation between governments, not on the emergence of a superstate; or something in between, not exactly a superstate, but evolving towards one. The idea of a federal state had strong backing in Germany and was forcefully expressed by the German foreign minister, Joschka Fischer, in May 2000. Fischer argued that the problems of a Union of 25 states could best be resolved by the establishment of a Federation of Europe, with a president elected by universal suffrage, a government and a two-chamber parliament. He acknowledged that not all countries would accept such a proposal; but maintained that those which did could go forward as a body, leaving others to follow when they saw fit.[5] The opposing view, that the EU should not become a federation but form a body to promote close intergovernmental cooperation, was maintained by the British and the Danes, and by some of the new candidates for membership – for example, President Krasniewski of Poland and the president of the Czech Republic, Václav Klaus.[6] An intermediate and less clear-cut point of view was set out by President Chirac of France, in an address to the German Bundestag in June 2000. Replying directly to Fischer's proposals, Chirac accepted the idea of a group of states moving more rapidly than others towards integration, and assumed that France and Germany would lead such a group; but he was less precise than Fischer on the issue of a federation, suggesting something more flexible. For Chirac, it was a positive virtue of European institutions that they were in a state of constant evolution – a striking idea, which had widespread appeal because it avoided reaching any final decisions.

The complex and obscure terms of the Treaty of Nice did nothing to resolve the differences between advocates of federalism, intergovernmental cooperation or something in between. A year after the Nice summit, a meeting of EU leaders at Laeken agreed to try a new course by establishing a convention to draft a constitution for the Union. A former president of France, Valéry Giscard d'Estaing, was appointed to preside over the convention, which was made up of representatives of governments, national parliaments, the European Parliament and the European Commission. Candidate states were to nominate members, without the right to vote. Giscard, in his role as president, went out of his way to claim far-reaching significance for the work of the convention, deliberately drawing a parallel with the Philadelphia Convention of 1787, which drew up the Constitution of the USA. The European Convention began its debates on 28 February 2002, and presented a draft constitution to a summit meeting of EU leaders in Thessaloníki on 20 June 2003. Delays and disagreements followed, so that a revised text was not finally accepted until June 2004 (see below, pp. 252–4).

DOUBT AND DIVISION

In the meantime, the European Union passed through a period of difficulties and vicissitudes. There were signs that popular opinion was divided on the issue of further integration. Some were minor, or difficult to interpret. In France there was a sharp shock to the orthodox political classes in the presidential election of May 2002. In the first round the far-right National Front candidate, Jean-Marie Le Pen, won 4.8 million votes (16.86 per cent), and beat the Socialist Lionel Jospin into third place – an astonishing result. In the second round, the incumbent President Chirac gained a massive victory over Le Pen, by 82.15 per cent to 17.85; but even so Le Pen increased his vote to a formidable 5.5 million.[7] Le Pen fought his campaign on a mixed bag of issues, notably immigration and crime, and so the significance of the vote was unclear; but it was certain that a part of his appeal lay in his opposition to the EU and the erosion of French sovereignty. In Greece, in 2000, the Archbishop of Athens organized vast demonstrations against a government proposal to remove a statement of religious affiliation from identity cards, to bring them into accord with EU practice. The archbishop declared that this was an attack on Greek identity, and asserted that 'our inspiration comes largely from the East and not from the West, which is undermining our traditional values'.[8] The Church collected some 3 million signatures for a petition to hold a referendum on the question. In the event, the government refused a referendum, the courts upheld the new form of identity card, and the wave of protest died away. It had been briefly impressive, but was perhaps no more than a passing disturbance.

There were clearer and more serious developments in Denmark and Sweden, where referendums were actually held on the question of whether to adopt the euro. In Denmark, the government, the main political parties and most of the press advocated a change to the euro; but the vote (28 September 2000) resulted in 53.1 per cent 'no' against 46.9 per cent 'yes', on a remarkably high turnout of 87.5 per cent of the electorate. This majority against the euro was large enough to cause the prime minister to assure the country that he would not seek another vote on the issue in the near future.[9] In Sweden, a referendum on the adoption of the euro was held on 14 September 2003. The government and most of the media supported the change, but the result, on a high turnout of 81 per cent, was a decisive 'no', by 59 per cent to 41 per cent. The government acknowledged that the margin was so wide that the result should stand for at least two parliamentary terms, that is, until 2013.[10] Meanwhile in Britain there was no referendum on the adoption of the euro, partly because the economic circumstances were held to be unsuitable, but mainly because the prime minister (Tony Blair), who was in favour in principle, felt that in practice he was unlikely to win a vote. In a way, this failure to hold a referendum was as significant as the actual rejections in Denmark and Sweden, because it showed that the government recognized the degree of public hostility to the single currency.

These diverse events were signs of a gap between elites (politicians, administrators and academics), who were pressing on towards ever closer union, and peoples who followed, sometimes reluctantly, behind. Jacques Delors, the president of the European Commission from 1985 to 1995, and an open advocate of a European federation, is said to have observed with regret that Europe had advanced behind a mask, creating an atmosphere of mistrust; and in some countries there was indeed a sense of alienation which posed a problem for the European Union. Further and weightier evidence of the gap between elites and peoples was to follow in 2005, when the electorates of France and the Netherlands rejected the proposed European Constitution in referendums (see below, p. 253).

At the same time, the member states of the European Union were deeply, and sometimes bitterly, divided on the major international issue of 2002–3: the American invasion of Iraq. This operation was being prepared towards the end of 2002 and early in 2003, and was launched on 20 March 2003, achieving rapid military success and overthrowing Saddam Hussein and his regime. These events split the EU. Before hostilities began, eight governments (five members of the EU – Britain, Denmark, Italy, Portugal and Spain; and three which were due to join the next year – the Czech Republic, Hungary and Poland) issued a public appeal for unity in support of American policy. They did not even trouble to invite France and Germany, the leading countries in the European Union, to take part; and indeed the French and Germans would not have done so. On 10 March President Chirac declared publicly that France would veto a Security Council resolution authorizing war against Iraq. Even so, the invasion went ahead. Among the countries of the EU, Britain committed substantial forces to the battle and the subsequent occupation. Other member states (Italy, Spain, Poland, the Netherlands, Denmark, Estonia, Latvia and Lithuania) sent contingents which were smaller in number but important symbolically. Hungary and Greece supported the operation by allowing the Americans to use their air bases. France, on the other hand, maintained a determined opposition to the American invasion and was strongly supported by Germany; Belgium and Sweden were also in the opposition camp. These divisions persisted into 2004. In March that year the Spanish Socialist Party won a general election, and the new prime minister,

Zapatero, declared that he would withdraw Spanish troops from Iraq, and attacked Bush and Blair for launching a war based on lies. On the other hand, the prime minister of Italy, Berlusconi, reaffirmed his determination to keep Italian troops in Iraq, and the Latvian parliament voted to keep the country's token force in Iraq until June 2005. The British government continued to stand firmly by the USA. On the most important foreign policy issue of the time, the states of the EU were gravely divided, and a single EU foreign policy would have to deal with other and lesser issues.

EU ENLARGEMENT OR UNIFICATION

Different aspects of the development of the European Union were on display in the eventful year 2004. On 1 May an unprecedented wave of new members joined the Union: from north to south, Estonia, Latvia, Lithuania, Poland, the Czech Republic, Slovakia, Hungary, Slovenia, Malta and Cyprus. These accessions had been approved in referendums held during 2003. In Poland, the 'yes' campaign was supported by General Jaruzelski, the last communist ruler, *and* by Pope John Paul II – an unlikely but powerful combination. The result was 77.5 per cent in favour, 22.5 per cent against. Other countries showed even higher majorities – 84 per cent in Hungary, 90 per cent in Slovenia and 92.5 per cent in Slovakia.[11] It was striking that most of the governments concerned wanted to go the whole hog and adopt the euro as soon as possible.

Among the existing states of the European Union, these events were usually called 'enlargement'; but the new members preferred 'unification' or 'reunification', signifying the restoration of a European unity which had been severed by the Iron Curtain. Either way, the accession of the ten countries – more than ever before at one time – was a remarkable event. Something of its meaning may be understood by looking at the new nominees to the European Commission. The Latvian nominee had been born in Siberia, where her parents had been deported by the Soviets. The Hungarian, by contrast, had been a diplomat under the communist regime and retained his position in the new order. One nominee had been educated at the universities of Leningrad and Moscow in the Soviet Union; another had taught at the universities of Berkeley in California and Sussex in England. One was a banker, another a lawyer, and yet another a militant ecologist who had served his apprenticeship in the hostile environment of communist Czechoslovakia. They certainly brought new blood to the Commission; and a training in east European politics doubtless did not come amiss in Brussels, where the existing EU members were scrambling for the most influential posts, and the corridors of power could be tortuous and murky.

The new adherents to the EU were poor in comparison with the existing members. Average GDP per head across the ten states was estimated at no more than 40–45 per cent of that in the 15 they were joining. Cyprus, Malta and Slovenia were the wealthiest, and the three Baltic states the poorest. On the other hand, most of the new members were achieving strong economic growth. In 2002 Estonia, Latvia and Lithuania produced increases in GDP between 5.8 and 6.8 per cent; and all the others except Poland managed growth rates which were higher than the average for the 15 previous EU members.[12] Reactions to the enlargement among the existing members were mixed. Portugal and Greece, which had done well in the past out of EU regional and structural funds, were dismayed at the arrival of poorer countries competing for the same resources. Most countries in western Europe were afraid of a sudden influx of immigrants from the new member states, and put up temporary barriers to prevent it. On the other hand, some industrialists were eager to look eastwards, and to open factories in the new countries, where wages and other costs were lower than in the West.

All in all, and despite misgivings in some member states, 1 May 2004 was an occasion for public rejoicing. The Irish government, which presided over the EU at the time, gave a spectacular party in Dublin, and the new entrants celebrated with music and fireworks. The contrast between the Europe of May 2004 and that of 20 years before (Orwell's fatal year of 1984) was remarkable. Europe had been transformed, and there was a real sense that members of a single European family had come together again after a period of harsh and difficult separation.

INDIFFERENCE?

But the roller coaster swung downwards again almost at once. Between 10 and 13 June 2004 the states of the European Union held elections for the European Parliament, and the response of the electorate was in most cases one of resounding indifference. Across all 25 countries, the turnout was only 44.2 per cent; even though in six countries (Belgium, Cyprus, Greece, Italy, Luxembourg and Malta) voting was compulsory. Turnout was particularly low in some new member states: 16.7 per cent in Slovakia, 20.4 per cent in Poland, 26.9 per cent in Estonia, 28.3 per cent in the Czech Republic and 28.3 per cent in Slovenia. Some of the founder members of the EEC, with long histories of commitment to European integration, showed little enthusiasm: turnout in the Netherlands was 39.1 per cent, in Germany 43 per cent and in France 43.1 per cent. Even countries where voting was compulsory produced some remarkable variations: the dutiful Luxembourgers achieved a 90 per cent turnout, the individualist Greeks only 63.8 per cent.[13]

Even those voters who troubled to turn out showed no sign of forming a conscious European electorate voting on European issues. Campaigns were mainly on domestic questions, and there was a strong tendency for electors simply to vote against the existing government – for example, in France the Socialists did well against a right-wing government, while in Germany the Christian Democrats gained support against a Social Democrat government. Moreover in some countries the opponents of the European Union itself scored modest but telling successes. In Britain, the United Kingdom

Independence Party won 12 seats out of 78; in France the National Front won 7 seats out of 78; in Sweden the 'sovereignty' party won 3 seats out of 19; and in Poland the Populists won 6 seats out of 54. These gains made little impact on the total make-up of the European Parliament, but were signs of dissent from the current consensus. All in all, the European parliamentary elections showed a large degree of indifference and a dash of hostility to the European project.

A EUROPEAN CONSTITUTION

But this setback was followed at once by another uprush of the roller coaster, with a long step forward by the European Union. A summit meeting of EU leaders (now representing 25 states), held at Brussels on 17–18 June 2004, agreed on the text of a constitution for the European Union, which was signed in Rome in November and was to be submitted for ratification in the various states by the end of 2006. This lengthy document comprised 448 articles, plus 35 protocols and 50 declarations. It provided that the EU was to assume a legal personality, and that EU law was to have primacy over national law in areas set out in the constitution. This was to some extent balanced by the principle of subsidiarity, by which the EU was to act only in areas where objectives could not be achieved at a lower level. On issues of principle, the EU Charter of Fundamental Rights, adopted in Nice in December 2000, was to be incorporated in the constitution; but there was no reference to the Christian roots of Europe, as had been proposed in May 2004 by seven member states.

On institutional matters, the constitution provided for the establishment of a new post of president of the European Union, to be elected by heads of government for a term of two and a half years, renewable for one further term; and also for the appointment of a minister of foreign affairs. The European Parliament was to have powers of 'co-decision' with the Council of Ministers. The national veto was to be retained on decisions on foreign and defence policy, direct taxation and financing the EU budget. Subject to this national veto the EU was to devise and implement a common foreign and security policy, and to make progress towards a common defence policy. Other provisions dealt in detail with the make-up of the European Commission and the rules for qualified majority voting in the Council of Ministers. The EU was to be open to all European states which respect its values; on the other hand, any member state had the right to leave the EU by negotiation.[14]

The significance of this document for the European Union, and the sort of European organization it signified, were uncertain at the time of its acceptance by the EU governments in June 2004, and became more so in the course of the next year. Advocates of federation expressed disappointment that the constitution left too much scope to the national veto. Opponents argued that it marked steady progress towards a European superstate, with a president, a foreign minister, a stronger Parliament and the prospect of a common defence policy.

The treaty establishing the constitution was to be ratified by all the signatory states – in ten countries by referendums, and in 15 by parliamentary means. It was due to come into force on 1 November 2006, *provided that* all the instruments of ratification had been deposited by that date; or, if not, at a later date following the deposit of the last ratification.

The process of ratification began smoothly. Spain approved the treaty by a referendum on 22 February 2005, by a vast majority of 77 per cent 'yes' to 23 per cent 'no', though on a low turnout of 42 per cent. Austria, Germany, Greece, Hungary, Italy, Lithuania, Slovakia and Slovenia all accepted the treaty by parliamentary votes, often by overwhelming margins. In Lithuania, for example, which was the first country to accept the constitution, the parliamentary vote was 84 to 4 in favour. The Hungarian National Assembly accepted by 322 votes to 12. In Germany the vote in the Bundestag was 569 to 23, and in the Bundesrat (representing the separate states) there were no votes against and only 3 abstentions.[15]

Nine states had thus approved the treaty before 29 May 2005, when the French electorate voted in a referendum. Despite a vigorous 'yes' campaign by President Chirac and the government, the result, on a high turnout of 69.3 per cent, was 54.68 per cent 'no' and 45.32 per cent 'yes'; or in number of votes, 15,450,279 to 12,806,394. On 1 June a referendum in the Netherlands produced an even greater majority against the constitution: 61.54 per cent to 38.46 per cent, on a turnout of 62.8 per cent.[16] In both countries, the 'no' vote was drawn from widely different groups across the political spectrum, but the results were none the less decisive for that. They were also impressive because France had taken the lead in the whole process of European integration from the Schuman Plan of 1950 onwards, and the Netherlands had long been regarded as committed to the same cause. Immediately after the French vote, the British prime minister, Tony Blair, called for a period of reflection before any further action; and on 6 June the Foreign Secretary, Jack Straw, announced in the House of Commons that legislative plans for a British referendum on the constitution were to be 'shelved'. In the course of a few days, therefore, two states rejected ratification by decisive margins, while a third deferred putting the question to the electorate.

These events left the European Union in a state of uncertainty, veering towards confusion. The policy of the presidency of the EU, held at the time by Jean-Claude Juncker, the prime minister of Luxembourg, and of the president of the European Commission, José Barroso, was to maintain that the treaty was not dead, and that the process of ratification by the various member states should continue. Indeed, on 2 June (the day after the Dutch referendum), the Latvian parliament voted in favour of ratification by 71 votes to 5. The Cyprus parliament accepted the treaty on 30 June and the Maltese parliament on 6 July. On 10 July the Luxembourg electorate voted 'yes' in a referendum, by 56 per cent to 44 per cent. On the other hand, a substantial body of opinion regarded the constitution as effectively dead. A number of states deferred the ratification process rather than proceeding with it. Finland postponed its parliamentary ratification indefinitely. The Czech Republic, Denmark, Poland and the United Kingdom similarly deferred their referendums indefinitely.[17] The Union itself was in disarray on the issue; though under the surface the momentum towards greater integration was maintained, impelled by most member governments and the existing European institutions.

THE IDENTITY OF THE EUROPEAN UNION

What then was the state of the European Union in the middle of 2005? It comprised 25 states, covering a large part of geographical Europe. Its ten recently joined members had shown great determination in their applications for membership, showing that the EU responded to something important in their needs and aspirations. It had acquired several of the features of a state: a parliament, an executive body and a bureaucracy; a court whose rulings are binding on member states and their peoples; a flag and an anthem. Twelve of its members shared a central bank and a common currency; though the cohesion thus established was being undermined by the failure of the Stability and Growth Pact, whose provisions were largely abandoned in March 2005 (see above, p. 244). The governments of all member states had agreed on a constitution, which is one of the characteristics of a state, but the fate of this document remained in doubt, and member governments took different views as to whether or not to continue the process of ratification.

The European Union had thus moved a long way towards integration, and had acquired some of the characteristics of a state. What it lacked was a European people, with a conscious outlook, identity and loyalty. *The Economist*, broadly pro-European in its views, observed in September 2004 that 'there is no real European *demos* – a population with a sufficiently strong European identity to breathe life into common democratic institutions'.[18] This verdict has been powerfully reinforced by the French and Dutch referendums, in which the demos spoke loudly against the latest 'European' proposals.

Indeed, it is hard to see how the different peoples within the EU can identify with a body whose own character remains uncertain. The institutions of what began as the EEC, and became the EC and is now the EU, have always been in a state of transition, constantly on a journey towards an unknown (or perhaps unstated) destination. British supporters of European integration have often made use of metaphors drawn from transport – catching or missing the European train was at one time a favourite figure of speech. But one wonders how many people actually want to live on a train, moving at an uncertain speed towards an unnamed destination. In these circumstances the identity and ultimate character of the European Union remain in doubt, and the gap between the advocates of ever closer unity and disgruntled or dubious public opinions seems to be growing wider.

The European Union thus has a developing but still uncertain identity, which characterizes one part of geographical Europe. The rest of the continent displays a wide diversity.

EUROPE OUTSIDE THE UNION

We may start with Norway and Switzerland, which are models of the values claimed by the EU, and are geographically embedded within it, but maintain their independence from it. They are the most European of the outsiders. There are also the mini-states – Andorra, Monaco, San Remo, Liechtenstein – which maintain their separate identities; and the exceptional case of the Vatican, less than a square mile in area but worldwide in its influence and significance. These countries remain a testimony to the diversity of Europe, and a tribute to the tolerance of many of its states.

The Balkan countries form a very different and multifarious group. Romania and Bulgaria are not yet sufficiently stable as democracies or as market economies to satisfy the demands of the European Union, but have been moving steadily towards membership, which they hope to attain within a few years. Among the successor states to the former Yugoslavia, Slovenia is already a member of the EU. Croatia applied to join in February 2003, but was a doubtful starter, partly because of its failure to track down those charged with war crimes committed during the conflicts of the 1990s. Bosnia-Herzegovina is still suffering the consequences of those conflicts, and is administered as a sort of mandate of the United Nations under the High Representative of the Bosnian Peace Implementation Council, Lord Ashdown, a former leader of the British Liberal Democratic Party. This is an active, not merely an honorific post. In April 2004 the High Representative dismissed the head of the armed forces of the Republic of Srpska for failing to provide information about the massacre at Srebrenica in 1994; and in June he removed no fewer than 60 Serb politicians and officials on the grounds that they were helping Radovan Karadzic and others accused of war crimes to avoid arrest.[19] The country is in better shape than it was in the 1990s, but is not yet, by EU standards, a normal state. To the south, Macedonia presented a formal application for EU membership in March 2004, but is still politically unstable and in serious economic difficulties, with high unemployment and a weak currency.

Serbia is in a difficult situation. In February 2003 the remnant of the Federal Republic of Yugoslavia was dissolved and replaced by the Union of Serbia and Montenegro, which may dissolve in its turn because the new constitution authorizes the two states to hold referendums on separation in 2006. The problem of Kosovo remains unresolved, in that the province is still part of Serbia, but comprises a population of only about 100,000 Serbs and 1.8 million Albanians. In the first part of 2005 Serbia-Montenegro was still insisting on some status less than independence for Kosovo, while the Albanian population demanded unconditional independence. There is little sign in this situation that the independent nation state has become a thing of the past.

Albania remains *sui generis*, politically unstable and finding it difficult to function as an organized state. The government tried to move towards international respectability in 2003 by opening negotiations with the European Commission for an association agreement with the EU, and by sending 70 Albanian soldiers to take part in the occupation of Iraq. But for the most part the country lives on the margins of European politics and economic life.

RUSSIA AND ITS NEIGHBOURS

Russia and its near neighbours, Ukraine, Belarus and Moldova, continue to raise in difficult forms the questions of the identity of Europe and the boundaries of the European Union. In November 2002 the then president of the European Commission, Romano Prodi, said in public that he did not envisage Russia, Ukraine, Belarus or Moldova becoming members of the European Union.[20] This reflected a widespread view at the time that these states were part of geographical Europe but outside the political and economic sphere of the EU, and so outside the institutional scope of Europe itself.

This situation changed somewhat in 2004–5. The European Union gained ten new members, mostly in eastern Europe, raising the question of where the ultimate frontier of the Union was to be drawn. Russia was certainly still excluded. There was no move within the EU to extend membership to Russia, which seemed unassimilable to the EU's norms. It was at best a country of striking contradictions. In some respects, Russia had achieved a successful transition from a communist dictatorship to a multiparty democracy. A presidential election in March 2004 was contested by six candidates, and President Putin was confirmed in office by a majority of 49.6 million (71 per cent) against 9.5 million (14 per cent) for the nearest challenger; but observers from the Organization for Security and Cooperation in Europe and from the Council of Europe had serious doubts about the conduct of the election.[21] Democracy in Russia was certainly not of the kind practised in most of Europe; though the Russians could claim with truth that their presidential elections attracted a voter turnout higher than in the USA. Putin himself acted as a sort of elected autocrat, using arbitrary and authoritarian methods. In economic affairs, Putin aimed at developing a market economy by authoritarian methods, on the hopeful analogy of Singapore, though so far without the same success. Putin waged an unrelenting struggle against Chechen separatists, which allowed him to claim (with some success) that he was on the same side as the West in the conflict against Islamic extremists. But Russian methods often offended EU views on human rights, and victory proved elusive. The Chechens struck back in 2003 with ten large-scale attacks against the Russians, including two in Moscow itself; and in 2004 they achieved two bombing attacks on the Moscow underground system. The Chechen conflict continued to align Russia with the West in some respects, but to isolate it in other ways.

In foreign policy, Russia maintained formal relations with NATO on a level of equality through a joint council set up in 2002, and in public, at any rate, the Russian foreign ministry claimed to be unperturbed by the eastward extension of the NATO alliance, even as far as the frontier of Russia itself. Russia also dealt with the European Union on an equal footing, holding regular twice-yearly meetings with EU representatives, with businesslike but unspectacular results. For example, in May 2004 the EU agreed to support Russian accession to the World Trade Association, and in return Russia opened parts of its telecommunications and financial services to EU participation.

Nearer home, Russia set out to establish its influence over the neighbouring states of Belarus and Ukraine. In September 2003 Russia, Ukraine, Belarus and Kazakhstan agreed to set up a 'Single Economic Space', in which the member states would harmonize their legislation on tariffs and customs dues, in order to create a free trade area, and eventually to coordinate their economic policies. The agreement also provided that the members would eventually give up some powers to a council of heads of state; though the Ukrainian president insisted that this process would be optional for the various states involved. By May 2004, when the four presidents met again, all the countries had ratified the agreement, but looked at it in different ways: Putin sought to press on towards a supranational body, while the others preferred to call a halt at a free trade area.

Certainly it was clear that Russia was seeking to restore some of the authority lost when the Soviet Union broke up. Of the states in the Single Economic Space, Belarus was most closely bound to Russia and very vulnerable to Russian pressure. As early as January 2003 the presidents of the two countries had actually agreed that their governments should draw up a joint constitution, unify their tariffs, customs and even their tax systems, and cooperate on the transfer of Russian gas exports across Belarus territory. Belarus also agreed to introduce the Russian rouble as the country's currency from January 2005. Progress in bringing these agreements about proved slow, and early in 2004 the two countries were still in dispute over gas prices and payments for moving gas across Belarus. The Russians showed they carried a big stick by cutting off all gas supplies to Belarus in February 2004, in freezing temperatures. By June 2004 agreement had been reached on prices and transit costs, and the two governments continued to work on a joint constitution; but the adoption of the Russian rouble as their single currency was put off to 2008, or perhaps even later. Belarus thus retained some room for manoeuvre, but in the last resort Russia carried great weight, and its influence was almost certain to prevail. Moreover, there was little chance of Belarus being able to balance between East and West. President Lukashenka ran an authoritarian form of democracy, which was unpopular in the European Union; and in 2004 three different organizations (the United Nations Human Rights Commission, the Helsinki Federation for Human

Rights and the Parliamentary Assembly of the Council of Europe) all published critical reports on the state of human rights in Belarus.

Ukraine was in a very different position. The country had a population of 49 million; valuable economic resources; and a strong geographical position – for example, the Russian Black Sea Fleet is still based at Sebastopol, in the Crimea, cut off from its homeland by the whole north–south width of Ukraine. Ukraine also extends far to the west, towards central Europe, sharing frontiers with Poland, Slovakia and Hungary. The population itself is divided, with a substantial Russian-speaking minority in the east and south, and a religious split between Catholics in the west and Orthodox in the east. Russia is a dominant neighbour (and the former ruling power) to the north. To the west, the European Union exercises a strong attraction, largely on economic grounds. In the late 1990s, the Ukrainian government showed a keen interest in making approaches to the EU, and in June 1998 a formal presidential statement declared that Ukrainian national interests required the securing of full membership. In practice, this ambition made little progress. Ukraine was far from meeting the conditions normally required for EU membership, and the EU itself showed no interest in extending its enlargement (which already had its problems) to include Ukraine.

This situation changed to some degree at the end of 2004 and early in 2005. In November 2004 a presidential election produced a narrow victory for Viktor Yanukovych, who advocated close ties with Russia, over his Western-oriented opponent, Viktor Yushchenko. The result was strongly disputed on grounds of fraud – some reports alleged that as many as 3 million votes had been cast by falsely registered electors. There were immense demonstrations in favour of Yushchenko in the streets of the capital, Kiev. From outside, the Russian government congratulated the victor, but the European Union and the USA declared the results invalid. The protesters gained their point, and a new election was held on 26 December 2004, resulting in a victory for Yuschenko by 52 per cent against 44 per cent.[22] The new president visited Brussels in February 2005, and declared his intention of seeking close relations with the European Union and NATO, and eventual Ukrainian membership of both bodies. He received a friendly welcome from EU leaders, and the Poles went so far as to propose offering Ukraine a clear prospect of future membership. Most member states were more cautious, preferring to make guarded references to association, and to including Ukraine in the EU's 'neighbourhood' policy. Meanwhile, Yuschenko himself was careful to face both ways, and his first official visit abroad as president was to Moscow. Russia for its part continued to press Ukraine to consolidate its position within the Single Economic Space. In May 2005 the Russians made a telling intervention when the Russian companies which supplied some 80 per cent of Ukraine's fuel suddenly reduced their deliveries, in reply to a Ukrainian proposal to control prices. The European Union, however attractive in many respects, could wield no such influence. Meanwhile the internal divisions within Ukraine, on lines of geography, language and religion, persist. For all these reasons, a clear-cut decision by the Ukrainian government and people, for or against close relations with the EU or Russia, remains difficult to reach.

Moldova, a comparatively small state of about 4.5 million people, was historically in an ambiguous position, having been at different times part of Romania and the Soviet Union. After becoming independent when the Soviet Union broke up, the country stood rather uneasily between Ukraine and Romania, and also looked towards Russia for support – in 2001 the president, Vladimir Voronin, was elected with Russian assistance. But the country also began to look hopefully towards the European Union. In elections in March 2005 the three main political parties (the only ones which actually won seats) all advocated seeking membership of the European Union.

Among these three countries (Belarus, Ukraine and Moldova), it is Ukraine, by reason of its population and geographical position, that presents the key problem for European identity. For the European Union – the Europe of economic unity, common values and elaborate institutions – the inclusion of Ukraine would be an enlargement even more drastic than that achieved in 2004. For that very reason, it is unlikely to be acceptable among the existing member states, where 'enlargement fatigue' is widespread and deep-seated.[23] For Russia, to retain its own sphere of influence among its near neighbours is a vital part of its great-power status; and its influence in Ukraine, in particular, will not be given up easily. There is here a continuing line of division, and a potential source of dispute, which is likely to persist.

THE QUESTION OF TURKEY

There remains the difficult question of Turkey, whose governments have been seeking membership of the EEC/EC/EU since the 1960s. In December 1999 the EU leaders took the important step of agreeing that a Turkish application for membership should be considered according to the same criteria as those applied to other candidates, with the implication that they saw no obstacle in principle to Turkish membership. The Turks for their part increased their efforts to meet the criteria required by the EU. They strengthened their democratic credentials by introducing legislation (October 2001) to make it more difficult to ban political parties. In 2002 the law was changed to allow the use of Kurdish and other minority languages in broadcasting and teaching. In the same year Turkey abolished the death penalty – a crucial matter for the EU, which specifically ruled out the death penalty in all member states. In 2003 the Turkish government redefined the powers of the National Security Council, in order to emphasize the subordination of the armed forces to the civil authority. In 2004 the National Assembly accepted a large number of changes to the penal code and agreed to drop a proposal by the ruling party (the Islamist Justice and Development Party) to make adultery a crime – to which the European Commission had specifically objected.

14   The European Union flag in Istanbul: is this the shape of things to come?
© Fatih Saribas/Reuters/Corbis

Despite all these measures, the EU leaders still moved cautiously. In 2002 they agreed to admit ten new members in 2004, but with regard to Turkey they limited themselves to a guarded statement that if the country had fulfilled the necessary conditions on human rights by December 2004 the EU would open negotiations for Turkish entry without delay. Finally, in October 2004, the European Commission agreed to recommend that negotiations should begin in 2005; but the Commission warned that negotiations would be suspended if Turkey did not introduce further reforms. Moreover, the Commission suggested that permanent safeguards against Turkish immigration should be established. The EU leaders accepted these recommendations at a summit meeting in Brussels in December 2004. They set 3 October 2005 as the date for the start of negotiations for Turkish membership. But they also emphasized that there was no guarantee that the negotiations would lead to admission, and that the talks would be suspended if Turkey offended against EU criteria on human rights. They also agreed that permanent safeguards would be introduced which would allow individual member states to deny Turks the right to live and work in their country, which would be a departure from the normal EU rules about freedom of movement and employment for EU citizens. They also imposed the condition that Turkey must recognize the Greek Cypriot government in Cyprus.[24]

Meanwhile, in the background to these events, President Chirac of France undertook on 1 October 2004 that France would hold a referendum on Turkish membership, and Austria later made the same commitment. The Turkish government for its part agreed to open negotiations on the set date, but complained that the opposition to free movement for its citizens and the insistence on referendums by France and Austria were forms of discrimination against Turkey – which was surely true.

It is plain that the arguments about Turkish admission to the EU are far from being resolved. On the Turkish side, advocates of entry argue that it would strengthen the country's economy and mark the acceptance of Turkey as a modern, European-style state, which had long ago been the object of Kemal Atatürk. On the EU side, supporters of Turkish membership argue that the Union is a community of values; and since Turkey has adopted those values, in terms of human rights and the rule of law, the country therefore has the right to join the community. To accept the Turkish candidacy would also be an impressive gesture, contradicting theories about a 'clash of civilizations' between Christianity and Islam, and showing that the European Union is not a Christian club. To reject Turkish membership would have the opposite effect, and precipitate a clash of civilizations, to the detriment of both sides. This argument is particularly strongly urged by the British government.

Opposition to Turkish entry arises in part from doubts about Turkey's record on human rights, and an unwillingness to import the long-running Kurdish dispute within the EU. But there are deeper issues. On the economic side, Turkey would be by far the poorest state yet admitted to the EU, with an income per head of only about one-quarter of the average for the EU in 2004. To bring the country up even to the level of the poorer existing members would be a difficult task, and would absorb funds which would otherwise go elsewhere. The sheer size of the Turkish population is also daunting. The total stood at almost 70 million in 2003, and was predicted to reach 84–86 million by 2020, more populous than Germany, and thus entitled to commensurate voting weight in the Council of Ministers and representation in the European Parliament. Moreover the vast majority of this population are Muslims. This fact is usually discounted in principle, because the Turkish state is secular and most EU governments have no wish to make religion a central issue in the Turkish application; but in practice popular opinion is at best uneasy about the prospect of admitting 70 million more Muslims to the EU. This issue carried considerable weight in the French and Dutch referendum campaigns in 2005, and the no vote on the European constitution in both countries cast serious doubt on any further enlargement, and especially enlargement to include Turkey.

Behind all these arguments and problems lies the fundamental question of whether Turkey is a European country or not. Geographically, almost all its territory lies in Asia, with Turkey in Europe making up only 3 per cent of its area. The adhesion of Turkey would bring the European Union up to the frontiers of Syria, Iraq and Iran. Historically, the long defence of Europe against Turkish invasion, and the struggles of Balkan nationalists against the Ottoman Empire, have left a lasting mark; though other historic enmities have been overcome in the movement towards European integration. Whatever one's views on these matters, the fundamental fact is that the issue of Turkish membership of the European Union is more than a practical question open to pragmatic answers. It raises the questions of what it means to be European, and what sense the European Union attaches to its own name. These issues have yet to be fully put to the public opinion of any state in the EU. To do so would certainly prove divisive and disturbing; but to avoid them might well prove to be even more dangerous.

UNANSWERED QUESTIONS

The questions 'What is Europe?', 'Where are Europe's borders?' and 'What does it mean to be European?' have never been more important. Yet the answers to these questions remain uncertain. The European Union seeks to offer precise definitions, in terms of institutions, economic rules and a code of values; and yet its proposed constitution is in limbo, its economic rules are often broken and its code of values is open to question. The EU has by no means decided where its border should be fixed. Sometimes it seems near to adopting the watchword 'wider still and wider', raising no geographical obstacle to the entry of Turkey, which would carry the frontier of Europe further than has ever been conceived previously. But against this it is clear that there is widespread public unease at the prospect of further enlargement – 'enlargement fatigue' has set in and will not pass away quickly. The future relations of Russia and its near neighbours with the EU are difficult to predict, and the old question as to whether Russia is more than geographically part of Europe remains open. In mid-2005 the condition of Europe, in its unity and divisions, is best characterized by a series of question marks.

All these events and debates took place, and still lie, under the shadow of an impending demographic catastrophe. In 1989 Michel Rocard, then the premier of France, declared that the countries of Europe were committing suicide without even realizing it.[25] The statistics make grim reading. In the 1990s, the rate of reproduction across geographical Europe, in all countries, was below the rate of 2.1 which would secure even the replacement of the population. In 1996 the number of deaths exceeded that of births in 11 European countries, including Germany and Italy. In 1997, for the first time in three centuries, the population of the continent actually declined. Moreover, the population is ageing. In the whole world, Europe is the continent with the smallest proportion of children and the largest of old people. It is true that other countries (for example, Japan, Australia and the USA) also have ageing populations; but Europe is in the most advanced stage.[26] The contrast between Rocard's chilling pronouncement and the intense activity of European politicians as they pursued integration is stark. The Europe that is making a fresh start is also withering away. To provide the dying continent with new institutions is ominously like allocating staterooms on board the *Titanic*. To the question 'What is Europe?' must be added the further and grimmer question: 'In the long run, will it matter?'

CONCLUSION

Unity and division have been constant themes in European history in the twentieth century, running alongside one another in varying forms. Fervent nationalism and powerful ideologies have intensified divisions and conflicts, sometimes to the point of war. Yet even amid these times of dissension the concept of European unity has persisted and even flourished, in diverse ways – sometimes rhetorical, invoking the sentiment of a European family or sketching visionary schemes for federal union, and sometimes more akin to engineering, concerned with the nuts and bolts of trade and economics.

Before 1914 Europe possessed a sort of coherence and unity that was largely taken for granted. Europeans knew that they were different from (and usually felt superior to) Asians or Africans. A conscious sense of being European was strong among aristocrats, intellectuals and other elites; and Europeans felt little need to define their identity except in the broad sense that they were the heirs of ancient Greece, classical Rome and Christianity. Nor did they seek to establish political institutions to consolidate their unity – the furthest they went was to set up a Telegraphic Union or an International Railway Convention, for simple practical purposes.

The First World War destroyed this relaxed, almost unthinking, sort of unity. The continent tore itself apart in what amounted to a European civil war. There followed a time of troubles, during which Europe was rent by conflicting ideologies, economic rivalries and finally by the Second World War, which wrought even greater havoc (moral and material) than the First. Yet paradoxically, even in the course of this destruction, new aspirations to create a European identity and unity took shape. Visionaries like Coudenhove-Kalergi and Aristide Briand sketched their equivalent of cloud-capped towers, with not much by way of foundations. Communists, Fascists and Nazis all had their own, very different, concepts of what Europe should look like, if only they could lay their hands on it and shape it according to their will. For a short time during the Second World War, indeed, it seemed as though Nazi Germany was about to impose its own brand of unity upon Europe. These movements came to nothing: the idealistic aspirations because they lacked substance; the Nazi despotism because Germany lost the war.

Then after 1945 there came the drastic division of Europe into East and West along lines which were ideological, political and economic. On each side of the Iron Curtain there took shape an attempt to define a partial European identity. The countries of the Soviet zone in eastern Europe adopted a system based on economic and ideological conformity, imposed on them from without by Moscow, but also largely accepted within. In western Europe, which was itself divided along a number of different lines, the six countries which concluded the Treaty of Rome in 1957 (France, West Germany, Italy, Belgium, the Netherlands and Luxembourg) set up the European Economic Community, boldly laying claim to a title for which at the time they had little justification. But within this organization there took shape a combination between idealists and power-brokers, economists and bureaucrats (a sort of union of aspirational engineers), creating an entity which over a period of years attracted other countries, so that by 1986 the number of members reached 12.

At the end of 1989 the Iron Curtain suddenly vanished, and the countries of eastern Europe were released from the Soviet straitjacket – or in the case of Yugoslavia and Albania, from communist regimes outside Soviet control. The subsequent course of events in relation to European unity was striking. In western Europe, despite continuing diversity among the different nations, the drive towards creating a particular form of European unity, deliberately engineered and constructed, has intensified. This entity has a new name – the European Union. Many of its members have adopted a single currency – the euro. It has assumed new powers, notably in social policy, and seeks to take over other functions in foreign policy and defence. It has devised criteria to which its existing members must conform, and which aspiring applicants must show that they possess. Moreover, this entity has exercised a compelling attraction for most of the ex-communist states of eastern Europe, which showed unremitting persistence in seeking membership, sometimes in face of a grudging and reluctant welcome. Their motives were mixed. A lingering fear of Russia impels governments to seek security in the EU. More important, most people hope for economic advantage, encouraged by the almost legendary reputation of the EEC and EU as creators of wealth – east Europeans hope that the Midas touch will still work. There is also some sense, especially among intellectuals, that their countries are rejoining the European mainstream, which was why the new member states preferred to describe their entry as the 'reunification' of Europe rather than the 'enlargement' of the European Union.

Whatever the motives, a new form of European unity has taken institutional shape in a body which in 2004 included 25 states, stretching from the Straits of Gibraltar to the Baltic Sea and from Ireland to Hungary. The European Union has many shortcomings. It is far from including the whole geographical continent of Europe. The vision to which it aspires is shared by elites rather than by majorities, embodied in cumbersome and defective institutions and sometimes interpreted by bureaucrats in ways which are pettifogging or absurd. The whole project (indeed the whole continent) is threatened by a demographic disaster which is advancing inexorably upon it. But despite these problems the European Union presents a form of European unity more significant and influential than anything seen since before 1914, and quite different in character. Its institutions confer upon it a weight and a momentum which were absent when Europe was something simply taken for granted.

From this story of the past century two salient points emerge. First, the periods when there was more that united Europe than divided it have been comparatively short, limited to the few years before 1914 and after 1990. In the long intervening period Europe was torn by dissensions and conflicts, and movements towards unity were the province of the rhetoric of idealists on the one hand and the mailed fist of Nazi Germany on the other. Out of just over a hundred years, the impulse towards unity as against division has prevailed only for a little over a quarter of a century – 14 years before 1914 and another 14 after 1990.

Second, there has been no linear progress or evolution towards European unity. It is true that there has been a development from the original six countries of the European Economic Community to the present 25 of the European Union, accompanied by a substantial increase in the functions, powers and influence of the Community and Union. But in the wider perspective of a century of European history, the story has been one of fits and starts, uncertainty and unpredictability. Before 1914, when Europe seemed coherent and even to some degree united; but it went on to tear itself apart. Later, even in the midst of the ideological and military conflicts of the 1930s and early 1940s, aspirations towards unity took shape. After 1945 the continent was grievously and apparently permanently divided, but eventually the walls came tumbling down in a way that almost no one had foreseen. Who knows when events will take another unexpected turn? If there is one thing certain at the present time, it is that nothing is certain. The danger of a European unity which is embodied in complex institutions and elaborate regulations is that it may not adapt to the sort of transformations which have occurred during the past hundred years. The story of Europe has not been one of historic evolution but of erratic and unpredictable change. It seems highly unlikely that such a fluid and changeable continent – or even a large part of it – can now be contained within a single mould.

NOTES

Preface

1. Pieter Geyl, 'The historical background of the idea of European unity', in Geyl, *Encounters in History* (London, 1967), 363. Geyl had experienced his full share of European history, in Buchenwald and in the Dutch Resistance.

2. The *Shorter OED* cautiously defines Eurospeak as 'the allegedly unattractive language used by Eurocrats'. Dr Johnson, an earlier lexicographer, would surely have omitted 'allegedly'.

Introduction

1. Oscar Halecki, *The Limits and Divisions of European History* (London, 1950), 8. Italics added.

2. Norman Davies, *Europe: A History* (Oxford, 1996), 15. Italics added.

3. Luigi Barzini, *The Europeans* (New York, 1983), 12. Italics added.

4. De Gaulle, speech at Strasbourg, 23 November 1959, cited in Antony Jay (ed.), *Oxford Dictionary of Political Quotations* (Oxford, 1996), 112.

5. H.A.L. Fisher, *A History of Europe* (new edn in 2 vols, London, 1943), 4.

6. Dmitri Obolenski, *Bread of Exile: A Russian Family* (London, 1999), 211.

7. G.M. Trevelyan, *History of England* (3rd edn, London, 1945), 138. On this school of historical thinking, see P.M.H. Bell, 'A historical cast of mind', *Journal of European Integration History*, 1996, vol. 2, no. 2, 5–19.

8. P.M.H. Bell, *France and Britain, 1940–1994: The Long Separation* (London, 1997), 235; Gérard-François Dumont (ed.), *Les Racines de l'identité européenne* (Paris, 1999), 227.

9. Barzini, *Europeans*, 64–5.

10. Statute of the Council of Europe, in J.A.S. Grenville, *The Major International Treaties, 1914–1973: A History and Guide, with Texts* (London, 1974), 401.

11. See pp. 259–62.

12. Jean Barrot, Bernard Elissalde and Georges Roques, *Europe, Europes: Espaces en recomposition* (Paris, 1997), 70. The figures are necessarily rough. Another estimate is that in 1900 Europe made up between a quarter and a fifth of the world's population, and in 1990 between a ninth and a tenth – J.M. Roberts, *The Penguin History of Europe* (London, 1996), 472.

Chapter 1

1. Robert Gildea, *Barricades and Borders: Europe 1800–1914* (Oxford, 1987), 278–9; B.R. Mitchell, *European Historical Statistics, 1750–1970* (abridged edn, London, 1978), 3–11. The population of Asiatic Russia in 1897 was approximately 20 million.

2. Gildea, 283; J.-M. Gaillard and A. Rowley, *Histoire du continent européen de 1850 à la*

fin du XXe siècle (Paris, 1998), 167; Richard Vinen, *A History in Fragments: Europe in the Twentieth Century* (London, 2000), 19.

3. J.-P. Bardet and J. Dupâquier (eds), *Histoire des populations de l'Europe*, vol. III: *Les temps incertains, 1914–1998* (Paris, 1999), 325.

4. Figures for the external trade of European countries in Mitchell, *European Historical Statistics*, 303–7.

5. Asa Briggs, 'The world economy', in *The New Cambridge Modern History*, vol. XII, *The Shifting Balance of World Forces, 1878–1945* (revised edn, Cambridge, 1968), 40.

6. A.J.P. Taylor, *The Struggle for Mastery in Europe, 1848–1918* (Oxford, 1954), xxv, xxx.

7. John Maynard Keynes, *The Economic Consequences of the Peace* (London, 1920), 9, 13.

8. Arno J. Mayer, *The Persistence of the Old Regime: Europe to the Great War* (London, 1981), 23.

9. Gordon Brook-Shepherd, *Royal Sunset: The Dynasties of Europe and the Great War* (London, 1987), 98–9.

10. Stanley Leathes, 'Modern Europe', in *The Cambridge Modern History*, vol. XII, *The Latest Age, 1870–1910* (Cambridge, 1910), 5, 7. Leathes assumed that, in the context of democratic government, the USA was part of the European tradition. He added that 'few would assert with confidence that democracy was suited to Asiatics...none perhaps would venture to propose its general application to communities of African negroes.'

11. Dominic Lieven, *The Aristocracy in Europe, 1815–1914* (Oxford, 1992), 248.

12. Mayer, *Old Regime*, 23; Paul Bairoch, 'Agriculture and the Industrial Revolution', in Carlo M. Cipolla (ed.), *The Fontana Economic History of Europe*, vol. 3, *Part I, The Industrial Revolution, 1700–1914* (London, 1976), 463–5.

13. John Gooch, *Armies in Europe* (London, 1980), 142. In actual sums, as distinct from proportions of the budget, German expenditure was by far the larger: the equivalent of 99 million French francs as against 38 million for France.

14. Leathes, 'Modern Europe', *CMH*, vol. XII, 7.

15. Gaillard and Rowley, *Continent européen*, 133–4.

16. Annie Kriegel and Jean-Jacques Becker, *1914: La guerre et le mouvement ouvrier français* (Paris, 1964), 200.

17. Text of the Stuttgart resolution in James Joll, *The Second International* (revised edn, London, 1974), 206–8.

18. Quoted in ibid., 112.

19. Richard J. Evans, *The Feminists: Women's Emancipation Movements in Europe, America and Australasia, 1840–1920* (London, 1992), 58.

20. James F. McMillan, *Twentieth-Century France* (London, 1992), 58.

21. See F.S.L. Lyons, *Internationalism in Europe, 1815–1914* (Leiden, 1963), 39–64, 120–1, 156.

22. Quoted in Geoffrey Blainey, *The Causes of War* (London, 1973), 24.

23. See I.F. Clarke, *Voices Prophesying War* (London, 1966), for some novelists who sensed impending catastrophe.

24. Leathes, 'Modern Europe', in *CMH*, vol. XII, 5.

25. D.K. Fieldhouse, *Economics and Empire* (London, 1973), 3.

26. P.E. Roberts, 'The British Empire in India', in *CMH*, vol. XII, 499.
27. A.P. Thornton, *Imperialism in the Twentieth Century* (London, 1978), 92.
28. A.P. Thornton, *The Imperial Idea and its Enemies* (Oxford, 1954), 294.

Chapter 2

1. J.E.C. Bodley, *France* (2nd edn, London, 1899), 45.
2. George Dangerfield, *The Strange Death of Liberal England, 1910–1914* (London, 1935).
3. Oil production, B.R. Mitchell, *European Historical Statistics, 1750–1970* (abridged edn, London, 1978), 197; urban population, Paul Hayes, 'Russia and Austria-Hungary', in Hayes (ed.), *Themes in Modern European History, 1870–1914* (London, 1992), 65.
4. Barbara Tuchman, *The Proud Tower: A Portrait of the World Before the War, 1890–1914* (pbk edn, London, 1980), 113.
5. H.A.L. Fisher, *A History of Europe* (revised edn, London, 1943), vol. II, 1092.
6. Raymond Carr, *Spain, 1808–1939* (Oxford, 1966), 400, 35.

Chapter 3

1. Lord Grey of Falloden, *Twenty-Five Years, 1892–1916* (London, 1925), vol. I, 89.
2. See Geoffrey Blainey, *The Causes of War* (London, 1973), especially Book One; R. Wohl, *The Generation of 1914* (London, 1980); Rupert Brooke, *Collected Poems* (London, 1918), 5.
3. Modris Eksteins, *Rites of Spring: The Great War and the Birth of the Modern Age* (London, 1989).
4. Gerard de Groot, *Blighty: British Society in the Era of the Great War* (London, 1996), 3. This book treats its subject with an admirable combination of good sense and sound scholarship.
5. Blainey, *Causes of War*, 36–7.
6. The text of the German ultimatum, which still repays reading, may be found in Imanuel Geiss (ed.), *July 1914. The Outbreak of the First World War: Selected Documents* (London, 1967), 231–2.
7. For events in Belgium and the deliberations of the Crown Council, see Robert Devleeshouwer, *Les Belges et le danger de guerre, 1910–1914* (Louvain and Paris, 1958), 265–331. The Crown Council was a hastily summoned gathering, chaired by the king and including government ministers and other politicians, senior army officers, and prominent persons from various Belgian institutions. King Albert's remark is quoted in John Keegan, *The First World War* (London, 1998), 91.
8. E.H. Kossmann, *The Low Countries, 1780–1940* (Oxford, 1978), 538.
9. See Jean-Jacques Becker, *1914: Comment les Français sont entrés dans la guerre* (Paris, 1977), a work of historical reconstruction on a massive yet always human scale.
10. Quoted in de Groot, *Blighty*, 9.
11. Ian Beckett, 'The nation in arms', in Beckett and Keith Simpson (eds), *A Nation in Arms: A Social Study of the British Army in the First World War* (Manchester, 1985), 8.
12. Peter Buitenhuis, *The Great War of Words: Literature as Propaganda, 1914–18 and After* (London, 1989), 14–15. All who attended the meeting agreed to keep it a secret, which they appear to have done in a manner remarkable for some highly voluble men.

13. Gordon A. Craig, *Germany, 1866–1945* (Oxford, 1978), 339–40.
14. Georges Lefranc, *Le Mouvement syndical sous la Troisième République* (Paris, 1967), 197. Merrheim (whom Clemenceau described during the war as 'the pacifist leader of those who make shells') was addressing the Congress of the Confédération Générale du Travail on 18 September 1919.
15. Herbert Butterfield, 'The scientific versus the moralistic approach in international affairs', *International Affairs*, October 1951, vol. XXVII, no. 4, 417.
16. See F.R. Bridge, 'The foreign policy of the monarchy', and F. Tibor Zsupan, 'The Hungarian political scene', in Mark Cornwall (ed.), *The Last Years of Austria-Hungary* (Exeter, 2002), 33–6, 110; Stevan K. Pavlowitch, *A History of the Balkans, 1804–1945* (London, 1999), 209.

Chapter 4

1. Gerard de Groot, *The First World War* (London, 2001), 24–5, 51–2.
2. J.M. Bourne, *Britain and the Great War, 1914–1918* (London, 1989), 156–7.
3. Quoted in John Keegan, *The First World War* (London, 1999), 133.
4. Michael Brown, *Verdun 1916* (London, 1999), 158–9.
5. French infantryman, ibid., 161; German soldier's letter, 12 March 1916, 109; French lieutenant's diary, 22 May 1916, 71.
6. A.H. Farrar-Hockley, *The Somme* (pbk edn, London, 1966), 252–3.
7. Brown, *Verdun*, 178–9.
8. C.R.M.F. Cruttwell, *A History of the Great War* (Oxford, 1934), 185. Russian casualty figures can only be estimated very roughly – Norman Stone, *The Eastern Front, 1914–1917* (London, 1975), 91, describes the problems of the records.
9. H.H. Herwig, *The First World War: Germany and Austria-Hungary* (London, 1997), 209. The figures are approximate. Keegan, *First World War*, 328, puts the Austrian losses even higher, at 600,000 killed and wounded plus 400,000 prisoners.
10. For these events, see pp. 68–9, 75–6.
11. G. Hardach, *The First World War, 1914–1918* (London, 1997), 91.
12. Paul Kennedy, *The Rise and Fall of the Great Powers* (pbk edn, London, 1989), 333.
13. Ibid., 345.
14. The right of conscientious objection, primarily on religious grounds, was provided for in the conscription legislation – an important concession to liberal sentiment and a significant precedent.
15. Some figures for German food production (in metric tons) in 1913 and 1917, respectively: wheat 5,094,000 and 2,484,000; rye 12,222,000 and 7,003,000; potatoes 54,121,000 and 34,882,000 – sources: Kennedy, *Great Powers*, 349; B.R. Mitchell, *European Historical Statistics, 1750–1970* (abridged edn, London, 1978), 113.
16. J.M. Winter, 'Some paradoxes of the First World War', in Winter and W. Wall (eds), *The Upheaval of War: Family, Work and Welfare in Europe, 1914–18* (Cambridge, 1988), 40.
17. Kennedy, *Great Powers*, 340.
18. Guy Pedroncini, *Les mutineries de 1917* (Paris, 1967), provides the most authoritative account of these events; for the number of divisions affected, see 63.

19. Bourne, *Britain and the Great War*, 68; E.L. Woodward, *Great Britain and the War of 1914–18* (London, 1967), 338–9.

20. Lord Newton, *Lord Lansdowne* (London, 1929), 467.

21. *Speeches of Lord Oxford and Asquith, selected by Basil Herbert* (London, 1927), 224. Italics added.

22. Z.A.B. Zeman, *The Making and Breaking of Communist Europe* (Oxford, 1991), 65.

23. Lord Grey of Falloden, *Twenty-Five Years, 1892–1916* (London, 1925), vol. II, 103; Falkenhayn quoted in Arthur S. Link, *Woodrow Wilson*, vol. III, *The Struggle for Neutrality* (Princeton, NJ, 1960), 406–7.

24. Marc Ferro, *The Great War, 1914–1918* (London, 1979), 129.

25. Herwig, *First World War*, 397–8, 420.

26. Jean-Jacques Becker, *The Great War and the French People* (Leamington Spa, 1985), 260–301; the quotation is from 301.

27. See p. 75. A useful summary of the Fourteen Points may be found in Harold Nicolson, *Peacemaking 1919* (London, 1933), 39–41.

28. There was here another 'might-have-been'. If the Germany of Hindenburg and Ludendorff had emerged as the final victor of the war, it is unlikely that it would long have tolerated the Bolshevik regime in Russia. The Western Allies, by their victory in France, in all probability saved the Bolshevik revolution, though they received no credit for it! It remains an intriguing thought that there should have been statues in Red Square to Foch, Haig and Pershing, or perhaps a poilu, a British Tommy and a doughboy.

Chapter 5

1. Quoted in Alan Sharp, *The Versailles Settlement: Peacemaking in Paris, 1919* (London, 1991), 156.

2. Quoted in Margaret Macmillan, *Peacemakers* (London, 2001), 19.

3. H.W.V. Temperley (ed.), *A History of the Peace Conference of Paris*, vol. III, 187, 214. The text of the treaty is printed in the same volume, 105–336.

4. Quoted in Klaus Schwabe, 'Germany's peace aims and the domestic and international constraints', in Manfred F. Boemaker, Gerald D. Feldman and Elizabeth Glazier (eds), *The Treaty of Versailles: A Reassessment after 75 Years* (Cambridge, 1998), 64.

5. Jean-Pierre Bardet and Jacques Dupâquier (eds), *Histoire des populations de l'Europe*, vol. III, *Les temps incertains, 1914–1998* (Paris, 1999), 635.

6. Figures from the census of 1930, Royal Institute of International Affairs, *Bulletin of International Affairs*, vol. XIII, 747.

7. Norman Davies, *Europe: A History* (London, 1996), 928–9.

8. The figures for debt were as follows. Owed to the USA: by Britain, $4661m; by France, $3991m; by Italy, Russia and other states, $3209m. Owed to Britain: by France, $3030m; by Italy, Russia and other states, $8141m. Owed to France: by Italy, Russia and other states, $3463m. A. Sauvy, *Histoire économique de la France, 1919–1939* (Paris, 1965), vol. I, 169.

9. Norman Davies and Roger Moorhouse, *Microcosm: Portrait of a Central European City* (London, 2002), 332.

10. Z.A.B. Zeman, *The Making and Breaking of Communist Europe* (Oxford, 1991), 94.

Notes

11. See, generally, Charles S. Maier, *Recasting Bourgeois Europe: Stabilisation in France, Germany and Italy in the decade after World War I* (Princeton, 1975).

12. Ute Daniel, 'Women's work in industry and family: Germany, 1914–18', in Jay Winter and Richard Wall (eds), *The Upheaval of War: Family, Work and Welfare in Europe, 1914–1918* (Cambridge, 1989), 267–96; Gerard de Groot, *Blighty: British Society in the Era of the Great War* (London, 1996), 128; James F. McMillan, *Twentieth-Century France* (London, 1992), 84–5.

13. On this general question of attitudes, see Georges Duby and Michelle Perrot (eds), *A History of Women in the West*, vol. V, *Toward a Cultural Identity in the Twentieth Century* (Cambridge, Mass., 1996), 21–38, 92–119.

14. Martin Pugh, 'The rise of European feminism', in Pugh (ed.), *A Companion to Modern European History, 1871–1945* (London, 1997), 166; Richard J. Evans, *The Feminists: Women's Emancipation Movements in Europe, America and Australasia, 1840–1920* (London, 1977), 232–5.

15. See the differing casualty figures in Bardet and Dupâquier, *Histoire*, vol. III, 7, J.M. Winter, *The Great War and the British People* (pbk edn, London, 1987), 75 and Derek Aldcroft, *The European Economy, 1914–1990* (London, 1993), 6–7.

16. Aldcroft, *European Economy, 1914–1990*, 6.

17. Bardet and Dupâquier, *Histoire*, vol. III, 95.

18. Milos Macura, 'Population in Europe, 1920–1970', in Carlo M. Cipolla (ed.), *The Fontana Economic History of Europe: The Twentieth Century*, part 1, 22. The figures in Bardet and Dupâquier, *Histoire*, vol. III, 11, differ only slightly.

19. Bardet and Dupâquier, *Histoire*, vol. III, 11.

20. John Lukacs, *The Last European War* (London, 1976), 174; Macura in Cipolla, *Twentieth Century*, part 1, 43–5.

21. Ibid., 18; A. Armengaud, *La Population française au XIXe siècle* (Paris, 1971), 41, 48.

22. Macura in Cipolla, *Twentieth Century*, part 1, 54.

23. Bardet and Dupâquier, *Histoire*, vol. III, 248, 325, 330–1. Figures for immigration present many difficulties: countries use different definitions of an immigrant; illegal immigrants often escape detection; naturalizations change the statistics, but not the underlying facts.

24. S.K. Pavlowitch, *A History of the Balkans, 1804–1945* (London, 1999), 239; Bardet and Dupâquier, *Histoire*, vol. III, 65–6. The criterion for transfer of populations under the Treaty of Lausanne was religion, not language, so large numbers of the new arrivals in Greece spoke no Greek.

25. Bardet and Dupâquier, *Histoire*, vol. III, 50, 57–8, 193–4; Lukacs, *Last European War*, 175.

26. Philippe Bernard, *La Fin d'un monde, 1914–1929* (Paris, 1975), 139–41; Aldcroft, *European Economy, 1914–1990*, 50. The 'gold exchange standard' meant that a country tied its currency to gold indirectly, through a currency which was itself on the 'gold bullion' standard.

27. Cipolla, *Twentieth Century*, part 2, tables on 687 ff.

28. See the analysis in Stephen J. Lee, *The European Dictatorships, 1918–1945* (London, 1987), xi.

29. The following voting figures in various countries are from Donald Sassoon, *One Hundred Years of Socialism: The West European Left in the Twentieth Century* (London, 1996), 43, and Chris Cook and John Paxton (eds), *European Political Facts, 1900–1996* (London, 1998), chapter 5.

30. Eamonn Duffy, *Saints and Sinners: A History of the Popes* (London, 1997), 260–1.

31. Ibid., 261.

32. Ralph White, '"Cordial caution": The British response to the French proposal for European Federal Union of 1930', in A. Bosco (ed.), *The Federal Idea*, vol. I, *The History of Federalism from the Enlightenment to 1945* (London, 1991), 237–62.

Chapter 6

1. Derek Aldcroft, *The European Economy, 1914–1990* (3rd edn, London, 1993), 67.

2. Charles P. Kindleberger, *The World in Depression, 1929–1939* (London, 1973), 171. The precise figures were: January 1929, $2997.7 million; January 1933, $992.4 million.

3. B.R. Mitchell, *European Historical Statistics, 1750–1970* (abridged edn, London, 1978), 64–9.

4. Brian Porter, *Britain, Europe and the World, 1850–1982* (London, 1983), 94.

5. Hubert Bonin, *Histoire économique de la IVe. République* (Paris, 1987), 24–25.

6. Aldcroft, *European Economy, 1914–1990*, 64. The Soviet government claimed a 67 per cent increase in industrial production, 1929–32, when the capitalist economies were all in trouble; but there are difficulties with the Soviet statistics, and the results of the first five-year plan were certainly exaggerated.

7. Alan Cassels, *Ideology and International Relations in the Modern World* (London, 1996) is an excellent guide.

8. Stephen J. Lee, *The European Dictatorships, 1918–1945* (London, 1987), 300, sets out these four characteristics. Norman Davies, *Europe: A History* (Oxford, 1996), 946–8, provides a list of no fewer than 18 points which communism, Fascism and Nazism had in common.

9. Quoted in Robert Service, *A History of Twentieth-Century Russia* (London, 1997), 88.

10. Figures in Jean-Pierre Bardet and Jacques Dupâquier, *Histoire des populations de l'Europe*, vol. III, *Les temps incertains, 1914–1998*, (Paris, 1999), 670.

11. François Furet, *The Passing of an Illusion: The Idea of Communism in the Twentieth Century* (London, 1999), 272. Furet wrote as a former communist and knew what he was talking about.

12. Quoted in Paul Hollander, *Political Pilgrims: Travels of Western Intellectuals to the Soviet Union, China and Cuba, 1928–1978* (Oxford, 1981), 95.

13. John Roberts, *The Penguin History of Europe* (London, 1996), 528.

14. Davies, *Europe*, 963.

15. See Ernst Nolte's 'fascist minimum', quoted in Stanley G. Payne, *A History of Fascism, 1914–1945* (London, 1996), 5, and Payne's own list of 'fascist negations', ibid., 7.

16. Quotations from Adrian Lyttleton (ed.), *Italian Fascisms from Pareto to Gentile* (London, 1973), 53, 42.

17. R.J.B. Bosworth, *Mussolini* (London, 2002), 222–3. Payne, *History of Fascism*, 117, puts the figure for political executions at 26.

Notes

18. Giolitti quoted in Bosworth, *Mussolini*, 156; Gasparri in Anthony Rhodes, *The Vatican in the Age of the Dictators, 1922–1945* (London, 1973), 41.
19. Quoted in Federico Chabod, *Italian Fascism* (London, 1963), 80.
20. See the English translation of Adolf Hitler, *Mein Kampf*, with an introduction by Donald Cameron Watt (London, 1974); Adolf Hitler, *Hitler's Secret Book* (New York, 1962); and the reflections on Hitler and the Jewish question in John Lukacs, *The Hitler of History* (New York, 1997).
21. Quotations from *Hitler's Secret Book*, 145, and Jeremy Noakes and Geoffrey Pridham (eds), *Documents on Nazism, 1919–1945* (London, 1974), 509.
22. Chris Cook and John Paxton (eds), *European Political Facts, 1900–1996* (London, 1998), 207.
23. In 1933, when the Nazis were in power, they won only 17,277,000 votes (43.9 per cent), despite organizing the elections themselves.
24. *Fontana Economic History of Europe* (London, 1976), vol. 6, part 2, Statistical Appendix, 690; Mitchell, *European Historical Statistics*, 68–9.
25. T.K. Derry, *A History of Scandinavia* (London, 1979), 320. During the Second World War, the name of 'Quisling' became synonymous in Britain with 'collaborator', or more simply 'traitor'.
26. Richard Griffiths, *Fellow Travellers of the Right: British Enthusiasts for Nazi Germany, 1933–39* (pbk edn, Oxford, 1983); the quotation from Lloyd George is on 224.
27. See John Lukacs, *The Last European War* (London, 1976), 290, for this largely unrecognized point.
28. W.H. Auden, 'September 1, 1939', in *Another Time* (London, 1940), 112.
29. Mussolini in Galeazzo Ciano, *Ciano's Diary, 1939–1943* (London, 1947), 10; Hitler in Ian Kershaw, *Hitler*, vol. II, *Nemesis* (London, 2000), 208.

Chapter 7

1. *Spectator*, 1 December 1939, 774. Nicolson was later a junior minister at the Ministry of Information in Churchill's wartime administration.
2. See the account of Federal Union by John Pinder in Walter Lipgens (ed.), *Documents on the History of European Integration*, vol. II, *Plans for European Union in Great Britain and in Exile, 1939–1945* (New York, 1986), 26–34.
3. C.R. Attlee, *Labour's Peace Aims* (London, 1940); an extract is printed in Lipgens, *Documents*, vol. II, 167–8.
4. Michael Dockrill, *British Establishment Perspectives on France, 1936–1940* (London, 1999), 154.
5. Martin Gilbert, *Finest Hour: Winston S. Churchill, 1939–1941* (London, 1987), 467; David Low, *Low's Autobiography* (London, 1956), 337.
6. Ian Kershaw, *Hitler*, vol. II, *Nemesis* (London, 2000), 400.
7. Walter Lipgens (ed.), *Documents on the History of European Integration*, vol. I, *Continental Plans for European Union, 1939–1945* (New York, 1985), 72. Seyss-Inquart was the German Commissioner for the Occupied Netherlands, making a speech on the programme for a new Netherlands Union.
8. John Laughland, *The Tainted Source: The Undemocratic Origins of the European Idea* (London, 1997), 27.

9. J. Förster, 'Croisade de l'Europe contre le bolchevisme', part 2, *Revue d'Histoire de la Deuxième Guerre Mondiale*, April 1980, no. 118, 1–26; A. Merglen, 'Soldats français sous uniformes allemands', ibid., October 1977, no. 108, 71–84; Norman Davies, *Europe: A History* (Oxford, 1996), 71–84.

10. On the numbers of Jewish dead, J.A.S. Grenville, *The Collins History of the World in the Twentieth Century* (London, 1994), 281–7; Lucy Davidowicz, *The War Against the Jews, 1933–1945* (London, 1974), 480, which puts the figure with great precision at 5,933,900; and Davies, *Europe*, 1021, 1328, presenting a minimum of 4,871,000 and a maximum of 6,271,500, and concluding that the figure of 5,850,000 used at the Nuremberg Trials was probably about right.

11. Stalin's post-war attempt at European domination came from outside Europe, and stopped (or was stopped) at the Iron Curtain.

Chapter 8

1. Goebbels quoted in Hugh Thomas, *The Armed Truce: The Beginnings of the Cold War, 1945–46* (pbk edn, London, 1988), 699; Churchill's telegram in *Winston S. Churchill, The Second World War*, vol. VI, *Triumph and Tragedy* (London, 1954), 498–9. Churchill later used the phrase in his speech at Fulton, Missouri in March 1946 – see Martin Gilbert, *'Never Despair': Winston S. Churchill, 1945–1965* (London, 1988), 192–206; it then became part of the language.

2. See the analysis in Derek Aldcroft, *The European Economy, 1914–1990* (London, 1993), 110–14; and the vivid account in D. Cameron Watt, *How War Came: The Immediate Origins of the Second World War* (London, 1989), 3–10.

3. Casualty figures in J.-P. Bardet and Jacques Dupâquier (eds), *Histoire des populations de l'Europe*, vol. III, *Les temps incertains, 1914–1998* (Paris, 1999), 82–5; Aldcroft, *European Economy, 1914–1990*, 108–9; I.C.B. Dear and M.R.D. Foot (eds), *The Oxford Companion to the Second World War* (Oxford, 1995), 289–91. For a long time the figure for Soviet war dead was widely accepted as about 20 million, but this has been revised upwards, on convincing evidence.

4. Bardet and Dupâquier, *Histoire*, vol. III, 66; Aldcroft, *European Economy, 1914–1990*, 134–5; Dear and Foot, *Oxford Companion*, 935–6.

5. Quoted in Stephen Hawes and Ralph White (eds), *Resistance in Europe, 1940–1945* (London, 1975), 22. I am grateful to Ralph White for drawing this passage to my attention.

6. John Lukacs, *The Last European War, September 1939–December 1941* (London, 1976), 178–82; Bardet and Dupâquier, *Histoire*, vol. III, 381 (Sweden), 401 (Britain), 488 (France), 512 (Portugal), 589 (Switzerland). The figures for birth rates per thousand population in 1940 and 1945 respectively, are: Sweden, 15.1, 20.4; Britain, 14.5, 16.1; France, 13.7, 16.2; Portugal, 24.3, 26.0; Switzerland, 15.2, 20.1.

Chapter 9

1. See Alan Milward, *The Reconstruction of Western Europe* (London, 1987), 1–17, for the argument that there was no severe economic crisis in western Europe, except for a shortage of foreign exchange, which itself arose from an increase in investment.

Notes

2. Forrest C. Pogue, *George C. Marshall*, vol. IV, *Statesman, 1945–1959* (New York, 1987), 200.

3. The presence of Turkey at the Marshall Plan conference was something of an anomaly, because Marshall's offer was made to European countries, and most Turkish territory lay outside Europe; but the USA was already committed to the economic support of Turkey.

4. V. Molotov, *Molotov Remembers: Inside Kremlin Politics. Conversations with Felix Chuev*, ed. Albert Resis (Chicago, 1993), 62.

5. Summaries of the results of the Marshall Plan in William I. Hitchcock, *The Struggle for Europe: The Turbulent History of a Divided Continent, 1945–2002* (London, 2003), 134–9; Maurice Vaïsse, *Les relations internationales depuis 1945* (3rd edn, Paris, 1994), 19; for France, Hubert Bonin, *Histoire économique de la IVe. République* (Paris, 1987), 153–4.

6. Table in J.A.S. Grenville, *The Collins History of the World in the Twentieth Century* (London, 1998), 541; B.R. Mitchell, *European Historical Statistics, 1750–1970* (abridged edn, London, 1978), 915, 918–20 for Scandinavia, the Low Countries and Portugal.

7. Grenville, *World in the Twentieth Century*, 536; Harold James, 'The fall and rise of the European economy in the twentieth century', in T.C.W. Blanning (ed.), *The Oxford Illustrated History of Modern Europe* (Oxford, 1996), 198; Hitchcock, *Struggle for Europe*, 142.

8. Timothy Garton Ash, *In Europe's Name* (New York, 1993), 21.

9. I.C.B. Dear and M.R.D. Foot (eds), *The Oxford Companion to the Second World War* (Oxford, 1995), 1275–82.

10. Martin Pugh, 'The rise of European feminism', in Pugh (ed.), *A Companion to Modern European History, 1871–1945* (Oxford, 1997), 166; Georges Duby and Michelle Perrot (eds), *A History of Women in the West*, vol. V, *Toward a Cultural Identity in the Twentieth Century* (Cambridge, Mass., 1996), 513–18.

11. For the Zurich speech, Martin Gilbert, *'Never Despair': Winston S. Churchill, 1945–1965* (London, 1988), 265–6.

12. List of member states, Chris Cook and John Paxton (eds), *European Political Facts, 1900–1996* (4th edn, London, 1998), 17.

13. Raymond Poidevin, *Robert Schuman: homme d'état, 1886–1963* (Paris, 1986), 423.

14. For the Treaty of Rome, see J.A.S. Grenville, *The Major International Treaties, 1914–1973* (London, 1974), 412–17; William Nicoll and Trevor Salmon, *Understanding the New European Community* (London, 1994), 15–20, 59–99; and Mark Gilbert, *Surpassing Realism: The Politics of European Integration since 1945* (Boulder, Colo. and Oxford, 2003), 70–5, 146.

15. Pierre Gerbet, *La construction de l'Europe* (3rd edn, Paris, 1999), 201.

16. J.-R. de Salis, *Switzerland and Europe: Essays and Reflections* (London, 1971), 17–18.

17. See the essay by Anselm Zurfluh, 'Les territoires alpins et l'identité européenne', in Gérard-François Dumont (ed.), *Les Racines de l'identité européenne* (Paris, 1999), 64–89.

18. Quoted in J.P.D. Dunbabin, *The Post-Imperial Age* (London, 1994), 6.

19. Christian Pineau, *Suez 1956* (Paris, 1976), 191.

Chapter 10

1. Pieter Geyl, 'The historical background of the idea of European unity' (first published in 1959), in *Encounters in History* (London, 1963), 368.

2. John Lukacs, *Decline and Rise of Europe* (New York, 1965), 44–5, and Jacques Rupnik, *The Other Europe* (London, 1988), xv, both emphasize this neglected but crucial point.

3. Geoffrey Swain and Nigel Swain, *Eastern Europe Since 1945* (2nd edn, London, 1998), 34.

4. For these election figures, see Chris Cook and John Paxton, *European Political Facts 1900–1996* (4th edn, London, 1998), 173–4 (Bulgaria), 214–15 (Hungary), 244–5 (Romania).

5. Quoted in William I. Hitchcock, *The Struggle for Europe: The History of the Continent Since 1945* (London, 2003), 114.

6. Figures in Cook and Paxton, *European Political Facts*, 180–1.

7. Quoted in R.J. Crampton, *Eastern Europe in the Twentieth Century* (London, 1994), 262.

8. Accounts of the purges may be found in ibid., 261–74, and Swain, *Eastern Europe*, 61–6.

9. See Philip Longworth, *The Making of Eastern Europe: From Pre-History to Post-Communism* (2nd edn, New York, 1997), 4, for this striking phrase.

10. Richard Vinen, *A History in Fragments: Europe in the Twentieth Century* (London, 2000), 406 and, generally, 410–13.

11. Rupnik, *The Other Europe*, 196–7 (musical five-year plan); Robin Okey, *Eastern Europe, 1740–1985* (2nd edn, London, 1986), 202–3 (Romanian language).

12. Swain, *East Europe*, 112.

13. The membership of COMECON in 1949 was: Albania, Bulgaria, Czechoslovakia, Hungary, Poland, Romania and the Soviet Union. East Germany joined in 1950; Albania left in 1961. The organization was later joined by Mongolia (1962), Cuba (1972) and Vietnam (1978); but in the 1950s it was a Soviet and east European body.

14. Mark Kramer, 'The Soviet Union and Eastern Europe', in Ngaire Woods (ed.), *Explaining International Relations Since 1945* (Oxford, 1997), 111–13, provides a lucid explanation of a complicated subject.

15. Tables on economic planning and collectivization in Swain, *East Europe*, 100–1.

16. Derek Aldcroft, *The European Economy, 1914–1990* (London, 1993), 173.

17. Crampton, *Eastern Europe*, 301.

18. William Colby, quoted in Gabriel Partos, *The World that Came in from the Cold* (London, 1993), 108.

19. Table in David Miller, *The Cold War: A Military History* (London, 1998), 342.

Chapter 11

1. Derek Aldcroft, *The European Economy, 1914–1990* (London, 1993), 221.

2. Ibid., 221 (GDP), 252 (unemployment), 201 (inflation).

3. Ibid., 234. The average figures concealed some big differences between regions and groups of workers – these were bad years for the old heavy industries like coal-mining and steel manufacture.

Notes

4. J.-P. Bardet and Jacques Dupâquier, *Histoire des populations de l'Europe*, vol. III, *Les temps incertains, 1914–1998* (Paris, 1998), 250; see 251–3 for tables of types of employment in different countries.

5. François Furet, *The End of an Illusion* (London, 1999), 16; William I. Hitchcock, *The Struggle for Europe* (London, 2003), 248.

6. Table in Georges Duby and Michelle Perrot (eds), *A History of Women in the West*, vol. V, *Toward a Cultural Identity in the Twentieth Century* (Cambridge, Mass., 1996), 500. The elections referred to took place between 1987 and 1992.

7. For this striking point, see Eamonn Duffy, *Saints and Sinners: A History of the Popes* (London, 1997), 275.

8. Mark Gilbert, *Surpassing Realism: The Politics of European Integration since 1945* (Boulder, Colo. and Oxford, 2003), 119.

9. Jean Chombert de Lauwe, *L'Aventure agricole de la France de 1945 à nos jours* (Paris, 1979), 300.

10. Quoted in Julius W. Friend, *The Linchpin: Franco-German Relations, 1950–1990* (New York, 1991), 39.

11. Quoted in Gilbert, *Surpassing Realism*, 109; see 106–11 for an incisive account of the whole crisis.

12. Quoted in ibid., 111.

13. Joao de Deus Pinhero, 'L'identité portugaise', in Gérard-François Dumont (ed.), *Les Racines de l'identité européenne* (Paris, 1999), 214–15.

14. See the summaries of the Single European Act and its background in William Nicoll and Trevor C. Salmon, *Understanding the New European Community* (London, 1994), 48–51; and Stephen George and Ian Bache, *Politics in the European Union* (Oxford, 2001), 116–19. In the EEC of 12 members in 1985, a qualified majority was made up of 70 per cent of the votes of the member states, weighted roughly according to size. West Germany, France, Italy and the UK had 10 votes each; Spain 8 votes; Belgium, Greece, the Netherlands and Portugal 5 votes; Denmark and Ireland 3 votes; Luxembourg 2 votes.

15. See the discussion in Gilbert, *Surpassing Realism*, 177.

16. Romain H. Rainero, 'La difficile identité italienne', in Dumont, *Racines*, 172.

17. Figures in Françoise de la Serre, *La Grande-Bretagne et la Communauté Européenne* (Paris, 1987), 217.

18. Quoted in John Lukacs, *The Decline and Rise of Europe* (New York, 1965), 275.

19. Quoted in Nicoll and Salmon, *New European Community*, 339–40; cf. comment on 306.

20. J.-R. de Salis, *Switzerland and Europe: Essays and Reflections* (London, 1971), 60.

21. Werner Ross, 'Europe's multilingual future', *Daedalus*, 1979, vol. 108, no. 2, 151–4.

22. Stanley Hoffmann, 'Fragments floating in the here and now', *Daedalus*, 1979, vol. 108, no. 1, 2–3, 8.

23. Table in Nicoll and Salmon, *New European Community*, 70.

24. Ibid., 72.

25. See the definition of *acquis communautaire* in George and Bache, *European Union*, 91.

26. Andrew Shonfield, *Europe: Journey to an Unknown Destination* (London, 1973).

27. Paul Kennedy, *Rise and Fall of the Great Powers* (pbk edn, London, 1989), 495.

28. Jean-Marie Benoist, *Pavane pour une Europe défunte*, quoted in Denis Lacorne, Jacques Rupnik and Marie-France Toinet (eds), *The Rise and Fall of Anti-Americanism: A Century of French Perception* (London, 1990), 19.

29. Gabriel Partos, *The World that Came in from the Cold* (London, 1993), 49; Tim Garton Ash, *In Europe's Name* (London, 1993), 61–2, 142–6.

30. Statute of the Council of Europe, in J.A.S. Grenville, *The Major International Treaties, 1914–1973* (London, 1974), 401–5.

Chapter 12

1. Paul Kennedy, *Rise and Fall of the Great Powers* (pbk edn, London, 1989), 554–5.

2. Seweryn Bialer, *The Soviet Paradox: External Expansion, Internal Decline* (London, 1986), 77.

3. J.-P. Bardet and Jacques Dupâquier (eds), *Histoire des populations de l'Europe*, vol. III, *Les temps incertains, 1914–1998* (Paris, 1999), 695. The figures for life expectancy in the USSR, for male and female respectively, were: 68.5 and 74.5 (1970); 61.5 and 73 (1980); 62.9 and 72.7 (1985); 63.8 and 74.3 (1990). Infant mortality, per 1000 births, was 23 in 1970, rising to 27.7 in 1980, and then falling to 26 in 1985 and 21.8 in 1990.

4. Paul Marer, 'The economics of eastern Europe and Soviet foreign policy', in Seweryn Bialer (ed.), *The Domestic Context of Soviet Foreign Policy* (London, 1981), 277–9; Philip Longworth, *The Making of Eastern Europe: From Pre-History to Post-Communism* (2nd edn, New York, 1997), 67.

5. Quoted in Alan Cassels, *Ideology and International Relations in the Modern World* (London, 1996), 222.

6. Flora Lewis, *Europe: A Tapestry of Nations* (New York, 1987), 461.

7. Quoted in Tim Garton Ash, *The Uses of Adversity* (London, 1989), 46.

8. Bialer, *Soviet Paradox*, 198.

9. Robert Service, *A History of Twentieth-Century Russia* (London, 1997), 443.

10. Quoted in Archie Brown, *The Gorbachev Factor* (Oxford, 1996), 95.

11. List in Gabriel Partos, *The World that Came in from the Cold* (London, 1993), 243.

12. Lewis, *Europe*, 346.

13. Polish election system and results, *Annual Register*, 1989, 111–12.

14. R.J. Crampton, *Eastern Europe in the Twentieth Century* (London, 1994), 408. The plainest wording was on 5 July in Paris: 'What the Poles and Hungarians decide is their affair, but we will respect their decision whatever it is'.

15. See Peter G. Boyle, *American–Soviet Relations: From the Russian Revolution to the Fall of Communism* (London, 1993), 230. The reference was to Frank Sinatra's famous song, 'I did it my way'.

16. *Keesing's Record of World Events*, vol. 35, no. 6, 36752.

Chapter 13

1. Peter G. Boyle, *American–Soviet Relations: From the Russian Revolution to the Fall of Communism* (London, 1993), vii.

2. Text in *Annual Register*, 1990, 569–76.

3. Martin Malia, 'Leninist endgame', *Daedalus*, Spring 1992, 60.

Notes

4. See the exposition of this theme in Erazim Kohak, 'Ashes, ashes...Central Europe after forty years', ibid., 197–215.

5. The economic and electoral statistics in the following passages on Poland are taken from the relevant volumes of the *Annual Register*.

6. Ibid., 1992, 145–8.

7. See V. Meier, *Yugoslavia: A History of its Demise* (London, 1999); Misha Glenny, *The Fall of Yugoslavia: The Third Balkan War* (London, 1994); Noel Malcolm, *Bosnia: A Short History* (London, 1994).

8. Quoted in Mark Gilbert, *Surpassing Realism: The Politics of European Integration Since 1945* (Oxford, 2003), 209.

9. For Dayton agreement, see *Annual Register*, 1995, 126–8; the agreement was initialled at Dayton, 21 November 1995, and formally signed at Versailles, 14 December 1995.

10. See e.g. Noel Malcolm, 'The case against "Europe"', *Foreign Affairs*, vol. 74, no. 2, March–April 1995, 52, where the author argues convincingly that the EU was moving towards a European state, 'with its own constitution, government, parliament, currency, foreign policy and army'.

11. Gilbert, *Surpassing Realism*, 212.

12. Quoted in *Annual Register*, 1999, 425.

13. See the summary in Gilbert, *Surpassing Realism*, 238.

14. Figures in *Annual Register*, 1994, 422; 1999, 428.

15. Figures in Sabine Strauss, 'Le sentiment de l'identité européenne', in Gérard-François Dumont (ed.), *Les Racines de l'identité européenne* (Paris, 1999), 357.

16. Unemployment figures in *Annual Register*, 1993, 405; 1997, 533.

17. Election results in Henry Ashby Turner, *Germany from Partition to Unification* (New Haven, Conn., 1992), 245–6.

18. Timothy Garton Ash, *In Europe's Name: Germany and the Divided Continent* (New York, 1993), 385–6.

19. Figures for household assets in *Annual Register*, 1995, 50.

20. French referendum figures in *Keesing's Record of World Events*, 1992, vol. 38, 39081–2. Votes totalling 909,377 were declared invalid, and there were suspicions of malpractice in the votes cast in the overseas departments.

21. Figures for the two Danish referendums, *Annual Register*, 1992, 70; 1993, 70.

22. Ibid., 1993, 81; 1994, 83.

23. Finnish referendum figures, ibid., 1994, 83.

24. Norwegian referendum figures, ibid., 78.

25. Swiss referendum figures, ibid., 1992, 81–2.

26. Ibid., 1999, 430.

27. Figures taken from the articles on the relevant countries in *Annual Register*, 1993 and 1999.

28. Richard Vinen, *A History in Fragments: Europe in the Twentieth Century* (London, 2000), 625.

29. William I. Hitchcock, *The Struggle for Europe: The History of the Continent Since 1945* (London, 2003), 347.

Chapter 14

1. *Keesing's Record of World Events*, vol. 51, 46539–40, for changes to the Stability and Growth Pact.

2. Text in *Annual Register*, 2000, 509–17.

3. Ibid., 73–4. The memory of this episode still rankled in Austria at the tenth anniversary of the Austrian entry into the EU in March 2005.

4. See the summaries of these complicated arrangements in Mark Gilbert, *Surpassing Realism: The Politics of European Integration since 1945* (New York and Oxford, 2003), 242–4; Stephen George and Ian Bache, *Politics in the European Union* (Oxford, 2001), 416–17.

5. *Keesing's*, vol. 46, 43594. Fischer was careful to say that he spoke only as a private individual, not as foreign minister; but such a distinction was almost impossible to maintain.

6. Speech by Krasniewski, advocating a 'Europe of homelands', *Annual Register*, 2002, 97; Klaus in *Le Figaro*, 15 July 2003, declaring that he needed neither a European constitution nor a European passport.

7. Figures for French election in *Annual Register*, 2002, 55–6.

8. Quoted in ibid., 2000, 92.

9. Ibid., 67, 401–3. In 1992 the Danes had rejected the Treaty of Maastricht in a referendum, but were asked to vote again on amended terms in 1993. The prime minister was rejecting any attempt to repeat these events.

10. Figures for Swedish referendum in *Keesing's*, vol. 49, 45606.

11. Figures for east European referendums in *Annual Register*, 2003, 96, 98, 101, 103, 105, 119. Turnouts were between 50 and 60 per cent, except in Hungary where it was only 46 per cent.

12. See the figures for GDP and economic growth in *Le Monde: Economie*, 27 April 2004, and *The Economist*, 1 May 2004. These vary in minor respects, but present basically the same picture.

13. Figures for European Parliament elections in *Keesing's*, vol. 50, 46067–72. *Le Monde: Cahier Résultats*, 15 June 2004, did not indicate which states operated compulsory voting.

14. British Management Data Foundation, *The European Constitution in Perspective* (Stroud, 2004) provides the full English text of the Treaty establishing a Constitution for Europe, with all protocols and declarations, signed in Rome on 29 October 2004. This runs to a total of 266 pages. There is a compact summary in *Keesing's*, vol. 50, 46072.

15. *Keesing's*, vol. 51, 46480 (Spain); vol. 50, 46328 (Lithuania); vol. 50, 46379 (Hungary); vol. 51, 46640 (Germany).

16. Ibid., vol. 51, 46634 (France); 46695 (Netherlands).

17. See Ross Cowling and Robert Broadhurst, 'In the other member states', *The European Journal*, vol. 12, no. 6, June–July 2005, 10–11, for a summary of the position at the end of July 2005.

18. *The Economist*, 'Survey of the European Union', 25 September 2004, 14.

19. *Keesing's*, vol. 50, 45973, 46087. One of those dismissed in June was the Speaker of the

Notes

Serb Assembly, Dragan Kalinic, who said that Karadzic was 'protected by God and the angels' rather than by any human agency – which confirms the distinctive nature of the situation in Bosnia.

20. *Annual Register*, 2002, 135.
21. *Keesing's*, vol. 50, 45920–1.
22. Ibid., 46322–3, 46383–4.
23. Karen Smith uses this telling phrase in 'The outsiders: The European neighbourhood policy', *International Affairs*, July 2005, vol. 81, no. 4, 758.
24. *Keesing's*, vol. 50, 46380–1, provides a summary of this crucial EU statement on Turkey.
25. Quoted in Gérard-François Dumont and Anselm Zurfluh, 'L'identité socio-démographique de l'Europe', in Gérard-François Dumont (ed.), *Les Racines de l'identité européenne* (Paris, 1999), 348–9.
26. J.-P. Bardet and Jacques Dupâquier (eds), *Histoire des populations de l'Europe*, vol. III, *Les temps incertains, 1914–1998* (Paris, 1998), 8, 21, 255–6, 701, 707; Dumont and Zurfluh, in Dumont, *Racines*, 344–5, 348–9. Figures for the different continents in 1997 were:

	Africa	North America	Latin America	Asia	Europe	Oceania
Population growth (%)	2.6	0.6	1.8	1.6	−0.1	1.1
Index of reproduction	5.6	1.9	3.0	2.9	1.4	2.4
Pop. over 60 years (%)	3.0	13.0	5.0	5.0	14.0	10.0

SUGGESTIONS FOR FURTHER READING

The following is a small selection from the vast literature available on the subject of this book. It is limited to English-language books, and is drawn from the works that I have found most useful and interesting – of necessity, a somewhat arbitrary choice. The place of publication is London unless otherwise indicated.

ASPECTS OF EUROPEAN HISTORY

General histories of Europe:

Blanning, T.C.W. (ed.), *The Oxford History of Modern Europe*, Oxford, 1996.
Davies, Norman, *Europe: A History*, Oxford, 1996.
Rietbergen, Peter, *Europe: A Cultural History*, 1998.
Roberts, J.M., *The Penguin History of Europe*, Harmondsworth, 1996.

Europe in the twentieth century:

Hitchcock, William I., *The Struggle for Europe: The Turbulent History of a Divided Continent, 1945–2002*, 2003.
Judt, Tony, *Postwar: A History of Europe since 1945*, 2005.
Mazower, Mark, *Dark Continent: Europe's Twentieth Century*, 1998.
Vinen, Richard, *A History in Fragments: Europe in the Twentieth Century*, 2000.

Reflections on European identity:

Albrecht-Carrié, René, *The Unity of Europe: An Historical Survey*, 1966.
Halecki, Oscar, *The Limits and Divisions of European History*, 1950.
Hay, Denis, *Europe: The Emergence of an Idea*, Edinburgh, 1968.
Lukacs, John, *Decline and Rise of Europe*, Westport, Conn., 1965.
Lyons, F.S.L., *Internationalism in Europe, 1815–1914*, Leiden, 1963.

Economic history:

Aldcroft, Derek H., *The European Economy, 1914–1990*, 1993.
Cipolla, Carlo M. (ed.), *The Fontana Economic History of Europe: The Twentieth Century, Parts 1 and 2; Contemporary Economies, Parts 1 and 2*, 1976.
Mitchell, B.R., *International Historical Statistics: Europe, 1750–1993*, 1998.
Venn, Fiona, *Oil Diplomacy in the Twentieth Century*, 1986.

Suggestions for further reading

Political and social movements:

Buchanan, T. and Conway, Martin (eds), *Political Catholicism in Europe, 1918–1965*, Oxford, 1996.

Cassels, Alan, *Ideology and International Relations in the Modern World*, 1996.

Caute, David, *The Fellow Travellers*, 1973.

Duby, Georges and Perrot, Michelle (eds), *A History of Women in the West*, vol. V, *Toward a Cultural Identity in the Twentieth Century*, Cambridge, Mass., 1996.

Duffy, Eamon, *Saints and Sinners: A History of the Popes*, 1997.

Evans, Richard, *The Feminists: Women's Emancipation Movements in Europe, America and Australasia, 1840–1920*, 1977.

Furet, François, *The Passing of an Illusion: The Idea of Communism in the Twentieth Century*, 1999.

Hargreaves, J.D., *Decolonization in Africa*, 1988.

Holland, R.F., *European Decolonisation, 1918–1981: An Introductory Survey*, 1985.

Joll, James, *The Second International, 1889–1914*, 1955.

Kedourie, Elie, *Nationalism*, 4th edn, Oxford, 1993.

Lee, Stephen J., *The European Dictatorships, 1918–1945*, 1987.

Marwick, Arthur, *War and Social Change in the Twentieth Century*, 1974.

Overy, Richard, *The Dictators: Hitler's Germany and Stalin's Russia*, 2004.

Payne, Stanley G., *A History of Fascism, 1914–1945*, 1996.

Rhodes, Anthony, *The Vatican in the Age of the Dictators, 1922–1945*, 1973.

Sassoon, Donald, *One Hundred Years of Socialism: The West European Left in the Twentieth Century*, 1998.

CHRONOLOGICAL PERIODS

The First World War:

Becker, Jean-Jacques, *The Great War and the French People*, Leamington Spa, 1985.

De Groot, Gerard, *Blighty: British Society in the Era of the Great War*, 1996.

De Groot, Gerard, *The First World War*, 2001.

Herwig, Helger H., *The First World War: Germany and Austria-Hungary, 1914–1918*, 1997.

Keegan, John, *The First World War*, 1998.

Strachan, Hugh, *The First World War*, vol. I, *To Arms*, Oxford, 2001.

Winter, Jay, *Sites of Memory, Sites of Mourning: The Great War in European Cultural History*, Cambridge, 1998.

Winter, Jay and Wall, W. (eds), *The Upheaval of War: Family, Work and Welfare in Europe, 1914–18*, 1988.

Peacemaking and between the wars:

Bell, P.M.H., *The Origins of the Second World War in Europe*, 2nd edn, 1997.

Boemeke, Manfred F., Feldman, Gerald D. and Glaser, Elizabeth (eds), *The Treaty of Versailles: A Reassessment after 75 Years*, Cambridge, 1998.

Boyce, Robert, and Maiolo, Joseph (eds), *The Origins of World War Two: The Debate Continues*, 2003.

Clavin, Patricia, *The Great Depression in Europe, 1929–1939*, 2000.

Kindleberger, Charles P., *The World in Depression, 1929–1939*, 1973.

Knox, James Macgregor, *Common Destiny: Dictatorship, Foreign Policy and War in Fascist Italy and Nazi Germany*, Cambridge, 2000.

Macmillan, Margaret, *Peacemakers: The Paris Conference of 1919 and its Attempt to End War*, 2001.

Marks, Sally, *The Ebbing of European Ascendancy: An International History of the World, 1914–1945*, 2002.

Marks, Sally, *The Illusion of Peace: International Relations in Europe, 1919–1933*, 2nd edn, 2003.

Northedge, F.S., *The League of Nations: Its Life and Times, 1920–1946*, 1986.

Sharp, Alan, *The Versailles Settlement: Peacemaking in Paris, 1919*, 1991.

Steiner, Zara, *The Lights that Failed: European International History, 1919–1933*, Oxford, 2005.

The Second World War:

Calvocoressi, Peter and Wint, Guy, *Total War: Causes and Courses of the Second World War*, 1972.

Dear, I.C.B. and Foot, M.R.D. (eds), *The Oxford Companion to the Second World War*, Oxford, 1995.

Foot, M.R.D., *Resistance: European Resistance to Nazism, 1940–45*, 1976.

Keegan, John, *The Second World War*, London, 1989.

Lukacs, John, *The Last European War, September 1939–December 1941*, 1977.

Overy, Richard, *Why the Allies Won*, 1995.

Purdue, A.W., *The Second World War*, 1999.

Post-war, 1945 to the present:

Ash, Timothy Garton, *In Europe's Name: Germany and the Divided Continent*, 1993.

Gaddis, John Lewis, *We Now Know: Rethinking Cold War History*, Oxford, 1997.

George, Stephen and Bache, Ian; *Politics in the European Union*, Oxford, 2001.

Gilbert, Mark, *Surpassing Realism: The Politics of European Integration since 1945*, Boulder, Colo. and Oxford, 2003.

Goldstein, Erik (ed.), *The End of the Cold War*, 1994.

Laughland, John, *The Tainted Source: The Undemocratic Origins of the European Idea*, London, 1997.

Maier, Charles S., *Dissolution: The Crisis of Communism and the End of East Germany*, Princeton, NJ, 1997.

Maier, Charles S. (ed.), *The Cold War in Europe: Era of a Divided Continent*, 3rd edn, Princeton, NJ, 1996.

Milward, Alan S., *The Reconstruction of Western Europe, 1945–51*, 1987.

Milward, Alan S., *The European Rescue of the Nation State*, 1992.

Nicoll, William and Salmon, Trevor C., *Understanding the New European Community*, 1994.

Suggestions for further reading

Pryce-Jones, David, *The War that Never Was: The Fall of the Soviet Empire, 1985–91*, 1995.
Remnick, David, *Lenin's Tomb: The Last Days of the Soviet Empire*, 1993.
Urwin, Derek, *Western Europe Since 1945: A Political History*, 4th edn, 1989.
Young, John W., *Cold War Europe: A Political History*, 1991.
Zeman, Z.A.B., *The Making and Breaking of Communist Europe*, Oxford, 1991.

INDIVIDUAL COUNTRIES AND AREAS

Austria-Hungary:

Okey, Robin, *The Habsburg Monarchy, c.1765–1918: From Enlightenment to Eclipse*, 2001.
Sked, Alan, *The Decline and Fall of the Habsburg Empire, 1815–1918*, 1989.

The Balkan States:

Glenny, Misha, *The Balkans, 1804–1999: Nationalism, War and the Great Powers*, 1999.
Jelavich, Barbara, *A History of the Balkans*, vol. II, *The Twentieth Century*, Cambridge, 1983.
Mazower, Mark, *The Balkans*, 2002.
Meier, V., *Yugoslavia: A History of its Demise*, 1999.
Pavlowitch, Stevan K., *A History of the Balkans, 1804–1945*, 1999.

The Baltic States:

Hiden, John and Salmon, Patrick, *The Baltic Nations and Europe*, 1994.

Britain:

Morgan, Kenneth O., *The People's Peace: British History, 1945–1990*, rev. edn, Oxford, 1992.
Taylor, A.J.P., *English History, 1914–1945*, Oxford, 1965.

Eastern Europe:

Crampton, R.J., *Eastern Europe in the Twentieth Century*, 1994.
Longworth, Philip, *The Making of Eastern Europe: From Prehistory to Postcommunism*, 2nd edn, 1997.
Okey, Robin, *Eastern Europe, 1740–1985: Feudalism to Communism*, 2nd edn, 1986.
Rupnik, J., *The Other Europe*, 1989.
Swain, Geoffrey and Swain, Nigel, *Eastern Europe Since 1945*, 2nd edn, 1998.
Wandycz, Piotr S., *The Price of Freedom: A History of East Central Europe from the Middle Ages to the Present*, 1993.

France:

Kedward, Rod, *La Vie en bleu: France and the French since 1900*, 2005.
McMillan, James F., *Twentieth-Century France*, 1992.

Germany:

Burleigh, Michael, *The Third Reich: A New History*, 2000.

Craig, Gordon, *Germany, 1866–1945*, Oxford, 1978.
Kershaw, Ian, *Hitler*, vol. I, *1889–1936, Hubris*, 1998; vol. II, *1936–1945, Nemesis*, 2000.
Nicholls, A.J., *The Bonn Republic: West German Democracy, 1945–1990*, 1997.
Turner, Henry Ashby, *Germany from Partition to Unification*, 1992.

Italy:

Bosworth, R.J.B., *Mussolini*, 2002.
Clark, Martin, *Modern Italy, 1871–1995*, 1995.

Poland:

Davies, Norman, *God's Playground: A History of Poland*, vol. II, *1795 to the Present*, Oxford, 1986.
Davies, Norman and Moorhouse, Roger, *Microcosm: Portrait of a Central European City*, 2002 [i.e. Breslau/Wroclaw].

Portugal:

Birmingham, David, *A Concise History of Portugal*, 2nd edn, Cambridge, 2003.
Gallagher, T., *Portugal: A Twentieth-Century Interpretation*, 1983.

Russia/Soviet Union:

Acton, Edward, *Rethinking the Russian Revolution*, 1990.
Brown, Archie, *The Gorbachev Factor*, Oxford, 1996.
Service, Robert, *A History of Twentieth-Century Russia*, 1997.
Service, Robert, *Lenin: A Biography*, 2000.
Ulam, Adam B., *Stalin: The Man and His Era*, 1974.

Scandinavia:

Derry, T.K., *A History of Scandinavia: Norway, Sweden, Denmark, Finland and Iceland*, 1979.

Spain:

Carr, Raymond, *Modern Spain, 1875–1980*, Oxford, 1980.
Preston, Paul, *Franco: A Biography*, 1993.

Switzerland:

Butler, Michael, Pender, Malcolm and Charmley, Joy (eds), *The Making of Modern Switzerland, 1848–1998*, 2000.
Salis, J.-R. de, *Switzerland and Europe: Essays and Reflections*, ed. and introduction Christopher Hughes, 1971.

Turkey:

Mango, Andrew, *Atatürk*, 1999.
Mango, Andrew, *The Turks Today*, 2004.
Zürcher, Erik J., *Turkey: A Modern History*, 1993.

INDEX

Index

Index

Index

Index